OUTDOOR PLAYSCAPES

Breaking New Ground

Lynn Wilson

NELSON / EDUCATION

NELSON EDUCATION

ISBN-13: 978-0-17-657381-2
ISBN-10: 0-17-657381-X

Consists of Selections from:

Outdoor Playscapes: Breaking New Ground, 1st Edition
Lynn Wilson
ISBN 10: 0-17-650718-3, © 2014

Cover Credit:

Courtesy of Lynn Wilson

This book is dedicated to the visionaries to come, those who value the development of the whole child through active, lifelong engagement with the out-of-doors—nurturing the growth of the body, mind, and spirit. Adventures await!

CONTENTS

EXHIBITS, FIGURES, AND TABLES

The creation of this book has been a long journey. I grew up in Toronto on the edge of a forest, a wonderful secret place with a stream that ran through it. This was a refuge, a place to imagine, a green haven. I spent countless hours there until the forest was plowed under to become a garbage dump. In those days there were no marches in the streets or signs protesting the destruction of my forest and so our tranquil space became a very different environment, a very different playground. Each day the trucks would come and dump more and more refuse. There were treasures to be found everywhere and, with the adaptability of children, my friends and I became explorers of a different kind. Today, the dump has long been grassed over and is now Amesbury Park.

My first teaching job was at a school on the banks of the Humber River and it wasn't long before my children and I were knee deep in water, studying the plants and looking for wildlife. We started a local campaign to clean up the river and we never looked back. We prepared for months for a week-long camping adventure that was the highlight of the year! I had found my forest again and so had my children!

Today we are faced with many environmental issues that have a direct impact on our families, homes, and the global community. Climate change and our contribution to it cannot be ignored; the depletion of potable water and natural resources, endangered species, air quality, ozone depletion, deforestation—the list is long and compelling. In our work with young children we cannot expect them to repair the damage that we adults have created but we can help them to connect with nature in a meaningful way so they develop a love of the Earth and understand the need to protect it. They will protect what they know. We have a responsibility to help create a future generation of children who love this planet!

This ebook is filled with stories of adventurers, visionaries, believers, and dreamers who all know the power of outdoor environments for young children. Their research, narratives, and models reinforce what we all know to be true—that we need to engage young children in the natural world where their mental, physical, and spiritual health can thrive. I hope that *Outdoor Playscapes* will inspire you to explore and nurture the natural world in the lives of the children with whom you are working. We have a tremendous responsibility as educators and research helps us understand that we need to be passionate advocates for the nature connection between children and the world in which they live. Imagine, hope, dream!

I dedicate this book to my children who have wandered in the wilderness with me, for their understanding and support and, most importantly, for their love and connection to each other.

A special thanks is necessary to my partner, Charlie Dougall, and many friends who helped me find and photograph playgrounds on our travels together.

ABOUT THE TEXT
CHAPTER OVERVIEW

In **Chapter 1** of the ebook, we examine the historical foundations of outdoor playscapes and gardens for children and identify key informants and their influence in the development of the outdoor play movement. In **Chapter 2** we look at the ways in which outdoor play for young children has changed over time. We investigate the challenges that families face in providing an active healthy lifestyle for themselves and for their children. Through extensive research, we analyze the implications of inactive children and their health risks. **Chapter 3** investigates the children's physical, social/emotional, and cognitive gains when involved in outdoor environments and analyze the impact of interacting in nature on families and communities. **Chapter 4** compares Canada's efforts in regards to outdoor environments to other *Organisation for Economic Cooperation and Development* (OECD) countries. We also look at different types of playgrounds and their play value. We begin to examine the elements of creating a successful playscape and explore a variety of tools that help us to access outdoor environments. **Chapter 5** outlines the zone approach to effective outdoor design. We examine each zone and the benefits it provides to young children. In **Chapter 6** we assess the benefits of greening outdoor playscapes, its impact on children and adults, and the elements that contribute to successful natural design. **Chapter 7** focuses on the adults working with young children and examines the barriers to effective outdoor experiences and ways in which educators can support positive play opportunities. We discuss the emergent curriculum approach and its role in planning meaningful experiences for young children. **Chapter 8** looks at toys and materials that enhance the outdoor experience. We discuss loose parts in detail and the criteria for the selection of outdoor materials. A variety of prop boxes, collections, Porta Paks and Story Boxes are highlighted. The final section of the book, **Curriculum Experiences for Play Zones**, is filled with more than 700 experiences for children. Creating outdoor curriculum requires knowledge and skill, and this section is organized by zones to support educators.

The zones are:

- Environmental
- Physical/Active Motor
- Social/Dramatic Play
- Cognitive/Construction
- Art
- Quiet/Communication

Each zone is differentiated with its own colour bar across the top of the page and an icon in a matching colour along the bottom, allowing students and instructors to quickly and easily access their zone of interest. This collection provides a springboard to respond to children's needs and skill development based on the educator's insightful observations. While the ideas presented will provide you with a wide range of experiences, I hope that you will see not only the ideas, but also the opportunity to expand and build on the observed needs and interests of a child in your care.

The numerous colour photographs throughout this ebook beautifully illustrate the concepts presented. You can view a gallery of images that further illustrate particular concepts discussed by selecting the **Additional Photos** icon, where available. This online image library includes hundreds of images that strengthen the concepts presented in the ebook.

For Additional Photos

Embedded throughout the text are readings that relate to the content. These are denoted by an **Additional Readings** icon, which takes the reader to a listing of recommended readings as well as children's story books.

For Additional Reading

Throughout the text, the **www** icon will appear in order to highlight websites of interest. You may click on the icon to access the link.

THE INSTRUCTOR'S MANUAL

The accompanying Instructor's Manual outlines strategies for in-class exercises on a chapter-by-chapter basis. The manual contains examples for classroom discussions, assignments, and additional material that supplements the text. It is available as a downloadable resource on the faculty companion website at www.ece.nelson.com/9780176507183/instructor.

ACKNOWLEDGMENTS

This book would not have been possible without the support of the educators in the George. Brown College's lab schools. While it is impossible to list everyone involved, I would like to acknowledge Mary Bianchi and Kelly Antram for their incredible enthusiasm and support for many of the photographs that appear in this book.

I also want to thank all of the staff at Nelson Education for their unwavering support and enthusiasm for this project: Developmental Editor Alisa Yampolsky, Managing Developmental Editor Sandy Matos, Marketing Manager Terry Fedorkiw, Executive Editor Lenore Taylor-Atkins, Senior Content Production Manager Imoinda Romain, Permissions Researchers Daniela Glass and Sheila Hall, Copy Editor Karen Rolfe, and Project Manager Shanthi Guruswamy at Integra.

I would also like to acknowledge the following people who were instrumental in the development of this book:

- Kelly Antram, George Brown College—Queen Street Child Care Centre
- Heidi Campbell, Evergreen Brick Works
- Brenda Huff, St. Clair College

- Leslie Kopf-Johnson, Algonquin College
- Barb Pimento, George Brown College
- Sue Narozniak, Red River College
- Julie Valerio, Humber College

ABOUT THE AUTHOR

Lynn recently retired from teaching in the School of Early Childhood at George Brown College after a 44-year career in education that involved teaching in a wide variety of settings including kindergarten classrooms, parent cooperative programs, child care, college classrooms, and international settings including work in Bosnia, Jamaica, and China. In 2006, the Association of Canadian Community Colleges awarded Lynn a National Teaching Excellence award. She has also authored an early childhood education textbook through Nelson Education: *Partnerships: Families and Communities in Early Childhood*.

Chapter 1

HISTORICAL AND THEORETICAL PERSPECTIVES ON OUTDOOR PLAY

Power of One — RYAN HRELJAC

"Let nature be your first teacher."

—*St. Bernard of Clairvaux (1090–1153)*

Ryan Hreljac of Ryan's Well, giving water to African children

Ryan's Well Foundation www.ryanswell.ca

Ryan Hreljac is an outstanding example of the Power of One. As a six-year-old, Ryan was significantly influenced by his Grade One teacher who spoke of the need for clean water for children and families in Africa. By the time Ryan was seven years old, he had collected enough money from his family, friends, and community to build his first well at Angolo Primary School in northern Uganda. This was only the beginning: since then, Ryan has helped build over 700 wells and 830 latrines, and has brought safe water and improved sanitation to over 736,000 people. Today Ryan is a student at King's College in Halifax, Nova Scotia, where he is studying international development and political science. He continues his work with Ryan's Wells and speaks around the world on issues about water and how important it is for each and every one of us to make a difference, no matter how old you are!

OUTCOMES:

1. To examine the historical foundations of outdoor playscapes and gardens for children.
2. To identify key informants and their influence in the development of the outdoor play movement.
3. To analyze a variety of approaches to providing outdoor experiences for young children.

AN HISTORICAL PERSPECTIVE

In order to understand our present-day approach to outdoor experiences and naturalized environments for children, it is important that we consider this type of play from an historical perspective. Modern humans evolved and have lived in intimate contact with nature, in the savannahs and forests, for almost our entire 120,000-year history. When children were free to play, their first choice was often to flee to the nearest wild place—whether it was a big tree or brushy area in the yard or a watercourse or woodland nearby (Pyle, 2002). Two hundred years ago, most children spent their days surrounded by fields, farms, or in the wild nature at its edges (White, 2004). For most of our history and indeed all of our pre-history, we have had an intimate connection with nature and the natural world; from an evolutionary perspective, it would be no surprise to still find echoes of this in our behaviour (Frumkin, 2001, in Lester & Maudsley, 2006). From the earliest times, all great civilizations had gardens. In ancient Egypt, the earliest surviving garden plan dates from 1400 BC; the Hanging Gardens of Babylon in Iraq were considered one of the Wonders of the Ancient World. The idea of the garden as paradise is a very early one, too, far earlier than the Bible. The word *paradise* didn't appear in the Bible until the Greeks translated it from the Hebrew in the second century AD. The word comes from *pairidaeza,* a word in the ancient Persian religious language *Zend*, and means an enclosure or walled garden. Later, when the Arabs conquered Persia in AD 637, they took the basic idea of the paradise garden—essential in their climate—and refined it. Their love of mathematics, and the fact that the Koran forbids the making of any image in human or animal form, led them to value geometric patterns, resulting in some of the exquisite tiled courtyard gardens that still survive in North Africa and Spain. Gardens were central to the religion of Islam and appear often in the Koran. As the Arabs conquered parts of Asia, North Africa, and Spain, during the sixth and seventh centuries AD, they built gardens as they travelled. In India, gardens around temples and tombs were already similar in many ways—walled, symmetrical, with water (symbolic as well as practical for worshippers to cleanse themselves before worship)—and the styles merged.

Although private houses and public arenas of ancient Greece and Rome had gardens, these were relatively simple until the influence of the ornate pleasure gardens (those not serving a spiritual purpose) of the East in the third century BC. When the Romans invaded Britain in 55 BC, they brought with them their ideas of how gardens should be built. By the fourth century AD, the arrival of Christianity in Britain led to the development of monastic gardens, which combined the formal layout of the Roman model with the practical and spiritual needs of Christianity. For the monks and nuns who made and cared for them, these gardens were an opportunity to create paradise in miniature, with God, nature, and humanity united in a common purpose. Although different in many ways to western gardens, the gardens of China and Japan too have a

Ryoan-ji, Kyoto, Japan

similar spiritual goal—to help people, through contemplation, ultimately achieve a state of divine emptiness or "no mind" as it's called in Taoism (Search, 2002). The gardens evoke the essence of mountains and water. One of the most famous is *Ryoan-ji* in Kyoto, Japan. Here there is very little vegetation, but an enclosed courtyard contains 15 rocks placed in drifts of moss that rest on a bed of raked gravel. *Ryoan-ji* is considered to be one of the most significant traditional dry gardens in Japan and is thought to aid monks in the meditation rituals associated with Zen Buddhism (Herrington, 2009).

More recently, formal gardens such as those at Versailles became the dominant style in Europe. Today, more than 3 million people visit Versailles annually (http://travel.nationalgeographic.com/travel/world-heritage/versailles)

Artwork from ancient Greece shows teachers and pupils learning in small groups outside. In Austria as early as 1879, Erasmus Schwab published *The School Garden: Being a Practical Contribution to the Subject of Education* stating that "school gardens are a fountain for the knowledge of nature and its consequent pleasure, and an excellent means of training." As the centuries passed, however, "school" became identified with an indoor setting. Bigger groups of students were easier to manage in a confined space and learning became associated more with memorization than with experience (Broda, 2007, p. 25).

THOSE WHO LED THE WAY

From the earliest times, many individuals have played a significant role in our understanding of outdoor experiences for young children—Plato, Aristotle, Comenius, Locke, Pestalozzi, and many others helped shape our understanding of children's play. More recently, the concept of outdoor learning owes much to many educators, researchers, and enthusiasts—too many to name—who have laid the groundwork for innovative and exciting learning opportunities for young children. While it is not possible to include all of them, the following is a selection of those who have made noteworthy contributions, along with movements that encouraged active outdoor experiences for young children.

Jacques Rousseau (1712–1778) is credited with distinguishing childhood as a separate stage of life. He emphasized both the influence of nature on learning and the need to balance intellectual growth with physical well-being. Rousseau believed that sending boys to a remote rural area where they could learn from nature was more beneficial than formal schooling. According to Rousseau, education came from three sources: nature, people, and things (Wellhousen, 2002).

> "Childhood has its own way of seeing, thinking, and feeling, and nothing is more foolish than to try to substitute ours for theirs."
>
> **—Jean Jacques Rousseau**

Influenced by Rousseau, *Friedrich Froebel* (1782–1852) emphasized nature in learning. As a young man, he apprenticed to a forester and had the opportunity to formally study vegetation and other elements of nature. These experiences were a significant part of his theory used to devise the concept of *kindergarten (children's garden)*. He opened kindergartens in Germany and incorporated indoor and outdoor activities. Kindergarten children were introduced to nature study, planted and watered seeds, observed the changes as the seeds sprouted, and cared for the growing seedlings. Nature walks in which the children and teacher explored natural surroundings were also routine. Froebel's nature walks were not to give lessons in plants and birds but rather to listen to the children, to what they found interesting, and to create curiosity and discovery in the landscape.

> "Play is the highest expression of human development in childhood for it alone is the free expression of what is in a child's soul."
>
> **—Friedrich Froebel**

A hundred years ago, when most Canadians were still reading by gaslight and a railway to the Pacific was only a national dream, physician *Marie Zakrzewska* (1829–1902) disembarked from a steamship in Boston harbour with an idea that would change the face of North America. Fresh in her mind were the public parks she had visited in the German capital of Berlin, delightful green spaces dotted with *sand gardens*. Zakrzewska's movement persisted and spread, led by social reformers appalled by the overcrowded conditions in the nation's industrialized cities. Fearing that the devil would make work for the idle hands of children recently released from their gruelling factory jobs, philanthropists pressed for open public spaces where kids could play in sand gardens. By 1889 there were 21 sand gardens in Boston and one in New York. (Mohr, 1987, p. 12)

From this initiative, The Playground Association of America was established in 1906.

> "In 1886 Dr. Marie E. Zakrzewska wrote to the chairman of the executive committee of the Massachusetts emergency and hygiene association, saying that in the public parks of Berlin there were heaps of sand in which children, rich and poor, were allowed to dig and play, as if on a mimic seashore, under the care of the police of the city."
>
> —Joseph Lee (n.d., p. 8)

John Muir (1838–1914) was a Scottish-born American naturalist, author, and early advocate of preservation of wilderness in the United States. His letters, essays, and books telling of his adventures in nature, especially in the Sierra Nevada mountains of California, have been read by millions. Muir believed it was our responsibility as citizens to protect our natural surroundings. His activism helped to preserve the Yosemite Valley, Sequoia National Park, and other wilderness areas. The *Sierra Club*, which he founded, is now one of the most influential grassroots conservation organizations in the United States.

> "Thousands of tired, nerve-shaken, over-civilized people are beginning to find out going to the mountains is going home; that wilderness is a necessity …"
>
> —John Muir

John Dewey (1859–1952) emphasized the importance of planning curriculum around the interests of children. Dewey established an experimental school at the University of Chicago in 1896 where emphasis was placed on the need for outdoor physical exercise during the school day. He believed that children should participate in meaningful projects and learn by doing by finding problems and solving them. Warde (1960) states that Dewey believed that "participation in meaningful projects, learning by doing, encouraging problems and solving them, not only facilitates the acquisition and retention of knowledge but fosters the right character traits: unselfishness, helpfulness, critical intelligence, individual initiative, etc. Learning is more than assimilating; it is the development of habits which enable the growing person to deal effectively and most intelligently with his environment."

> "Education is a social process; education is growth; education is not preparation for life but is life itself."
>
> —John Dewey

Margaret McMillan (1860–1931), along with her sister Rachel, established the first nursery school in Peckham, England in 1914. The concept of their *Open-Air Nursery School and Training Centre* was that taking children from the crowded, unhealthy conditions of their homes would improve their health. The McMillans believed that the environment in which education was to take place had to be conducive to learning. The school was "nursery garden education" where the real learning environment was outside.

The garden was arranged on different levels, on grass and hard surfaces. There were paths, steps, logs, trees, shrubs, ponds, seats, tables, slides, ropes, swings, playhouses, planks, ladders, barrels, blocks. There was a kitchen garden, a wild garden and a rock garden. There was a plethora of natural materials—twigs, leaves, stones, bark, seeds and so on. The movable equipment included trucks, wheelbarrows and bicycles. Children used real tools. Sand, water and builders' bricks were available. Children had access to dressing-up materials. The garden naturally attracted birds and they were further encouraged with bird boxes, bird baths and bird tables. Animals, including chickens, tortoises, rabbits and fish, were kept. Children had access to scientific equipment and to small games apparatus.[*] (Bilton, 2010, p. 2)

The fresh air, the physical activity, and the space ensured that the children did indeed become healthier as hoped. Margaret is seen as the originator of the nursery school concept and provided teacher training in her centre. She wrote *The Nursery School* in 1919 and *Nursery School: A Practical Handbook* in 1920. She also encouraged parents to watch their children at play in the hopes they would learn by watching and provided a parents' room so they could also be educated.

> "The best classroom and the richest cupboard is roofed only by the sky."
>
> —Margaret McMillan

---

[*]Bilton, H. 2010. *Outdoor Learning In The Early Years. Management And Innovation*. Routledge Taylor And Francis Group. p. 72.

Patty Smith Hill (1868–1946) was a kindergarten teacher who trained under the Froebelian system; however, after studying the work of John Dewey she incorporated many of his progressive ideas and became a leader of the progressive kindergarten movement in the United States. She thought that children needed to play freely to develop to their full potential. Outdoor activities, socialization, and open-ended play became increasingly important and highly valued. Equipment such as slides, jungle gyms, seesaws were designed to encourage free, large motor movement. She introduced the *Patty Hill Blocks*, which were large enough for children to construct structures and play inside them. The children in her classrooms played with many items they would experience in everyday life. Her emphasis on creativity and the natural instincts of children in contrast to the more structured educational methods of the time initiated curriculum reforms that permanently changed kindergarten education in the United States.

> Hill is perhaps best known along with her sister for co-writing the tune to the song "Good Morning to All." The tune became even more popular as "Happy Birthday to You."

Maria Montessori (1870–1952) significantly influenced the field of early childhood education. Her focus was on biology, the scientific study of life and living organisms. She relied on hands-on experiences based on the child's innate interest in understanding more about the world around him. She emphasized the importance of valuing and respecting the whole of nature. Children would be given live specimens of animals and plants, care for classroom pets, and participate in field trips during which they could further explore. "The child who has felt a strong love for his surroundings and for all living creatures, who has discovered joy and enthusiasm in work, gives us reason to hope that humanity can develop in a new direction" (Montessori, 1932, p. 58). Through her teaching, she nurtured the spiritual force that created a reverence to protect the earth and its living creatures, and to promote peace. Clearly, her hope was to not only encourage a deep respect for the earth but also that the children would also become peacemakers. Maria Montessori was nominated for a Nobel Peace Prize in 1949, 1950, and 1951. "Today there are more than 25,000 Montessori schools worldwide in 110 countries reaching millions of children. Thousands more are in home school" (Pathways for Families, 2012).

> "Education is a natural process carried out by the child and is not acquired by listening to words but by experiences in the environment."
>
> —**Maria Montessori**

The first professional landscape architect in the United States was *Frederick Law Olmsted* (1822–1903). He anticipated the social and health problems caused by increasingly crowded and polluted industrial cities, and he knew that these problems would be exacerbated over time. He put this theory to work along with architect Calvert Vaux when designing Central Park, in New York City, the first major public park in the United States. People visiting New York today might think that the park was in place and the city was built around it; nothing could be further from the truth. This is an example of human ability to alter landscape in significant ways—changing 341 hectares of swamp land and rock outcrop into one of the world's most famous green spaces.

> These transformations involved the importation of four million cubic meters of dirt for fill and hill creation, rock blasting that required 350 metric tons of gunpowder, planting 270,000 trees and shrubs, and tragically, the removal of one of Manhattan's first African American villages, Seneca, which was home to 1600 people. (Herrington, 2009, p. 30)

> "The enjoyment of scenery employs the mind without fatigue and yet exercises it; tranquilizes it and yet enlivens it; and thus, through the influence of the mind over the body gives the effect of refreshing rest and reinvigoration to the whole system."
>
> —**Frederick Law Olmsted**

While Copenhagen was under German occupation during World War II, Danish landscape architect *Carl Theodor Sorensen* (1893–1979) developed the first adventure playground in the Emdrup section of the Danish capital.

> Known commonly as "junk playgrounds," these facilities were the perfect solution for a country at war. Sorensen established an enclosed area, slightly over one acre in size, where a play leader gave children useless fragments of wood, metal, or masonry. The same person dispensed a few building implements such as hammers, saws, and nails. … given

all this latitude, children became the self-directors of everything that they produced. Their camaraderie and uncontrolled creativity became the essence of their play experience. (Solomon, 2005, p. 12)

> "Carl Theodor Sorensen is one of the great landscape architects of the 20th century. His work is at once monumental and modest, artful and humane, refined and original, serious and playful, restrained yet free."
>
> —**Ann Whiston Spirn**

Rachel Carson (1907–1964) was perhaps one of the most influential persons in the environmental movement. With an M.A. from Johns Hopkins University, she worked at Woods Hole Marine Biological Laboratory and taught at both the University of Maryland and Johns Hopkins and worked with the U.S. Bureau of Fisheries. In her first book *Under the Seawind*, she wrote about the beauty and wonder of the oceans. This was followed by *The Edge of the Sea*. But Rachel Carson is best known for her book *Silent Spring*. In this book she documents the dangers of pesticides and herbicides and showed the long-lasting presence of toxic chemicals in water and on land, and the presence of DDT even in mother's milk. Carson presented evidence that some human cancers were linked to pesticide exposure. There was great resistance in the United States from the agricultural chemical industry but her work moved then President John F. Kennedy, who ordered a Science Advisory Committee that backed Carson's scientific claims. Although she would not live to see it, DDT was banned in 1972. After her death, an essay she'd written was published in book form as *Sense of Wonder*. "Rachel Carson's literary legacy is only four books. But those four books are enough to have changed how humankind regards the living world and the future of life on this earth" (Lear, 1998, p. ix).

> "If a child is to keep alive his inborn sense of wonder, he needs the companionship of at least one adult who can share it, rediscovering with him the joy, excitement, and mystery of the world we live in."
>
> —**Rachel Carson**

According to Ken Worpole (2006), Dutch architect *Aldo van Eyck* (1918–1999) "put the needs of the child and neighbourhood democracy at the centre of town-planning and urban renewal." In 1947, van Eyck joined the Office for Public Works in Amsterdam, a city that had been ravaged by World War II. Worpole (2006) evocatively described this world: "Images of starving children scavenging for food in barren streets, haunted the nation, and immediately after the war, politicians, artists and intellectuals called for a 'new open-heartedness' in social policy." Van Eyck was delighted with the popularity of his first project—a small playground. Over the next 30 years, he would go on to construct 700 more. For a pictorial record of van Eyck's achievements, refer to *The Playgrounds and the City*. Worpole (2006) ends his article by using van Eyck's own words: "In one of his essays van Eyck wrote of cities: 'If they are not meant for children, they are not meant for citizens either. If they are not meant for citizens—ourselves—they are not cities.'"

> "A city that has no room for the child is a diabolical thing."
>
> —**Aldo van Eyck**

Loris Malaguzzi (1920–1994) is seen as the leading influence in the development of the Reggio Emilia Schools in Italy. A primary school teacher who also studied psychology, he brought his many interests such as journalism, sports, politics and theatre into his work with young children. Malaguzzi and his creative and dedicated staff have influenced early childhood educators around the world. With the support of the local government that believed that investment in children is a fundamental cultural and social investment and with the support and the commitment of local parents and the community, it has ensured the continuation of one of the most outstanding examples of quality early childhood programs.

There is an emphasis on expression and children's utilization of multiple symbolic languages; the development of long-term projects as contexts for children's and teachers' learning and research; and careful attention to the role of the environment as it supports relationships between teacher, parent and child. (OECD, Bennett & Leonarduzzi, 2004, p. 12)

Before van Eyck

After van Eyck

What is truly significant in this model is the emphasis on the environment, which is seen as the "third teacher," including both the garden and the town. Information for one special project, the *Amusement Park for Birds* can be found at

 http://www.videatives.com/store/product_info.php?cPath=1&products_id=97

> "The pleasure of learning and knowing, and of understanding, is one of the most important and basic feelings that every child expects from the experiences he confronts alone, with other children or with adults. It is a crucial feeling which must be reinforced so that the pleasure survives even when reality may prove that learning, knowing and understanding involve difficulty and effort."
>
> **—Loris Malaguzzi**

Edward O. Wilson (1929–), Harvard biologist, introduced and popularized the term *biophilia* in his book of the same name. Biophilia helps us to understand our need to connect with other species (*bio = life*; *philia = love*). Wilson believes that we are genetically predisposed to make these connections because of our evolutionary roots. Yet it would appear that particularly in cities, we work against this philosophy by creating *biophobia*, a fear of nature, a fear of other species. For example, we warn children against touching and getting dirty, and instill fear that an insect might bite.

Evidence of biophilia has been observed in children even younger than two (Moore & Marcus, 2008).

> "It's obvious that the key problem facing humanity in the coming century is how to bring a better quality of life—for 8 billion or more people—without wrecking the environment entirely in the attempt."
>
> **—E.O. Wilson**

You can view a powerful speech by Edward O. Wilson in a TED conversation in support of life on Earth:

http://www.ted.com/talks/e_o_wilson_on_saving_life_on_earth.html

David Weikart (1931–2003), an American psychologist, was the creator of the internationally known early childhood model known as cognitively oriented curriculum or *High Scope Research Foundation Curriculum*. It is the most well-known early childhood model based almost completely on Jean Piaget's theories on child psychology and cognitive development and supports the concepts of active learning where children have hands-on experiences. Having children *plan*, *do*, and then *review* their experiences is integral to this program. In 1962, Weikart collaborated with a committee of elementary education leaders to create the *Perry Preschool Project* in Ypsilanti, Michigan. In the High Scope Program, children and adults spend time outside every day to engage with nature in all its forms.

> "The outdoor play space is a wonderful place for children to test their voices, exercise their muscles, explore nature, and interact with others. Children have the opportunity to use toys and equipment that are not typically available or used during indoor play. They are free to engage in vigorous and noisy play, challenge their physical capabilities, and experience nature with all of their senses."
>
> —High Scope Early Childhood Curriculum (2009)

David Suzuki (1936–) is an academic, science broadcaster, and environmental activist and is perhaps best known for hosting CBC's *The Nature of Things*, which is seen in over 40 countries. A long-time activist to reverse global climate change, Suzuki cofounded the *David Suzuki Foundation* in 1990 to work to find ways for society to live in balance with the natural world that sustains us. He is the author of 52 books, 15 of which are for children, and the recipient of 24 honorary degrees and the Order of Canada. He states that many environmentalists are concerned with the way young people are growing up. Computers, television, video games, and the Internet offer information and entertainment in a virtual world without the hazards or discomfort of mosquitoes, rain and cold, steep climbs, or "dangerous" animals of the real world—and without all the joys that the real world has to offer. He encourages us to expose our children to reconnect with and appreciate the natural world; otherwise, we can't expect them to help protect and care for it (Suzuki & Moola, 2010).

For Additional Reading

> "The way we see the world shapes the way we treat it, and we will only protect what we know and love."
>
> —David Suzuki

Dr. Joe Frost is a Professor Emeritus at the University of Texas at Austin and has been a leader in the field in early childhood and children's play environments for more than 30 years. A prolific writer, he has written or cowritten 20 books, many translated into other languages. Although he retired in 2000, he continues to produce countless papers, reports, and articles as well as design children's playgrounds in the United States and worldwide. He is a past president of the Association for Childhood Education International and the International Play Association, and has received numerous honours and awards (Frost Play Research Collection, 2012).

> "Children need playgrounds that help them develop a sense of beauty. Some of them look like concentration camps. Children are engaged longer, suffer fewer injuries and have fewer behavior problems on playgrounds that are broad, expansive and designed for all the developmental needs of kids."
>
> —Joe Frost (as cited in Scott, 2000)

For Additional Reading

Robin C. Moore (1969–) is a leading expert in the field of children's play and play environments. He is perhaps best known for his visionary playscape, the *Environmental Yard* in Berkeley, California. This adventure playground reflects a space that engages a full range of children's behaviours in a rich, diverse environment that includes open-ended materials. The inclusion of places where children can interact with nature are critical to his designs. His work is revered in many countries around the world and he has lectured extensively on the issues of childhood and environmental design. An important achievement has been the development of the *Natural Learning Initiative* at the University of North Carolina's College of Design. "The purpose of the Natural Learning Initiative is to promote the importance of the natural environment in the daily experience of all children, through environmental design, action research, education, and dissemination of information" (Natural Learning Initiative, n.d.).* Learn more about the Natural Learning Initiative at

http://naturalearning.org

> "Children have a natural affinity towards nature. Dirt, water, plants, and small animals attract and hold children's attention for hours, days, even a lifetime."
>
> —Robin C. Moore and Herb H. Wong

Anita Rui Olds (1940–1999) was one of the strongest contemporary influences on program environments that continue to inspire us today.

---

*© Natural Learning Initiative/North Carolina State University.

Self-taught in architecture and interior design, she taught others how to create environments for children that comfort, heal, and inspire them (Curtis & Carter, 2003). With a doctorate in Human Development and Social Psychology from Harvard University, she was the founder and director of the Child Care Institute, an annual training program for designers and child-care professionals.

> "Children are miracles. Believing that every child is a miracle can transform the way we design for children's care. When we invite a miracle into our lives, we prepare ourselves and the environment around us. We may set out flowers or special offerings. We may cleanse ourselves, the space, or our thoughts of everything but the love inside us. We make it our job to create, with reverence and gratitude, a space that is worthy of a miracle! Action follows thought. We can choose to change. We can choose to design spaces for miracles, not minimums."
>
> —Anita Olds (as cited in Curtis & Carter, 2003, p. 1)

For Additional Reading

Richard Louv (1949–) has had an enormous influence on our understanding of the importance of nature and its impact on children. The author of eight books, he is perhaps best known for his book *Last Child in the Woods: Saving Our Children from Nature Deficit Disorder*. This book is a must-read for everyone working with children. Louv has lectured tirelessly around the world in his efforts to re-engage children with nature. His call to action has prompted the creation of the *Children and Nature Network* at

 http://www.childrenandnature.org

"It is leading a movement to connect all children, their families and communities to nature through innovative ideas, evidence-based resources and tools, broad-based collaboration and support of grassroots leadership" (Children and Nature Network, n.d.).*

---

*Richard Louv is the author of eight books about nature and development including *Last Child in the Woods: Saving Our Children from Nature-Deficit Disorder* and *The Nature Principle: Human Restoration and the end of Nature-Deficit Disorder*. For more information on the movement to connect children with nature, see www.richardlouv.com or www.childrenandnature.org.

> "Not too many years ago, a child's experience was limited by how far he or she could ride a bicycle or by the physical boundaries that parents set. Today ... the real boundaries of a child's life are set more by the number of available cable channels and videotapes, by the simulated reality of videogames, by the number of megabytes of memory in the home computer. Now kids can go anywhere, as long as they stay inside the electronic bubble."
>
> —Richard Louv (1991)

Jim Greenman (1949–2009) was senior vice president for education and program development at *Bright Horizons Family Solutions*. He had more than 30 years' experience as an early childhood teacher, administrator, researcher, program and facility designer, college professor, and consultant (Greenman, 2005, p. 1). His insightful thinking about what makes for the best environments for children and families, both environmentally and programmatically, pushed the field toward higher and higher standards of caring. Despite his early death, his books will continue to inspire early childhood professionals.

> "No matter where you are on the globe, no matter what infinitesimally small time and space you occupy out of the millions of years life has existed on earth, nature is there, connecting all life. Nature is present in our history, stories, myths, and dreams."**
>
> —Jim Greenman (2007, p. 284)

For Additional Reading

Sharon Gamson Danks is an environmental planner. She has visited schools in Canada, England, Sweden, Denmark, Norway, and the United States. In 2005 she was hired by the San Francisco Unified School District to plan its green schoolyard programs for 16 elementary schools. "Since 2001, Sharon and her firm, *Bay Tree Design*, have assisted over three dozen schools, using a participatory master planning process to help them transform their grounds from ordinary asphalt

---

**Greenman, J. 2007. *Caring Spaces, Learning Places: Children's Environments That Work*. Exhange Press Inc. p. 284.

into vibrant ecosystems for learning and play" (Gamson Danks, 2011). Her book, *Asphalt to Ecosystems,* is an important contribution to our understanding of how to transform playscapes for young children!

> "The ecological schoolyard paradigm shift revisits the way our children play on school playgrounds, seeking to add diversity to the existing single-purpose designs that emphasize competitive sports and standardized play structures. In green school-yards, these features are balanced with age-old 'nature play' elements— boulders, logs, sand, mud, plants, water— that provide children with physically challenging play opportunities, while also engaging their creativity and sense of adventure."
>
> —Sharon Gamson Danks (*Asphalt to Ecosystems*, 2010, p. 2)

For Additional Reading

Rusty Keeler is an artist/designer with a unique sensitivity to the sights, sounds, and experiences of childhood. His natural playscapes journey began in the play equipment manufacturing industry as a conceptual industrial designer for the Danish play equipment manufacturer *Kompan.* He has a deep belief in the beauty and importance of play in children's development and his designs reflect his desire to create a more beautiful world in which to grow and explore. Keeler works throughout the world creating play environments for children and lectures at colleges and conferences internationally. His *Natural Playscapes* book is a visually powerful resource filled with hundreds of compelling pictures of children engaging in nature.

> "We can do it. We can create extraordinary places for young children to discover themselves and the world around them. We can create places for children that tickle the imagination and surprise the senses. We can make places for children of all abilities to interact with nature as they play on the planet. We can craft these spaces with love, collaboration, and care."
>
> —Rusty Keeler (2008, p. 15)

For Additional Reading

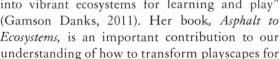

FURTHER INFLUENCES ON PLAYSCAPES

After World War II, many people involved in recreation, artists and architects joined forces with manufacturers to create "novelty" play structures that were expensive, massive, made of metal and often unsafe. These structures, designed by adults without any input from children, were intended to encourage imaginative play and encourage a connection with the past by representing historical and cultural events with play structures that included items such as farm equipment, rocket ships etc. As well, large concrete and rock outcroppings that were to represent animals, shapes and fantasy figures etc. were scattered throughout the playground. These structures were fixed and lifeless, and no action on the part of the children could change or alter the equipment. They were largely ignored by the children, who preferred whatever natural elements might be available on the playground. Children needed a much more diverse environment (Frost, 2006).

During the 1970s and 1980s, there was a resurgence of wooden play equipment. The structures combined physical play features by incorporating swivel swings, tires, slides and climbing apparatus with dramatic play areas by adding hiding places and shapes to the architecture, such as castles and ships. The structure, combined with sand piles, tricycle paths and space for materials with loose parts became the standard. These play works were intended to provide rich play experiences for children (Frost, 2006, p. 3.).

Forest Schools originated in Scandinavia where outdoor living and learning is embedded in society: there is a strong belief that nature and movement are essential to a child's overall development and well-being. Forest schools originated in Sweden in the 1950s when a retired soldier started to teach children about the natural environment through stories, songs, and hands-on experiences. This idea was adopted by Denmark in the 1980s as a solution to the lack of buildings available for the number of nursery places required. The philosophy of the forest school was based upon the desire to provide young children with an education that encouraged appreciation of the wider, natural world and which would encourage responsibility for nature conservation in later life. The concept of Forest Schools was then introduced in the United Kingdom. Children freely exploring their environment were seen to grow in confidence, take responsibility for their own learning

Forest School, Sweden

and show a greater appreciation for the natural world. Forest schools have been rapidly developing in the United Kingdom, where trained and accredited Forest School leaders devise a learning program tailored to children's interests and individual needs. Children are allowed to work at their own pace and the repetitive nature and routine embedded in the program allows the children to build their confidence and self-esteem as well as their social skills. Research has also shown that children with emotional, behavioural, and learning difficulties especially benefit from the Forest School approach.

Canadian Carp Ridge Forest Preschool in Ottawa is situated on 190 acres of land and offers children aged two to six a chance to play in the woods on a daily basis. Children will throw in their plastic toys for tree branches and their sneakers for boots, to head out and explore the great outdoors. They'll do things like hiking, nature crafts, outdoor yoga, shelter-building, gardening, snowshoeing and much more. In an age where families worry about childhood obesity, over-usage of technology, environmental toxins, and climate change, this program offers something different. "As a society, we're greatly impacted by our lack of connection to the outdoors. Children are growing up in manufactured environments where they're disconnected from nature, which can lead

to all kinds of social issues," said Marlene Power, Founder and Director of the Forest Preschool and mother to three-year-old Emry and six-year-old Hazel. She became involved with the Ecowellness Centre after visiting many preschools in the Ottawa area. She felt disenchanted by the lack of natural space for children to play, and the lack of emphasis on environmental principles within conventional preschools" (Canadian Carp Ridge Forest Preschool, media release, 2013).

In 1990, a movement to improve the quality of school grounds was initiated in Britain under the *Learning through Landscapes* (http://www.ltl.org .uk/index.php) program.

The group provides training, resources, and support, and develops programs and research that advance understanding in the better use, designs and management of school grounds. They were inspirational to many working in this field, and there was soon a worldwide interest in their success. Many schools began to look at their asphalt environments and plan for a different outdoor environment for young children. Joining a global movement to re-green our schools is a hopeful act. Green environments become outdoor classrooms where children can socialize, learn about the world around them, and get their hands in the dirt. Green playscapes can "teach civic virtues; the private care of public property, economy, honesty, application, concentration, self-discipline, civic pride, justice, the dignity of labour, and the love of nature. In other words, school gardens formed good, responsible citizens who would contribute to society" (Coffey, A. 2001. *Transforming School Grounds In Greening School Grounds: Creating Habitats For Learning*. Grant, T. & Littlejohn, G. (Eds). Toronto. Green Teacher. P. 7.).

CANADIAN PLAYGROUND STANDARDS

In response to the number of childhood injuries, in the early 1990s the first set of playground safety standards were developed by the *Canadian Standards Association* (CSA). These standards, known as CAN/CSA-Z614-07, are the only ones nationally recognized for children's play spaces and equipment. The standards are guidelines intended "to promote and encourage the provision and use of play spaces that are well-designed, well-maintained, innovative, and challenging, and, in so doing, contribute to the development of healthy children in the broadest sense of the word" (Canadian Standards Association, 2008, p. 2). The

Woodbine Park, Toronto

standards are continuously updated and are applied to public playgrounds, such as those on school grounds, in parks, and in early childhood learning centres. Some provinces, such as Ontario, require early learning and child care centres to meet the CSA Standard before an operating license is issued (Dietze & Kashin, 2012).

Many people and organizations have changed the way we see gardens and natural environments and continue to do so. An avid gardener, the artist *Monet*, famous for his paintings of his gardens in Giverny, France, traded bulbs with the Emperor of Japan. *Frank Lloyd Wright*, architect and interior designer, created his homes with a direct connection to nature. *Vita Sackville West*'s gardens at *Sissinghurst Castle* in Kent draw thousands of visitors each year. Today, *Mike Dixon*'s *Space Garden* at the University of Guelph is creating a space greenhouse that will feed the astronauts on their way to Mars. *Parks Canada* manages 42 National Parks (including seven National Park Reserves), four National Marine Conservation Areas and one National Landmark U.S. First Lady *Michelle Obama* created a renewed interest as she planted her fourth garden in 2012 at the White House with local children. She has also written a book about her experience: *American Grown: The Story of the White House Kitchen Garden and Gardens Across America*. Are there people in your community who are making a difference?

UN CONVENTION ON THE RIGHTS OF THE CHILD

The UN Convention on the Rights of the Child is an international treaty that sets out universally accepted rights for children. It is a benchmark against which a nation's treatment of its children can be measured. In 1989, the United Nations Convention on the Rights of the Child stated that play and age-appropriate play opportunities were important rights of the child.

Article 29 states:

1. States Parties agree that the education of the child shall be directed to:
   (a) *The development of the child's personality, talents and mental and physical abilities to their fullest potential;*
   (b) *The development of respect for human rights and fundamental freedoms, and for the principles enshrined in the Charter of the United Nations;*
   (c) *The development of respect for the child's parents, his or her own cultural identity, language and values, for the national values of the country in which the child is living, the country from which he or she may originate, and for civilizations different from his or her own;*
   (d) *The preparation of the child for responsible life in a free society, in the spirit of understanding, peace, tolerance, equality of sexes, and friendship among all peoples, ethnic, national and religious groups and persons of indigenous origin;*
   (e) *The development of respect for the natural environment.*

Article 31 states:

1. *States Parties recognize the right of the child to rest and leisure, to engage in play and recreational activities appropriate to the age of the child and to participate freely in cultural life and the arts.*
2. *States Parties shall respect and promote the right of the child to participate fully in cultural and artistic life and shall encourage the provision of appropriate and equal opportunities for cultural, artistic, recreational and leisure activity.*

First Lady Michelle Obama and White House Horticulturist Dale Haney work with children from Washington's Bancroft Elementary School to break ground for a White House garden.

UNITED NATIONS DECADE OF EDUCATION FOR SUSTAINABLE DEVELOPMENT (2005–2014)

"After observing the planet for eight days from space, I have a deeper interest and respect for the forces that shape our world. Each particle of soil, each plant and animal is special. I also marvel at the creativity and ingenuity of our own species, but at the same time, I wonder why we all cannot see that we create our future each day, and that our local actions affect the global community, today as well as for generations to come."

—Roberta Bondar (cited in Government of Ontario, 2007, p. 2)

As we near the end of the *UN Decade of Education for Sustainable Development*, governments across Canada and around the world have introduced a wide variety of environmental education and sustainability initiatives. For example, in Ontario, Dr. Roberta Bondar, the first Canadian female astronaut in space, chaired an expert panel to analyze needs and research successful approaches to teaching and learning about the environment in elementary and secondary schools. The panel's report—*Shaping Our Schools, Shaping Our Future*—was published in 2007.

The environmental education framework addresses the need for a unified and cohesive approach that will ensure consistent province-wide implementation. There were five guiding principles:

1. Environmental education is not only about visible environmental issues but also about their underlying causes, and so places an emphasis on personal and social values and active stewardship.

2. Student engagement and leadership are central to environmental education.

3. Leadership by example means integrating elements of environmental education and responsible environmental practices into all decisions and actions.

4. Environmental education must be implemented locally so that it is meaningful and relevant to our diverse communities.

5. Realizing environmental education in Ontario schools is a long-term, ongoing process that will evolve over time.

This framework will enable Ontario's young people to develop the skills, knowledge, and perspectives they will need to become engaged and environmentally responsible citizens. (Government of Ontario, 2009, p. 25)

SUMMARY

There is no question that early visionaries understood the importance and impact of outdoor play and nature experiences for young children. We owe much to the dreamers and creative thinkers who have come before us; because of their influence, today we see a growing international nature community that is providing leadership and guidance as we work together to provide vibrant outdoor environments for all children.

Inside LOOK

Evergreen!

Since 1991 the *Evergreen Foundation* has been engaging Canadians in creating and sustaining dynamic outdoor spaces—in schools, communities and homes. By deepening the connection between people and nature, and empowering Canadians to take a hands-on approach to their urban environments, Evergreen is improving the health of our cities—now and for the future. Through *Evergreen Common Grounds and Toyota Evergreen Learning Grounds*, Evergreen is a leading national funder and facilitator of local, sustainable greening projects in schoolyards, parks and communities across Canada. Evergreen has helped fund over 3,000 School Ground Greening Projects and over 2,000 Community Greening Projects in parks and public spaces. (Evergreen, 2012)

Heidi Campbell is the senior designer, *Learning Grounds* at Evergreen Brick Works Centre for Green Cities in Toronto. Heidi has been an integral part of the design of the *Children's Garden in Chimney*

(continued)

Court, which provides an urban context for children to discover and connect to nature. The key program themes in Chimney Court are food, water, and handwork; the areas include a child-sized greenhouse, a traditional bake oven and outdoor kitchen, vegetable and flower gardens, a fire pit, a chipmunk maze, a hobbit house made out of mud and straw, an outdoor workshop including large stores of natural materials, and a sand and water play area. Using a variety of natural materials—logs, branches, bark, stone, clay, sand—children are the primary architects and builders of creative and traditional structures and objects.

Inside LOOK

World Forum Foundation

With ever-increasing environmental challenges, the World Forum's initiative "*Raising Environmentally Passionate Future Generations*" is an important step forward. The goal is to recruit, motivate, and train environmental stewards—236 teams from 93 nations to reconnect over two million children with nature. In partnership with the *Nature Conservancy* and the *International Federation of Landscape Architects*, the teams will comprise educators, environmental scientists, community health care workers and landscape architects. Over a five-year period, teams will receive training and interactive tools to implement projects such as conferences, community forums, and public policy initiatives, and then come back together to analyze their projects and plan for future developments (World Forum Foundation, 2011).

Inside LOOK

Scotland—Curriculum for Excellence Through Outdoor Learning

Scotland has become a world leader in its approach to outdoor learning. The country's outstanding document, *Curriculum for Excellence Through Outdoor Learning* helps educators understand the important role that they play in an integrated hands-on approach to outdoor experiences. At the core of this philosophy is "challenge, enjoyment, relevance, depth, development of the whole person and an adventurous approach to learning. The following are fundamental principles:

- *Smarter*—Outdoor learning encourages the interplay and relationship between curriculum areas. This awareness promotes lifelong learning and develops critical thinking skills.
- *Healthier*—Learning outdoors can lead to lifelong recreation. Activities such as walking and cycling which are ideal for physical and emotional well-being contribute to a healthier Scotland.
- *Safer and Stronger*—Outdoor learning activities span social divisions and can help build stronger communities. Some organizations have therapeutic programmes where outdoor learning plays a central role with opportunities to develop skills to assess and manage risk when making decisions.
- *Greener*—Frequent and regular outdoor learning encourages children and young people to engage with the natural and built heritage. Scotland's countryside and urban areas provide ideal settings for children and young people to understand the global significance of sustainability issues and inform personal decisions that contribute towards a greener Scotland.

- **Wealthier and Fairer**—The outdoors provides excellent opportunities to use a wide range of skills and abilities not always visible in the classroom. Becoming aware of such skills can fundamentally change personal, peer and staff perceptions and lead to profound changes in life expectations and success.[*] (Learning and Teaching Scotland, 2010, p. 5)

[*]Learning and Teaching Scotland, 2010. p. 5: http://www.educationscotland.gov.uk/images/cfeoutdoorlearningfinal_tcm4-596061.pdf. © Crown copyright 2012.

Inside LOOK

Toronto District School Board

Canada's largest school board, The Toronto District School Board is the first to have a department dedicated to Environmental Education. Their vision for the development of human-environmental curriculum is:

1. **Sense of Place** to explore and see our immediate surroundings, both natural and built, and to look beyond the immediate to the larger landscape.
2. **Ecosystems Thinking** to help us examine how nature works and to understand how natural and human systems are interconnected and interdependent
3. **Human Impact** to weigh the consequences, both helpful and harmful, of human interventions into natural systems.[*]

There is no question that green environments including school gardens provide opportunities to include all of these elements. The day-to-day interactions between children and their garden provide powerful learning opportunities. With the addition of a butterfly meadow, a pond, wall murals, rock gardens, a stage for dramatic play, nesting boxes and bird feeders, roof top gardens, container gardens, nature trails—the possibilities are endless (Houghton, 2003, p. 21).

[*]Houghton, E. 2003. A Breath Of Fresh Air Celebrating Nature and School Gardens. The Learnxs Foundation & Sumach Press, Toronto District School Board. p. 21. © E. Houghton.

 http://michigantelevision.org/childrenplay/index.html

"Where Do the Children Play?" is a PBS documentary on the history, psychology, and politics of children's free play and the growing movement to bring it back into children's lives.

Courtesy of Angie Valente

Children's artwork: Angie

Chapter 2

CHALLENGES TO OUTDOOR PLAY

Bindi Irwin

Bindi Irwin was born July 24, 1998, in Queensland, Australia. Both of Bindi's parents were involved in Australia's animal conservation movement. Her father, Steve, hosted several television programs before his death in 2006 after being stung by a stingray while snorkelling near the Great Barrier Reef. He and Bindi had been working on a wildlife show for children, which featured Bindi as the host. From the first episode of *Bindi: The Jungle Girl*, which debuted in 2007, it was clear that she had inherited her father's adventurous spirit. The program was intended to educate young viewers about wildlife and their habitats. In 2008, she received a daytime Emmy Award as Outstanding Performer in a Children's Series, the youngest performer to win this award. She also appears with her mother on *Planet's Best with Terri and Bindi* on the Animal Planet cable network. *Bindi's Bootcamp* is one of her most recent ventures, a game show that requires participants to demonstrate their wildlife knowledge. Among her many other environmental projects, she supports *Wildlife Warriors Worldwide,* a conservation group started by her father (Biography.com, 2012).

ZUMA Wire Service/Alamy

OUTCOMES:

1. Identify the ways in which outdoor play for young children has changed over time.

2. Examine the challenges for families in providing an active healthy lifestyle.

3. Identify the implications of inactive children and their health risks.

> "Every child should have mud pies, grasshoppers, water bugs, tadpoles, frogs, mud turtles, elderberries, wild strawberries, acorns, chestnuts, trees to climb. Brooks to wade, water lilies, woodchucks, bats, bees, butterflies, various animals to pet, hayfields, pine-cones, rocks to roll, sand, snakes, huckleberries and hornets. And any child who has been deprived of these has been deprived of the best part of education."
>
> **—Luther Burbank (American horticulturalist and botanist, 1849–1926)**

Snow!

Lynn Wilson

CHILDREN AND PLAY

> "The world is rich with learning opportunities for children. And yet, our eagerness to expose children to the wonders of our technological society, coupled with our fears of ever-lurking strangers, means more children than ever before have never experienced the thrills of woods, fields, or streams, not to mention the very neighborhoods in which they live."*
>
> **—Rhoda Redleaf (2010, p. 1)**

PLAY DEFINED

Play is defined as an activity in which children are actively engaged, that is freely chosen, intrinsically motivated, nonliteral and serves the child's needs for pleasure, emotional release, mastery or resolution. (Johnson, Christie, & Wardele, 2004, p. 42)

Children play within their personal codes of behaviour, as well as those of their culture and society. At times, play tests those codes, and this gives rise to one of the community's key concerns about play and how adults manage it. Play is important to the child in providing an arena for behaviour

that is not overwhelmingly dominated by adult views and values. It is an important part of the experience, which may look like mistakes or bad behaviour from other points of view, from which children learn the appropriate behaviours for their own adulthood. Some boundaries are required, but these need to be skilfully drawn and applied if the benefits of play for the child are not to be eroded. (National Play Fields Association, 2000, p. 7)

Play is important for healthy personal development. *The Mental Health Foundation,* National Health Service, United Kingdom (1999) identified some children who "are more resilient in the face of stressful life events than others, e.g., poverty or family discord will impinge more on some children than others," Many of the attributes enhanced by play are found to be helpful in developing resilience: "those children who have good communication skills, a positive attitude, a problem solving approach and the capacity to reflect tend to be more resilient. The ability to plan, a belief in control, a sense of humour are all qualities that can lead to resilience. (Mental Health Foundation, 1999, p. 10)

Children prefer to be outside and unsurprisingly gravitate toward natural areas (Evans, 2006) where they feel excited by the chance of finding something new and the opportunity to explore and discover things for themselves.

---

*Hey Kids! Out the Door, Let's Explore! By Rhoda Redleaf (2010), pg. 1. © Redleaf Press.

PLAY IN NATURE

All of us in the field of early childhood understand the importance of play in children's development. In his book *Caring Spaces, Learning Places* (2007, pp. 284–286), Jim Greenman eloquently states the following qualities of the natural world to explain why it is so rich in play potential:

- Nature is universal and timeless
- Nature is unpredictable
- Nature is bountiful
- Nature is beautiful
- Nature is alive with sounds
- Nature creates a multitude of places
- Nature is real
- Nature nourishes and heals*

Theemes (1999, p. 3) would add that play includes the following basic elements:

- Play is pleasurable and gratifying
- Play is self-directed and engaged in freely
- Play is intrinsically rewarding for children
- Play is challenging, active and engaging
- Play is imaginative**

Because young children learn primarily through their senses and through motoric manipulation, they are excellent candidates for nature education experiences. The elements of the natural world offer raw materials to manipulate, and best practices in early childhood education promote the hands-on approach to learning. Robin Moore, a leading expert in this field states:

> Children live through their senses. Sensory experiences link the child's exterior world with their interior, hidden, affective world. Since the natural environment is the principal source of sensory stimulation, freedom to explore and play with the outdoor environment through the senses in their own space and time is essential for healthy development of an interior life ... the content of the environment is a critical factor in this process. A rich, open environment will continuously present alternative choices for creative engagement. A rigid, bland environment

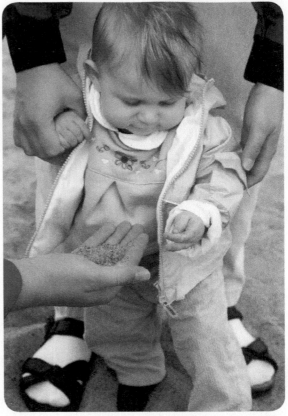

Sensory experiences abound in the outdoor playscape.

will limit healthy growth and development of the individual or the group. (Moore, 1997, p. 203)

The younger the child the more the child learns through sensory and physical activity; thus, the more varied and rich the natural setting (e.g., rocks, running water, varieties of colours and sounds, and the wide range of permitted activities), the greater its contribution to the physical, cognitive, and emotional development of the child (Rivkin, 1997, p. 61).

When the senses become dulled through lack of participation, a young child may lose forever the ability to find satisfaction from his environment.

OUR CONNECTION TO THE OUT-OF-DOORS

All human cultures are impacted by wildlife and its habitat since we all share a need for food, water, shelter, and space. Our values, traditions, legends, myths, and religious teachings inform and instruct us on how we are to interact with the environment in which we live. We all are impacted by the same environmental influences—both positive and negative.

---

*Greenman, J. 2007. *Caring Spaces, Learning Places: Children's Environments That Work*. Exchange Press Inc. pp. 284–286.

**From *Let's Go Outside: Designing the Early Childhood Playground*, p. 3 by Theemes, T., Ypsilanti, MI: HighScope Press. ©1999. HighScope Educational Research Foundation. Used with permission.

BIOPHILIA VERSUS BIOPHOBIA

Edward O. Wilson and evolutionary psychologists use the term *biophilia* to refer to the innate, hereditary emotional attraction of humans to nature and other living organisms. Biophilia is the biologically based human need to affiliate with nature and the genetic basis for humans' positive responses to nature. The opposite, *biophobia* is the aversion to nature. White (2004) explains that this deep psychological link with the natural world from a young age is seen as fundamental in understanding the world and an individual's role within it.

> Efforts to teach about "environmental issues" abstractly and at too young an age can result in individuals becoming dissociated from or even anxious about nature with the potential for biophobia—from wonder and enjoyment to fear and dislike. Biophobia ranges from discomfort in natural places to active scorn for whatever is not man-made, managed or air conditioned. Biophobia is also manifest in the tendency to regard nature as nothing more than a disposable resource.* (Wilson, 2007, p. 141)

Biophobia at work!

Fifty-three percent of children in a worldwide study expressed feelings of fear about natural processes such as rain, wind, and snow (World Forum Foundation, n.d.).

NATURE DEFICIT DISORDER

In his book *Last Child in the Woods* (2008), Richard Louv coined the phrase *nature deficit disorder*. "It describes the human cost of alienation from nature, among them: diminished use of the senses, attention difficulties, and higher rates of physical and emotional illnesses. The disorder can be detected in individuals, families, and communities" (Louv, 2008, p. 15). In calling for a "nature–child reunion," Louv talks about "how blessed our children can be—biologically, cognitively, and spiritually—through positive physical connection to nature" (as quoted in Wilson, 2009, p. 34). In Louv's book *The Nature Principle* (2011), he suggests that in an age of rapid environmental, economic, and social transformation, the future will belong to the nature-smart—those individuals, families, businesses, and political leaders who develop a deeper understanding of nature, and who balance the virtual with the real.

James Cameron, the film maker of *Avatar*, one of the most-watched films in history supports the principles Louv outlined in his work. Cameron believes that this movie awakened in us a knowledge that

> the endangered human species is paying an awful price as it loses touch with nature. It asks questions about our relationship with each other, from culture to culture, and our relationship with the natural world at a time of nature-deficit disorder. This collective disorder threatens our health, our spirit, our economy, and our future stewardship of the environment.** (Louv, 2011, p. 4)

THE TIMES THEY ARE A-CHANGING!

Years ago our grandparents wandered the streets involved in active and imaginative play with often nothing more than sticks, ropes, rocks, stones, and bicycle rims—yet their play was vibrant, inventive, and engaging.

Today's children are living a childhood of firsts. They are the first day care generation; the first truly multi-cultural generation; the first generation to

---

*Wilson, R. 2007. *Nature and Young Children – Encouraging Creative Play and Learning in Natural Environments*. Routledge Taylor and Francis Group London and New York. p. 141.

**From THE NATURE PRINCIPLE by Richard Louv. © 2011 by Richard Louv. Reprinted by permission of Algonquin Books of Chapel Hill. p. 4.

Children's cart, 1911

grow up in an electronic bubble, the environment defined by computers and new forms of television; the first post sexual revolution generation; the first generation for which nature is more an abstraction than reality; the first generation to grow up in a new kind of dispersed, deconcentrated city, not quite urban, rural, or suburban. (Louv, 1991, p. 5)

Our relationship with the outdoors has changed because times have changed. Just ask any Boomer parents and they will tell you about the unstructured freedom of outdoor play. "Come home when the street lights go on" was a familiar parental phrase. We were raised with an intimate contact with natural environments. We walked or rode our bikes just about anywhere; the fields, ball parks, empty parking lots, and the woods were our playgrounds. We explored, took risks, and discovered—all without parent supervision—and were intimately connected to our territory, in rhythm with the passing of the sun and the changing of the seasons.

Peter McDonnell (2005) at the Johns Hopkins University School of Medicine states that

today our society seems to believe there should be no risks; the corollary of this belief is that if something untoward occurs, someone must be forced to pay. If a child falls off a swing at the park and hurts him or herself, the city must pay. In a previous town where I lived in California, city parks were actually being closed because the city could no longer obtain insurance against playgrounds lawsuits.

THE IMPACT OF TECHNOLOGY

Researchers believe that the amount of time that children spend at daycare, the increases in television viewing, the fact that children have fewer siblings

to play with than children of previous generations, the greater parental constraints in play places, and safety concerns have resulted in dramatic increases in sedentary behaviour.

Any school-age child will be able to tell you the names of a favourite television show or video game but very few would be able to name the flowers or trees that grow in their own backyards.

The world at large is becoming more impersonal; sounds of nature come from TV screens rather than real experiences. Children today are the first generation for whom nature is more abstract than a reality. The use of the television and the Internet in the home is having a dramatic impact on physical activity and our connection with the natural world. TVs and DVDs are often used to entertain children as parents cope with their busy lives. Changes in family structure and many more mothers being employed outside the home mean that many children return to an empty house after school and are warned about going outside for fear of them coming to harm. Children with computers and TV sets in their bedrooms spend more time away from other family members and friends.

- In 1971, the average age at which children began to watch TV was 4 years, today, it is 5 months.

- More than 90% of children begin watching TV before the age of two, despite recommendations that screen time should be zero for children under two, and limited to 1 hour for children 2–5.

- The National Longitudinal Survey of Children and Youth (NLSCY) indicates that 27% of those aged 2–3 and 22% of those aged 4–5 are watching more than 2 hours of TV per day. (Active Healthy Kids Canada, 2010)

There's no denying the benefits of the Internet. But electronic immersion, without a force to balance it, creates the hole in the boat—draining our ability to pay attention, to think clearly, to be productive and creative. The best antidote to negative electronic information immersion will be an increase in the amount of *natural* information we receive. The more high-tech we become, the more nature we need.* (Louv, 2011, p. 4)

---

*From THE NATURE PRINCIPLE by Richard Louv. © 2011 by Richard Louv. Reprinted by permission of Algonquin Books of Chapel Hill. p. 24.

The Forecast*

Perhaps our age has driven us indoors.
We sprawl in the semi-darkness
Dreaming sometimes
Of a vague world spinning in the wind.
But we have snapped our locks,
Pulled down our shades,
Taken all precautions.
We shall not be disturbed.
If the earth shakes, it will be on a screen;
And if the prairie wind spills down our streets
And covers us with leaves,
The weatherman will tell us.

Daniel F. Jaffe

THE USE OF THE CAR

Researchers repeatedly tell us about the reduction in outdoor opportunities for young children. Often children are driven to school, losing the chance to walk and socialize with their friends, both valuable learning opportunities. According to Active Healthy Kids (2011), in a regional study, 42 percent of children are driven to school but would allow their children to walk or cycle if they were not alone, due to concerns about safety. In their own neighbourhoods, some parents are reluctant to let children use their local parks for the same reasons.

> Pabayo et al (2011) found that children in Quebec who used active transportation—walking or riding their bikes to school—over three years had fewer weight issues and consistently had a lower body-mass index growth curve. He found that children from poorer socio-economic backgrounds, those with a single parent and those with an older sibling were more likely to fall into the active category. Children in British Columbia, Saskatchewan and Manitoba were significantly more likely to use active transportation and children in the Atlantic provinces were less likely. Urban children are walkers and bike riders to a greater extent than their counterparts in rural areas where greater distances make buses, cars, and trucks necessary. The number one predictor of use for active transportation to school is the distance between home and school. Walking to school declines after age 11 because middle schools and high schools are often farther from home. (Tobin, 2011)

*© Daniel F. Jaffe. Reprinted by permission.

THE ROLE OF FAMILIES IN OUTDOOR EXPERIENCES

The role of parents has become more and more complex. We live an increasingly hurried and pressured lifestyle. There is enormous pressure for academic performance and the role that "good" parents play in building every skill and aptitude that a child might need from the earliest age. "'Helicopter parents' can be found hovering protectively over their offspring, ready to swoop in and rescue them at the first sign of trouble. They pave their way, fight their battles for them, and generally deny them free rein to succeed or fail on their own" (Mercogliano, 2007, p. 5).

Today so many children live restricted lives and many of the traditional places where children used to play are now lost to them. For some children, the hallway in their apartment building is their "outdoor" play space.

> While current crime rates in Canada are about equal to what they were in the 1970s, the increase in news coverage of crime has fuelled parental fears of letting their children outside. Among mothers, 82% cite safety concerns and almost half of parents cite fear of exposure to child predators as reasons they restrict outdoor play. [Fifty-eight percent] of Canadian parents agree they are very concerned about keeping their children safe and feel they have to be over-protective of them in this world. (Active Healthy Kids Canada, 2012, p. 13)

Wells and Evans (2003) discovered that 5-year-old children who, due to dangerous traffic conditions, could not easily play outdoors unsupervised exhibited poorer social, behaviour, and motor skills and had fewer playmates than children with easy access to the outdoors. For those living in

Safe risk taking is an important life skill.

Ingrid Crowther

the suburbs, explosive growth patterns, increased traffic, great distances to be covered to reach recreational facilities or friends creates a dependence on the car rather than places to ride bikes, walk, or play.

In rural communities, children are often limited in their mobility. They may live far from friends and must rely on a car to connect with others, and walking or biking may be limited due to concerns about their safety and the long distances that they must travel.

And so, many children experience physical activity in a structured environment—swimming lessons, soccer games, gymnastics class, dance and music lessons—and adults are almost always present, given their concern about children's safety and security. Many children live in this world of organized experiences in groups almost from birth; through enrichment activities and organized child care. Free play is very different: in free play, children make the rules; in sports and organized activities, adults make and enforce the rules.

Weather plays a role in outdoor play. When properly dressed in rain gear, playing in a warm rain and splashing in puddles is an engaging activity. Playing outside should not be restricted to warm, dry weather; late autumn, winter, and early spring present their own unique opportunities for learning and active imaginative play. Being active in winter is an important part of enjoying life for Canadians but many families spend most of their leisure time indoors. Many of us grew up with the myth that going out in cold or wet weather causes colds and other illnesses. However, fresh air and active outdoor play, even if it's cold outside, can help keep us healthy.

ROLE OF EARLY CHILDHOOD ENVIRONMENTS

Child care facilities clearly have an important role to play in physical activity opportunities. Bower et al. (2008) identified those children at facilities with high physical activity environment scores as assessed using the *Environment and Policy Assessment and Observation Instrument* (a unique measure of nutrition and the physical environment) as receiving approximately 80 more minutes of moderate physical activity per week. Similarly, Dowda et al. (2004) identified that those preschoolers attending facilities that offered more

Ingrid Crowther

Winter provides many outdoor play opportunities.

resources and better-educated teachers experienced significantly higher levels of physical activity.

> Given the large numbers of Canadian preschoolers attending daycare and the possible variation in resources, quality and outdoor time, policies and procedures that support play and activity are important and necessary. The potential implications of preschoolers' insufficient activity for the current obesity epidemic are staggering; if nearly half of our preschoolers are not "catching on" to the joy and habit of engaging in regular physical activity now, it is startling to think about what will happen to their body compositions as they enter and advance through the more sedentary homework years. (Tucker & Irwin, 2009, pp. 141–142)

The *Active Healthy Kids Canada Report* (2011), which focused on the after-school period from 3:00–6:00 p.m., states:

- Children in lower income families are less able to participate in organized sport and physical activity after school.
- 72% of parents say their children don't have access to a supervised program after school.

Outdoor Play

Growing up in central Ontario cottage country, I spent my childhood exploring and playing outdoors. A philosophy that I have embraced throughout my life is that there isn't bad weather just bad gear. You have to be prepared before heading outside. This philosophy stuck with me as I started my career in Early Childhood Education. First I worked as an Early Childhood Educator in programs located in downtown Toronto; later in Nunavut where I supported and licensed Early Childhood programs; and in Winnipeg, Manitoba, where I taught at a college in the Early Childhood Education program. All these experiences made me realize that it doesn't matter where you live or the weather conditions, you need to be prepared. This applies to children as well as the caregivers supervising them.

As an ECE, the key for me was being comfortable enough to explore and enjoy myself outdoors with the children, being able to embrace time outside in all seasons, and not being afraid to get dirty/wet/cold. Getting children ready to head outside for time outdoors is a challenge, no matter where you live in Canada. However, the culture that surrounds your community can make a difference.

In Nunavut the Inuit embrace living out on the land—even in the cold of the winter or early spring. Inuit Qaujimajatuqangit (IQ), Inuit traditional knowledge, has a set of guiding principles that incorporate Inuit social values. One of the guiding principals is Avatimik Kamattiarniq, the concept of environmental stewardship. It supports the relationship Inuit have with the land and themselves. This concept is woven into daily living within Nunavut communities. Children come to child care settings prepared to spend time outdoors, to explore, and to learn more about the world they live in. The children and child care staff members view outdoor play as integral to the early childhood setting.

Exploring the outdoors; having fun in the puddles left on the tundra from melting snow.

Sarah McMahon

Contributed by: Sarah McMahon, Pangnirtung, Nunavut

www

http://www.gov.nu.ca/hr/site/beliefsystem.htm

http://www.turtletrack.org/Issues01/Co01132001/CO_01132001_Inuit.htm

- Fewer than half of the after school programs reported had physical activity as a primary purpose.

- Boys are more likely than girls to engage in physical activity in the after school period.

According to the 2007–2009 *Canadian Health Measures Survey*, Statistics Canada (2010), 6–19-year-olds in Canada spend an average of 8.6 hours per day, or 62 percent of their waking hours, in sedentary pursuits.

The Ontario Supplement to the Active Healthy Kids Canada (2011) Report Card on Physical Activity for Children and Youth states that

in its report to the government of Ontario the *Ontario Chronic Disease Prevention Alliance* states that there are emerging concerns in the

Balls are Banned!

A Toronto elementary school banned most balls from its playground, citing the need to protect staff and students after a parent got hit in the head with a soccer ball.

The new policy has infuriated parents and students, and exposes what child-health researchers say is a growing focus on child safety that is keeping kids from being physically active. Earl Beatty Junior and Senior Public School principal Alicia Fernandez sent home a note warning parents their students are no longer allowed to bring soccer balls, basketballs, baseballs, footballs and volleyballs to school. All balls that weren't made of sponge or nerf material would be confiscated. The Toronto school isn't the only one to ban balls over concern for student safety. Last year, an Ottawa public school banned balls on the playground during winter. In June, a public school St. Catharines, Ont., banned balls after a girl got hit in the head while watching a schoolyard soccer game. Both bans were overturned after students at the schools started a petition.

"It sends the wrong message that playing these unorganized games or even some form of reasonably organized sports is dangerous and generally speaking that's not true," said Dr. Mark Tremblay, chief scientist at Healthy Active Living Kids Canada. "The health benefits far exceed the risks associated with them."

Source: Adapted from McMahon, T. 2011. Parents Cry Foul After Elementary School Bans Balls Over Playground Safety. National Post. November 16. Reprinted with the express permission of: National Post, a division of Postmedia Network Inc.

12 indicators of the status of physical activity of children and youth. Less active are girls, adolescents, those with lower family income and parent education levels. The report also states that those who are less able, those who are overweight and those with disabilities are often excluded from active play and have difficulty finding integrated physical activity opportunities.

Parents worry that something is wrong with children, especially boys, when they cannot sit still and focused in a classroom for hours at a time deciphering and manipulating symbols. However, scores of studies show that natural environments heighten mental acuity, diminish stress and even speed up physical healing. There is even evidence that nature's ever-changing cycles—full of visual, olfactory, and physical complexity—can increase intelligence. People and animals in complex, constantly changing environments show an increase in the number and complexity of the neural connections in their brains: they become smarter! Conversely, creatures in stagnant environments show a decrease in neural complexity: they become both more listless and more violent. Human beings simply seem wired to work better mentally, physically and emotionally with steady infusions of nature. Researchers say that this is because we are genetically predisposed to feel most fully at ease in environments that would have facilitated survival for our earliest human ancestors (Dannenmaier, 1998, p. 12).

LACK OF OUTDOOR ACTIVITY— A GLOBAL PHENOMENON

"Today just one in five children regularly play outside in their neighbourhood. The rest are denied the chance to get out of the house and have the everyday adventures that, to people of my generation, are what childhood is all about."

—David Cameron, British Prime Minister, 2009

"The cost of physical inactivity in England has been estimated at £8.2 billion a year" (Fields in Trust, 2010). "In one global study, playing with friends was the single favourite pastime of kids around the world" (*Active Healthy Kids Report Card*, 2012, p. 13).

> [Ninety-two percent] of Canadian children said they would choose playing with friends over watching TV. Given the choice, 74% of Canadian kids in Grades 4 to 6 would choose to do something active after school, with 31% choosing to play with their friends at the playground. (*Active Healthy Kids Report Card*, 2012, p. 13)

Most people would agree that, despite our scientific knowledge, the general state of physical and mental well-being in Western society is pretty poor. The World Health Organization describes health as "the condition of perfect bodily, spiritual and social well-being and not solely the absence of illness and injury" (Geneva Foundation, n.d.).

SEDENTARY BEHAVIOUR

Parents and teachers' potential overestimation of physical activity levels in children may result in a decreased emphasis placed on the importance of encouraging and supporting active lifestyles (Tucker, 2008). Typical physical activity of preschoolers is often characterized by short, intermittent bouts of intense movement between longer bouts of lower-intensity movement. This was recently demonstrated in a Canadian study that found that 95 percent of moderate to vigorous activity occurred in chunks of time that lasted 15 seconds or less (Obeid et al., 2011). Based on several preschooler studies from the literature, young children now typically spend a lot of time in sedentary behaviours, with estimates ranging from 74 percent to 84 percent of the day (Timmons et al., 2011). According to Active Healthy Kids Canada (2010), Canadian data indicate that fewer than half of children aged 4–5—and just one-third of 2–3-year-olds—participate in regular, unorganized sports and other physical activities each week. And in child care facilities, where more and more children spend their days, physical activity levels are low, with as much as 89 percent of children's time spent sitting still. The NLSCY concurs with this data, indicating that only 36 percent of 2–3-year-olds and 44 percent of 4–5-year-olds regularly engage in unorganized sport and physical activities each week.

"Studies of sedentary behaviour suggest that sitting for extended periods of time increase[s] a person's chances of developing a wide range of illnesses and diseases, including several types of cancer, cardiovascular disease, obesity and Type II diabetes" (McGinn, 2011).

In 2011, "The Canadian Society for Exercise Physiology's (CSEP) released the *Canadian Sedentary Behaviour Guidelines for Children and Youth* the first, systematic evidence-based sedentary behaviour guidelines in the world for children 5–11 years and 12–17 years" (CSEP, 2011). These guidelines provide recommendations for limiting sedentary behaviour and will be welcomed by those working to improve the health and well-being of our children.

CHRONIC ILLNESSES

Today, chronic illnesses and allergies are on the increase and there is a renewed interest in holistic medicine and the wisdom of our elders for healthy alternative solutions to our health issues. A study published in 2003 concluded that the rate at which American children are prescribed antidepressants almost doubled in five years; the steepest increase—66 percent—was among preschool children (Rawlings, 1998, p. 6). Louv (2005) indicated that "although countless children who suffer from mental illness and attention disorders do benefit from medication ... new evidence suggests that the need for such medications is intensified by children's disconnection from nature" (p. 48).

PHYSICAL ACTIVITY

There is no question that the benefits of children's participation in physical activity are well documented. There is a reduction in obesity, depression, and anxiety and an improvement in musculoskeletal health and fitness, cardiovascular health, self-esteem, play and academic performance. While everyone over the age of 2 benefits from daily activity, only 38 percent of girls and 49 percent of boys are sufficiently active and these numbers decline during adolescence (Tucker, 2010). According to Tucker:

> Play in natural settings as opposed to traditional style playgrounds is associated with:
>
> - **Improved motor fitness**
> - **Improved balance**

Keeping active keeps us healthy.

- Improved co-ordination
- Reduced ADHD
- Increased imaginative play
- Brain development and function
- Knowledge gain—science learning and literacy.

Spontaneous exploration—such as riding a tricycle on a winding path—connects physical movement with the mind. Frost and Klein found that

> perceptual abilities are learned and depend upon movement as a medium for this learning. Conversely, movement involves a perceptual awareness of sensory stimulation. All of these enhance or improve perceptual motor functioning—gross motor, fine motor, spatial awareness activities, directional awareness, balance, integration (hitting a moving ball), expressive activities. (Frost & Klein, 1979, p. 40 in Herrington & Beach, 2007)

A growing number of children suffer from **motor illiteracy**. Children who do not play actively outdoors consumers do not become proficient in motor skills (Pereira, Fale, & da Guia Carmo, 2002). This becomes a lifelong issue and affects skeletal and muscular development (Dietze & Kashin, 2012, p. 136).

Inside LOOK

Dr. Evelyn Bak

A growing health concern is the lack of physical activity among children. This lack of exercise and sedentary lifestyle is not only causing a growing number of health problems related to obesity and putting our children at risk of developing adult health problems such as heart disease, type 2 diabetes, stroke, and several types of cancers, but also exposing them to a myriad of other physical changes that carry their own risks. As children spend less time being active and more time being sedentary (watching television and playing computer and video games), their growing and developing bodies become deconditioned and adapt poor postures, leading to decreased joint movement, wasting of trunk muscles, decreased muscular strength and endurance, muscular pain, and stiffness of joints and ligaments. As a health practitioner dedicated to the treatment and prevention of musculoskeletal injuries, I know these physical changes may translate into higher incidences of injuries and illness with longer healing times. The general finding from various studies conducted is that children are suffering from headaches, low back, and neck pain at much earlier ages and eyestrain/visual disturbances and repetitive strain injuries involving the elbows, wrists, and hands are steadily on the rise.

It is evident that more research is required to look into the short- and long-term health effects of a physically inactive, technology-oriented society, especially in our children.

Dr. Evelyn Bak is the owner, founder and resident chiropractor of Balance Health Group in Toronto. Dr. Bak specializes in providing non-invasive treatment and rehabilitative care to patients suffering from an array of symptoms or injuries resulting from sports, motor vehicle accidents, acute and chronic ailments, and more. http://www.thinkbalancehealth.com

Physical activity is important to integrate into the lives of children. It sets the foundation for facilitating and maintaining healthy active living through childhood and adulthood (Cragg & Cameron, 2006; Stolley et al., 2003) and physical activity levels have been shown to remain relatively stable from year to year. Specifically, the physical activity behaviours of preschoolers have been identified as similar to or the same as activity levels during their childhood years (Pate, Baranowski, Dowda, & Trost, 1996 in Tucker, 2008). Physical development has also been linked to bone strength in later life. In a study that examined connections between physical activity and bone density measures in 368 preschool children, researchers found statistically significant correlations between physical activity and optimal bone development (Janz et al., 2010).

Dale, Corbin, and Dale (2000) state that children who engage in physical activities at school tend to engage in more energetic activities at home, while children who have child care and school experiences that lack active physical activity engage in more sedentary behaviours at home, such as watching TV and computer use. Children who play outdoors tend to have more positive attitudes about their physical environment; they are more likely to grow up as adults who are concerned about conservation issues (Louv, 2008, 2011; Suzuki & Vanderlinden, 1999; Wilson 2009).

HOW MUCH ACTIVITY IS ENOUGH?

According to Active Healthy Kids Canada (2010), while international guidelines vary, the global consensus is that all children aged 1 to 5 should get at least two hours of physical activity each day, spread over recreational activities, active transportation, and playtime. Yet recent physical activity recommendations for preschoolers from Australia and the United Kingdom state that preschoolers should be physically active at least three hours every day (Timmons et al., 2011).

Canada's *Physical Activity Guidelines* (2012) for the early years provide us with recommendations for active play. The Canadian Society for Exercise Physiology (CSEP) and ParticipACTION produced the guidelines, with support from the Children's Hospital of Eastern Ontario Research Institute's Healthy Active Living and Obesity Research Group (CHEO-HALO).

Physical activity early in life sets the stage for a healthy lifestyle.

FOR CHILDREN 0–4 YEARS:

- Infants (aged less than 1 year) should be physically active several times daily—particularly through interactive floor-based play.

- Toddlers (aged 1–2 years) and preschoolers (aged 3–4 years) should accumulate at least 180 minutes of physical activity at any intensity spread throughout the day, including:

  - A variety of activities in different environments;
  - Activities that develop movement skills;
  - Progression toward at least 60 minutes of energetic play by 5 years of age.

FOR CHILDREN 5–11 YEARS:

- 60 minutes of moderate to vigorous-intensity physical activity daily
- This should include:

  - Vigorous-intensity activities at least 3 days per week

– Activities that strengthen muscle and bone at least 3 days per week.[*] (CSEP, 2012)

More detailed information is available at

[www] http://www.csep.ca/english/view.asp?x=804

According to newly released data from the *Canadian Health Measures Survey*, only 9% of boys and 4% of girls meet the new Canadian Physical Activity Guidelines. Each of Canada's provinces and territories provide(s) legislation or guidelines for early learning and child care programs that address the recommended outdoor playtime required daily, the minimum types and standards of the equipment for outdoor play, and the maintenance regime required for equipment and outside play space (Dietze & Kashin, 2012, p. 133).[**]

Regulations are in place to ensure a healthy and safe environment for young children in daycares and public playgrounds. The challenge in Canada is the variation in regulations in support of physical activity and outdoor playtime. Only 8 of the 13 provinces and territories have physical activity guidelines and Ontario is the only province that has an outdoor play-time requirement:

every child over thirty months of age that is in attendance for six hours or more in a day plays outdoors for at least two hours each day, weather permitting, unless a physician or parent of the child advises otherwise in writing. (*Day Nurseries Act* Reg. 262ms. 53[4])

OVERWEIGHT AND OBESE CHILDREN

According to the World Health Organization (2012),

In 2010, more than 40 million children under five were overweight. Once considered a high-income country problem, overweight and obesity are now on the rise in low- and middle-income countries, particularly in urban settings. Close to 35 million overweight children are living in developing countries and 8 million in developed countries.

Lack of exercise plus greater consumption of unhealthy food is leading young children down the path of obesity. Obesity among the Canada's children has reached historic highs, with diseases once associated with the middle-aged now affecting teenagers and young adults. Obesity among children and adolescents is tracking at an even faster pace than obesity among adults; according to Health Minister Leona Aglukkaq, in 2012 more than one in four young Canadians is overweight or obese (Xinhua, 2012). Pediatric Surgeon Dr. Kellie Leitch conducted a comprehensive study in 2007 for Health Canada to examine obesity in children. Leitch reports that

we are doing surprisingly poorly when compared to other OECD and countries in measures of the health and wellness of children and youth. Among 29 OECD nations:

- Canada ranks 22nd when it comes to preventable childhood injuries and deaths;
- Canada ranks 27th in childhood obesity; and,
- Canada ranks 21st in child well-being, including mental health. (Leitch, 2007)

According to the World Health Organization, being overweight due to poor nutrition and lack of physical activity is one of the greatest health challenges and risk factors for chronic disease in the twenty-first century. Many life-long diseases begin in childhood. Given the prevalence of childhood obesity, and given its contribution to many diseases, *this is the first generation that may not live as long as their parents*. Obesity is now having a huge life expectancy impact, which was not foreseen 10 years ago.

More than 60 per cent of 860 pediatricians and family doctors in Canada who were surveyed in a study published last year identified parents who are overweight themselves— parents who become defensive when the topic of their child's weight is raised and parents who show little interest in helping their child lose weight—as fundamental barriers to curbing the growing numbers of children who are growing up fat. (Kirkey, 2011)

We know that childhood obesity can present many challenging and often dangerous health issues for even our youngest children—diabetes, heart disease, liver disease, eating disorders, sleep issues, depression, etc.

According to Statistics Canada, 17 per cent of children in Canada are overweight; nine per cent are obese. The proportion of teenage boys

---

[*]Canadian Physical Activity Guidelines, © 2011, 2012. Used with permission of the Canadian Society for Exercise Physiology, www.csep.ca/guidelines.

[**]Dietze, B., Kashin, D. 2012. *Playing and Learning in Early Childhood Education*. Pearson Canada Toronto. p. 133. Reprinted with permission by Pearson Canada Inc.

classified as overweight or obese has more than doubled since 1981, climbing to 31 per cent in 2009. Among teenage girls, it increased to 25 per cent from 14 per cent. Researchers who followed more than 1,700 Ontario high school students for one year found that overweight and obese boys were twice as likely than their healthy-weight peers to be hit, kicked, pushed or shoved around. They also were two times more likely to suffer "relational" bullying—being shunned or excluded from groups and activities. Obese girls, meanwhile, were three times more likely than healthy-weight girls to become the perpetrators of relational bullying—a kind of psychological torment that can cut as deeply as any physical wound.* (Kirkey, 2012)

Leitch's 2007 report also makes recommendations for children with disabilities to participate in physical activity, and specifically

- **Provide infrastructure support for the development of skills development and recreation facilities that allow children with disabilities to fully experience recreation and sport activities; and,**
- **Create an incentive for NGOs to operate programming that is accessible to children with disabilities.**

Further information on playgrounds and obesity can be found at:

 http://childcarecanada.org/documents/childcare-news/11/08/study-suggests-traditional-playgrounds-contribute-childhood-obesity

STRESS AND SICK DAYS

Children who attend *Forest Schools*, common in Europe, had 25 percent fewer sick days than the city children.

One reason for this is that the air is nearly always better outside than indoors because outside a child is less likely to be exposed to virus [sic] and bacteria and not so likely to be infected by other children. Another reason may be that, since stress has been shown to have a negative effect on the immune system, high stress levels may be having a weakening effect on the ability [of] the city children to resist infection (Forest Schools, n.d.).

---

*Kirkey, S. 2012. Canadians Starting to View Overweight as Normal, Doctor's Study Suggests. August 13. Material reprinted with the express permission of: Postmedia News, a division of Postmedia Network Inc.

Wells and Evans (2003) explored the role of nature in reducing life stress. They found that children who were more active in nature were rated lower in symptoms of psychological distress by their mothers. The children themselves saw themselves as being higher in self-esteem. People became less stressed and calmer in natural settings. Their blood pressure and heart rate dropped, and they were more able to focus. The researchers also found that ill people recovered more quickly, and required less medication and follow-up treatment when they spent more time in natural settings.

NEARSIGHTEDNESS

Researchers have found that nearsightedness occurs less often when children spend more time outdoors. Of growing concern is research that indicates that large numbers of East Asian children and youth from countries such as China, Taiwan, Japan, Singapore, Hong Kong, and South Korea are being diagnosed as shortsighted. Myopia has been thought to be related to genetics, but there is a growing concern that screentime and a lack of outdoor light is preventing the release of retinal dopamine, which may prevent myopia (Vieira, 2012, p. 50).

AIR QUALITY AND ASTHMA

In urban settings, children are exposed to outdoor air pollution from industry and traffic exhaust fumes on their way to school, idling behaviour of vehicles outside the centre, and possible outdoor air pollutants inside the classroom. Air pollution is a global health threat to children. *The Physical School Environment* (World Health Organization, n.d.) states that

nearly 80% of 105 European cities surveyed exceeded World Health Organization air quality standards for at least one pollutant. Air pollution in developing world cities is estimated to be responsible for 50 million annual cases of chronic coughing in children younger than 14 years of age. Many schools should be concerned with outdoor air quality. Equipped with some knowledge about air quality in their area, schools may choose to avoid involving students in intensive outdoor exercise during periods of high air pollution. Ozone levels usually peak between midday and evening. Avoiding outdoor activities during high pollution periods and in areas adjacent to highways or near other sources of air pollution will help to minimize asthma attacks in sensitive children and other short- and long-term health effects associated with exposure to air pollutants. (p. 14)

This is also a concern in Canada where "asthma rates have increased four-fold over the last 20 years. Approximately 12% of children and 8% of adults have asthma. Asthma is one of the leading reasons for school and work absenteeism and for hospital admissions among children" (CHealth, 2012).

Depending on the physical environment and location, indoor air quality has been found to have two to five times more pollutants than outdoor air quality levels (World Forum Foundation, 2011). Lack of adequate air filtration and ventilation and the presence of dirt, moisture, and warmth encourages the growth of mould and other contaminants. High levels of CO_2 in playrooms can create health issues such as headaches, dizziness, lethargy, and difficulty breathing. This continues to be an area that educators and health care professionals must monitor in order to provide a safe and healthy environment for the children in their care.

SUN EXPOSURE AND NATURAL LIGHT

Evidence suggests that natural light increases children's cognitive and academic performance, social skills, calmness, and overall psychological wellness. The human body is nourished directly by the stimulation of sunlight. Too much sun exposure can be harmful but too little time outside can also be a concern. Vitamin D, important to healthy development, occurs naturally in our bodies as we absorb its benefits from the sun. There is a concern that Canadians, particularly new Canadians, who do not participate in regular outdoor exposure, are at risk of acquiring diseases due to vitamin D deficiency. Canadians native to northern latitudes have lighter skin, giving them the natural ability to absorb vitamin D. However, many new immigrants require more exposure to the sun because of their skin pigmentation. For example, Vieth (2010, p. 22) indicates, "people from India or equatorial Africa require six times the sun exposure to make the same amount of vitamin D as a white person" (Dietze & Kashin, 2012, p. 137).[*]

Heschong et al (2002) in their study of primary school children in two districts in America found that overall, elementary school students in classrooms with the most daylight showed a 21% improvement in learning rates compared to students in classrooms with the least daylight. This research indicates that daylight has a positive effect on pupils in terms of learning.[**] (Bilton, 2010, p. 20)

Educators should be aware of the benefits of sun exposure while using sunscreen as directed and encouraging the use of clothes, large sun hats, and sunglasses that can reduce exposure to the damaging effects of ultraviolet radiation when necessary. It is important to target children's attitudes and behaviour at a young age, particularly during primary school, when they tend to be most receptive. Preventive health habits developed at a young age may persist into adulthood and can enable healthy adulthood and aging. Schools are vitally important settings to promote sun protection, as during the first 18 years of life a significant proportion of time is spent at school where sun exposure may occur.

Lynn Wilson

Appropriate clothing is essential.

---

[*]Dietze, B., Kashin, D. 2012. *Playing and Learning in Early Childhood Education*. Pearson Canada Toronto. p. 137. Reprinted with permission by Pearson Canada Inc.

[**]Bilton, H. 2010. *Outdoor Learning In The Early Years. Management And Innovation*. Routledge Taylor And Francis Group, p. 20.

TOXICITY

According to the World Health Organization (n.d., p. 11):

> Children are in a dynamic state of growth and their nervous, immune, respiratory, endocrine, reproductive and digestive systems are still developing. Their ability to detoxify and excrete toxins differs from that of adults. Exposure to environmental toxicants during certain stages of development can irreversibly damage the normal development of organs and systems.
>
> - **Young children breathe faster, and eat and drink more in proportion to their body weight than adults. They drink 2.5 times more water, eat 3 to 4 times more food, and breathe 2 times more air. Children therefore absorb more toxicants contained in air, water or food, which makes them more vulnerable to acute and chronic effects of environmental hazards.**
> - **Children often have a greater exposure to environmental hazards than adults: they are closer to the ground where many contaminants settle and young children commonly put their hands into their mouths.**

An important organization is the *Canadian Partnership for Children's Health and Environment* (CPCHE). CPCHE works with community partners such as the *Canadian Association of Physicians for the Environment* and the *Environmental Health Institute of Canada* to coordinate and protect children's health from environmental contaminants. The organization also keeps environment issues in the forefront when governmental policies are being developed.

PRESCRIPTIONS FOR OUTDOORS

A new strategy has been added to a doctor's tool box—prescriptions for outdoor activities!

> In 2010, the *National Environmental Education Foundation* (NEEF), working with the *American Academy of Pediatrics*, launched a training program for paediatricians, focused on prescribing outdoor activities. In Norway, general practitioners can prescribe their patients a stay in a *Care Farm*. In the Netherlands, six hundred health farms are integrated into the health service. In 2006, a group called the *Forest Therapy Executive Committee*, made up of researchers and others began to give forest access to people in Japan to forests that had the greatest therapy benefits and called them *Forest Therapy Base* or *Forest Therapy Road*. In the UK, a growing "green care" movement encourages therapeutic green exercise activities, therapeutic horticulture, animal-assisted therapies, ecotherapy and care farming. The more exercise someone does, the more the cell releases antioxidants to protect it. So a child who plays outside in a natural green space will reduce the chance of developing chronic diseases later in life.[*] (Louv, 2011, pp. 81–86)

Nature prescriptions are becoming more commonplace to alleviate stress and depression and boost physical activity. Dr. Conrad Sichler, a family physician and psychotherapist in Burlington, Ontario, states that "the outdoors can give people a space to simply be apart from the hectic demands of their daily lives. It can also put people in touch with

---

[*]From THE NATURE PRINCIPLE by Richard Louv. © 2011 by Richard Louv. Reprinted by permission of Algonquin Books of Chapel Hill. pp. 81–86.

Inside LOOK

SunSmart Schools—Australia

In Australia, where skin cancer incidence is the greatest in the world, the SunSmart Schools programme emphasizes a sun protection policy that involves the whole school community. Students in SunSmart schools wear sun-protective clothing, hats and sunglasses, apply sunscreen, avoid outdoor activities when the sun is at its highest, plant trees for shade, and study ultraviolet radiation levels at different times of the day. Such schools can apply for accreditation as a SunSmart School and receive a SunSmart School sign. (World Health Organization, n.d.)

a sense of beauty and reverence that can enhance their mental and emotional health" (Gordon, 2011b, p. A14). In Portland, Oregon, Park Rangers are teaming up with doctors to respond to "Park Prescriptions" that are signed off by rangers after the visit ensuring that the doctor's orders for a "hike" have been followed. Another addition to the job descriptions of Park Rangers: they are now health care professionals!

While there are many challenges facing Canadian families and educators alike, there is renewed interest in finding ways to engage young children and start them and their families on a path to a more healthy and active lifestyle.

Inside LOOK

Tracking Schoolchildren with GPS

In the fall [of 2011], researchers at the University of Western Ontario will resume a study in which they plant global positioning systems on elementary school children in London, Ontario in an effort to understand how their environment influences their activity levels. The study, which is in its first phases, is the largest of its kind in Canada and will explore factors at school and in the surrounding community. The goal is to help researchers understand how playsets can be intimidating, why some kids who live only a kilometre away get a ride to school every day, and how to make changes that encourage a healthy lifestyle. Climbing childhood obesity rates—Statistics Canada says about one-in-four Canadian school-aged children are overweight—as well as evidence that exercise and greenery can be a boon to student learning have helped fuel interest in building exercise-friendly spaces for children. But change in the schoolyard—which is supposed to foster an active break from indoor lessons—is likely to be slow, with outdoor spaces low on the priority list in an era of budget crunches and crumbling infrastructure. Most Canadian school playgrounds are built in the if-you-build-it-they-will-play tradition of schoolyard architecture: Flat, barren expanses of asphalt with little seating, less shade, and one monolithic metal play structure. During recess time in the spring there's no shade, and in winter, "Half the school population is waiting for it to end, plastered against the door," said Cam Collyer, program director for *Evergreen*, a national charity that has rebuilt nearly 3,000 playgrounds. He said that for many years, playground design amounted to picking a gym set out of a catalogue. "It's been done one way for a long time, it's like a bad habit." Although some school boards have begun working with Evergreen, some community groups are taking matters into their own hands, funding changes to playgrounds through grants and bake sales. Evergreen designers replace concrete with winding pathways, stone artwork, diverse but robust greenery and open-ended play elements like wood posts. The charity has 18 designers across the country, and Mr. Collyer said "Their dance cards are full." Until recently, the number of playgrounds in a neighbourhood was assumed to have a correlation with the activity levels of its youngest residents, said Jason Gilliland, director of the *University of Western Ontario's Urban Development Program*, and leader of the GPS study. By tracking school children with GPS, Dr. Gilliland and his colleagues are using data to turn that assumption on its head. GPS data have helped researchers discover that some kids won't use the jungle gym because the older kids are monopolizing it, and that tree-lined streets make a child more likely to walk to school because they feel more shielded from traffic. "Cities and policy makers are clamouring for this kind of information," he said.[*] (Hammer, 2011)

---

[*]Hammer, K. 2011, Aug. 20. "Study Suggests Traditional Playgrounds Contribute To Childhood Obesity." *The Globe and Mail Inc.* All Rights Reserved.

Caitlin Chandler

Children's artwork: Caitlin

Chapter 3

BENEFITS OF OUTDOOR PLAY

Power of One WANGARI MUTA MAATHAI

Wangari Muta Maathai

jeremy sutton-hibbert/Alamy

Wangari Muta Maathai (1940–2011) was born in Nyeri, Kenya, and among her many academic accomplishments was the first woman in East and Central Africa to earn a doctorate degree. As founder of the Green Belt Movement, Maathai's vision was to provide income and sustenance to millions of people in Kenya through the planting of trees. The organization also conducts educational campaigns to raise awareness about women's rights, civic empowerment, and the environment throughout Kenya and Africa. Winner of many notable prizes, Maathai's most prestigious award was the Nobel Peace Prize in 2004 awarded "for her contribution to sustainable development, democracy and peace" ("I am a Hummingbird" campaign, n.d.). Her untimely death brought heartfelt condolences from many dignitaries, and the comments by then–U.S. Secretary of State Hillary Rodham Clinton best underscore Maathai's influence:

I was deeply saddened to learn of the death of Wangari Maathai. The world has lost a powerful force for peace, democracy and women's rights. From early on, Dr. Maathai was a tireless advocate for the environment, for women and for all those in the developing world who are unable to realize their potential. She founded the Green Belt Movement that has planted millions of trees and helped women throughout Africa improve their lives and the futures of their families and their communities. She understood the deep connection between local and global problems, and she helped give ordinary citizens a voice. Her death has left a gaping hole among the ranks of women leaders, but she leaves behind a solid foundation for others to build upon. I was inspired by her story and proud to call her my friend. (http://wangari.greenbeltmovement.org).

To honour the memory of Wangari Maathai, the *"I am a Hummingbird"* campaign, a tree-planting campaign in Kenya, and internationally, has been launched. This initiative brings together Kenyans, friends, and supporters from around the globe to plant one billion trees in memory of Wangari Maathai ("I am a Hummingbird" campaign, n.d.).

OUTCOMES:

1. Evaluate the physical, social/emotional, and cognitive gains for children involved in outdoor environments.

2. Analyze the impact of interacting in nature on families.

3. Examine the ways in which communities benefit from a stronger connection to nature.

PHYSICAL BENEFITS OF OUTDOOR PLAY

> "A skinned knee or a twisted ankle in a challenging and exciting play environment is not just acceptable, it is a positive necessity in order to educate our children and prepare them for a complex, dangerous world, in which healthy, robust activity is more a national need than ever before."
>
> —RoSPA (2007)

Children need open spaces and materials to help them use large motor skills by climbing, jumping, running, and swinging in a variety of situations. The greater space of the outdoors can potentially counteract the effects of relatively crowded indoor environments. The outdoor physical environment needs to challenge even the youngest children by exposing them to a variety of different paths for moving and for riding bicycles or pulling wagons; places to balance, hop, skip, and dance; hills to roll on; tunnels to crawl through; and great places to swing and hang in support of their gross motor skills. Green grass and soft spaces outdoors are wonderful opportunities for babies on their tummies to explore the world around them. Watching a baby step in bare feet onto grass for the first time is a wonderful experience!

"Playground equipment offers exercise that challenges growing toddler muscles—pushing on swings, climbing steps before swooping down the slide. Outdoors, toddlers learn to trust their bodies as they attempt more and more kinds of movement" (Honig, n.d.).

Ingrid Crowther

Infants need opportunities to explore.

These opportunities provide a basis for sensory motor coordination. Fine motor skills and hand–eye coordination can also be improved as children engage in throwing and catching, kicking and pulling. Fine motor skills are strengthened when crumbling earth, holding plants, patting down the earth—the opportunities are endless. Cardiovascular endurance and stretching physical limits are only some of the benefits of outdoor experiences.

GENDER DIFFERENCES IN HOW CHILDREN PLAY IN THE OUTDOORS

In Tucker's 2008 review of 39 primary studies involving over 10,000 children from seven countries, one clear finding was that male preschoolers are more active than female preschoolers.

> Studies have noted that boys, from infancy through adolescence, tend to participate in more physically active play than do girls (Campbell & Eaton, 1999; Frost, 1992; Lindsey & Colwell, 2003). ... [D]uring recess times, boys more often played games requiring higher levels of physical activity than did girls. Girls played less strenuous games or held conversations as they walked around the playground. These results suggested that during times of unstructured activity, such as recess, boys tend to choose more active play than girls do.[*] (Riley & Jones, 2007)

[*]Riley, Jeanetta G. Jones, Rose B.: When girls and boys play: what research tells us. (review of research). *Childhood Education Fall 2007*. Reprinted by permission of the publisher (Taylor & Francis Ltd, http://www.tandf.co.uk/journals).

Bilton (2008) states that research on the workings of the brain has shown that boys' brains mature in a different sequence than girls' and, in some areas, at a slower rate. This can have a direct bearing on how boys learn.

Boys first develop the part of the brain for knowing about movement and the space in which they move themselves and other things. Consequently, Bilton suggests that boys feel more secure in the outdoor environment where there is space for them to learn through movement; "Pellegrini and Smith (1993) suggest that boys tend to prefer playing outdoors, due to the need for open space to participate in their active games" (Riley & Jones, 2007). Boys tend to engage in rough-and-tumble play more than girls do. "Rough-and-tumble play involves such activities as grabbing and wrestling and may be a socially acceptable way for boys to physically demonstrate their feelings of friendship" (Reed, 2000, in Riley & Jones, 2007).[*]

Cullen (1993) found that the play of boys and girls outdoors followed the stereotype established indoors, with boys playing with the more active equipment and girls tending to stay with the more home-type play.

Lynn Wilson

Boys often engage in more active play.

Lynn Wilson

Girls often engage in home-type play.

[*]Riley, Jeanetta G. Jones, Rose B.: When girls and boys play: what research tells us. (review of research). *Childhood Education Fall 2007.* Reprinted by permission of the publisher (Taylor & Francis Ltd, http://www.tandf.co.uk/journals).

Conventional design features of school grounds are not serving girls well. It is critical for staff to model and promote nonstereotypical play and the need for effective interventions (see Chapter 7) and programming to promote healthy levels of activity in young girls. All children need to be introduced to active women who are athletes, coaches, and leaders in sports.

In their research on greening environments in the Toronto District School board sites Dyment and Bell (2006) noted that

before greening, the school ground favoured the play activities of boys who dominated large open spaces with competitive, rule-bound games such as hockey, baseball, and soccer. When the school ground was transformed, the school ground provided a diversity of spaces that better accommodated the play interests and abilities of both girls and boys. For instance, there were places where children could play in a manner that was more nurturing, more cooperative and less competitive.

These findings support the work of Moore and Wong (1997), who found that a green school ground in Berkeley, California, allowed boys and girls to expand the play repertoire by engaging them in less organized play and more unorganized "free" play.

On the green school ground, the researchers observed an increase in active play, creative play,

Here boys and girls work cooperatively to build a log house.

pretend play, exploratory play, constructive play, and social play as compared with the original school ground. While it is important not to reinforce simplistic gender stereotypes, the findings from this study point to the value of offering a diversity of spaces to accommodate a range of active and quiet play activities, irrespective of gender.*

IMPACT OF OUTDOOR PLAY ON POSITIVE SELF-IMAGE AND SELF-ESTEEM

The Ontario Physical and Health Education Association (OPHEA) makes the connection between motor competence and self-esteem. As noted by Best Start (2005, p. 3):

> While adults base feelings about themselves on their physical, social, family, personal, school/work, and moral ethical experiences, the very young child is most likely to evaluate him/herself based on family and physical experiences. A child perceives competence in physical activity by his/her ability to perform simple tasks (such as making contact with the ball), trying hard, learning a new athletic skill, enjoyment of the activity, and receiving positive feedback and reinforcement from parents and teachers.
>
> Physical activity influences self-esteem as it:

- helps decrease feelings of anxiety, tension and depression

Bicycles provide ample opportunities for active play.

- is related to a general sense of optimism and contributes to feelings of well-being
- is an avenue for expression of anger, aggression and happiness
- is a means for self-discovery and social interaction
- positively influences academic achievement, creativity, and problem-solving
- improves self-discipline
- improves fitness levels which are related to positive mental health
- has a positive impact on behaviour and healthy lifestyle choices in later years, such as the decision to smoke, drink alcohol and take drugs.

It is important for all adults in the child's life to avoid focusing on body shape or size as a measure of self-esteem. Discourage teasing and putdowns; let children know that making comments about people's weight, shape, or size is unacceptable; and teach that people come in all shapes, weights, sizes and colours. It is also important to be aware of gender biases—a girl's self-esteem is often linked

---

*From Our garden is colour blind, inclusive and warm: reflections on green school grounds and social inclusion by Dyment, Janet E.; Bell, Anne *International Journal of Inclusive Education*, Mar 01, 2008, vol. 12,2. reprinted by permission of the Taylor & Francis Ltd, http://www.tandf.co.uk/journals.

to physical appearance, whereas a boy's self-esteem is more likely to be linked to talents and abilities.

It is important to encourage children to focus on their abilities rather than on their appearance, helping them identify things they like about themselves. Teachers and parents also need to be positive and accepting of themselves, by not discussing diets and making negative comments about their own bodies.

SOCIAL/EMOTIONAL BENEFITS OF OUTDOOR PLAY

> "While our physical reliance on nature for survival has never been seriously questioned, our emotional and spiritual ties to the natural world have not been as clearly understood. From a holistic health promotion perspective, addressing the social dimensions of health goes hand in hand with addressing the physical dimensions. If the social environment is fun, peaceful and welcoming, and children are feeling emotionally safe, then their interest in play and physical activity will undoubtedly increase. Conversely, if a play space is hostile, exclusive or overly challenging, then children will be less inclined to actively participate."
>
> **—Janet Dyment and Anne Bell (2007, p. 8)**

Engaging in social play is so important because it nurtures not only the child's intellectual development but also her emotional intelligence. It teaches children about conflict resolution and problem solving in

Infants need many opportunities to explore the world around them.

Ingrid Crowther

Rope climbing supports upper body strength.

a positive nurturing environment. Learning to negotiate and solve problems is an important life skill.

Outdoor play is just as critical for the overall development of infants and toddlers as it is for older children. Younger children are very keen to watch what others are doing, engage with adults, and enjoy interactions with nature. Toddlers tend to want to play alone but can learn important social skills through outdoor play: outdoor play offers the children time to begin to learn about sharing, getting along with others, and other important social skills. Seeing and smelling are pleasing experiences for infants and toddlers outdoors; therefore, pushing strollers to places where young children can see, touch, and smell flowering plants is an important sensory experience and provides the benefits of interacting with attentive adults.

Young children need positive connections with nature in order to thrive. There is considerable research to suggest that separation from nature has negative effects on our emotional well-being and that, to some extent, our happiness and mental health is mediated by our relationship with the natural world (Kaplan, 2001; Laumann et al., 2001; Nisbet et al., 2011). Over the past few years, there has been a growing awareness of children's need to interact with nature both physically and emotionally (Wilson, 2009).

The outdoor environment allows children an opportunity to play out their experiences and work through difficult or troubling feelings by engaging in imaginative play. Play is also an expression of creativity and is how children learn, how they cope, and how they discover who they might be.

The space available outdoors is directly related to fewer constraints of children's behaviours and enables them to find solitude away from other children and adults, engage in solitary activity, or be in small, intimate groups. Such opportunities for solitary pursuits and experience of privacy are necessary for young children (Greenman, 1988). When children choose to play with others, they learn to negotiate, cooperate, compete, and resolve conflicts. By providing gathering places and choosing equipment that allows for socialization, we incorporate important elements into the playscape.

Emotional benefits also include reduced aggression and increased happiness. Research tells us that enriching the outdoor environment reduces antisocial behaviours such as violence, bullying, vandalism, and littering. Boredom has been recognized by both children and adults as one of the main causes of all kinds of inappropriate behaviour. "Opportunities for free play with limited adult intervention provide time for children to explore which behaviors are accepted among their peers" (Wortham, 2002, in Riley & Jones, 2007, p. 38). Through their years of research, Hirsh-Pasek and Golinkoff (2003) have concluded that "play is to early childhood what gas is to a car. It is the very fuel of every intellectual activity that our children engage in" (p. 214). The frequency and quality of children's positive outdoor social play is linked to the range of materials available. Comparisons of children's play behaviours and equipment/materials choices on different types of playgrounds reveal that both boys and girls engage in more cooperative and sociodramatic play in environments containing a rich array of fluid materials (sand, water, etc.), portable materials (blocks, containers, etc.) and vehicles (tricycles, wagons, etc.) than in those featuring large fixed equipment (climbers, slides, etc.) (Frost, 1992).

> Good education is holistic; it is concerned with mind, body and spirit. Motivation and enthusiasm are essential ingredients of effective learning. Adventure is a great motivator. Time spent alone or in small groups in natural areas also motivates. Young people who under-achieve in the classroom may suddenly come alive and show a range of skills

Empathy and caring for each other is a critical life skill.

> that have remained hidden in formal teaching. They develop a stronger sense of self, gain confidence and trust. Learning in the outdoors is active, co-operative and relevant. (Cooper, n.d.)

Emotional benefits include stress reduction, reduced aggression, and a happier frame of mind. Children have an opportunity to enhance their feelings of self-esteem and to express their feelings through dramatic play and art experiences. In a positive environment, caring adults will ensure that the children are encouraged to take pride in their accomplishments and take appropriate risks to challenge themselves. The development of empathy—learning to consider other points of view—should be encouraged.

NATURE AND ITS IMPACT ON STRESS

> "[R]esearch on people of different cultures, demographics and gender demonstrates not only a common preference for natural environments, but also that there are patterns in these preferences ... sweeping vistas, open water, secluded hiding places, mysterious passageways—these are the environmental features that appear to contribute most to our physical and mental well-being."
>
> —Edward Cheskey (1994)

Over 2000 years ago, Chinese Taoists created gardens and greenhouses to improve human health. Researchers have found that the brain is relieved of "excess" circulation (or activity), and nervous system activity is also reduced when people contemplate nature (Louv, 2011).

Wells and Evans (2003) studied rural children and found that even a view of nature—green plants and vistas—helps reduce stress among highly stressed children. Further, the more plants, green views, and access to natural play areas, the more positive the results. Restak and Mahoney (1998) explain that it is no longer just common sense to avoid stress; paying attention to stress is necessary because stress results in the loss of brain cells. Restak and Mahoney advise that the best stimulant is exercise: getting up and moving around. Estroff Marano, editor-at-large of *Psychology Today* (2004), states that parents who allow their children to find a way to deal with life's day-to-day stresses by themselves are helping them develop resilience and coping strategies. We should begin by considering the benefits of *learning injuries*—children learn a great deal from their encounters on the playground! Children need to be gently encouraged to take risks and learn that nothing terrible happens says Michael Liebowitz, clinical professor of psychiatry at Columbia University and head of the *Anxiety Disorders Clinic* at New York State Psychiatric Institute. "'They need gradual exposure to find that the world is not dangerous. Having overprotective parents is a risk factor for anxiety disorders because children do not have opportunities to master their innate shyness and become more comfortable in the world.' Otherwise, children never learn to dampen the pathways from perception to alarm reaction" (quoted in Marano, 2004).

> Excessive fear can transform a person and modify behavior permanently; it can change the very structure of the brain. The same can happen to a whole culture. What will it be like for children to grow up in socially and environmentally controlled environments—condominiums and planned developments and covenant-controlled housing developments surrounded with walls, gates, and surveillance systems, where covenants prevent families from planting gardens? One wonders how the children growing up in this culture of control will define freedom when they are adults. (Louv, 2008, p. 127)

New research supports the contention that nature therapy helps control pain and negative stress. Direct contact with the natural environment, particularly in challenging situations, can be inspirational and lead to feelings of belonging or oneness with the Earth. According to "*Green Exercise and Green Care*," a 2009 report by researchers at the Centre for Environment and Society at the University of Essex, there are many benefits to exposure to nature. More than 1,850 participants in their study showed an improvement in their psychological well-being,

increased self-esteem and mood, and a reduction in feelings of anger, confusion, depression, and tension. Another health benefit was the reduction of blood pressure and the burning of calories (Louv, 2011).

Kuo and Sullivan (2001) argue that natural environments help to decrease the irritability and mental fatigue inherent in stressful situations such as living in public housing, a long-term care facility, or a prison. The researchers note that gardens have been associated with decreases in violent outbursts among Alzheimer patients (Mooney & Nicell, 1992) and prison inmates (Rice & Remy, 1998).

Connecting the indoors physically and visually to the exterior brings the outside in, contributing to the restorative potential of the indoor environment (Herrington & Beach, 2007). In more than 100 studies conducted on outdoor experiences, the results consistently indicate that outdoor experiences produce "positive physiological and psychological responses in humans, including reduced stress and a general feeling of well-being" (White & Stoecklin, 2008, p. 2).

> "Nature comes in many forms: a new calf steaming, a pet that lives and dies, a woods with beaten paths and stinging thistles. Whatever form nature takes, it offers children a world separate from parents and older than them—a kind of greater father and mother; it gives children a sense of their place in time. Unlike television, nature does not steal time from adults or children; it augments that time, makes the time fuller, richer. And for those children for whom family life is destructive, nature can offer healing."
>
> —Richard Louv, *The Web of Life, Weaving the Values That Sustain Us* (quoted in Little Eyes on Nature, 2009)

THE IMPACT OF NATURALIZED PLAYSCAPES ON SOCIAL/ EMOTIONAL DEVELOPMENT

> "Children who are closely connected to nature and "who dwell ... among the beauties and mysteries of the earth are never alone or weary of life. ... They find reserves of strength that will endure as long as life lasts."
>
> —Rachel Carson (1956, p. 88)

Eco- and Outdoor Camps

Katelyn Brown is a recreation programmer for the Municipality of Clarington, Ontario, and she outlines the benefits of camp experiences for young children.

I see kids who've attended our Eco and Outdoor based camps leaving with a newfound sense of ownership and pride for their environment. They are excited and motivated to change things for the better. They can be overheard reminding their parents to turn off the lights when they leave a room, and discouraging them from buying bottled water. Our Outdoor Camps allow kids the opportunity to be outside all day, every day of the week. They swim, run and play outside for the seven and a half hours per day they are with us. Energy levels are high—the lethargic lack of energy observed at many of the indoor locations where kids are "cooped up" inside is absent at our Outdoor Adventure Camp. The overwhelming response from parents is that their kids leave camp exhausted, that they sleep much better, and wake up the next day with more energy and excitement than the day before. These kids are the future of our planet, and when you teach them the skills at a young age they buy in. Their passion and enthusiasm for change is infectious (Katelyn Brown).

Outdoor-adventure programs stimulate the development of interpersonal competencies, enhance leadership skills, and have positive effects on adolescents' senses of empowerment, self-control, independence, self-understanding, assertiveness, and decision-making skills. These changes were shown to be more stable over time than the changes generated in more traditional education programs (Brown, 2012).

A study of 15 summer residential camp programs that provided specialized programs for children with a wide range of disabilities demonstrated improved initiative and self-direction that continued when they returned home (Louv, 2010).[*]

[*]Adapted from "Last Child in the Woods" and "The Nature Principle". Richard Louv is the author of eight books about nature and development including *Last Child in the Woods: Saving Our Children from Nature-Deficit Disorder* and *The Nature Principle: Human Restoration and the end of Nature-Deficit Disorder*. For more information on the movement to connect children with nature, see www.richardlouv.com or www.childrenandnature.org.

The majority of Canadians live in urban areas and have limited access to natural settings; however, a movement to "green" the playscapes of schools and child care centres across the country has provided many urban children and adults access to natural environments in their own communities.

School grounds projects designed to bring nature back into our daily lives are crucial for the long term conservation, protection and restoration of wild places. Most young people never have the opportunity to experience wilderness; many living in urban settings have very limited opportunities to explore natural environments. As visits to outdoor education centres become limited by financial constraints, the danger exists that learning about the natural world will increasingly depend upon printed and electronic materials. Teaching in this way is largely an academic abstraction; it cannot foster the kind of lifelong ecological consciousness derived only from learning through the senses in natural settings throughout childhood. Nature, it has often been repeated, is our best teacher.[*] (Coffey, 2001, p. 10)

It's not so much what children know about nature that's important, as what happens to them when they are in nature and not just in it, but in it by themselves, without grownups. Experts are beginning to suggest that when kids stop going out into the natural world to play, it can affect not just their development as individual but society as a whole. (Henley, 2010, p. 2)

Most children experience primitive fears such as being alone, being in the dark, falling, monsters or wild animals, loud noises, or getting lost. Yet many children are beginning to see nature as

[*]Coffey, A. 2001. *Transforming School Grounds In Greening School Grounds: Creating Habitats For Learning*. Grant, T. & Littlejohn, G. (Eds). Toronto. Green Teacher. P. 10.

Full engagement with water and earth provide immeasureable learning opportunities.

leading, negotiating, and making friends. Children discover what they like to do and which experiences require risk taking; they learn how to make up games and rules, and stretch their imaginations. One child may play a lead role while another may learn how to stand up for himself.

"As they experience joy, togetherness, and accomplishments, they develop a positive sense of self and a zest for living in an ever-changing and challenging world" (Wilson, 2008, Preface).[*]

There are some indications that connecting children with nature can also contribute to the development of a more peaceful society (Wilson, 2009).

> Passion does not arrive on videotape or on a CD; passion is personal. Passion is lifted from the earth itself by the muddy hands of the young; it travels along grass-stained sleeves to the heart. If we are going to save environmentalism and the environment, we must also save an endangered indicator species: the child in nature.
>
> —**Richard Louv (2005)**

our natural enemy, which generates feelings of fear and helplessness. Aboriginal cultures teach us to care for Mother Earth but too often we warn children away from the Earth—*don't go outside, it's too cold, you will get dirty if you play in the mud,* etc. and warn them of the dangers of water and the woods. Exploration can help children to relate to nature and to learn and understand about food, shelter, reproduction, and death. Children learn how nature cares for them and at the same time can be destructive. This is particularly true for children who live in areas where natural disasters have occurred or where tornadoes or hurricanes, for example, are common.

Playing in a real world also makes a child more capable of dealing with challenges. The natural environment is not the same at all times, which forces a child to think creatively to meet these changes. This fosters a sense of calm that often continues into adult life. Nature also allows children to move freely, make noise, and engage in boisterous play in ways that may be discouraged inside. Children also test their courage and practise cooperation and sharing,

In their study of children, parents, and staff at 45 schools, Dyment and Bell (2006) note that

"greened" school grounds were more inclusive of people who may feel isolated on the basis of gender, class, race or ability [and] suggest that these spaces promote, in a very broad sense, social inclusion. Some participants commented that green school grounds helped to provide an inclusive space for people with other "differences" as well, noting that they were welcoming of people of all ages, sexual orientations and religions. They observed more inclusive play and gathering of community members. Green school grounds provide a more diversified environment with a broader choice of play activities. These factors appear to foster the type of positive social dynamics that support more socially inclusive behaviour. Study participants reported that when students were learning and playing on a green school ground, they were being more civil (72%), communicating more effectively (63%) and were being more cooperative (69%). These improvements were noted not only among students;

[*]Wilson, R. 2008. *Nature and Young Children: Encouraging Creative Play and Learning in Natural Environments.* Routledge. Taylor and Francis Group. P. preface.

interactions between students and teachers were also enhanced (69%).[*]

These findings are consistent with those of Netta Weinstein and her colleagues (2009) at the University of Rochester, who found that contact with nature can have humanizing effects, fostering greater authenticity and connectedness. These findings of increased cooperation, greater inclusion, and decreased aggression in naturalized playgrounds have been observed elsewhere. Natural environments not only restore us, reduce our irritability, and enhance our concern for others, but also engage us because as Rachel and Stephan Kaplan (1989) have pointed out, they are fascinating. Our fascination with the natural world explains why, when only a small part of a playground is naturalized (e.g., 10%), children play in the naturalized areas for more than half of their time outdoors (Houghton, 2003). Nature captivates our imaginations and provides the perfect materials for play.

From the early childhood literature, we know that young children construct their own knowledge and build a sense of rightness and responsibility from the inside out versus having knowledge and ethics handed to them from the outside. And from the environmental education literature, we know that environmental stewardship is rooted in a sense of appreciation and caring. Fear and mandates have not been effective in developing strong commitments to protecting the environment; early positive experiences in natural environments have proven to be a far more effective way of fostering environmental stewardship (Chawla and Hart, 1995; Wilson, 2008). Once children learn to love and respect the Earth, they are likely to care deeply about its well-being. This is the essence of an environmental ethic. However, Save the Earth campaigns are not appropriate for very young children. Placing this burden on children asks them to fix something that they didn't break and assigns them a task they are not equipped to handle.

A SENSE OF PLACE

Some of the most fundamental geographical concepts to be acquired by the child are those concerned with a sense of place. The child's sense of place refers to his/her understanding of, and feeling for,

the essential character of different places: an understanding of how landscapes have been formed and shaped by the interaction of natural processes and human activity, and an appreciation of the distinctive contribution made by the motivations, beliefs, values and attitudes of people. (National Council for Curriculum and Assessment, 2010)

As children in early learning centres develop a sense of place—an environment that they can influence and control, add to and manipulate— each child soon feels a sense of ownership and the environment becomes "my space"!

HOW LIVING THINGS SUPPORT SOCIAL/EMOTIONAL DEVELOPMENT

Children's fascination with natural environments is that they are alive! They are filled with a variety of living things—animals, plants, birds, fish, and insects. The unpredictability of living things can sometimes create fear in young children, especially children with limited experiences in nature. Insects, animals, and unfamiliar surroundings can sometimes cause children to be hesitant and adults, whose aim is to protect children, can inadvertently increase children's fears by describing forests as dark scary places, unnecessarily restricting children's exploration outdoors or expressing fear and disgust when presented with natural materials such as soil, rocks, small animals, spiders, and bugs. Nature is not an enemy to be avoided or conquered but a part of our world to be understood, respected, and appreciated. Children living in northern communities often have more experience playing outdoors, climbing on rocks and in trees, whereas children in cities are often more restricted, and their limited experiences can make natural environments unfamiliar and fear-provoking, at first (Dietze & Kashin, 2012). Adults can help to alleviate these fears by acting as role models in their appreciation and respect for nature, and they can provide children with opportunities to explore natural environments.

There is very little research regarding the benefits of animals and children in child-care settings; most research addresses the health benefits associated with animal-assisted therapy for children who are special needs, dealing with trauma, etc. For example, Martin and Farnum (2002) studied the interaction between dogs and children with pervasive developmental disorders (PDD), disorders characterized by lack of social communications and abilities. Results

[*]From Our garden is colour blind, inclusive and warm: reflections on green school grounds and social inclusion by Dyment, Janet E.; Bell, Anne International *Journal of Inclusive Education*, Mar 01, 2008, vol. 12,2. reprinted by permission of the Taylor & Francis Ltd, http://www.tandf.co.uk/journals.

show that children exhibited a more playful mood, were more focused, and were more aware of their social environments when in the presence of a therapy dog. Sams, Forney, and Willenbring (2006) have found similar results with children with autism.

Sobel (2002) advocates that in addition to regular contact with nature, one of the best ways to foster empathy during early childhood is to cultivate children's relationships with animals. Young children feel a natural kinship with, and are implicitly drawn to, animals, especially baby animals (Rosen, 2004, Sobel, 2002).

Animals are an endless source of wonder for children, fostering a caring attitude and sense of responsibility toward living things. Children interact instinctively and naturally with animals, talk to them, and invest in them emotionally (Sobel, 2002). Studies of the dreams of children younger than age 6 reveal that as many as 90 percent of their dreams are about animals (Acuff, 1997; Patterson, 2000). Additionally,

the importance of animals is reinforced by the fact that animals constitute more than 90 percent of the characters employed in language acquisition and counting in children's preschool books (Kellert, 1983).

There is no question that critters from goldfish to chickens to worms found in the garden provide incredible opportunities to connect with nature and our feelings of empathy. Of course, any pet or animal should be in good health and have all the proper immunizations where required. The living space for the animals should be cleaned regularly, and hand washing is a must. Obviously, wild or dangerous animals should not be kept in child care and this includes ferrets, turtles, and birds of the parrot family. Children should be cautioned about approaching animals on their walks. While teachers will always have to be concerned about allergies or sensitivities, animals have much to teach us.

The death of a pet in child care will be a difficult time for everyone but it provides an opportunity

Inside LOOK

Teacher Comments

One teacher commented on the benefits of animals in his program, stating that he sees the children comforting and nurturing the animals, demonstrating respect for the animal that often transfers into their interactions with each other. A sense of responsibility was enhanced and relying on a daily schedule for feedings etc. provided a sense of structure. All of the children were delighted by the antics of the animals.

Another teacher also commented on the connection that a child made with a rabbit in the room that helped to decrease her loneliness and isolation from the group. Her mother had recently passed away and she was comforted by the rabbit's responses to her. Because of the children's interest in animals, this teacher expanded the collection to include mice, fish, a guinea pig, a lizard, and a snake. She was also able to find a number of puppets that matched their animals and this expanded their dramatic play as well as their story writing and artwork. Veterinarian visits to the playroom also expanded the children's understanding of how to provide even better care for their animals.

A teacher observed communication between the children and their pet as secrets were whispered into the ear of their guinea pig. She also noted an incredible change in a child who, prior to the animals in the room, was aggressive and destructive. Introducing animals into this environment made a tremendous difference to all the children but to this child in particular who was given responsibilities for caring for these pets. His empathy for the pets began to carry over into his interactions with the other children.

Lynn Wilson

The Glass Garden at the Rusk Centre

Chicks Hatching!

Hatching chicks was a positive and exciting process for the children in one child care centre. The children learned so much during this project. They exhibited patience as they waited for the eggs to hatch; counting how many days were left before the chicks would be born. This process involved empathy for those chicks that did not hatch and a greater understanding of the cycle of life. Physically chasing the chicks, carefully and gently lifting them into their carrying boxes, and talking with each other about how much food they eat expanded both mathematics and language development. Drawings and dictated stories and documentation panels explained the childrens' experiences to their families. Social skills were required as they took turns and supported each other. The project ended with the chicks being taken to a farm with the children experiencing a great deal of sadness as their hatchlings moved to a more appropriate setting. The teacher created a "Smilebox" presentation on a CD for each family so that they would always have a memory of the project. This was an incredible learning experience for the children and their teachers.

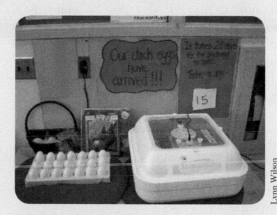

Hatching chicks!

Lynn Wilson

to talk to the children about reproduction, birth, illnesses, accidents, death, and grieving. Children will have many questions about death and the teacher's role is to help them learn that death is a natural part of life. If teachers anticipate that death may be imminent, they can begin to prepare the children for this loss by explaining that the animal is very ill and may die. Since many children will personalize these experiences, they may also need some reassurance that being ill doesn't necessarily result in death. Being honest with the children and making every attempt to answer their questions is important. This also gives an opportunity for families to share their spiritual beliefs with their children about death and dying. Teachers also need to be aware of children in the group who may be experiencing other difficult situations in their own homes such as a recent death of a member of the family or a pet of their own. These children will need extra support. Very young children do not have the life experiences to help them understand the meaning of death and will react to the response of the adults around them. It is very important that the children have an opportunity to talk about their feelings. Many young children

do not have a concept of the permanence of death and they should be reassured that they were in no way responsible for the passing as some children have confusing thoughts about their role in death. Making a memory book for older children may help them deal with their emotional state; drawing pictures, writing stories about their feelings for the pet, and adding photographs may be helpful. Some children may want to plan a memorial, or bury the pet in a special place. Planting a tree or a garden in memory of the pet is also a positive response. Teachers also need to be aware of their own feelings as a pet's death may trigger memories from their own childhood about loss and grief. There are many books now available to help children understand more about death and dying.

GIRLS AND BOYS AND SOCIAL INTERACTIONS DURING PLAY

For Additional Reading

Even very young children tend to be socially influenced by playing with same-sex peers. For example, Martin and Fabes' (2001) investigation of preschool and kindergarten children at play indicated that playing with same-gender peers affects play behaviours. Their research findings added to the evidence (e.g., Boyatzis, Mallis, & Leon, 1999; Thorne, 1993) that children often choose to play with same-sex peers, whether indoors or out. Additionally, Martin and Fabes found gender-typical behaviours for children who more often played with same-sex peers. For instance, the girls who most often played with other girls were generally less active during play and chose to play in areas close to adults. Boys who played with other boys more often engaged in play that was more aggressive and farther from adult supervision.

> In an early study examining gender and play, Lever (1978) found several differences in how 5th-grade girls and boys play. For example, boys played more competitive, rule-oriented, group games than did girls; girls interacted in smaller groups, had conversations, and walked and talked with friends more often than did boys. Lever concluded that the nature of boys' team games and their experiences with rule-dictated play: *1) allowed for the development of cooperation skills between peers with differing ideas, 2) afforded them opportunities to work independently to accomplish a common task, and 3) provided motivation to abide by established rules.*[*]
> (Riley & Jones, 2007 [emphasis added])

Other recent studies have found similar results. A study by Goodwin (2001) notes that boys gravitated to form social structures, with boys who had the greatest skills often taking the lead and directing others in their play. Boys with less skills were allowed to play but not as leaders. Girls, on the other hand, did not depend on skill level to direct the games but Goodwin found that girls were more likely to exclude others from their play. Therefore, it is easy to see that not all children will have positive play experiences. Some children struggle with the social skills necessary to successfully enter play situations (Blatchford, Blaines, & Pellegrini, 2003).

Children who do not have sufficient outdoor play experiences generally have

> poorer ability in motor tasks, lower levels of physical activity, poorer ability to deal with stressful or traumatic situations and events, poorer ability to access and manage risk and poorer social skills, leading to difficulties in negotiating social situations such as dealing with conflict and cultural differences. (Dietze & Kashin, 2012, p. 134)

---

[*]Riley, Jeanetta G. Jones, Rose B.: When girls and boys play: what research tells us. (review of research). *Childhood Education Fall 2007*).

Evergreen Foundation

Some children struggle to find ways to enter into play and are often excluded.

These circumstances can provide opportunities for guided interventions from sensitive educators. Some children will need support in their attempts to enter into other children's play situations.

For some children, the child care experience can at times be overwhelming; they need opportunities to withdraw and self-regulate. A well-designed outdoor space provides opportunities for them to find sheltered spaces to be alone.

> My first garden was a place no grown-up ever knew about, even though it was in the backyard of a quarter-acre suburban plot ... to a four year old the space made by the vaulting branches of a forsythia is as grand as the inside of a cathedral, and there is room enough for a world between a lilac and a wall. Whenever I needed to be out of range of adult radar, I'd crawl beneath the forsythia's arches, squeeze between two lilac bushes, and find myself safe and alone in my own green room.
>
> **—Michael Pollan (1991, p. 7)**

SELF-REGULATION

Self-regulation is the process of adaptation that guides and organizes emotional, social, and cognitive growth. In secure relationships, children are equipped with the skills necessary to regulate behaviour, to manage feelings, to interact, and to meet the demands of exploration (Sroufe, 1995). Self-regulation is part of adapting and reacting to the demands of life, tolerating being alone for a reasonable amount of time, making friends, and sustaining motivation and interest in learning. It is the basis of coping and competence, and includes abilities to regulate behaviour, emotions, and attention. Individual differences exist in the child's ability to self-regulate; biology and experience account for this difference. How children regulate is influenced by their past experiences and their level of development, circumstances, the people present, and the children's personal goals.

Culture is also responsible for differences in regulation. In their families, children learn the shared meaning and values of their culture. Culture establishes standards for the interpretation and display of emotions, facial expression, and actions. Culture may assign meaning to events that influence individual responses, such as who deserves respect and therefore requires restrained behaviour; or what constitutes an insult and what action is required. Family and culture must be considered when understanding, observing, and interpreting behaviour.

The relationship between the design of school grounds and student behaviour seems clear: playgrounds become much more peaceful and harmonious when play spaces are diversified. In a study of 41 programs, it was found that in lower quality outdoor environments children engaged more in functional or repetitive play, while in higher quality outdoor environments, children showed a tendency to display more constructive play. As the quality of the outdoor program decreased, the frequency of negative behaviours increased (DeBord, Hestenes, Moore, Cosco, & McGinnis, 2005). Boredom can result when children play in poor quality environments, which, in turn, may result in aggressive and destructive behaviour. "Children tend to bridge their differences more easily in a natural environment; fights and accidents—so common on asphalt yards—give way to more constructive play" (Hines & Malley-Morrison, 2005, p. 8). "As younger children associate in play situations, they begin to realize that play ends if they do not negotiate behaviors and cooperate; therefore, play helps children learn to regulate their behaviors in order to continue playing together" (Riley & Jones, 2007, p. 38).*

Teachers everywhere acknowledge that enriching students' outdoor learning environment reduces anti-social behavior such as violence, bullying, vandalism and littering. It has been proven that physical movement in playgrounds is slowed by "obstacles" in the form of trees in planters, paving paintings, movable building objects and informal seating arrangements for passive pursuits. This child-calming effect has cut down the number of "knock and bump" accidents in paved playgrounds by up to 80%. Over the years, decreases in juvenile delinquency have been reported during periods of school and community gardening. Similarly, teachers today report that social stresses in the classroom are diminished when young people are engaged in learning through improving their surroundings. In Britain, research shows that both absenteeism and dropout levels are in decline as school life grows more meaningful for older students; and teachers and students alike are discovering that hands-on activities in outdoor classrooms make learning more interesting. Creating an outdoor classroom may not actually lessen teachers' workload, but it changes the nature of the work by taking the pain out and putting the joy and excitement of learning back in.** (Coffey, 2004, p. 8)

A teacher from a school with a community watershed restoration project on adjoining parkland reported that "the children might not be having a successful day, but when we go into the garden and get the time to explore physically, there is a calming effect; it become a different environment and place." Another teacher from the same school described the naturalized area's particular magic as important "for my sixty second vacations—taking a moment to look out the window and catch my breath!" (Houghton, 2003, p. 28).†

In their research in the Toronto District School Board's green schools, Dyment and Bell (2006) note that

---

*Riley, Jeanetta G. Jones, Rose B.: When girls and boys play: what research tells us. (review of research). *Childhood Education Fall 2007*.

**Coffey, A. 2004. *Asking Children Listening to Children. School Grounds Transformation*. Canadian Biodiversity Institute. P. 8).

†*A Breath Of Fresh Air Celebrating Nature and School Gardens*. The Learnxs Foundation & Sumach Press, Toronto District School Board. P. 28. © E. Houghton.

improved social and behavioural skills were heightened through active student involvement in the process of greening. When students were given opportunities to work with other students, teachers, parents and community members on greening projects, they learned important life skills. They learned, for example, that through teamwork, cooperation and dedication they could make a difference. At one school, the green school ground was used as part of a behavior modification program for students who were having difficulty working with other students and teachers in a conventional classroom setting. Students in this program were involved in all aspects of the greening project, and the social benefits of the program were clear. One parent commented "everyone can join us in the garden. What a great place for a disenfranchised child to meet new people, dig and plant. Our garden is colour blind, inclusive and warm. Anyone can help us, and they do."* (p. 10)

Children have opportunities to develop social skills as they engage in play with their peers, and Moore (1996) suggested that children who play together in nature have more positive feelings toward one another. Researchers have concluded that play in diverse, natural environments tends to reduce or eliminate antisocial behaviours such as bullying and violence (Coffey, 2001; Malone & Tranter, 2003; Moore & Cosco, 2000).

> Children can be as prone as adults to the overstimulation given by urban settings. The wilder places can help them to wind down and increase their awareness of other things, where to get wet or dirty is expected rather than deplored. Children with ADHD may benefit enormously from this type of exposure. (Bell, Taylor & Francis Group, 2008, p. 96)

In Canada, 5 to 15 percent of school-age children are affected by ADHD, which occurs more frequently in boys than girls.

> With these children there are often accompanying challenges, for example, 25% of these children will suffer from anxiety disorders, 20–30% with depression, conduct disorders and approximately 25-30% will have a learning disability. At the Human-Environment Research Laboratory at the University of Illinois, researchers have discovered

that children show a significant reduction in the symptoms of attention-deficit disorder when they engage with nature. (Faber Taylor, Kuo, & Sullivan in Louv, 2011, p. 29)

Kuo and Faber Taylor's 2004 research suggests daily doses of "green time" may have a positive impact on children with these symptoms and "nature treatments" could supplement current treatments. Outdoor play has been found to benefit the memory levels of a child. In fact, all-round learning skills show improvement. The vitamin D from sunlight also contributes to memory retention and as such is useful in treating children with Attention Deficit Disorder. A more recent study by Kuo and Taylor (2011) of more than 400 children diagnosed with Attention Deficit Hyperactivity Disorder found a link between the children's routine play settings and the severity of their symptoms. Those who regularly play in outdoor settings with lots of green (grass and trees, for example) have milder ADHD symptoms than those who play indoors or in-built outdoor environments. The association holds even when the researchers controlled for income and other variables.

COGNITIVE BENEFITS OF OUTDOOR PLAY

> "Scientific understanding is not going to change our habits or give us the political will to change our life—even the hard facts which tell us we shouldn't do this or that, don't actually persuade people as much as a spiritual experience can. You have to reach the hearts of the people."
>
> —Jagjit Chulian, artist

The study of relationship between mental acuity, creativity, and time spent outdoors is a frontier for science. But new research suggests that exposure to the living world can enhance intelligence for some people. This probably happens in at least two ways: first, our senses and sensibilities are improved through our direct interaction with nature (and practical knowledge of natural systems is still applicable in our everyday lives); second, a more natural environment seems to stimulate our ability to pay attention, think clearly, and be more creative, even in dense urban neighborhoods. This research has positive implications for education,

*From Our garden is colour blind, inclusive and warm: reflections on green school grounds and social inclusion by Dyment, Janet E.; Bell, Anne *International Journal of Inclusive Education*, Mar 01, 2008, vol. 12,2. reprinted by permission of the Taylor & Francis Ltd, http://www.tandf.co.uk/journals.

for business, and for the daily lives of young and old." (Louv, 2011, p. 27)

Berman, Jonides, and Kaplan (2008) state that simple and brief interactions with nature can produce marked increases in cognitive control. Wells (2000) shows that proximity to, views of, and daily exposure to natural settings increases children's ability to focus and therefore enhances cognitive abilities. As well, there is considerable evidence these natural settings such as wilderness areas, community parks, and even views of nature and indoor plants have cognitively rejuvenating effects (Cimpich, 1993; Hartig, Mang, & Evans, 1991; Kaplan, 1984; Lohr, Pearson-Mims, & Goodwin, 1996; Miles, Sullivan, & Kuo, 1998; Tennessen & Cimprich, 1995).

The growing body of research on young people shows there is now a consistent pattern; a correlation between physical activity or fitness and a modest improvement in academic achievement. Mark Tremblay, who leads the *Healthy Active Living and Obesity Research Group* at the Children Hospital of Eastern Ontario states that "it appears that academic performance proceeds at a faster rate when exposed to physical activity" (McIlroy, 2010). Schools in Finland have 15 minutes of play after every hour of class, and students there regularly outperform kids from around the world in international education studies (ibid.). The type of workout may make a difference. Getting the heart rate up is important, but in one German study, games that required complex skills—such as throwing and catching while moving—led to a greater improvement in focus and concentration than more rote exercise (McIlroy, 2009, p. A4). There clearly is a positive link between nature exposure and the development of a sense of wonder that can lead to motivation for lifelong learning.

Adults who understand the importance of outdoor play will create environments that encourage children to be curious and freely explore. Children need opportunities to act on and change their environment with the use of loose parts, real tools, and materials that reflect their interests. Children should be encouraged to observe their environment, noting changes that take place and to discuss and record their observations. Their vocabulary increases as they label and identify plants, animals, and objects they find. They quickly begin to integrate early math and science language and develop an understanding of the principles of concepts such as size, shape, number, etc. There is no question that experiences in green environments contribute to improved learning, behaviour, and teamwork.

Gerald Lieberman and Linda Hoody were among the early researchers to focus on the environment as a learning context rather than as a curriculum topic. Their 1998 research study, published in a report titled *Closing The Achievement Gap: Using the Environment as an Integrating Context for Learning*, found intriguing data that definitely supports the use of the outdoors for instruction. Their study included forty schools from thirteen states, representing all grade levels (K–12). The outcomes indicate that students learn more within an environment-based context than within a traditional educational framework.** (Broda, 2007, p. 19)

Studies have shown that outdoor experiences can lead to a stronger internal locus of control, improved personal and social adjustment, and an enhanced perception of self. Research by Lieberman and Hoody (1998) (see http://www.seer.org) states that children actively engaged in the outdoor environment demonstrate:

- Stronger problem solving skills
- Improved critical thinking skills
- Better mastery of math skills
- More enthusiasm for studying math
- Increased creativity
- Increased engagement and enthusiasm
- Questions that are thought provoking
- Better understanding of connections and interrelationships
- Improved retention of knowledge
- The ability to transfer their learning to other aspects of their lives
- Greater pride and ownership in their environment.

The impact of increased environmental education was also felt by teachers who demonstrated more enthusiasm and greater engagement in their

*From THE NATURE PRINCIPLE by Richard Louv. © 2011 by Richard Louv. Reprinted by permission of Algonquin Books of Chapel Hill. p.27 International Journal of Inclusive Education, 1 http://dx.doi.org/10.1080/13603110600855671.

**Broda, Herbert W. 2007. *Schoolyard-Enhanced Learning: Using the Outdoors as an Instructional Tool, K-8*, © 2007 Stenhouse Publishers. All rights reserved. No reproduction without written permission from the publisher. P. 19.

The Eighth Intelligence

Psychologists and educators who have studied Howard Gardner's idea of being "nature smart", his eighth intelligence—*The Naturalistic Intelligence*—suggest the following descriptors of children with naturalistic intelligence. They:

- Display keen sensory skills (sight, sound, smell, taste, and touch)
- Readily notice and categorize elements of the natural world
- Enjoy being outdoors and engaging in such nature-related activities as gardening, exploring natural areas and observing natural phenomena (e.g.: movement of clouds, singing of birds, effects of wind and rain etc.)
- Easily notice patterns in their natural surroundings (differences, similarities, linkages etc.)
- Display an interest in and care about animals and plants
- Enjoy collecting nature-related specimens (e.g. leaves, rocks, shells, seeds etc.)
- Express awareness of and concern for the well-being of the natural world
- Easily learn new information about natural objects and species and understand ecological concepts
- According to Gardner's theory, everyone has each type of intelligence to varying degrees, but culture and experience play a role in the development of a particular type of intelligence. Each type of intelligence needs a stimulating physical and social environment to foster that particular area of development.[*] (Wilson, 2007, p. 10)

[*]Wilson, R. 2007. *Nature and Young Children – Encouraging Creative Play and Learning in Natural Environments.* Routledge Taylor and Francis Group London and New York. P. 10.

teaching. They learned new subject material and were more willing to pursue new teaching methods.

Dr. John Ratey calls it "Miracle-Gro for the brain." In his 2008 book *Spark: The Revolutionary New Science of Exercise and the Brain*, the Harvard Medical School professor argues that we turn on our "thinking brain" when we run, skip, or cycle to get the heart pumping. Exercise boosts blood flow, which carries more oxygen and nutrients to the brain. It also increases levels of a protein called brain-derived neurotrophic factor, which nourishes brain cells and promotes the growth of new neurons and synapses. So as well as boosting efficiency and speed, exercise helps the brain get bigger. It also helps kids become more alert, focused, and motivated by elevating and balancing the neurotransmitters that influence emotions and attention (Gordon, 2011a).

PLAY IN NATURE AND LANGUAGE SKILL DEVELOPMENT

As noted by Riley and Jones (2007):

Play is a natural environment for children's language development (Perlmutter & Burrell, 1995).

Children use language during their solitary play as well as in social play encounters (Piaget, 1962). Both expressive and receptive language skills are needed to plan, explain, and execute play activities. Language skills give children the ability to cooperate in creating and prolonging their play episodes (Van Hoorn, Monighan-Nourot, Scales, & Alward, 2003).

Nind's (2001) research focused on language development in an early-years unit and suggests that children may be more confident in their use of language outdoors than indoors because of a perceived independence from adult control. Developing language skills facilitates peer relationships. According to Riley and Jones (2007):

Piaget (1962) theorized that the talk of preschool-age children is egocentric (i.e., talk that is not for the sake of communicating with others). Very young children verbalize without a need for others to enter into the conversation; however, as older children begin to interact more often with adults and peers, the need to communicate arises. Egocentric speech gradually subsides and social speech takes over as children practise using language (Ginsburg & Opper, 1979).

Lynn Wilson

Materials should be available for children to engage in print in support of their play.

Lynn Wilson

Ryann

I was helping to collect so many things on the nature walk. I helped find so many pinecones, sticks, rocks, and pine needles. I helped clean the garden too. When I was looking for things I see some bugs in the dirt. I saw one really big squishy worm.

Language learning takes place as Ryann tells his story.

Language is a major factor in social play scenarios, such as sociodramatic play in which children create pretend play episodes and take on the roles of others. Language in the context of play provides children with the ability to develop strategies for cooperation, engage in varied and complex play themes, and share perspectives about their world (Van Hoorn et al., 2003). Children's language guides their play and provides the communication needed for the continuation of the play (Guddemi, 2000; Heidemann & Hewitt, 1992). Language usage during play allows children to develop and test their verbal skills.

Children experiment with language by babbling, cooing, telling jokes and riddles, reciting chants and poems, and making up words both indoors and outdoors.

As children use language during play, they develop their understanding of how language affects their ability to communicate (Frost, 1992). Additionally, playing with language develops children's phonological awareness (the conscious sensitivity to the sound structure of language); this includes the ability to auditorily distinguish parts of speech, such as syllables and phonemes by allowing for experimentation with the sounds of words.

Lynn Wilson

Word and picture cues can support children's independent learning.

Children learn that sounds can be manipulated when they rhyme. There is no question that a garden provides opportunities to learn new words in context. Children will continue to learn new vocabulary related to plant care, science, math, and other topics in a concrete rather than abstract way. They have an opportunity to learn the names of plants in more than one language, words for tools needed to tend the garden, and the names of birds and butterflies and other critters that visit.

Lynn Wilson

There are so many print resources about nature available to encourage language acquisition.

Research indicates that the types of games in which girls often engage may support language development differently than the types of games boys typically play. Blatchford, Baines, and Pellegrini (2003) studied playground activities of children in England during the year the children turned 8 years old. The researchers found that girls held significantly more conversations and played significantly more verbal games than did boys. Goodwin (2002) also found that 4th- through 6th-grade girls spent most of their playtime talking with one another. Their games tended to require close proximity to one another, thus allowing for extended conversations. Conversely, some studies found that the games boys tended to choose often involved language usage that was more instruction-oriented, with boys verbally directing the play actions of one another. (Goodwin, 2002)

As children age and engage in games with rules, the explanation of the games becomes more complex and so does the children's language.

NEW CANADIANS

Mary Meyers is a leading advocate and author in the field of English language teaching and learning. She developed *Mainstreams Publications,*

the only elementary-focused publisher in Canada to address a need for resources and educator guidance for Teachers of English to Speakers of Other Languages (TESOL). See

http://www.mainstreamspublications.com

As a primary teacher who specialized in TESOL, Mary initiated several in-school Reception Centres for newly arrived immigrant and refugee children. In her first award-winning book, *Teaching to Diversity: Teaching and Learning in the Multi-Ethnic Classroom* (1993), Mary states how field trips to wooded parks, and ravines with hiking trails improve students' language development and builds cohesion in the group:

> Outdoor education is a wonderful way to acculturate new Canadians to the new country, our land (topography), animals, and weather. Seasonal trips to the apple farm, spring farm animals, and wooded park lands with ravines allow teachers to prepare students for the classroom follow-ups in speaking, viewing, stories, arts and drama.
>
> Outdoor trips early in the year allow children to bond with each other and develop different friendships; the result is that during classroom activities students will show greater collaboration and verbalizing. This only happens though when students are not compelled to partner, line up and shush.
>
> Initially, outdoor trips should allow for opportunities so children may behave naturally; to run, shout, explore, investigate, discover, roll or lay down to look at the sky and clouds; in short, so youngsters will lose some of their timidity and follow their natural inclination to find out about their world. That kind of freedom and behavior works best in the open space of a large wooded park after a guided hike. Outdoor education does not refer to a plastic playground or a soccer field.
>
> Observation is a wonderful tool, and natural outdoor environments show teachers as well as other children a side of new students that is often not apparent inside the walls of their classroom. It's like the thrill of the first snow—the shy child suddenly smiles and shouts, the timid child watches with sheer delight before participating in the glee, and the follower takes on the lead while another suddenly becomes a helper for someone else.
>
> Walk slower on a trail or a stretch of beach and let students touch the acorns, peer into holes and turn over rocks and logs. Use burrs as a lesson for the discovery of Velcro. Use everything they

touch and are interested in as lessons. Introduce new words for things, nouns and verbs, and commands and phrases that will be reinforced back in classroom arts, self-made books and literacy.

It became a running joke that my class was on trips more than in the school, but the fact is once is not enough when it comes to certain experiences. When students have a chance to re-visit an outdoor place once again, they'll do so with an increased sense of wonder and language facility to share in further learning.

The experiences that teachers plan for outdoor instruction relies on the best attributes of *Active Learning* in that students experience meaningful interaction with content, materials and peers. Essentially, Outdoor Learning is Active Learning:

- allowing different rates of learning
- providing open-ended, multi-level learning opportunities allowing for different learning styles, and activities recognizing student strengths, talents and interests
- providing multi-sensory modes of receiving and producing communication, providing meaningful contexts and scaffolds for language acquisition
- creating opportunities for peer collaboration, interaction and support
- linking and extending meaningful language experiences to literacy development.[*] (Meyers, 2012)

---

[*]Mary Meyers

Reading in every season!

Ingrid Crowther

One challenge facing newcomer families is Canadian winters; they are a source of significant concern for most immigrants, especially those from countries where it never snows. There is no denying that the winter months can be bitterly cold. But properly attired, many immigrants are surprised by how well they cope with winter in Canada, and children are joyful in snow play.

Inside LOOK

Improving Health Outcomes by Connecting to Nature

Based on the transformative powers of nature, we can reshape our lives now and in the future. The following suggests strategies for accomplishing this:

- As technology plays a more integral role in our lives, the more we need nature. Nature awakens our senses
- We know that we are "hard wired" to connect with nature regardless of our cultural background or geographical location.
- Nature heals. People who are ill and in hospital recover more quickly and need less pain medication when they are in rooms with views of trees as compared with those patients with views of brick walls. Richard Louv calls this our need for Vitamin N.
- Vitamin N can also benefit those who work in office environments. When nature is introduced, employees are more productive and spend less time away from work due to illness.

(continued)

- Nature can help to decrease depression and improve our well-being. Researchers in Sweden found that joggers who ran in natural green environments felt more restored, and less anxious, angry, or depressed compared to joggers who ran in city streets even though they all burned the same calories.
- Nature can also help us build communities. Neurochemicals and hormones associated with social bonding are increased when we engage with nature. Many clubs are being formed where families gather to hike, garden, or bicycle. Some engage in outdoor green gyms.

If we are able to reconnect with nature, the planet will benefit from it. Our future is at stake.

The opportunities to reduce stress and conflict in nature are well documented.

Adapted from Louv, 2011, p. 5; and Louv, 2012.

BENEFITS FOR FAMILIES

> It is paradoxical that many educators and parents still differentiate between a time for learning and a time for play without seeing the vital connection between them.
>
> —Leo F. Buscaglia

Time in nature gives both parents and children time to be together in meaningful ways, reducing stress and providing shared opportunities that children may remember well into adulthood. But very often, access to nature is limited and more and more children are playing in indoor play gyms, activity centres in malls, etc. Cultural and institutional barriers (including the growing practice of litigation), trends in education that marginalize direct experience in nature, and the structure of cities are limiting our connection with nature. Personal or familial barriers include time pressures and fear. Many parents are caught up in the "waste no time" syndrome. They feel that to get ahead, children's lives should be carefully programmed. Many parents pressure their children to excel in school, emphasizing high grades and test scores; "just playing" is considered a waste of valuable time.

As discussed earlier, Tucker et al. (2006) state that childhood obesity is on the rise and interventions targeted at preschool-aged children are essential for the primary prevention of this disease. The researchers found that parents agreed that physical activity programming was an ideal way to combat obesity in preschoolers. Suggestions from parents included involving them in the program planning and operation, increasing accessibility to programs, providing more facilities, and better promotional strategies such as the use of a television commercial and resources/ideas to engage children in the home particularly during the winter months. It was also noted that there are few educational materials available for parents to use. Many parents also mentioned that they relied on their child care centres to ensure their preschooler is achieving the recommended level of physical activity. Available programs could be marketed and publicized through physicians and a partnership between child care and local physical activity programmers is critical.

Given that the health-related behaviours of preschool-aged children are predominantly under the influence and control of their parents, parents' activity patterns are closely associated with those of their offspring, and overweight preschool-aged boys and girls are 6.1 and 3.8 times, respectively, more likely to have at least one obese parent. According to the 2007–2009 *Canadian Health Measures Survey* from Statistics Canada, only 15 percent of Canadian adults meet the Canadian physical activity guidelines, suggesting that many parents are not acting as good active-living role models for their children. Moore et al. (1991) determined that children who had physically active mothers were twice as likely to be active as those with inactive mothers. Children who had physically active fathers were 3.5 times more likely to be active than those with nonactive fathers; however, children whose parents were both physically active had an almost sixfold increase in likelihood of being active. Consequently, parents' involvement in healthy bodyweight promotion in children is critical (Irwin et al., 2005).

The same study (Irwin et al., 2005, p. 299) cites nine barriers to adequate physical activity:

- *Age:*
  Some organizations required that all participants be toilet trained and there was very little available for the age group.

- *Season and weather:*
  Warmer seasons were more conducive to physical activity and the colder weather provided more challenges—in some cases the preschoolers were willing to go outside but the parents were not.

- *Daycare:*
  Parents believed that enrolling their children in some form of daycare facilitated their children's physical activity. Access to affordable child care was an issue.

- *Siblings:*
  Having more than one child presented problems when trying to enroll in structured programs. However, for some parents having multiple children made physical activity easier because the children had siblings to be active with.

- *Financial costs:*
  Although parents recognized the value of physical activity, the costs were a barrier, particularly for single-income families.

- *Time:*
  Time for working parents was a problem for getting regular physical activity.

- *Society and safety issues:*
  Parents described a busier, less safe society and more alternatives than when they were children; however because of safety concerns, children have less freedom to play outdoors today than in the past.

Place (2000) found that the family outdoor experiences in early life are significant in determining whether individuals become "eco-centric" adults. The question then becomes, how can we support families in our communities to be more involved and more connected to nature?

Many parents are concerned about children taking risks. When we hear the term *risk taking* it is often considered to have a negative connotation. In fact, from the perspective of children, child development, and outdoor play, risk taking is a necessity. Children learn about new skills, try new ideas, and achieve new knowledge and skills by taking risks. They need gradual exposure to find that the world is not dangerous (Marano, 2004). In effect, children who have developed the confidence to embrace the challenges of the environment and accept that learning occurs with mistakes will further explore new possibilities. Risk taking must be thought of

Lynn Wilson

There are many ways for families to engage their children outdoors.

in healthy terms—providing children with the opportunity to discover, be adventurous, and build confidence in using their bodies—rather than as a possibility of injury. This can be achieved by managing safe risk opportunities. Attitudes toward risk taking are influenced by our cultural experiences.

BENEFITS FOR COMMUNITIES

> "[Eighty-one percent] of adults believe that children playing outside helps to improve community spirit [... and eighty-eight percent] of parents say that children playing outside help families to get to know each other in a community."
>
> **—Playday ICM Survey, 2010**

For Additional Photos

More than 95 percent of the Earth is under direct influence while only 3 percent of the surface is set aside as parks and protected areas (Baskin, 1997). Therefore, as advocates, we need to lobby our governments to protect and develop green spaces, particularly in urban environments. Incorporating nature trails, urban parks, and bike and walking paths is critical to foster a greater connection with nature.

> In many communities, the opportunity for children for spontaneous interactions with peers at home and outdoors in the neighbourhood are diminishing. This is due to factors such as the dominance of car traffic and the reduced availability of other children to play with and the parents' and children's concerns about children's safety outdoors. Stranger danger, neighbourhood park quality, pollution and badly planned urban environments are all contributing factors to the lack of community use of parks. (Kernan & Singer, 2011, p. 34)

In 1995, in his seminal book, *Bowling Alone*, Harvard sociologist Robert Putnam described the increasing isolation of life, how the associations that once held us together have fallen away. He pointed to plummeting membership in PTAs, Boy Scouts, and yes, bowling leagues. He used a variety of methods to measure *social capital*, a term that describes how well people in a community look out for one another.

More contact with nature within cities can also, in some settings, reduce violence. Research conducted in a Chicago public housing development compared the lives of women living in apartment buildings with no greenery outside to those who lived in identical buildings—but with trees and greenery immediately outside. Those living near the trees exhibited fewer aggressive and violent acts against their partners. The researchers suggest that natural settings assist in the recovery from mental fatigue and, given that aggression increases with mental fatigue, more exposure to nature would be valuable. The same researchers at the University of Illinois have also shown that play areas in urban neighbourhoods with more trees have fewer incidences of violence, possibly because the trees draw a higher proportion of responsible adults (Kuo & Sullivan, 2001).

The physical environment in and around the school can be used as a living laboratory for the study of natural phenomena. Whether the school is located in a densely populated urban area, a sprawling suburb, a small town, or a rural area, the environment can and should be used as a resource for science study (Broda, 2007, p. 204). The community may also benefit when harvest time approaches. Perhaps there is a food bank or a homeless shelter that would appreciate a donation from the children's garden. The garden is a unique place between the natural world and the social world.

A great resource is *How Walkable Is Your Neighbourhood* at http://www.walkscore.com where you can find out the resources that are available in your community—where to shop, what schools are available, where are the nearest parks etc. Find out your community score on a scale of 100.

Lynn Wilson

This addition to a billboard was done anonymously, reflecting care and concern for members of this community.

Nearby nature can be an antidote to obesity. A 2008 study published in *American Journal of Preventive Medicine* found that the greener the neighbourhood, the lower the body mass index of children. "Our new study of over 3,800 inner city children revealed that living in areas with green space has a long term positive impact on children's weight and thus health," according to senior author Gilbert C. Liu, MD. The results support those who believe that changing the built environment for inner-city kids is just as important as attempts to change family behaviour (Bell, Wilson, & Liu in Louv, 2008, p. 47).

Dyment and Bell (2006) note that

> green school grounds enhanced community connection by providing opportunities to meet new people, make new friends and strengthen old friendships. Through their involvement in regular greening committee meetings or weekly gardening sessions, adults had opportunities to spend time together while working towards a common goal. As noted by other researchers (Lewis, 1992; Barker, 1994; Shapiro, 1995; Glover, 2004), community greening initiatives create inclusive and friendly social environments. Glover (2004) even suggests that community gardening projects are less about gardening than they are about community. The green school ground was an especially important venue for inviting involvement from new Canadian parents. Given the tangible and physical nature of gardening, commonly cited impediments to their involvement in school activities, such as language barriers, were removed or mitigated.[*]

Experts in the community, garden clubs, and garden enthusiasts—even community groups such as Girls Guides or Boy Scouts or high school students needing to complete community hours—may be willing to help in your garden. Families in the centre may have connections or the ability to make significant donations to centre projects. One centre, Studio 1 2 3, was located in a building where several artists had their studios. An artist created a wonderful whimsical sculpture for the children's outdoor space.

According to Tucker et al. (2007), we need policy makers ensure that child care policies and programs mandate daily physical activity indoors and

Studio 1 2 3

Lynn Wilson

outdoors as well as incorporating parents' preferences into strategies for creating or modifying city parks to ensure that limited public resources are being targeted most effectively in support of children's physical activity. Public Health professionals should promote physical activity, active play, and less screen time as part of early years programs and ensure safe outdoor spaces for children to play. Early Childhood Administrators, Educators and Assistants must deliver training and resources to provide daily active playtime that involves free active play and structured activities, encouraging children to play outdoors whenever possible.

> Someday it may be common for farms and ranches to do double duty as schoolyards. Just as some ranchers charge fees for hunting on their land, farmers and ranchers might attract extra income by providing space for hands-on business retreats, nature therapy, or education and rural experiences for young city dwellers. In Norway, farmers and teachers are working together to create new curricula. Students there spend part of the school year on the farm, immersed in science, nature and food production.[**] (Louv, 2011, p. 277)

[*]From Our garden is colour blind, inclusive and warm: reflections on green school grounds and social inclusion by Dyment, Janet E.; Bell, Anne *International Journal of Inclusive Education*, Mar 01, 2008, vol. 12,2. reprinted by permission of the Taylor & Francis Ltd, http://www.tandf.co.uk/journals.

[**]From THE NATURE PRINCIPLE by Richard Louv. © 2011 by Richard Louv. Reprinted by permission of Algonquin Books of Chapel Hill. 81–86 P. 277.

Dufferin Grove Park

Dufferin Grove Park is a 14.2-acre city-owned park in the heart of Toronto. This park is a community hub that offers many options for children and their families. There is a farmer's market, a basketball court, a yearly Easter egg hunt, campfires, Art in the Park, an enormous sand pit, playground equipment, volleyball nets, a community garden, summer drop-in activities, an outdoor skating rink that shares space with a kitchen, a club house, and outdoor summer concerts, to name just a few of the activities in the park. But perhaps one of the most popular experiences is the Friday Night Supper where a wood-fired oven turns out pizzas! A donation is requested and all of the funds raised go back into the park; however, no one goes away hungry for lack of cash. Several awards have been bestowed on this community for its activism and commitment to neighbours and cooperative spirit.

Wood-oven pizzas are made here!

A large sand area makes for great family fun.

Connecting the World's Children with Nature—Environmental Action Kit

Planet Earth is vulnerable to environmental threats of monumental proportions. ... The World Forum Foundation has made a commitment to the Clinton Global Initiative to connect two million young children with nature in the next two years. In order to attain this goal, the World Forum Foundation worked, with the support of IBM, and collaboratively with the Nature Action Collaborative for Children (NACC) Leadership Team and the Dimensions Foundation Nature Explore staff to create [an Action] Kit. ... [T]his kit will serve as a helpful and important resource to people all over the world. (World Forum Foundation, n.d.)

Included in the kit is *An Eco-Friendly Guide for Early Child Programs* to assist programs to "go green."

It offers simple, common sense steps for getting started on this effort, and also provides guidance for those designing or re-designing a new child care center facility... Another section of the kit, called "Tools for Advocacy" includes a DVD... featuring wonderful photos from around the world. [T]he DVD uses words, pictures, and music to send powerful messages to educators, designers, and families. (World Forum Foundation, n.d.)

Two other tool *kits* are also now available: *Tool Kit for Families* and *Took Kit for Educators*, both are exceptional resources.* Much more information about this kit is available on the World Forum Foundation website:

http://www.worldforumfoundation.org/wf/nacc/ibm/story.php

*Reprinted with permission from the World Forum Foundation. Connecting the World's Children with Nature Environmental Action Kit.

Inside LOOK

The Community Greenhouse, Inuvik

Part of the problem in Inuvik is the over availability of non-healthy food.' In the Town of Inuvik, the Community Greenhouse gives local community members access to healthy, affordable food. Located on the Mackenzie River Delta, two degrees above the Arctic Circle, fresh, economical produce is often not available. The Community Garden Society of Inuvik (CGSI) is a non-profit organization formed in November 1998.

The Garden Society wanted to create a positive space for the community. With the help and support of Aurora College, they began converting a decommissioned arena, Grollier Hall, by removing the tin roof and replacing it with polycarbonate glazing. Slated for demolition, the group transformed the arena into a Community Greenhouse, which now serves as a focal point for community development.

The Greenhouse contains two main areas: 74 full-sized community garden plots on the ground floor, and a commercial greenhouse on the second floor. Garden plots are available to residents of Inuvik, and are also sponsored for elders, group homes, children's groups, the mentally disabled, and other local charities. Greenhouse members are required to do 15 hours of volunteer service for each plot they rent. This includes giving tours, watering, and taking care of the children's or elders' plots. The commercial Greenhouse produces bedding plants and hydroponic vegetables to cover operation and management costs. . . .

During the spring and early summer of 1999, the project progressed from the conceptual and feasibility stage, into the renovation and construction phase, and finally through to operation.

The Greenhouse serves as a community-development project that not only grows food, but plays host to school groups, workshops and tourists. Every Saturday, a community market is held to sell produce and other local

Inuvik Community Greenhouse Society

Courtesy of Phillipe Morin

(continued)

goods; as well, there is a carnival for the kids. This has helped bring more family culture into the community.[*]

---

[*]NORTHWEST TERRITORIES: Inuvik Community Greenhouse – Building a strong sense of community through recreational gardening, food production, knowledge sharing, and volunteer support http://www.phac-aspc.gc.ca/publicat/2009/be-eb/nwt-tno-eng.php Health Canada, 2002. Reproduced with the permission of the Minister of Public Works and Government Services Canada, 2012.

Inside LOOK

Robert Bateman

Robert Bateman, a Canadian artist and environmentalist, has created "The Robert Bateman Get to Know Program." Its purpose is to connect children with nature in the hopes that their greater understanding of wildlife will ensure that they will protect what they know. The website is filled with helpful information for educators:

 http://www.get-to-know.org

Aidan Fisk

I like watering the plants in the garden. I like to eat the crunchy salad for lunch.

Children's artwork: Aidan

"When we walk upon Mother Earth, we always plant our feet carefully because we know the faces of our future generations are looking up at us from beneath the ground. We never forget them."

—Oren Lyons, Onondaga Nation

PLAYSCAPE DESIGN

Power of One

SUE HUMPHRIES— COOMBES SCHOOL, ENGLAND

Susan Humphries is installed as Honorary Doctor in Landscape Planning at the Swedish University of Agricultural Sciences in Uppsala, Sweden, October 8, 2011.

© Stewen Quigley. Courtesy of The Coombes CE Primary School

At the Coombes School in southern England, the playground looks like an arboretum. Narrow paths snake through the shrubbery past apple, willow and walnut trees. There is a pond, two labyrinths, a garden and plenty of good spots to dig for worms. Lessons often take place outside. It is the creation of Sue Humphries, an educator who, over four decades, transformed the once barren yard into a verdant outdoor classroom because of her conviction that sitting in chairs is not the best way for children to learn.[*] (McIlroy, 2010, p. A4)

At the school, the students range in age from 3 to 11 and spend about half of their time outside over the course of the school year. Now retired from teaching, Ms. Humphries continues to work there voluntarily four days a week and is a governor with the responsibility for the school's outdoor environment. She has travelled throughout the world to offer practical advice on how to and create inviting landscapes even in small schoolyards. "It is important to raise children with other species, with fruits, flowers and gardens so they can plant and grow and understand something about the cycle of nature. We owe the world this as well as the children" (McIlroy, 2010, p. A4). Sue continues to serve as a Trustee of the *Learning Through Landscapes Trust*.

[*]McIlroy, A. 2010. Young Minds Bloom In Outdoor Classrooms. Saturday, November 13th. A4. The Globe and Mail Inc. All Rights Reserved.

Watch this YouTube video of Sue Humphries and the Coombes School:

http://www.youtube.com/watch?v=s0Jms8v4Sgo

OUTCOMES:

1. Discuss Canada's efforts with regard to outdoor environments in comparison to other *Organisation for Economic Cooperation and Development* (OECD) countries.

2. Compare different types of playgrounds and their advantages and disadvantages.

3. Examine the elements of successful playscape design.

4. Investigate the available tools for accessing outdoor playscapes.

> "Space speaks. Space speaks to each of us. Long corridors whisper "run" to a child; picket fences invite us to rail our hands along the slats. Physical objects have emotional messages of warmth, pleasure, solemnity, fear; action messages of come close, touch me, stay away; or identity messages of I'm strong, or I'm fragile … spaces do more than speak—they load our bodies and minds with sensory information."[*]
>
> **—Jim Greenman (2007, p. 13)**

PHYSICAL ENVIRONMENTS AND QUALITY EDUCATION AND CARE

Commitment to outdoor play in the early years can vary at both policy and practice levels. Countries vary in their policy commitment to outdoor play in ways that are likely to relate to longstanding curricular traditions.

For example France and several English-speaking countries focused on "readiness for school." In these countries, national policy is more likely to identify indoors as the main learning environment, designating outdoors as primarily a recreational space. In contrast, countries such as Norway, Denmark and Sweden, influenced by the Nordic social pedagogy tradition, are more likely to accord

equal pedagogical importance to both kinds of space, with a consequent financial commitment to the outdoors. (Garrick, 2009, p. x)

The Canada Country Note of the *Thematic Review of Early Childhood Education and Care* carried out by the *Organisation for Economic Cooperation and Development* (OECD) (Beach and Friendly, 2005) reaffirmed that the early learning physical environment is an important element of quality. The review team noted that facilities in Canada were generally poor even when they had been newly built, that resources and materials did not provide children with high quality experiences and that programs over-emphasized safety at the expense of opportunities for children to develop independence and autonomy. They also expressed concern about the lack of adequate and available outdoor space, so that children spent little time outdoors and had few opportunities to move freely between the indoors and outdoors. They pointed out that this is in contrast to other northern countries such as Finland and Sweden where children spend much of their day outside, including during the winter months, in regular early learning programs and in special programs such as "forest kindergartens." The OECD report made a number of suggestions to improve indoor and outdoor environments; these ranged from:

- considering the arrangement of space
- introducing more interesting materials
- allowing for more opportunities for physical activity, especially outdoors. (Beach & Friendly, 2005, p. 2)

All of the Canadian provinces and territories except for Newfoundland and Labrador have regulations in place for space requirements in early learning environments. The *Early Childhood Network* suggests that 6 square metres per child of outdoor spaces is desirable, as well as direct access from indoors to outdoors. Only Prince Edward Island, Manitoba, Saskatchewan, and British Columbia meet or exceed this standard (Beech & Friendly, 2005).

A POSITIVE EXAMPLE

The City of Vancouver plans for and coordinates development of child care facilities. Through the land use process, the city negotiates space, manages development projects and works with a design team

---

[*]Greenman, J. 2007. *Caring Spaces, Learning Places: Children's Environments That Work*. Exchange Press Inc. p. 13.

to ensure that facilities conform to its Childcare Design Guidelines (1993). These guidelines not only have space requirements that are approximately twice the provincial regulations but they also address the organization and arrangement of the space, the types of activity areas that should be provided and the relationship among them, the details of the outdoor space and its relationship to the indoors. In recent years, the city has been encouraging the creation of child development "hubs" with a mixture of child care, family resource programs and other family supports. (Beach & Friendly, 2005, p. 2)

Inside LOOK

Sandra Menzer, Executive Director, Vancouver Society of Children's Centres

The Vancouver Society of Children's Centres has developed a number of licensed child care programs in the downtown core of the city. The majority of our centres are part of commercial or residential high rises with roof top playgrounds usually on the 2nd, 3rd or 4th floors. As we work with our landscape architects to design fun, safe and creative playgrounds we are challenged with creating spaces where children can be surrounded by natural and lush green spaces within the concrete and glass world of our downtown. Our overall goal is to focus on elements that create an oasis of calm within our outdoor spaces. This means incorporating trees of varied heights, hedges and perimeters of bamboos, and a range of planters with ornamental grasses and places for perennial plantings. We create distinct play spaces by using natural materials such as logs and stones for borders, construct our climbing structures out of natural wood and place our climbers on the exterior walls of the outdoor space to create openness for the whole play space. We include a mix of ground covers, from sand to fibre to wood decking to stamped concrete with patterns so children can have a variety of experiences as they explore either on foot or on bike. We also put a focus on imaginative play opportunities by building large sandboxes with playhouses adjacent and offering some quiet areas for art, or story time. Our play spaces have become focal points within the downtown and we have successfully incorporated unique learning opportunities for children (and teachers) of all ages.

Lynn Wilson

Sapphire Roof Top Child Care Centre, Vancouver, British Columbia

Lynn Wilson

A spectacular playscape for the children at this early learning environment

Lynn Wilson

Atelier Child Care Centre, Vancouver, British Columbia

Contributed by: Sandra Menzer, 2012

For Additional Photos

TYPES OF PLAYGROUNDS

Traditional playgrounds are typically flat, barren open areas with various pieces of unrelated commercial, usually metal, large-muscle equipment such as slides, swings, bars, see-saws, and merry-go-rounds. These pieces of equipment are fixed and designed primarily for exercise, large motor play, and little else. In this environment the children play on one piece of equipment until they are bored and then move on to the next. There are often more injuries on this type of playscape since the surfacing is often inadequate. Risky behaviour is the by-product of boring traditional playgrounds that do not challenge or engage the children. If children are not able to manipulate or act on the equipment, they often act on the environment in unsafe ways—diving off the top of swing sets, hanging precariously from bars, etc. Unfortunately, adults often create environments for children from their memories of their own playground experiences where asphalt, fixed equipment, and concrete structures prevailed.

Creative or contemporary playgrounds are usually adapted to a particular site and incorporate some moving parts such as wooden bridges, nets, cable slides etc., which allow the children to have a greater impact on the environment. There are often game boards, tic-tac-toe panels, musical instruments, binoculars, and sound tubes, which enhances the play value of the equipment. These playgrounds are typically designed by professional architects or designers using manufactured equipment, usually wood, and expensive stone and timber terracing. They are intended to have high aesthetic appeal for adults.

📷 **For Additional Photos**

Jamie Bell Playground, High Park, Toronto

Sound experiments

PLAYGROUND STANDARDS

After the first mandatory Playground Safety Standard was adopted in West Germany in 1975, manufacturers soon implemented these standards to provide safer commercial structures and to reduce the number of legal challenges. There has been a trend toward plastics that would address the concerns about rotting wooden structures and more recently in neutral wood colors. Over the past decade the outdoor play spaces designed for children in Canada have been largely shaped by fear and profit, rather than by what we know about children's play and development. Since the early 1980s the Canadian Standards Association (CSA) has played an increasingly important role in this transformation as their technical standards for children's outdoor play spaces have been gradually adapted as policy by local and regional agencies. (Herrington & Nicholls, 2001, p. 1)

Ithaca, New York

ADVENTURE PLAYGROUNDS

"In a sense, you and I have always played in 'adventure playgrounds.' We created a fort in the kitchen cabinets, jumped from couch to couch across oceans; we snuck out through a hole in the fence to a new world. We climbed trees and hid in bushes. We played in the mud and the rain. We chased each other, made secret worlds with our own language. We created spaces with whatever we could find around us. Some of us played in abandoned buildings, or barns, or vacant lots between buildings, used what we found and made up stories of our lives to be. We looked everywhere to find our space."*

—Lia Sutton (2011)

Adventure Playground

The first Adventure Playground opened in Emdrup, Denmark in 1943, during World War II, and was inspired by the work of a Danish landscape architect, Carl Theodor Sorensen, and the idea eventually spread throughout Europe and, to a lesser degree, to Asia. In the devastation of World War II, children played in forbidden sites happily using dirt, scraps of metal, and wood in thoughtful creative play in preference to formal jungle gyms. Adventure Playgrounds are special playgrounds featuring trained play leaders or play workers. Children spend their time building dens, huts, and houses with tools and scrap materials; caring for animals; cooking over open fires; tending gardens; playing in water, sand, and dirt; and engaging in a wide variety of creative, challenging games and play activities. Indeed, a central quality in creating Adventure Playgrounds is recognizing that children's ideas are often better than those of adults (Norman, 2003; Frost & Klein, 1979; Bengtsson, 1974; Allen, 1968).

Lady Allen of Hurtwood of England was so impressed with her visit to Emdrup and the Adventure Playgrounds that she saw there that she brought the idea back to London. Adventure Playgrounds, which grew to include those for children with disabilities, have inspired

manufacturers to create more stimulating and interactive playground equipment. Today you will find Adventure Playgrounds in Denmark, Switzerland, France, the Netherlands, Japan, and England; however, Germany has more than any other country—with 400.

Unfortunately, Adventure Playgrounds failed to gain popularity in the North America because of adults' perceptions of their unsightly appearance, unsubstantiated safety concerns, lack of understanding of the value of spontaneous, creative play and games, and lack of funding. Despite their junk appearance and extensive challenges, "the *Royal Society for the Prevention of Accidents* (U.K.) confirms that the accident record of Adventure

Children's interpretation of the Three Little Pigs' stick house on an Adventure Playground

*Adventure Playgrounds. A Child's World In The City 2005. © Lia Sutton. 2012 Adventure Playgrounds. A Child's World In The City. http://adventureplaygrounds.hampshire.edu/aboutme.html.

Playgrounds is far better than that of other forms of provision" (Heseltine, 1998), and the incidence of lawsuits at such playgrounds is far lower than playgrounds in the United States. (Frost, n.d., p. 3)

Adventure Playgrounds provide opportunities to experiment and explore; providing risks for children to take.

Berkeley's Adventure Playground is one of a handful of playgrounds in the United States based on a concept that grew in popularity after World War II. Kids, whose lives are becoming increasingly structured by school, sports, music lessons, need time to do anything they want, and if it's not given to them, they will just take it. Berkeley's Adventure Playground opened in 1979. There is no equipment. Instead, kids are confronted with boards, spare tires, telephone poles, and lots and lots of mud. If they want a fort, they can put one together; if they want to splash in the mud puddle, no one is going to tell them not to. The freedom is liberating. It's also demanding: Skills like initiative and risk-taking are often unused, especially on a normal playground. The injury rate is something that would be bragged about at a union job site. Over a two-day period this summer, 700 children came through the Adventure Playground. The injury total was two fingers hit by hammers. By forcing kids to assess the possibility of risk, they play more safely while also learning how to take care of themselves. There are also trained "play workers" on site, supervising. Now, almost 30 years after its inception, ideas from the Adventure Playground are taking hold around the country. Loose parts, play workers, and the use of natural elements like mud and sand are all factoring into the next generation of parks.[*] (Clendaniel, 2008)

© John Rice

Berkeley, California, Adventure Playground

[*]© Clendaniel, M. 2008. "Adventure Playgrounds." *The Education Issue,* Issue 12, August 14th. http://www.good.is/post/adventure-playgrounds.

DESIGN OF PLAYSCAPES

"Playscapes for children of all ages need to be more than playgrounds. They should be 'habitats'—places where children can live."

—Mary Rivkin (2000, p. 4)

Sense of place is of critical importance to children who are beginning to understand their sense of the world. "What the natural world looks, feels, and smells like on our part of the planet, helps us distinguish how we are the same and how we are different from the rest of the world. Developing a sense of place is critical to a foundation of ecological awareness and responsibility" (Bucklin-Sporer & Pringle, 2011).

Rusty Keeler (2008) makes a case for the term *playscapes* rather than *playgrounds*; the latter conjures up the idea of an outdated play environment model. Also a term used by landscape architects and designers, *playscapes* reflect the natural environment. Using native plants, trees, hills, etc., every effort is made to engage children and adults in nature and to offer children a wide range of open-ended opportunities. The term *playscape* focuses us on the idea that the whole environment is taken into consideration, not just a section of the yard or the garden.

Martha Thorne, associate curator of Architecture at the Art Institute of Chicago, states that

we should value the design of spaces for play as much as we value the children who use those spaces. We need to recognize the substantial contribution carefully crafted urban spaces can make to our children's lives and the lives of our communities. And though children's playgrounds may not change the urban environment on a macro scale, they have the potential to change the world in small, meaningful ways. A well-designed playground offers a chance for a child—and a community—to explore, to imagine and to take risks. (Quoted in Solomon, 2005, p. 25)

Horticulturists too have also become more involved in playground design. Their skills lie in their ability to apply scientific knowledge to the cultivation and propagation of plants. They are able to provide technical information in the field of landscape design to create parks, gardens, and recreational areas, with concern for conservation and preservation of natural resources.

Architects Have Much to Contribute

For landscape architects designing outdoor playscapes for young children, one of the biggest challenges is to not *overdesign* the space. In general, one need only to create a spatial framework that allows for loose parts play, flexibility of use, and for the space to be continually modified and embellished by the children and their caregivers. Providing shade and shelter, and creating a variety of child-scale distinct spaces/places within the framework are all fundamental. Natural materials—trees, shrubs, grass, water, sand, mulch, flowers, mud, logs, and rocks—should all be present. Engaging the child care staff in a participatory design process provides invaluable insight, builds enthusiasm and helps to ensure that the playscapes will meet the needs of the users.

Contributed by: Kim Allerton, OALA Northwood Associates Landscape Architects Ltd. Kim has been providing consulting services on a wide variety of projects across southern Ontario since 1981.

Herrington and Lesmeister (2006) agree that landscapes designed for children's use should consider developmental and play needs and the unique contributions that landscapes can offer. They classify seven areas in which the quality of the outdoor play space can be assessed:

- *Character*
  —the feel and design intent of the space
- *Context*
  —the type of setting, number of children, location, degrees of sun and shade, etc.
- *Connectivity*
  —the physical, visual and learning pathways the space creates
- *Change*
  —the range of differently sized spaces and how these change over time
- *Chance*
  —the ability of children to create, manipulate, and leave an impression on the play space and for the space to stimulate spontaneity
- *Clarify*
  —the ability of children to understand how the space can be used and appreciate what can be done
- *Challenge*
  —both physical and cognitive provided by the space.

These seven Cs are a useful structure around which to describe and plan for an outdoor space.

There is much to be said about how a community views its children by the location of their playscapes; are they tucked away or are they part of the mainstream of life in the city?

For Additional Photos

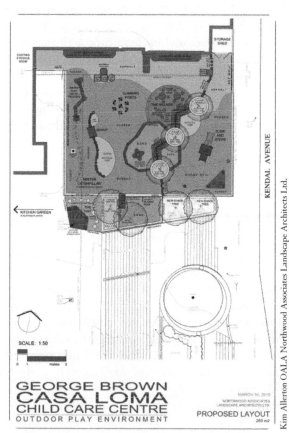

Evergreen Foundation Project, Kim Allerton, Northwood Landscape Architects Ltd.

CREATING CHANGE— PLANNING FOR NEW PLAYSCAPES!

We need dramatic and innovative change! This transition to inspired natural playscapes is the responsibility of the adults who care for children; their families, their community, legislators, health care professionals, landscape architects, horticulturalists, designers, nutritionists, educators, environmental activists, and government officials.

TOOLS THAT HELP
POEMS

POEMS—*Preschool Outdoor Environment Measurement Scale*—is an assessment tool for evaluating the quality of outdoor environments in child care centres for children 3 to 5 years of age (Debord, Hestenes, Moore, Cosco, & McGinnis, 2005). The items included in POEMS are designed to provide direction to educators who want to offer high-quality programs and hands-on interactions for children in outdoor learning environments. The items can serve as a menu of strategies to work toward higher quality outdoor activities. POEMS is also a reference tool for landscape architects and designers working with child care programs to design quality outdoor play and learning spaces. POEMS contains 56 items, which are grouped into five domains—physical environment, interactions, play and learning settings, program, and teacher/caregiver role.

For more information go to

http://www.poemsnc.org/ECA.html

GO GREEN RATING SCALE

Phil Boise (2010) wrote the *Go Green Rating Scale* and the accompanying Handbook, which is designed to provide early childhood environments with the healthiest of environments. Both these educational tools explain the importance of environmental health in early childhood settings, and the rating scale helps programs evaluate and improve the environmental health of their facilities. The scale is divided into nine sections, each of which addresses a major aspect of green—administration, green living and stewardship, cleaners and disinfectants, body care and hygiene products, air quality management, exposure to lead, exposure to chemicals found in plastics, pesticides, and other contaminants. For more information go to

http://www.gogreenratingscale.org

Other tools, such as the Harms and Clifford *Environment Rating Scale*, are also available. The Manitoba Family Services and Consumers Affairs website displays the *Best Practices Licensing Manual for Early Learning and Child Care Centres* and has information related to outdoor environments. Joe Frost's (2002) *Play and Playscapes* has an Infant and Toddler Playground Maintenance Checklist (p. 346) as well as an excellent comprehensive Playground Rating System for children 3 to 8 years of age (p. 107).

Further change may occur on children's playscapes when educators and administrators spend time examining sites such as the Berkeley Adventure Playground (see above) or visiting outstanding playscapes in their community.

A PROJECT BEGINS

Gathering the children's opinions and ideas is the first step toward involving everyone in the planning for a transformation process. A core team should be responsible for managing the project and overseeing the planning, fundraising, promotion, volunteer recruitment, etc. It is best to begin with two or three people who are passionate about this

These families donated funds and their names became part of the fence.

project—the manager, educators, PTA officials, family members, youth groups, elected officials, local celebrities, etc. Then expand the committee with individuals who bring expertise to the project. Are there artists, horticulturists, landscape architects, gardeners, sculptures in your community who would like to help?

Members of the team should start by making sure that they agree on the purpose for greening the grounds and that they share a common vision. Setting up a system to maintain communication within the group and with the broader community is critical. With this group, establish roles and responsibilities, create a timeline, and develop plans for fundraising. Establish a detailed budget/fundraising goal for the complete project. In addition to playscape materials and safe surfaces there will be other expenses—professional services, construction costs, writing funding proposals, etc. Most groups pay for their playground project through small grants, community-based fundraising, and in-kind donations such as products, services, and volunteer labour. Most projects will depend on volunteers, helping to create a sense of community ownership and reducing the costs; volunteers will be your most valuable resource!

Inside LOOK

Fundraising Ideas

Your local community recreation co-ordinator or municipal councillors can help you find out about funding that your centres can access. Below is a list to get you started!

Lowe's Toolbox for Education
Lowe's support program awards $5 million every year to more than 1,000 schools for new playgrounds, creating play spaces that are accessible and the repairing of old equipment. Each school may receive between $2,000 and $5,000 based on their application.

The Pepsi Refresh Project
This project allows Canadians every two months to submit their ideas for improved communities to http://www.refresheverything.ca. Once posted, Canadians can decide which ideas will receive one of ten grants by voting for their favourites. Over the course of a year, Pepsi will contribute more than $1 million.

Toyota Evergreen Learning Grounds School Ground Greening Grants
The Toyota grants are for schools wishing to create outdoor classrooms and food gardens to provide students with a healthy place to play, learn, and develop a genuine respect for nature. Amounts range from $500 to $3,500 for publicly funded Canadian schools (JK–12) and $500 to $2,000 for not-for-profit daycare.

Walmart—Evergreen Green Grants
Walmart provides funds for community-based restoration and stewardship initiatives in urban and urbanizing areas, including naturalization, restoration, and stewardship, and community food gardens in amounts up to $10,000.

Community Initiatives Program (CIP)
This program supports sports, health, recreation, libraries, arts, and culture. Grants for up to $75,000 can be applied for but must be matched by the community but not always with cash; volunteer services or donated materials would also be acceptable. For those who cannot match the funds, a $10,000 unmatched grant is also available.

Mountain Equipment Co-op
This organization also contributes funds to projects and to date has supported community efforts in 10 provinces.

Community Initiatives Fund–Physical Activity Grant Program
The CIF Physical Activity Grant Program supports strategic projects and initiatives that will advance the physical activity movement in Saskatchewan and increase the level of physical activity of Saskatchewan people. The program aims to engage and mobilize physical activity

(continued)

sector partners to foster collective will and leadership and increase community capacity through enhanced cross-sectoral cooperation.

Molson Community Cheer Program

Through the Molson Community Cheer Program, Molson Coors Canada is donating $1 million in support of a minimum of 20 projects, programs, and initiatives that promote active lifestyles across Canadian communities.

The North Face Co.

The company supports community efforts where young people are connected to nature as well as educating on environmental health.

General Mills Canada

General Mills Canada—Champions for Healthy Kids Grant Program encourages communities across Canada to improve the eating and physical activity patterns of young people ages 2–20. Twenty-five grants of up to $5,000 are awarded annually.

Let Them Be Kids

Across Canada, Let Them Be Kids, a volunteer non-profit organization, has helped to build playgrounds, skate parks, and fitness parks across the country.

ParticipACTION and GreenGym

ParticipACTION is encouraging communities to build outdoor fitness and gym equipment in environments where they will be accessible and easy to use. A new partnership with GreenGym provides a grant of up to 10 percent on the purchase of GreenGym outdoor fitness equipment.

TD Friends of the Environment Foundation

Providing environmental funding to non-profit organizations across Canada, the TD Friends of the Environment Foundation accepts applications for community projects. Non-profits, schools, municipalities, and First Nations groups are encouraged to submit applications for projects and initiatives that focus on:

- Protecting and preserving the Canadian Environment
- Assisting young Canadians in understanding and participating in Environmental activities
- Supporting urban renewal such as environmental projects to rejuvenate smaller or at-risk neighbourhoods and "main streets"
- Enhancing cooperation among Environmental organizations

World Wildlife Fund

Green CommUnity School Grants Program is offered by the WWF—Canada. The grants are awarded to communities that make an effort to reduce their impact on the environment, help to educate community members about environmental issues, encourage leadership, and support initiatives for change.

FIRST STEPS, EXPLORING THE SPACE—QUESTIONS TO ASK!!

CHILDREN FIRST!

- Are the children excited about going outside?
- Where do the children play and not play and why?
- What is stimulating and what is challenging!
- Is the outdoor space a sensory experience for the children? Do they experience a range of sounds, tastes, textures, colours, and smells?
- Does the space meet the needs of all the children including the youngest children and children with special needs?
- Do children have access to lose parts to expand their play?
- Are the children given large blocks of time to engage in uninterrupted outdoor time?

THE PHYSICAL ENVIRONMENT

- Where can we find people or organizations on the Internet or in our community who might support our work?

- How imaginative and creative can we be in the design? Do we have the people who can help us with this?

- Are there other successful projects for children in our neighbourhood that we should visit?

- Do we have access to the original site plans so we know where our boundaries lie?

- If we have a rooftop playscape, have we planned for shade, shelter, and wind conditions?

- Who do we need permission from to make changes?

- What utilities do we need to be aware of before we dig?

- Is the entrance to the playscape inviting to children, families, and the community?

Entranceways influence behaviour.

- Can we create a seamless transition from indoor to outdoor?

- Is there access to a washroom and water close at hand?

- Can we create an outdoor change table for infants and toddlers in a sheltered space so teachers don't have to come inside when changing needs to happen?

- Do we have adequate lighting?

- How will the space be timetabled; what groups of children go out together?

- What about seasonal changes? What kinds of play options would children have when it is raining and when it is very hot?

- Is there space for a wall mural?

- How will we design the space to maximize winter conditions?

- Are there large spaces for gathering and game playing and instructing a group of children as well as small spaces for one, two, or three children to play and rest?

- How will the space encourage prosocial behaviour?

- How can we encourage solitary and partner play?

Murals can reflect the community and the cultural groups present.

Murals can also be playful!

For Additional Photos

Grant MacEwan Child Care Centre, Edmonton, Alberta

For Additional Photos

- Are there places for children to take reasonable risks; does the space provide challenges?

- Consider traffic patterns—can the children see what their play options are and how to get to different areas?

- Will the existing fixed equipment stay? Does it have enough play value to keep it, and is it safe? Is there quality of workmanship and does it engage the children?

- Will school-agers be using the playscape? Their bodies are physically bigger, so the equipment needs to be sturdier. Is the equipment challenging and flexible, so they will not be bored and simply not use it?

- How do we provide for differing age groups on our playspace?

- Our site is flat; can dirt be hauled in to create low, rolling inclines? Can we include hills for winter sliding?

- Can we plan for a porch swing or hammock in a shaded area for feeding and nurturing babies

University of British Columbia Child Care Services, Vancouver

as well as being a comfortable place for the teachers and children?

- Where will the children eat when they are outside?

- Should we have wood or chain-link fencing? Solid wood fences are more expensive than chain-link ones and while they cut down on traffic or other noises they also prevent children seeing the world around them.

- What type of surfaces will we have—grass/loose natural materials such as wood chips, mulch, or sand, or hard materials such as asphalt, concrete, or resilient materials such as elastocrete?

- Can we provide shelter so the children can be outside even during inclement weather?

- Have we considered that all areas within a fall zone of moving and climbing equipment should be covered with highly resilient material?

- Are the paths accessible to children with special needs?

- What will we construct around different zones to keep loose material from scattering?

- Have we consider drainage since ideally the playscape should slope gently away from the building? Can we install gutters to channel run-off water away from the play area?

- Can we create a rain water catchment such as a barrel for watering the plants?

- Will steep sloping areas have enough vegetation to prevent erosion?

- What type of secure gates will we have? They should be self-closing and locked or secured from opening by young children.

- How will we maintain our playscape?

- How do we handle garbage, composting, and recycling?

- How do we separate trash from play areas to avoid contamination and stinging insects?

- Are we ready to map out our plan?

- Where is the sun and where is the shade? Where are the hot spots?

- How do we add even more shade to the space?

- Can we find a place to put the equipment that won't be too exposed to the sun? We want to avoid creating hot spots on equipment that could harm the children.

For Additional Photos

For Additional Photos

Shade is critical on the playscape.

Waterfront, New York City

- What vegetation can stay and what new plantings will we need?

GREENING THE SPACE

- What native plants can be incorporated to "green" the space?
- Where will we locate the gardens?
- How will we provide access to water for the gardens and water play?
- How will we provide drinking water for the children?

Billy Johnson Park, New York City

THE ZONE APPROACH

- What zones are we able to incorporate that will facilitate play and minimize conflict?
- How will we create a transition zone?
- Can we place compatible zones close together, with active zones separated from quiet zones?
- Is there appropriate accessibility to each zone?
- Can we use low, natural partitions and different surfacing to define zones?
- Is there a space for a quiet retreat?
- Is there a space for active games?
- Will there be places for the children and adults to sit?
- Can we take advantage of natural/prominent elements, slope of the land, etc.?
- How will this space encourage the children to take an active interest in nature?

STORAGE

- How can we store all of the loose parts that we know are essential for a vibrant play space?
- How can we locate the storage so practitioners don't need to carry everything outside each day?
- Can we purchase or build small storage pieces that are well constructed and safe from vandalism or gather other items for storage such as wicker baskets, nets, boxes on wheels, small suitcases, laundry baskets, or plastic stacking crates that can easily be moved from place to place by the children?

For Additional Photos

Queen Street Child Care Centre

An interesting way to use a canoe for storage!

Small Shakers

Small Shakers

Soft Blocks

Manipulatives for infants and toddlers

Ryerson Early Learning Centre

- How can children be involved in taking out and putting away the equipment? Can we organize it at their height (lower than 60 centimetres)?

- Can we double up on space with storage underneath and decking on top?

- Can we include trays that can hold any number of items and are easily carried from one area to another?

- Can we build or find trestles that are child size that can hold pieces of wood that can be laid across to provide an instant table?

- Where can we locate hooks and shelves that will help to keep the equipment well organized?

- How can we label areas of the outdoor space to create a print-rich environment?

- How can we label tubs and storage containers to help maintain a sense of order and help educators and children find what they need?

- Can we encourage the children to take photographs of the contents of the bins and match them to the bins?

Adequate, well-labelled storage enhances the play-scape experience.

- Where will we store the first aid equipment?
- Where will we locate the intercom system or store portable telephones?

One of the best possible resources to help you get started is Randee Holmes and Cam Collyer's book: *All Hands in the Dirt: A Guide to Designing and Creating Natural School Grounds*.

Another important resource is the Evergreen publication, *Small Wonders—Designing Vibrant, Natural Landscapes for Early Childhood*. It is free to download from the Evergreen website at

http://www.evergreen.ca/docs/res/Small-Wonders.pdf

ASK THE CHILDREN

> "By the end of grade six, children will have spent about 1,800 hours, or 257 entire school days in the schoolyard—a place that many describe as boring, dangerous, noisy, dull, uncomfortable and ugly. The design of the majority of school grounds virtually ignores students' social interests. School grounds are largely planned for active sports, most of which can only be pursued during the warmer months."*
>
> **—Ann Coffey (2004, p. 1)**

---

*Coffey, A. 2004. *Asking Children Listening to Children. School Grounds Transformation*. Canadian Biodiversity Institute. p. 1.

Mohr (1987) asked children in Grades Five and Six to draw their vision for a new playground. When the drawings were handed back, they reflected the traditional playground with swings and slides because the children had never seen anything else. Mohr recommends that instead of asking the children what they would like in their playground, ask them how they like to play and develop the design from that perspective.

So how do we help children feel that this space belongs to them? Asking what their favourite outdoor space is, what do they like to do outside, what would make the playground more fun is critical since no one will have more intimate knowledge of the space than the children. However, given Mohr's comments, a visit to local playgrounds, parks, nature areas, etc. may help the children form new ideas for their space. Storytelling; music making; using temporary accessories such as tents, tables, drums, or chimes; and involving children in the ongoing transformation of the site are all ways to set the stage for making the place their own. When children help look after a garden, paint a mural, create a sculpture, or put a hand print in a stepping stone, they feel connected to a place.

Children's ideas about their play environment are often insightful and thoughtful. They will explain what they want to do and experience on their play space. While construction of the play space may need adult involvement and supervision, it is important to include children whenever possible.

> Asking children to take part as genuine partners in transforming their school grounds can have powerful consequences. It is not just about "greening" the environment for its own sake. Involvement creates a sense of school ownership by the children. As a child, if you feel "this is my space, I am proud of it, I love being here," common sense tells us that such a child is more likely to succeed academically than the child who has no such feelings for their school. Several research studies in the last several years have presented convincing evidence that children are well aware of being listened to or ignored. Children readily notice when their needs are not being taken into account as when adults design and manage their environment without their input. The result of such environments (each of us can think of examples besides bland schoolyards) is boredom and alienation. (Robin Moore in Coffey, 2004, p. vii)

Children Speak!

The kindergartens look like they're in a cage. They should have a nicer space. They should be allowed to come out into our yard sometimes and we should be able to go in and sit and read to them and talk to them. We hated being caged up like that when we were little.

If adults had to be out here like us, they wouldn't sit in the dirt on the ground. They would make sure there was somewhere nice for them to sit!

There is a big rock by the trees and everyone likes sitting on it but it's out of bounds. All the nice shady places that we like are off-limits!

We need to improve the view of the yard. It is so ugly. We need to plant some trees to make the yard look better. The grass is muddy and wet in the Spring and then it turns yellowish-brown and smells bad. After that, it dries out and turns brown and looks completely dead. It makes us feel down.

We have no plants in the yard. No grass. No trees. No flowers. There is nothing outside for 'nice' animals. And it's not nice for us either!

We find broken glass in the yard from beer bottles. They don't care if we get cut by the glass. We don't like all the garbage in the yard or the seagulls, hornets and wasps that come to eat it. When I think about the yard, the first thing I think of is all the garbage.* (Coffey, 2004, pp. 17–24)

---

*Coffey, A. 2004. *Asking Children Listening to Children. School Grounds Transformation*. The Canadian Biodiversity Institute. pp. 17–24.

Early childhood environments are in a position to change outcomes for young children by designing outdoor playscapes that take their breath away. Do the children stand at the window looking out, knowing that wonderful things await them if they could just get outside, if teachers would just get out of their way?

For Additional Reading

CONSIDER THE WHOLE COMMUNITY

For Additional Photos

> "Never doubt that a small group of thoughtful, committed citizens can change the world. Indeed, it is the only thing that ever has."
>
> **—Margaret Mead**

Next, look beyond your immediate play area to the surrounding environment with these questions in mind:

- What is the character of the surrounding community? Is it industrial, rural, or inner city? Does it include many different cultures?

- Can this space reflect the values of the neighbourhood? How? For instance, in a predominantly Aboriginal village in northern British Columbia where community and co-operation are highly valued, the outdoor space, equipment, and activities promote these ideals.

- What play structures are already available for children? For example, does the local park already have tire swings and a fire engine? You might want to avoid duplicates of local playgrounds' equipment.

- What can your outdoor space provide that may be lacking in children's homes or community environments?

- Will the community use this space as well?

- How will your outdoor space be affected by other neighbourhood conditions including traffic patterns, residential units, businesses, etc.? Do these have implications for safety, acceptable levels of noise, hours of operation, and other considerations?

- Are families involved in outdoor play? If so, where?

A Community in Action

Despite the destruction caused by the fire, this action galvanized the community.

An arsonist who started a fire in the Jamie Bell Playground in Toronto galvanized this community. This playground was originally designed in 1999 with enormous input from the children. After a massive fundraising project, the playground was finally built with the help of citizens from all over the city. Many families have wonderful memories of time spent in the park. When the fire was discovered, the community once again sprang into action and with the support of organizations, construction companies, architects, and many private citizens, the structure has been rebuilt along with many other initiatives that have long been planned. This is a stellar example of the power of one community!

- How can our centre history and culture be incorporated?
- Will we take our children into the community to use the playground resources that are there?

Think about individuals, organizations, the landowner, and other stakeholders that may have an interest in a playscape project. Bring these potential partners together to talk about your ideas. Find out if they have knowledge, experience, funds, or enthusiasm to apply to your project.

Don't stop asking—check in with practitioners, families, neighbours, and community members who may have not only great ideas but also be able to contribute in some way. Link up with groups that might be willing to help. Ask if you might speak at one of their meetings and present your goals for the centre. You might try getting on a local radio or television show to ask for donations or volunteers. Newspapers might be willing to write a piece about your project. How could older children and youth be involved in supporting the project? Could local high school students provide supervision and activities to complete a community credit, or could a minimal salary be given? The more youth are involved in the process, the less likely vandalism will occur.

WHAT SHOULD PLAYSCAPES DO?
INTEGRATE A SENSORY APPROACH

"Through our senses the world appears."

—**Buddha**

For Additional Photos

For Additional Photos

Warm sun on faces. Squishy mud between toes. Crunch of a freshly picked carrot. Our senses gather information about the world and how it works. We use our senses every day as we make our way in the world—smelling, tasting, hearing, and looking (Keeler, 2008, p. 41).

Sensorimotor engagement resides in our own unconscious learning, our muscle memory that has been developed since infancy. Play experiences that enhance the senses are integral to human development. In sensorimotor learning, the young child is preoccupied with her senses and motor abilities. Ninety-five percent of the information we receive comes to us through seeing, touching, and hearing. Our sensory channels are our primary sources of learning. Such learning can be fostered through varied and stimulating experiences that engage the senses and invite movement in space. Because young children learn primarily through their senses and through motoric manipulation, they are excellent candidates for nature education experiences. Infants and toddlers are natural scientists, driven to investigate and experiment with everything they encounter. The natural world is full of sights, smells, sounds, textures, and tastes—so many enticing ways to engage the senses—and the playscapes for young children should reflect this!

Places that engage the senses—rich colour, fragrances, pleasant sounds, engaging textures, varied light qualities—heighten the enchantment and meaning of any experience: blooming flowers; soft music from a range of cultures; sensory walks; changes and contrast in scale, light, texture, and colour; fragrant herb gardens; a compost pile; mixing sand and water: water fountains; wind chimes; wind socks; ribbons hanging from trees; kites; birdfeeders; birdbaths; dark and bright spaces; sunlight through the trees; objects that are soft or prickly, flexible, large, and small.

Think about adding texture to the play space—grass, concrete, sand, large smooth rocks, leaves, bark, blankets, water, wooden decks, etc. Texture panels mounted in play structures or on walls, or textured tiles along the walls or fence is another sensory opportunity. Fastening kitchen pots, colanders, frying pans, and other identifiable materials to the fence or wall allows the children an opportunity to bang away, particularly infants and toddlers.

For Additional Photos

Instruments from a wide range of cultures can be included—bells (hang them from trees), chimes, maracas, rhythm sticks, a variety of drums, sitar, kalimbas, gongs, dried painted gourds, woven jute rattles, wooden flutes, conch shells, castanets, tambourines, triangles, cymbals, and old pots and pans. Large loose parts are important to infants and toddlers and so many items from the kitchen that are familiar to the children are perfect exploratory objects.

Opportunities to fingerpaint and experiment with mud and clay will foster exploration and expression. Draw the attention of the children to outdoor sounds such as birds, car noises, buzzing insects, etc. Expand children's perceptions of the world and lend a sense of specialness by providing unusual or unexpected items; for example, totem poles, tire animals, pipe telephone systems. Children love surprises and discovery. Consider how the play yard might remain a bit secret

and obscure, through nooks, crannies, and an enchanted forest (Frost & Talbot, 1989).

For interesting information about a musical environment for children with autism and their peers visit the *Music Hut* at

http://www.musictherapy.biz/Dr._Petra_Kern/Music_Hut.html

Lynn Wilson

A sound wall, Princess Diana Playground, London, England

Lynn Wilson

An opportunity to create interesting sounds at the Rusk Institute of Rehabilitation Medicine, New York City

Tribal Thunder

Tribal Thunder, Heartbeat of the Earth is an organization that brings music, specifically drumming, to children and teachers alike. Oscar De Los Santos (2012) explains

> Of all the musical instruments in the world, the drum is found in every culture on the face of the planet. It is the unifying heart beat behind all music; the heartbeat of life and the pulse of creation. It has been my experience that people underestimate the power of music, however 80% of one's memories will be linked to sounds and songs that at once can trigger memory and strong emotion. (Tribal Thunder, n.d.)

This organization carries out a variety of workshops in schools and has a variety of traditional drums for sale, some of which can be installed in outdoor play spaces. More information is available at

http://tribalthunder.com

Lynn Wilson

Natural materials can be used to create sound.

Courtesy of Suzanne Ganse

Many new manufactured materials are also available.

PROVIDE AN ABUNDANCE OF MATERIALS

The playground should encourage and allow interaction among children, materials, and adults.

Children need an environment rich in possibilities with no sense of scarcity in terms of—storage, building supplies and tools, and vegetation. Having the materials readily available through effective storage means the children don't have to ask a teacher to help them and encourages self-help skills.

For Additional Photos

Children prefer real materials to plastic replicas— loose parts and simple tools are critical. Add materials that allow children to transform "junk" into personal creations. Open-ended materials are important; being open to many uses and interpretations, they give children the power to say what they will be or do—cardboard boxes, building blocks, logs, planks of wood, etc. Some sites contain an abundance of items—for example, tires—so how can these be used in innovative ways? (See Chapter 8 for more information about loose parts and other resources.)

Lynn Wilson

Adequate storage is critical to effective outdoor planning.

DESIGNING AND PLANNING FOR RISK

"The creeping culture of risk aversion and fear of litigation ... puts at risk our children's education and preparation for adult life. Children today are denied—often on spurious health and safety grounds—many of the formative experiences that shaped my generation. Playgrounds have become joyless, for fear of a few cuts and bruises. Science in the classroom is becoming sterile and uninspiring."

—**Judith Hackitt**

It is only by direct personal experience that children learn to assess and overcome danger and hazardous situations, and gain varied and flexible responses to the different situations in which they find themselves.

The playground has become so safe that it no longer allows children to take on challenges that will further educational and emotional development ... national and local safety guidelines have restricted their ability to craft imaginative areas in which kids can play. Their discontent is fueled by the specter of product-liability and personal-injury litigation. (Solomon, 2005, Introduction)

When we hear the term "risk taking" it is often thought of as having a negative connotation. In fact, from the perspective of children, child development, and outdoor play, risk taking is a necessity. Children learn about new skills, try new ideas, and achieve new knowledge and skills by taking risks. In effect, children who have developed the confidence to embrace the challenges of the environment and accept that learning occurs with mistakes will further explore new possibilities. Risk taking must be thought of in healthy terms—providing children with the opportunity to discover, be adventurous, and build confidence in using their bodies—rather than as a possibility of injury. This can be achieved by managing safe risk opportunities.* (Dietze & Kashin, 2012, p. 141)

For Additional Photos

Providing for exciting and challenging playscapes does not negate the need for safe environments. This includes not only the children's physical safety but also their emotional safety. The level of risk must be appropriate for the age group. The design of the site must meet all necessary safety and accessibility standards. The safest environment is one where site design and programming are tailored to children's needs and sensitive to their vulnerabilities. A space that offers plenty of different play opportunities in various parts of the site helps alleviate crowding, conflict and behaviour problems. It is also possible to

reduce risk by providing plenty of soft surfaces, providing adequate shade to protect the children's skin and eyes from harmful UV rays and avoiding potential toxins such as wood preservatives, pesticides and poisonous plants. A safe and healthy landscape is one where caring adults can easily observe, supervise and participate in children's activities. (Evergreen, 2004, p. 5)

In their text *Healthy Foundations in Early Childhood Education*, Pimento and Kernested (2010)

---

*Dietze, B., Kashin, D. 2012. *Playing and Learning in Early Childhood Education*. Pearson Canada Toronto. p. 141. Reprinted with permission by Pearson Canada Inc.

provide one of the richest and in-depth overviews of safety regulations. Educators are encouraged to consult this resource in their development of safe playscapes.

ENCOURAGE IMAGINATION

With the growth of early learning environments, there has been an increase in the development and design of outdoor play equipment. While new equipment may replace badly worn or even dangerous equipment, the result in many instances has been a cookie-cutter approach with sterile, plastic commercial environments. Children imagine through play, but the outdoor play spaces created for children's play increasingly lack the elements necessary to encourage imagination, such as mystery or material that can be shaped and formed, such as mud.

Visit these two websites for many more wide imaginative playscapes around the world:

www http://www.melbourneplaygrounds.com.au/melbourneplaygrounds-info.php?id=22766

http://www.mentalfloss.com/blogs/archives/34277

Sapporo-shi, Hokkaido, Japan

According to developmental psychologist Paul Harris, imagination is not only important in the creation of mental images, but the ability to put these images to use is a basic skill that we employ throughout our lives. Imagination forged during childhood is linked to the development of causal judgments, moral reasoning and language comprehension in adulthood. In this sense, imagination is instrumental to how we understand the world and conduct ourselves in it. (Herrington, 2008, pp. 91–92)

Novelty is ensured when environments include simple and complex features. There may be private, sheltered spaces for creeping babies and expanded spaces for crawlers. Screened-in porches allow places for infants to sleep while protected from insects and to play during inclement weather. Walking toddlers are active explorers and are challenged by new materials or environmental set–ups; for example, interesting materials in the sand area, containers for dumping and filling, and blocks to knock down and start building again. Providing ledges or railings at 36 to 40 centimetres for babies allow infants to pull themselves up and stand to explore the world from a different perspective.

Creating activity boards on fences with objects safely attached is a great opportunity for exploration. Planting unusual trees, or plants beside a fence, also engages the children. Interesting fencing materials can be used to separate areas on the playscape. Using Plexiglas allows young and older children to connect visually with each other.

The environment must be dynamic, providing graduated challenges, and it must be continually changing. Children should never feel bored in their playscapes. We need to create open, flowing, and

Brooklyn Botanical Gardens, New York City

For Additional Photos

Brooklyn Botanical Gardens, New York City

relaxed spaces, with appropriate equipment for the age group, and scaled to the child. The playscape should be physically challenging with adequate space to avoid conflict.

Children gain a sense of power by hearing stories about small versions of themselves—brownies, pixies, fairies—and feel a sense of magic in a place "inhabited" by them. Children value myths, fairy tales, and characters such as Anansi the Spider, or Curious George.

Universally employed in children's art is their symbolic play—stars, moon, trees. Age and history bestow a magical aura and so the connection with other times and places is important, as are old trees on the playground and old building materials.

Sculptors can help to create stimulating structures that relate to special characters and thereby add further interest. Hollow tree trunks and holes under root plates can be used for crawling through. As fairy tales abound in forests, gnomes, elves, or goblins can also be built into the play areas. Consider a maze cut among small trees, bridges that tilt as you walk along them, structures that blow in the wind.

Hollowed-out logs are great additions to the playscape, and provide countless drumming

opportunities. If there is a grassy area, you might also use a lawn mower to create another type of maze. A more elaborate maze using pathways and flowers, shrubs, and trees might also be constructed.

RESPOND TO CULTURAL INFLUENCES

No matter how you define play, it is a dominant activity of children's daily life in all cultures. Children play out personally meaningful experiences in their physical environment in their own way, while at the same time the sociocultural environment shapes children's play (Erickson, 1963; Vygotsky, 1977).

> Children's ethnic family culture always interweaves directly in their play and peer interactions. Culture is the contextual factor that influences all forms of adult-child, child-child, and child-children play. How we interpret child's play and development differs from culture to culture. Even defining child's play and a child's other activities differ depending on one's culture. For example, many families with Asian ethnic cultural influences tend to see play and academic activity separately. In contrast, from an Italian perspective, as in the Reggio Emilia schools in Italy, there is little distinction between play and a child's other activities, and rather a strong emphasis on social-interaction in child's play. (New, 1994)

We must also be mindful of newcomer families. For example, children who come from areas of the world where water is scare will have seen conservation of water modelled for them. These children may find it difficult to engage in water play or outdoor sprinklers. For many of these

The use of saris reflects the community and provides a welcome winter enclosure for the children.

families the lack of water may have meant the difference between life and death Children also learn cultural values related to how space is to be organized, valued, and shared. While in some countries direction is not an issue, in others direction is sacred and preferred; for example, Navajo doors must face east, Muslim mosques are oriented toward Mecca, and sacred rivers flow south in India. (Massad, 1979)

New Canadian children may not have had an opportunity to engage with nature in their home country if war or conflict was an issue.

Others may find it more difficult to be active in the outdoor environment because of their cultural practices, and this is particularly true for girls. In some cultures it's not accepted for females to be active in sport or active living. Clothing restrictions may also be a challenge as some girls cannot be seen in public in bathing suits, short sleeves, or shorts. In some sports, such as football (soccer), head coverings are not allowed at certain levels of play. Some older adults may view being active as dangerous to their health, although the opposite is usually true. Yet many of these barriers can be overcome. Girls can wear modified active wear. Sports and games can be adapted, and programs can offer games and

The playscape should reflect the cultural influences of the community.

experiences that different cultures enjoy. Games and activities popular in other parts of the world are also played in Canada. These games include cricket, boule, bocce, kabaddi (an ancient Indian game that combines wrestling and rugby), tai chi, yoga, and soccer (called football in most parts of the world). Educators can be allies for families in their communities to ensure that cities provide places for their games and activities.

Many schools and child care centres in urban environments are surrounded by housing and industrial development where children may live in dense housing units and not have access to green space; a green environment in their school or centre can have a major impact.

LEARN FROM ABORIGINAL TEACHINGS

Walk Slowly*

Walk slowly through life, little one
Stop to smell the wild flowers
Stop to listen to the birds
Stop to touch the animals
Stop to look around you.
Walk slowly through life, little one
Stop to smell the sweet grass
Stop to listen to the wind
Stop to touch the raindrops
Stop to look at nature.
Walk slowly through life, little one
Stop to smell
Stop to listen
Stop to touch
Stop to look
Walk slowly through life, little one.

Caroline Flett

All programs for young children can begin by keeping the tradition of the Elders

to teach children that there was no complete solitude. They made sure that children knew that wherever they went, they would be greeted by the warm, reassuring presence of local life-forms, geological features, natural forces, which were often as trusted, familiar and communicative with them as members

*Caroline Flett. "Walk Slowly." Winnipeg, MB: Manitoba Native Education Branch. 1985. Poster. Reproduced by Permission from Manitoba Education and the author.

of their families back home … An early understanding that we are of the soil and the soil of us, that we love the birds and beasts that grew with us on this soil, and that a bond existed between all living things because they all drank the same water and breathed the same air. (Suzuki & Knudtson, 1992, p. 103)

Inside LOOK

Our Children, Our Ways: Early Childhood Education in First Nations and Inuit Communities—Exploring the Natural World

Our Children, Our Ways, is part of a video series about ECE in First Nations and Inuit Communities developed by Red River College (2000). Filmed across the country in all four seasons, children and caregivers are seen involved in a wide variety of outdoor activities from ice fishing to planting a garden to exploring along wooded paths. Historically Inuit and First Nations children were taught how life survives, that each animate and inanimate form has a role to play in the survival of their natural world, and that all aspects of nature embody beauty, strength, and wonder. Although their world has changed a great deal, living in harmony with the natural world remains a fundamental value in First Nations and Inuit culture. It is a spiritual relationship rooted in survival. Children begin to build an understanding of life and death and their role in supporting the life cycles of living things through many experiences in their environment. Children learn about the natural world in a different but equally important way by hearing stories and legends—either told by elders or read by caregivers. Creatures such as bears, ravens, and fish are part of traditional First Nations and Inuit stories. By hearing the stories, children gain a deeper knowledge of the natural world and learn the worldview of their people that has been passed down for generations.

Inside LOOK

Aboriginal Peoples' Connection to the Land

John Beaucage, Grand Council Chief, helps us to understand the connection of Aboriginal people and the land.

At the time of Creation, Anishinaabe was given the responsibility to protect and look after *Shkagamikwe*, our Mother Earth. This was established in the form of a sacred covenant. As Anishinaabe's descendants, we, the Anishinabek are stewards of the land, the water and the air. We carry this responsibility to this day. We believe Mother Earth is the foundation of our people: the Anishinabek Nation. We regard every part of her as sacred. She is our historian, the keeper of events. She provides us with food, medicine, shelter and clothing. She is the source of our independence. We know that through the cord of life, all of humanity is connected to her. The well-being of our people today and generations to come, are directly related to our ability to live in balance and harmony with her. We are deeply concerned that our Earth has become a vulnerable and abused place. Her magnificent forests have been rapaciously felled, her rivers and oceans polluted and her delicate atmosphere is contaminated. Unfortunately, our children and our elders are among those most vulnerable and like many indigenous nations, who live so close to the land, our people have begun to experience the ill effects of an unhealthy environment. We invite all native people to join with us and reclaim their sacred responsibility as stewards of the land. Let us work together to preserve the Earth, to respect all life and to evolve new strategies for our survival. (Beaucage, 2009)

Aboriginal peoples in Canada suffer disproportionately high rates of various health problems including diabetes and heart disease. In an Aboriginal worldview which understands individuals, communities and land to be infused with an underlying spiritual unity, health can be understood to stem from a state of connectedness within individuals and between individuals, communities and land. (Stroink, Nelson & McLaren, 2009, p. 5)

Inside LOOK

Brenda Huff, ECE Programs Coordinator, Thames Campus, St. Clair College

The tie that binds First Nation children to their culture is the outdoors, their "Mother Earth." Historically, First Nation communities found everything they needed to sustain life within all of the living things that their mother the earth provided. People only took what they needed and always gave back to show respect. Young children need to experience the outdoors in order to make natural connections to nature, including access to the four elements of earth, air, fire, and water. First Nation children require opportunities that make linkages to the earth such as exposure to sand, water, dirt, rocks, stones, trees, flowers and other related materials. These open ended properties promote exploration, problem solving, and respect for nature as children grow in their understanding of the world around them. This kind of knowledge can be built wherever children live in the world regardless of whether they live in an urban or rural setting.

Educators can use these materials to create natural provocations for children to both incidentally and intentionally teach young children about the beauty of the outdoors and respect for all living things. During the outdoor experience children experience the element of air through the air they breathe during physical activity and exposure to the environment. As children participate in the outdoors they feel the sensation of the wind on their physical self and the impact it has on their activities. The element of fire can be incorporated through safe exposure to sun and the provision of contrasting shade features in a playground. The last element of water can be experienced with activities such as water play, and inclusion of water features, e.g. shallow pond, fountain, or watering plants.

Children find wonder in gazing at the properties of a rock or a pinecone. This kind of wonder can't be stimulated by a commercial toy that may have limited or repetitive purposes. The outdoors has the potential to be a naturalized environment that draws on all of the senses to encourage the development of a child's awareness and bank of information about nature.

The Kettle Point Aboriginal Head Start program has an exemplary outdoor play space that includes many natural elements. This type of outdoor play space supports the values that First Nation people place on respecting and connecting to nature.

Note: The First Nations teachings mentioned are part of an oral tradition that stem from a variety of First Nations, for example, Delaware, Chippewa.

(continued)

Kettle Point Head Start Day Care, on the shores of Lake Huron

Kettle Point Head Start Day Care

Contributed by: Brenda Huff, 2012

PROVIDE PLAYSCAPES THAT ARE ACCESSIBLE AND INCLUSIVE OF ALL CHILDREN

In many settings where young children are present, there will be children with special needs including those with physical, language, and developmental or learning challenges. Although play is a crucial life situation for all children, often the policy and physical environments that shape playgrounds exclude children with disabilities. Thirty-four elementary school playgrounds in Sudbury, Ontario, were audited using a modified version of the Ontario Parks Association *Playability Tool*. The findings indicate that there are significant barriers in terms of the quantity, quality, and diversity of types of play spaces available to children with physical disabilities. The findings depict playgrounds as precarious spaces for the protection of the participation and spatial rights of children with disabilities (Yantzi, 2009). As teachers we must provide teaching, learning, and play materials appropriate for children with disabilities and do all that is possible to help all children to develop to the best of their capabilities. In playground design, there is a growing movement toward *playability* a philosophy of removing barriers, providing supports, and increasing opportunities for people of all abilities to grow and learn together in play spaces. Many people can benefit from an accessible playground, including

- People who use strollers, wagons, or scooters;
- People who use wheelchairs, walkers, crutches, or canes;
- People who have cognitive disabilities, limited mobility, or other impairments;
- Small children, pregnant women, and people with respiratory challenges.

Special modifications of the playground space may need to be addressed to incorporate a plan for mobility of the children, ensure their accessibility

Slides constructed side-by-side allow adults to aid children who need additional support in this exciting experience.

Rusk Center, New York City

to equipment, and provide a challenge. Special attention to safety will also need to be considered.

For children in wheelchairs or walkers, a surface must be in place to support their ability to move throughout the playscape. The decisions you make about playability will influence the overall design of your playground. For example, loose-fill surfacing materials restrict the use of mobility aids such as wheelchairs, walkers, canes, crutches, and strollers; these devices require a firm, stable, and slip-resistance surface such as unitary manufactured materials. Consequently, sand, pea gravel, and other loose surfaces will not be appropriate; in fact, they can damage the moving mechanism of the wheelchair or walker.

- Doorways need to be wide enough to accommodate easy access.

- Attention to slope and width of ramps and paths must also be considered. Avoid steps and abrupt changes in the surface and levels of circulation paths.

- Include ramps to play structures so all children can participate.

- Wider balance beams with nonslip surfaces will support the child with balance and mobility challenges and those who are visually impaired.

- The addition of railings may make access safer and possible for children with balance and mobility challenges or for those who are visually impaired.

- Swings may be adapted to secure a child.

- Water and sand play tables, art tables, or gardens can be elevated so that wheelchairs can slide underneath or to provide an area for children to lean on.

- A simple adaptation may make play in the sand table possible for a child who has diffi-

culty grasping and holding smaller items—for example, securely tape foam pipe insulation around the handle of a sand shovel for easy handling (the same strategy can be used for paint brushes and other implements).

- For children with low vision, brightly coloured toys, material, and equipment (or contrasting colours—e.g., black and white) will be helpful—e.g. include bright balls, paint the steps of the ladder in bright or contrasting colours, etc. (Dombro, Colker, & Trister Dodge, 1997).

- Create playhouses accessible and large enough to accommodate a child in a wheelchair. Consider whether door openings are wide enough to accommodate a wheelchair or walker and whether door knobs are at a height that a child in a wheelchair can reach. These adaptations support independence and participation (ibid.).

- Hammock swings provide the support and stability a child needs to feel comfortable and secure while viewing the changing scenes on the playscape.

- Using Velcro to strap a child's feet onto the tricycle pedals helps the child to be able to ride more effectively. Some children with physical disabilities do not have the ability to control their muscles and cannot keep their feet on the pedals.

- Deflate balls slightly to make it easier to catch for a child with gross motor or coordination challenges.

- Bubbles are a fun activity for any child. Look for opportunities to engage the children.

- Balls with bells inside help a child who is visually impaired track the movement of the ball and will support her ability to catch or kick the ball and consequently to be actively involved in play.

- A therapy ball is a large ball that can be used to sit or lie on to challenge a child's balancing skills or to provide various forms of sensori-motor experiences. It also can be used to stimulate a child's motor reactions, or to relax a child with hypertonic reactions (spasms).

- Providing a child with autism with a "fidget" toy may help him stay focused—this could be a toy such a stress ball or a beanbag, which can also be used for more active play.

- Provide sensory alternatives for children who are adverse to touching sand by providing child-size gardening gloves or materials for manipulation inside zip-top bags.

- Provide wide slides so children can slide down with someone else if needed.

- Overhead ladders that are suspended above wheelchair height can provide opportunities to strengthen upper-body strength.

- A child who has seizure disorders or problems with balance may need to wear a helmet to protect her head in case she falls.

- To participate fully in some activities, and during small group times, children with physical disabilities may need assistance in order to sit. A beanbag chair or large pillow can be moulded to provide the support needed. There are also a variety of specialized chairs that may be helpful for some children.

- Strobe lights should be installed for hearing-impaired children and adults.

Consider some quiet outdoor spaces for children who may become overwhelmed by the sensory overload or lack confidence in their physical ability

University of British Columbia Child Care Services

to navigate the terrain and large-motor equipment in the busy outdoor environment. Teachers must be observant, realizing when, where, and how to assist but also when to back off and foster independence on the part of the child (Mitchell, 2008).

Remember to make simple adaptations to toys, materials, and equipment; for example, how can you add to, brighten, make bigger, add resistance, or stabilize the body or the toys, materials, or equipment to support the active involvement and engagement of children with a variety of special needs in play? The possibilities are endless! (Sources for lists in this section: Dombro, Colker, & Trister Dodge, 1997, pp. 113–114, and interview with Rita Barron, Faculty, George Brown College)

The child's family will be your best support in providing an inclusive environment as they know the child's needs best. Many communities have specialized resource teachers who are available to provide their expertise. It is advisable to consult with the child's physiotherapist to ensure that adaptations made to toys, materials, and equipment or the use of therapeutic materials or equipment are appropriate.

Dyment and Bell (2006) noted that green school grounds were more inclusive of people with intellectual disabilities; unlike conventional school grounds, the green school ground provides a diversity of play areas so that students with distinct needs were are able to find spaces that are safe and suitably challenging. Students could also choose from among a wider variety of activities to find one more in line with their abilities and needs.

An excellent resource on accessible playgrounds is available at this website:

http://www.accessibleplayground.net/about-2

Swings can be adapted to support children with special needs.

Shane's Inspiration—MyPlaygrounds are designed to be independently playable for children with special needs. Many playground examples are shown here:

http://www.shanesinspiration.org

Another helpful resource on accessible playground design is Robin Moore, Susan Goltsman, and Daniel Iacofano's *Play for All Guidelines—Planning, Design and Management of Outdoor Play Settings for All Children.*

Inside LOOK

Spiral Gardens

Spiral Garden and Cosmic Bird Feeder are integrated, outdoor programs at Bloorview MacMillan Children's Centre in Toronto since 1984. These programs bring together children aged 6–12 years with and without special needs to have a shared creative experience in a natural context, the garden. Spiral Gardens' philosophy states:

> Through the metaphor of the garden, we celebrate our interdependence with the natural world as the context for healing our children, ourselves, and the Earth. Through gardening, the arts and play we collectively explore and express ways to nurture all our relations. All aspects of the person—physical, emotional, spiritual, rational, and intuitive—are integrated in the process. (Holland Bloorview, 2004)

On any given day a whole range of activities are offered simultaneously. Activities range from familiar to challenging, individual to collective, and structured to unstructured. Children are free to decide which activities they would like to participate in as well as the rhythm with which they move in and out of activities. The people who make up the teams that run these programs reflect a diversity of backgrounds and experiences, and include visual artists, musicians, educators, therapists, and students.

Children's artwork: Fiza

PLAYSCAPES—A ZONE APPROACH

Power of One

FORMER GOVERNOR GENERAL—ADRIENNE CLARKSON

(CP PHOTO/Ottawa Citizen-Julie Oliver) The Canadian Press Images/Ottawa Citizen

Adrienne Clarkson. Many festive events have been held here in the gardens at Rideau Hall.

Rideau Hall is, since 1867, the official residence in Ottawa of both the Canadian monarch and the Governor General of Canada. It stands in Canada's capital on an 88-acre estate at 1 Sussex Drive. Former Governor General Adrienne Clarkson, ever since childhood

> has been entranced by growing things. … It's not surprising that she was thoroughly involved in the revamping of the gardens at Rideau Hall. … With the help of a legion of talented gardeners and arborists, the grounds were transformed. (Ottawa Citizen, 2010)

Clarkson also brought to the endeavour a gardener's knowledge of the importance of long-term planning. Thus her wise decision to plant formal perennial gardens rather than having to replant less appealing annuals every year. She also recognized the value of using indigenous plants, a choice that also promotes Canadian species. Each visiting dignitary to Rideau Hall was asked to plant a tree, mostly along the main drive which is dotted with nearly 130 trees with small plaques listing the name of who planted each particular tree. These include Queen Elizabeth; The Queen Mother; Diana, Princess of Wales; John F. Kennedy; Jacqueline Kennedy Onassis; Richard Nixon; Bill Clinton; Kofi Annan; and Vladimir Putin, to name a few. From these fields, plants, fruits, and edible flowers are used in the kitchens, and a greenhouse and the flower garden provide flowers for the hall and other government buildings in Ottawa. During the early spring months, the maples throughout the property are tapped for syrup making.

OUTCOMES:

1. Critique the zone approach to the design of outdoor playscapes.

2. Evaluate each zone area for the benefit it provides to young children.

3. Examine a variety of innovative playscapes for young children.

PROVIDE A ZONE APPROACH

A zone approach maximizes the design and utilization of outdoor playscapes. How these zones will be adapted in each individual program will reflect the site and its opportunities. Esbensen (1987) suggests seven play zones: *transition, manipulative/creative, projective/fantasy, focal/social, social/dramatic, physical,* and a *natural element.* Hill (1978) describes four categories of play and play space outdoors—*physical, social, creative,* and *quiet.* Bilton (2002) suggests "*an imaginative play area, a building and construction area, a gymnasium area, a small apparatus area, a horticultural area, an environmental and science area and a quiet area*" (Bilton, 2002, p. 48).

In this chapter, we outline the following:

- Transition zone

- Environmental zone

- Physical/active motor zone

- Social/dramatic zone

- Cognitive/construction zone

- Art zone

- Quiet/communication zone

- Sheltered zone

- Adult zone

When planning the zones, determine which activities and experiences work best next to each other and how the children will transition from one area to another. Organize compatible zones to facilitate play and minimize conflicts, with quiet play areas away from more active spaces. Children should be free to move resources from one zone to another when their play dictates this. All zones should provide opportunities for children to become detectives, investigating, questioning, exploring, perceiving, articulating, manipulating, imitating, adapting, collecting, and experimenting—individually and in a group. The zones should also allow for appreciating relationships, imagining, inventing, concluding, evaluating, risk taking, rebuilding, and reflecting. The possibilities are endless!

TRANSITION ZONE

For Additional Photos

The entrance way into the playscape should send the message that you are entering a special place. With so many playgrounds using a cookie-cutter approach, the entrance way is an opportunity to "take the children's breath away," and help them to create a sense of place that is all their own!

Due to the important developmental and health benefits of outdoor play environments, an outdoor play space contiguous to the interior classroom is a baseline requirement of child care centres in many environmentally progressive cities. Calgary and Toronto both advocate outdoor play areas contiguous to the indoors, requiring good justification if they do not connect. Unfortunately, not all Canadian cities have followed this cornerstone of quality care. In a comprehensive study of child care centres throughout Canada, Beach and Friendly (2005) found "children had little opportunity to move freely between the indoor and outdoor spaces" (p. 17). For example, having sliding glass doors at ground level that open to the outside allows children to move freely from one area to another as their play develops or changes course rather than standing in line inside the door waiting for all the children to be dressed before being able to venture out!

Connectivity between the indoors and outdoors also allows early childhood educators to communicate with greater ease and efficiency; they can easily convey to each other the needs of children indoors and outdoors. Connectivity also allows for greater supervision of both spaces, providing a safer play environment for the children (Herrington & Beach, 2007).

Lynn Wilson

An beautiful entrance to the playscape enhances the outdoor environment.

A seamless access, Tokyo, Japan

The Transition zone gives children enough time to move from quieter indoor play to louder, more active play outdoors and vice versa. A well thought out transition area allows children time and space to decide where they want to go as they enter the playground.

A hard surface at the doorway allows a carpet to be laid to catch sand or mud. Some centres locate children's cubbies in this transition area so children can easily slip on their boots and raincoats when necessary.

The addition of shrubs, trees, or planted beds outside makes play spaces safer by slowing the children's movements; changing hard surfaces to softer ones—such as wood chips or sand—creates places for children to tumble or fall with less chance of injury. Bathrooms and fountains should be easily accessible to the children in this transition area. A sheltered change table allows teachers to stay in the play area rather than having to take the child back inside. High-activity zones are best positioned away from the transition zone.

PATHWAYS

Pathways are important in creating clear routes around the playscape so that children do not interfere with each other. Long pathways encourage running so consider a variety of different "avenues" to get from place to place. Looping pathways can be created in many interesting ways, using stepping stones, cobblestones, coloured gravel, bricks, cement projects with embedded leaves or other natural materials, special objects the children have collected, hand prints, buttons, pieces of ceramics, etc.

For Additional Photos

Hard surfaces and softer surfaces (Elastocrete) can provide different play opportunities for children; simply removing asphalt or concrete will open up many possibilities. Design path surfaces to bring out the beauty of the surrounding vegetation and equipment. Some paths can offer surprises of

Brooklyn Botanical Gardens, New York City

Children have helped to create this pathway.

Jupiterimages/Getty Images/Thinkstock

Evergreen; an interesting way to create a pathway

Lynn Wilson

Pathways can lead to interesting places.

Lynn Wilson

These picket fences help to direct the children's movements in this playspace at Grant MacEwan Child Care Centre, Edmonton, Alberta.

Lynn Wilson

The use of coloured elastocrete creates pathways at Grant MacEwan Child Care Centre, Edmonton, Alberta.

Lynn Wilson

Pathways can also be created using water channels, as at this park in New York City.

their own: herbs growing between bricks or flagstones, mosaic tile patterns, interlocking wooden shapes. There is something magical about encountering beauty unexpectedly as one move through a space (Olds, 2001).

ENVIRONMENTAL ZONE

The Environmental zone opens up possibilities to interact with nature and its elements—earth, air, fire, and water. Nature offers levels of meaning far

beyond the artificial or manufactured—gardens, herbs, orchards, groves, streams. The elements of the natural world offer raw materials to manipulate. No matter where we live in the world, no matter what species of plants we eat, regardless of skin colour or language, we all have a basic need for plants to provide sustenance, clean air, and shelter. Growing things, and live animals that encourage interaction with and respect for nature, are the truly flexible elements of a good play environment.

"An outdoor environment that includes natural elements and provides opportunities for independent discovery, active experimentation and quiet contemplation to mull over new knowledge is an intellectually stimulating place for children" (Evergreen, 2004, p. 3). Sand, grass, nontoxic plants, flowers, and trees are important parts of the children's outdoor exploration. The entire outdoor space should contain a variety of natural elements. Digging, burying, making mud, making ditches and rivers, and finding life are critical elements in a successful outdoor play space!

Consider the impact of all types of weather on playground design, including shade and protection from the sun. Because "it has been estimated that one in six children in school today in Canada will get skin cancer in his or her lifetime" (Coffey, 2001, p. 31),[*] sun protection is critical. However, also consider sunlight in the playscapes design. Different plants need differing amounts of sunlight to grow well and many require a minimum of six hours to thrive. Observe the areas of outdoor space that are exposed to direct and indirect light and the areas that are shaded. Materials such as asphalt, concrete, cast iron, and steel may absorb too much heat and be uncomfortable surfaces for children. If you do use these materials, try to place them in areas that are shaded during the hot parts of the day and year.

In hot climates, choose materials chosen carefully. Shiny metal poles or slides can cause serious burns; materials such as wood, rope, grass, and some plastics may be better choices. Sheltered spaces are also important during the afternoon when the sun is at its peak. Trees, awnings, and trellises provide much-needed shade. "Large pieces of bright fabrics can also be hung and used as temporary shade structures when natural shade is not available" (Miller, 1989, p. 21).

In some communities, rain is as common as snow is in other parts of the country. Rain and

A simple tarp provides shade at Ryerson's Early Learning Program.

snow provide immeasurable opportunities for active engagement. There is no such thing as bad weather, only bad clothing! In some areas, wind is a critical factor; consider it when designing planting. Position tall, thick bushes and coniferous trees to block prevailing winter winds and control snow drifting for play while avoiding creating winter shade. Use fresh-fallen snow to create snow structures such as hills, tunnels, passageways, steps, etc.

Trees create interesting shadows as their leaves move in the breeze. Add to the shadow patterns by hanging coloured pieces of plexiglass, old CDs, or a crystal to make rainbows or to cast interesting coloured light. Coloured plexiglass hung from the fence allows crawling babies to look at the world in a different way.

WATER

Water is a magnet for everyone, especially children. Running water can be dammed or channelled, squirted, splashed, bridged, fished, and used in

Coram's Field, London, England

---

*Coffey, A. 2001. *Transforming School Grounds in Greening School Grounds: Creating Habitats for Learning.* Grant, T. & Littlejohn, G. (Eds). Toronto. Green Teacher. p. 31.

Teardrop Park, New York City

For Additional Photos

many creative ways. Pumps, taps, grooved and hollow logs, stones, and planks all help the imaginative use of water. The play space should have easy access to water; if it is available in more than one spot, all the better.

Water is needed for many reasons in the outdoor space; however, gardens will need substantial watering, depending on local weather conditions. Proper drainage is clearly an important consideration when planning a play space; you don't want to have areas that are flooded after each rainfall that may endanger growing plants or create unsafe situations during the colder months. A stream, pond, or contained marshy place will create a natural habitat for wildlife.

Bird baths, outdoor water tables, ponds, elevated streams, splash pools, fountains, etc., bring exciting elements to the play space. Ponds, which must be safely enclosed, are full of creatures that are fascinating to young children. A water pump adjacent to the sand area can enable children to

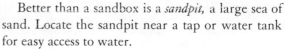

Access to water can enhance the play experience.

combine play with two elements. A water outlet can channel water flow to a sand area with children creating dams and barricades of rocks, boards, etc. Whether the water is flowing or still, it has special attractions—reflection, movement, drama, sound, and its cooling effect.

SAND AND ROCKS

Use good drainage to keep sand fresh but expose sand to the purifying rays of the sun for at least part of every day, and turn it over occasionally to ventilate it. Solid lids and tarps make the sandbox too dark and dank; a screen made of nylon netting or chicken wire effectively keeps out animals and debris without blocking fresh air and sunlight.

For Additional Photos

Better than a sandbox is a *sandpit,* a large sea of sand. Locate the sandpit near a tap or water tank for easy access to water.

Consider planting growing vines on a trellis or providing an umbrella over the sand area to provide shade when the sun is intense. Surrounding your sandpit with natural materials such as stones, tree stumps, decking, hedges, etc., and natural ground cover can expand the opportunities for children's play. Include boulders inside the pit to act as seats or tables for sand creations.

A water wall

Grant MacEwan Child Care Centre, Edmonton, Alberta

Langara Child Development Centre, Vancouver

Princess Diana Playground, London, England

Hudson River Park, New York City

Ryerson Public School, Toronto

Consider adding gravel and rocks to the playscapes where older children play. They can supply hiding holes, shelter, imaginary defences, castles, or dens. Smaller stones can be moved to build with, to dam a stream, or to make stepping stones or seats. Gravel and sand can be dug, shovelled, drawn in, made into hills, and used for all sorts of games. In many outdoor spaces children enjoy climbing on and manipulating rocks, boulders, flat limestone rocks with fossils, flagstones, etc.

Climbing walls are becoming more popular; Hudson River Park, New York City.

This sieve is an interesting addition to the sand pit.

A trip to a local quarry will provide an incredible array of interesting materials to enhance the outdoor play space. They may also be used to separate one area of the play space from another. Consider adding bamboo and mesh wire scoops, whisks, coconut shells, bamboo pieces, shells, sticks, spoons, and shovels—anything that inspires creativity!

FIRE

In a controlled environment, and particularly with older children, fire lighting and the safe use of fire can become a meaningful experience for children. It is not unusual for children to be curious about fire since we enjoy campfires and singing over birthday candles. Fire is used when camping, barbecuing, during dinner, and in many religious ceremonies. However, it is important to educate children about the dangers of fire and to teach

These children are re-enacting their camping experiences.

Borders between zones can be created in many different ways.

young children, including very young children, that fire is an adult tool and should be used only when an adult is present.

GROWING THINGS

Playscapes should have places for growing plants. This allows children to experience life cycles, to anticipate changes in seasons, and to tend and care for life. Here the children begin to appreciate the importance of the environment and recognize pattern, shape, and changes in the world around them.

For Additional Photos

Garden plots that can be reached easily from either side (about 60 cm wide) are recommended to prevent children from walking on the vegetation. Vegetables, bulbs, and hardy annuals that grow easily and quickly are good choices for young children. Gardens, flower patches and boxes, herb gardens, trees, vines, shrubs, and weeds provide beauty, life, and loose parts.

All vegetation should be safe and nontoxic. Organic methods of managing insects and weeds can be a powerful learning opportunity. A protected outdoor setting that allows the tending of rabbits, ducks, and even larger animals if space allows, is a wonderful laboratory for children. Concern for wild creatures and their habitats can promote greater fulfillment in one's life and a sense of caring for other people. Here children can observe, appreciate, and care for living things with

Coram's Field and the Harmsworth Memorial Playground, London, England

a sense of respect and wonder. Don't forget about spiders, worms, and birds!

There should be materials for collecting and carrying leaves, pebbles, shells, and rocks.

There should also be implements for measuring rain, temperature, wind, shadows, etc. Areas with tall grass, wild flowers, and bushes with safe berries will introduce a variety of insects, butterflies, and birds to the area. Feeding stations, nesting boxes,

Bird houses can be built in many different shapes and sizes.

and bird houses become wonderful opportunities and, when placed close to windows, it provides a year-round opportunity for the children to observe.

Composting is also a valuable learning opportunity. For more information on composting, go to the Compost Council of Canada at

http://www.compost.org/English/qna.html

Greening the outdoor playscapes is further developed in Chapter 6.

PHYSICAL/ACTIVE MOTOR ZONE

Activities that test the limits of capabilities, rough and tumble play, sports and games, and games of chase create a special atmosphere that sets this zone apart from the everyday world.

The lines of the Physical/Active Motor zone can be enhanced by incorporating curves, hanging shapes, and topsy-turvy—arched doorways, mobiles, and rolling hills. Hills provide a different perspective and their opportunities for play change over seasons. Objects or views that are framed by layers of foreground materials heighten a sense of depth, provide a feeling of richness, and increase the degree of complexity of the space through layers of vegetation,

Discovering critters in the playscape is an exciting experience.

Lynn Wilson

Wye Valley, Wales

Lynn Wilson

Princess Diana Playground, London, England

walls, and borders. Include changes in scales—the miniature, the child-sized, and the colossal—models, tiny animals, dinosaurs (Frost, 1992).

Choices for children in this zone are critical. Physical play must provide a variety of muscular activities that allow children to develop not only their physical strength, control, and balance but also an awareness of the importance of health and fitness.

The Physical/Active Motor zone should provide opportunities for:

- Walking, running, hopping, skipping, and galloping in open spaces, pathways, or tracks that allow for all kinds of movement. Toddlers and other unsteady walkers need smooth flat surfaces.

- Jumping and leaping from platforms and climbers over safe absorbent landings.

- "Bouncing and balancing on beams of different sizes, widths, and heights, logs, poles, boulders, ropes, wobbly balancing surfaces, moveable balance beams, spring platforms, [and] spring animals" (Greenman, 2003).

- Staying still—the most advanced level of balance and body coordination.

- Throwing, striking, and catching, and using small equipment such as nets, hoops, barrels, bean bags, balls, Frisbees, skittles.

- Hanging upside down.

- Turning somersaults and cartwheels.

- Swinging on swings with seats, tire swings, rope swings, porch swings, hammocks, bouncing swings (swing areas should be

Lynn Wilson

Balancing is an important motor skill.

bounded by wooden frames that signal a danger zone; when space is limited, consider the play value and space that swings require).

- Travelling, riding, transporting, racing, hauling, and ferrying with carts, wagons, and wheelbarrows on pathways and sidewalks.

- Pushing, pulling, lifting.

- Sliding on high, low, wide, narrow, curvy, straight, fast, or slow slides. Wide slides allow for more than one child to slide at the same time and slides that are embedded in hills allow easy access for younger children.

- Rocking, rolling, and tumbling—children love to roll themselves and objects down slopes.

- Walking, pulling, or hauling things up a slope provides challenges.

- Bending, twisting, turning quickly.
- Building/constructing—woodworking areas provide opportunities to strengthen both gross and fine motor skills.
- Moulding, hammering, bending—loose parts allow materials to be manipulated and strengthen fine motor skills.
- Climbing on trees, platforms, climbers, ropes, ladders, sculptures, nets, and rock walls.
- Planting, digging.
- Controlling tools and equipment.
- Playing team and individual sports, including yoga.

Children need physical challenge from the playground and opportunities to expand their visual-spatial skills, their kinesthetic skills, and body competence. They need the stimulus, risk, and opportunities to accept or reject challenges based on their skills as well as courage and supportive supervision.

Far too often, outdoor playscapes are dominated by a large piece of fixed equipment. "Research tells us that areas with the most fixed equipment have the lower levels of play and children are more active when they had equipment that could be manipulated" (Harriman, 2010, p. 7). It may be necessary to look for opportunities to adapt or completely remove this type of fixed equipment to maximize the play experience in a more natural environment.

Infants and toddlers are busy learning the mechanics of their bodies and developing strength and coordination. Babies who are crawling or creeping will enjoy moving over soft textured materials. You could make a texture path by providing different textures for the baby to crawl over and through—fake fur, floor mats, tires, cardboard boxes, and tunnels.

Infants need materials that are gentle for crawling and falling on, and cool for sitting. Children who are able to hold their heads up can lie on their tummies directly on the grass but, because of sensitive skin, babies should be wearing a soft shirt that covers the tummy entirely; also be conscious of the sun on delicate skin. Grass should be cleaned of any debris. Consider tall and short grasses that blow in the breeze to provide another opportunity to watch the wind at work.

"Think about adding variations in elevation such as ramps and wide low steps. This may be the best time to use infant seats or swings to give less-mobile babies a vantage point" (Gestwicki, 2011, p. 103). Swings provide children opportunities to experiment with balance, force, gravity, and resistance.

The overall environment should include support for a wide range of motor activities remembering that the first 60 cm from the ground should be assumed to belong to this age group. Mobility opens up new worlds for infants and toddlers as they investigate new objects, explore spatial awareness, and gain control over their environment. Provide interesting incentives to encourage crawling babies. Attach cruising bars to fences, walls, and play structures so they can pull up and support themselves as they move between areas. Logs and tree stumps allow children to pull themselves up, examine the surface, and roll off. Grass serves as a soft, textured, cool surface for crawling, and acts as a partial cushion if falls occur from ground level. Other cushioning materials such as pea gravel should be avoided with this age group as it will end up in their mouths, noses, ears, or they will vomit it. Wooden ramps, tunnels, decks, and stairs can be padded with outdoor carpet for comfort and to reduce heat in metal materials (Miller, 1989).

PLACES FOR TOYS WITH WHEELS

A hard surface is necessary for riding toys. Toddlers really enjoy pushing themselves along on low wheeled toys. Older children will enjoy more complex "road" opportunities with twists and turns. Providing duplicates of popular items will

For Additional Photos

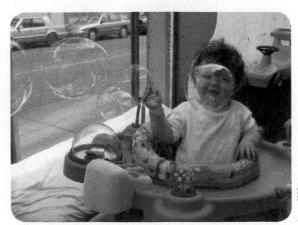

Lynn Wilson

Bubbles!

The children in this centre created their own licence plates for their bicycles.

minimizes a toddler's need to share, something for which they are not developmentally ready.

SOCIAL/DRAMATIC PLAY ZONE

For Additional Photos

Good playgrounds provide spaces for dramatic or symbolic play, which contributes to a range of communication styles, gender development, cooperation, perspective-taking ability, divergent thinking, creativity, and social and interpersonal problem-solving skills. Social play areas allow

University of British Columbia Child Care Services

Dramatic play experiences should be readily available in the outdoor environment.

children to develop social skills and language. Hirsh-Pasek et al (2009) examined three studies conducted between 1982 and 2002 and concluded that the prevalence of social, pretend play for 4- to 5-year-olds in community-based child care centres dropped from 41 percent to only 9 percent. With a greater focus on teaching academics, early childhood programs today have many more didactic components than they did 20 years ago.

Dramatic play in the outdoor environment may become more expressive because it permits more motor freedom and more sensual opportunities than inside play. In this zone, create a place where children can sit and talk with peers, share a discovery with an adult, or simply observe. There may be times when the children will come together to share stories, sing songs, carry out circle games, receive instructions, be reminded about safety issues, etc., so prepare an open area for this type of gathering.

Create opportunities for children to choose whether and when to play alone or with others, and to negotiate, cooperate, compete and resolve conflicts. Provide rest areas, equipment that invites

Lynn Wilson

Gathering places are important.

socialization and complements the social forms of play—solitary, private, meditation, cooperative, interrelationships—with individuals and groups of different ages, abilities, interests, genders, ethnicities, and cultures.

Lynn Wilson

Runnymede Public School

Lynn Wilson

A child having a rest at the University of British Columbia Child Care Services.

Lynn Wilson

A secluded gathering place

Lynn Wilson

Gathering places can take many forms.

Corsaro (2003) sees children as active agents in making social meaning from their play. Through their play activities, children construct their own peer culture, which he defines as "a stable set of activities or routines, artifacts, values, and concerns that kids produce and share in interaction with one another" (ibid., 2003, p. 37).

It is important that children develop their own authentic ways to interact, and build their social competence with peers. Research tells us that enriching the outdoor environment reduces anti-social behaviours such as violence, bullying, vandalism, and littering. Boredom has been recognized by both children and adults as one of the main causes of all kinds of inappropriate behaviour.

This zone allows the children to build their confidence and participate as part of a small or large group. It also provides a venue for forming positive relationships and developing independence. In older children, it allows for cooperating, tolerating, respecting, and appreciating others and their ideas, and a greater awareness of their own emotions and those of others. Initiating, risk taking, and taking responsibility for the development of a role or play concept allows children to act out day-to-day situations or something that might be challenging for them. This provides a cooperative problem-solving experience while children learn to sympathize and empathize with others. Social play areas also allow children to develop their social skills by organizing games, and developing rules for play.

Dr. Diamond, author of *Tools of the Mind* (2007) from the University of British Columbia, and other researchers have found that dramatic play helps children regulate their impulses and builds developmental flexibility. When they are playing at being a doctor or a patient, they have to inhibit the urge to act out of character. They also have to adjust quickly and flexibly to whatever plot changes may be introduced by another child. "Play is really important, and taking it out of the curriculum actually hurts academic performance" (McIlroy, 2009, L1).

Dramatic play is more than imitation and pretending; it often encompasses complex problem solving; science; and a range of motor, cognitive,

Providing materials and equipment that support side-by-side cooperative play enhances social interactions.

Rusk Institute of Rehabilitation Medicine, New York City

Telephone play is great fun!

Real objects are critical to imaginative play.

Children can help to create comfortable places to sit.

and sensory experiences. In many programs, dramatic play areas become exclusively housekeeping and dress-up areas. These are always appealing to children, reflecting the world they know best.

However, many children's active experience in the world outside the home is narrowing. Child care needs to widen the children's world by extending children's experience through walks, field trips, books, and subsequently offer dramatic play opportunities to allow children to absorb and reflect back the experience (Greenman, 2007).

Chimney Court, Evergreen Brick Works

Hohmann and Weikart (1995) "concluded that pretend play in the preschool years allows children to make a number of cognitive gains as they try out new ideas and skills" (p. 131). "Research supports the notion that when children learn concepts through play both their learning and memory seem to be fixed more strongly and last longer" (Brown & Vaughan, 2009, p. 102).

The Social/Dramatic Play zone should have areas for building lean-tos, cardboard castles, shelters and barricades, sculptures, and vehicles. Any furniture should be welcoming and comfortable to use, easy to maintain, and able to withstand ill treatment or theft. Moveable tables and benches allow worn grassy areas to recover by shifting the furniture to another place or to take enjoy locations with better sunshine.

> Child size picnic tables, a bench, and old tree stumps placed in a circle can make an inviting setting for discussion, observation, and quiet retreat. Picnic tables that are too large are often too heavy to move easily. Once you get the children considering alternatives to benches and picnic tables that they normally see outdoors, they think of items such as logs, stumps, rocks and small grassy hills.* (Coffey, 2001, p. 21)

---

*Coffey, A. 2001. *Transforming School Grounds In Greening School Grounds: Creating Habitats For Learning*. Grant, T. & Littlejohn, G. (Eds). Toronto. Green Teacher. p. 21.

Plantings have been incorporated into this seating area.

Tables provide opportunities for cooperative play.

Tables and benches should be easily accessible and the ground upon which they are placed should be flat. This is particularly important for children in wheelchairs. Tables with indentations around the edges also allow children with special needs to use the tables for balance. Castoff wire cable spools can be great tables; they are round so no one sits at the head of the table and they can be dug into the ground if they are too high.

Incorporate a wide variety of materials or loose parts such as blocks, planks, dowels; kitchen items such as chopsticks, rice bowls, woks, tongs, steamer baskets, tea boxes and tins, cans, rice bags; and cleaning items such as brooms, dustpans, buckets, mops, basins, sponges, etc. Encourage families to donate old clothing, purses, computer bags, jewellery, shoes, etc. By using a diverse range of materials from the children's homes, cultural awareness develops. Items such as saris, kimonos, woven vests, serapes, dashikis, shawls, tunics, moccasins, Chinese slippers, turbans, straw hats, knitted hats, jewellery, purses, ribbons, capes, fabric pieces, headdresses,

currency from various countries, and an unbreakable full-length mirror will engage the children.

Use large cardboard boxes and let the children design windows and doors to create "secret" entrances. Add woven mats, carpet pieces, cushions from a range of cultures, hammocks, blankets, sleeping bags, placemats, umbrellas, and baskets to extend the play.

Spaces such as a playhouse or treehouse often provide a rich opportunity for imaginary play. Rather than one playhouse, build several close together to better reflect a community and you will see an increase in the children's social interactions. You can control access to the playhouses with borders to allow privacy and to direct guests toward the front door. Locating playhouses near the sand garden also allows for more creative play.

Consider painting a mural on a wall to enhance the children's interest in a particular project idea; make it a pirate ship, a cave, or a garden centre! Screws in a wooden wall can support a washing line or the hanging of signs.

Rather than one house, a community is created here.

Boating adventures with friends!

Princess Diana Playground, London, England

Villa Borghese, Rome, Italy

Dramatic play costumes can be created with squares of sheets or large plastic bags to create wind costumes; ribbons and markers can embellish their play. Given the nature of outdoor play, dress-up materials should be sturdy to withstand frequent washings—another great practical outdoor play activity for the children! Capes are easily made and can be transformed based on the children's imaginations into just about anything; add sparkles and sequins for a more dramatic impact. Store dress-up items in labelled suitcases that are light enough for the children to manoeuvre.

Create a simple stage by building a frame, and nailing boards and wheels to it so it can be easily moved around the playground. Older children can use it to role-play with or without scripts; design costumes, scenery, music, and songs; prepare for an audience by singing, dancing, making music, and indulging in fantasy play and creative self-expression.

The Social/Dramatic Play zone provides an opportunity for the children to act out relevant festivals, religious celebrations, Mardi Gras, or celebrations that are important in their community. Too often, teachers remove these special materials as soon as the event has passed, when, in fact, this is when children engage in the richest play—after they have experienced the celebration. Observe the children carefully before removing the relevant materials.

Nothing provides for more social contact than preparing food and eating outside. The children learn how to shop for healthy ingredients, prepare food, and share their efforts with each other. Additional benefits include learning how to set a table, —one to one correspondence as well as practising table manners. More elaborate celebrations for families include menu planning with a focus on nutritious treats made by the children from their garden.

COGNITIVE/CONSTRUCTION PLAY ZONE

There are many ways to support cognitive growth, as this zone can support improvements in mental health, higher attention levels, and greater self-regulation, as well as develop a sense of place and sense of identity. The Cognitive/Construction Play zone enables children to satisfy their curiosity and test new ideas. It provides an opportunity to expand their logical thinking process through classifying and seriating, comparing, predicting, estimating, arranging, ordering; developing spatial and temporal concepts; and displaying and developing new language. Here, as in all zones, the children begin to develop a greater understanding of the world around them.

Mathematics is an integral part of most of the play and activities in which young children are involved in the outdoor space. Infants are beginning to understand spatial relationships when they

For Additional Photos

Blocks provide many opportunities to support cognitive development.

manoeuvre themselves into a position on the grass from which they can grab an attractive toy. When toddlers climb, crawl, and walk over, under, and around outdoor play toys and stack their rings and blocks, they discover more about the shape and size of the world in which they live. Older children begin creating very complex and intricate structures.

Whether the young child is digging in a sand pit, pouring water, or balancing on the edge of a board, he or she is experiencing new ideas that form the basis for developing mathematical concepts. Critical to the child's development is the mental structure of number that can only fully be realized with the handling of real objects. Acquiring physical knowledge is fundamental to the understanding of the quality of things and what they do. The development of logico-mathematical thought, which we might also think of as the ability to reason, ultimately enables children to develop ideas of relationships between objects. A child who thinks actively in his own way about all kinds of objects and events, including quantities, will inevitably construct number. According to Piaget, who is well known for his interactive learning theory, the opportunity to conduct spontaneous, uninterrupted actions in the real world of objects through the several stages of human development results in a mind that can think abstractly about science and mathematics (Piaget, 1936).

> We know that children are experimenters and testers from birth. As young children explore their world, they use same processes that adult "scientists" use—the hallmarks of the scientific method: observing, classifying, predicting, experimenting, drawing conclusions, and communicating ideas. (Neill, 2008, p. 1)

Fox Hollow Child Care Centre, St. Margaret Village, Nova Scotia

Children are quick to observe nuances in the playscape and are often engaged in classifying and comparing natural items such as leaves, rocks, etc. As their play expands, they are able to predict and experiment: how quickly their bicycles can reach the end of the pathway, how far the boat will float in the stream, how high they can swing, or how high the plant will grow. Their experiments help them to draw conclusions that scaffold their learning, and there is no question that young children enjoy communicating their successes with each other!

Involvement in science and technology will help and encourage children to appreciate the beauty and value of their natural environment, to have respect for living things, to respond constructively to changes effected through science and technology, and to develop the attitudes, skills, and knowledge required to make informed decisions. When children explore and investigate freely they learn that risk taking and unforeseen outcomes are valuable components of scientific endeavours and important parts of the learning process. When we present diverse content to match the diverse experiences, interests, and abilities of the children, we facilitate the development of language through science experiences.

Magnifying glasses attached to the table provide many opportunities for in-depth exploration.

Science in the Early Years

Preschoolers are conducting scientific inquiry whenever they are raising questions about objects and events around them, exploring objects, materials and events by acting upon them and noticing what happens[;] making careful observations of objects, organisms and events using all their senses[;] describing, comparing, sorting, classifying and ordering in terms of observable characteristics and properties[; and] using a variety of simple tools to extend their observations and make predictions, gather and interpret data. [T]hey recognize simple patterns and draw conclusions. They record observations, explanations and ideas through multiple forms of representation including drawings, simple graphs, writing and movement while working cooperatively with others, sharing ideas and listening to new perspectives. (Neill, 2008, p. 1)

Vygotsky's zone of proximal development refers to tasks that the child cannot yet accomplish on their own without the support of an adult or a more skilled peer. Vygotsky viewed scaffolding as a framework for all learning. Learning is a collaboration between an adult and child or a more experienced peer, which enables the child to perform beyond his or her independent capabilities. Older children should have opportunities to interact and support younger children in their explorations of their natural environment. Gathering up pine cones that have fallen into the yard and sharing them with the babies fosters a sense of empathy and connection with younger children. Harvesting greens such as bok choy or Swiss chard, for example, or fragrant herbs and offering them to a baby to explore is an opportunity to provide real objects to help infants and toddlers associate words with concrete objects. Having time with younger children provides an opportunity to describe flowers, birds, or butterflies and other events happening in the playscapes. These opportunities increase prosocial behaviours, leadership abilities, and communication skills for the older children. This may also be an opportunity for older children to connect with their younger siblings and the benefits that this brings. This is also particularly significant for children who speak languages other than English, and deepens the children's understanding of diversity.

This zone allows older children and younger children to connect with each other. Multi-age groupings also allow children to be in contact with other children who may have special needs; problems of stigmatization may be eliminated as the children become comfortable in caring for each other.

Nimmo and Hallett (2008) tell a story that illustrates the power of children of all ages working together.

After voting to construct trellises for the beans, the 5 year-olds and their teacher gathered tools, string, and sticks from the woods. As the older children collaborated on the first structure, some 3 year-olds from another classroom came out to watch. Before long they asked if they could help. The 5 year-olds responded, saying: "We'll show them how!" The teacher simply observed as the older children took the risk and built 7 foot structures without adult assistance. In so doing, they shared their knowledge, negotiated roles, and encouraged the younger children. (p. 3)

Taking advantage of nature, the busy city, behind the fence, the machinery of bikes or hinges or pulleys, the aerodynamics of kites allows for great discoveries even in small areas. Children in rural communities may well have a wider scope, given their access to more spacious terrain. Equipment and materials in these environments may well reflect the community interests, occupations, etc.

Creative play spaces should include materials that children can manipulate and shape as they experiment with a wide range of materials and learn about their properties. Here they solve problems by experimenting, asking questions, and making decisions. Large-scale construction elements—big barrels, crates, machine parts, and dead branches—can be used to encourage large-scale building and learning about construction principles. Building with these elements helps the children learn to estimate size, further develop their motor abilities, and learn about the world of work. This encourages children's interaction and cooperation, through learning to help and asking for help. Large unit blocks can be stored in milk crates for easy transport by the children. Skeletal structures such as platforms, dead trees, A-frames, ladders, etc., provide places for children to add to when loose parts are available.

Setting up a woodworking centre in the outdoor environment encourages the safe use of tools; also provide lots of glue and other loose parts for the wooden creations to keep the children thoroughly engaged. Children quickly learn to respect tools. Begin slowly with young children, introducing one tool and one skill at a time. Using real child-size tools is critical to success; there is nothing more frustrating than using a plastic replica. Children need to know that following the safety rules is critical; i.e., goggles must be worn at all times.

Using wood for the first time is exciting; there is so much to explore—the grain, the smell, weight, differences in types of wood, etc. Soft woods—pine, cedar, and fir—are best. You may want to limit the number of children in this area at first so that safe use of the tools can be reinforced. This is a great opportunity to expand vocabulary as you use the tools, explore and learn the names of different nails, screws, bolts, etc. This area also supports problem solving, eye–hand coordination, fine motor skills, imagination, and creativity. You may help young children begin by hammering nails with large heads into a wood stump. Some children find this a great way to work through stressful feelings! This area might be located close to the art centre where other loose parts can be added to the children's creations.

Collect cardboard boxes, logs cut into manageable rounds, and planks of wood to create a block area with a variety of loose parts. Block play provides opportunities for the development of motor skills and eye–hand coordination as well as a more concrete understanding of spatial arrangements and creative problem solving. Through experimentation children experience cause and effect, and their social interactions encourage collaboration through sharing ideas and plans. These experiences help the children begin to understand mathematical concepts such as less, more, tallest, shortest, shapes, sizes, and patterning, and well as directional clues and colours. Children will find ways of weighing objects and measuring things that are relevant to them.

Patterns are everywhere in nature and children can be encouraged to create all kinds of patterns, moving from simple to more complex. Use the children themselves to create patterns! In this area of discovery, learning proceeds in a continuum from concrete to pictorial to symbolic and from simple to complex, concrete to abstract.

Why? Young children ask the *Why* question many times each day. Children don't have to be taught to explore, question, or manipulate; they are born with an innate desire to do so. Children integrate information into pre-existing concepts and deepen their understanding about the world around them. Developing survival skills for an increasingly complex world, seizing a chance to emphasize conservation, and understanding the physical properties of the world around them prepares them for future action as adults.

ART ZONE

"It is not the language of painters but the language of nature which one should listen to … The feeling for the things themselves, for reality, is more important than the feeling for pictures."

—Vincent van Gogh

Young children are open, curious, and creative! Remember that children can be creative in many ways in many of the zones mentioned. Art experiences involve the children in sensorimotor learning through the use of an art tool and the thinking process involved in the creation itself. Through art, children problem solve, design, predict cause and effect, and learning about the materials themselves. Using a variety of materials encourages flexibility of thought. We want to encourage divergent thinking and focus on the process in their learning.

For Additional Photos

Children should be encouraged to express themselves openly with new ideas and new experiences. Educators are in an enviable position of fostering each child's creativity. A child who meets with unquestionable acceptance of her unique approach to the world will feel safe in expressing her creativity, whatever the activity or situation. Incorporating creativity into all areas of the curriculum contributes to a young child's positive attitude toward learning. Teachers who encourage children to work at their own pace and to be self-directed in a relaxed, nonjudgmental atmosphere are fostering creative development. (Mayesky, 2012, p. 30)

As children relate their stories about their experiences, their language skills also increase.

Observing Art in Nature

There are numerous art elements that a child can observe in nature: lines, shapes, colours, textures, patterns, forms, spaces, and movement. Looking for each of these elements in nature trains a child to acquire a discerning artist's eye in creating their own artwork, and additionally to develop an appreciation of a wide variety of forms and applications of art in nature. For example, a child is encouraged to find lines in trees—the straight, the crooked, and the jagged lines that define its form. A further step to explore nature involves discovering the shapes in nature of alphabet letters and numbers to facilitate literacy and numeracy. Children learn to look for these lines in the spaces and textures of rocks, streams, a pathway or clouds in the sky. It is through this outdoor exploration of nature that children can find patterns in leaves, or perhaps participate in the creation of a garden that alternates different flowers, vegetables or herbs. The child's wonder develops into knowledge of literacy, numeracy, science and, by sharing observations and experiences with peers—social cognition. Two art forms that lend themselves easily to the use of natural elements are collage and sculpture. Using recycled cardboard boxes or fallen pieces of birch bark (or other bark) a child can glue together various found materials based on their understanding of lines, shapes and forms as they exist in nature and create their own counting, patterned or open-ended collage, sculpture or mobile. The art elements are an integral part of a child's learning, to decode the environment around them and to use nature to facilitate an aesthetic sense for the world outdoors.

Dr. Miriam Melamed-Turkish

Setting up the zone will affect the enthusiasm with which the children will approach this area. Portable storage, activity boxes, and carts with multiple shelves will house many of the materials the children will need. Organize the materials so they are easily accessible and easy to tidy up. This zone should be placed close to a water source. A table can provide a space for art activities and a prop box with common items such as glue, scissors, paper, markers, crayons, etc. Where space is limited, a fold-down table is a great idea for maximizing surface area.

Easels can be incorporated in many areas throughout the playscape.

Toddlers using paint brushes with water on walls and on mural paper are beginning their first steps to writing, as are children who experiment with chalk. This zone allows children the opportunity to investigate, explore, manipulate, adapt, collect, experiment, and engage in creative problem solving. They are inventors, taking risks, reflecting, and rebuilding what doesn't work. They develop logical thinking skills such as classification, seriating, spatial concepts, predicting, estimating, and developing vocabulary, and they will enjoy displaying their creations, which demonstrate their thoughts, feelings, and emotions!

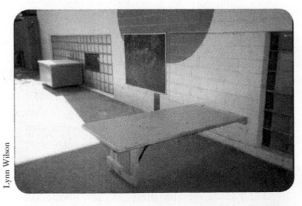

In this small space, the fold-down table is invaluable.

This large chalkboard is sensational!

Chalk at work; Esther Exton Child Care Centre

This easel is set up to engage the children in this stimulating environment at Ryerson's Early Learning Centre.

Clothes Peg Weaving

The fence becomes an integral part of the playscape.

Art is a means of conveying diversity; for example, by helping older children learn to make pottery, you are bringing many cultures together since this has been a common practice for thousands of years. Materials that reflect a variety of cultures include origami paper, rice paper, Chinese brushes, feathers, pine tree branches, clay, raffia, dried flowers, pine cones, dried grasses, seed pods, beads, crayons, markers, charcoal, paint rollers, brushes of all sizes, etc.

Older children may also enjoy batik, ceramics, clay modelling, découpage, macramé, oil painting, sand painting, beading, and working with recyclable materials, for example. Many art activities such as painting at an easel, modelling with clay, finger painting, and sponge painting can all be carried out outdoors without worrying about the mess they can often create. In the warmer weather use a hose to quickly and easily clean tables. Displaying the children's artwork in the outdoor environment allows families and the community to see the important connections that the children are making.

Fence art!

The back of the storage shed now has a creative use.

For Additional Photos

QUIET/COMMUNICATION ZONE

In a good playground, there should be places for children to just be—a quiet, private refuge or a nook or meeting place where two or more children can gather to talk and share their discoveries. Good playgrounds should be fun, a place to escape from routine mental fatigue and boredom, a place to relax and enjoy. Give children time for messing around with valued friends in enchanting places or places for doing nothing, dreaming, or imagining!

Most of us can remember playing "King of the Mountain"; nothing surpasses that one moment when you reach the top before all the other children. We need to provide places for children

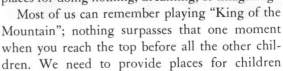

For Additional Reading

Inside LOOK

Environmental Art

The outdoors is a natural site for art to explore colour, texture, form, and space. Eco-art/environmental art education integrates art education for older children with environmental education as a means of developing awareness of and engagement with environmental concepts and issues, such as conservation, preservation, restoration, and sustainability. Environmental art

is art that helps improve our relationship with the natural world. There is no definition set in stone. This living worldwide movement is growing and changing as you read this. Much environmental art is ephemeral (made to disappear or transform), designed for a particular place (and can't be moved) or involves collaborations between artists and others, such as scientists, educators or community groups (distributed ownership). These variables can make exhibiting this work difficult for traditional museums so *greenmuseum.org*: an online museum for global the environmental art movement has been created.

Some environmental art:

- Informs and interprets nature and its processes, or educates us about environmental problems
- Is concerned with environmental forces and materials, creating artworks affected or powered by wind, water, lightning, even earthquakes
- Re-envisions our relationship to nature, proposing new ways for us to co-exist with our environment
- Reclaims and remediates damaged environments, restoring ecosystems in artistic and often aesthetic ways.* (Hull, 2010)

Older children especially will be interested in using the Internet to explore these ideas and concepts while creating their own projects.

At The Jamie Bell Playground, High Park in Toronto, the children's artwork helps to personalize the playscape.

*WHAT IS ENVIRONMENTAL ART © Lynne Hull, 2010. http://greenmuseum.org/what_is_ea.

UBC Child Care Services

to view the world from a different perspective. Generate things at different levels: tree forts; platforms; places to hide; trees, bushes, as well as things that have been made; and places to inspire mystery and imagination.

Outdoor environments must have places for children to retreat. For some, the busy nature of the day is overwhelming and they need physical environments where they can withdraw and self-regulate. Such spaces should be intimate and away from the active and high-noise play spaces. Preschoolers also often like to retreat to nest-like enclosures.

Studies have shown that noise level is a critical factor in children's health and well-being as well as their ability to learn. Providing quiet spaces should be an important element in every outdoor design (Coffey, 2001, p. 14).[*] Passive landscaping including lawn areas and trees as well as appropriately scaled benches, play equipment, and tables will satisfy this need for individual play and a quiet retreat. Plant string beans, sweet peas, or other runners at the base of branches formed into a tepee. The vines will cover the branches to create a green quiet space for the children.

Create other lean-tos using old blankets or sheets. Encourage the children to "feel" the quiet—listen to nature's sounds. It is common in European programs to sleep outside or on sleeping porches. Sometimes it is fun to just lie on the grass and talk with friends! Provide blankets, pillows, comforters, and books for the top of the climber or a quiet space on the playground. This area might also be a perfect spot to try yoga. OPHEA sells yoga alphabet cards to help K–12 children learn the basics of yoga in playful poses. Go to

http://www.ophea.net/category/program-name/activity-cards

Evergreen Brick Works: a teepee

Brooklyn Botanical Gardens

[*]Coffey, A. 2001. *Transforming School Grounds in Greening School Grounds: Creating Habitats for Learning.* Grant, T. & Littlejohn, G. (Eds). Toronto. Green Teacher. p. 14.

PLAYSCAPES—A ZONE APPROACH

Places for doing nothing

A puppet show at Langara Child Development Centre, Vancouver

Learning and language are integrally connected. Opportunities for speaking and listening and reading and writing are critical elements of this zone. Here the children have opportunities to negotiate plans, take turns in conversations, and build on their imaginary play. This area can be a place for storytelling with puppets and a puppet theatre, or an opportunity to tell a clothesline story with characters from their favourite story book, felt board stories, etc.

Provide quality nature-focused literature, including both fiction and nonfiction books. Children's understanding of the natural world can be extended through these books and stories. This may also be a good place for reference books as children attempt to learn more about their buildings, their garden, their woodworking projects, etc.

Writing materials may be organized here as well: a clipboard to record story ideas or draw the children's thoughts, dry erase boards, small

A special chair for storytelling

University of British Columbia Child Care Services

Game boards can be created anywhere!

A sheltered space at Simon Fraser Child Care Centre

blackboards, etc. Older children will enjoy a spot to play checkers, Bingo, chess, and lotto games; provide playing cards and materials to create their own games.

Create portable Story Boxes (see Chapter 8), which contain a book and a variety of props and materials that relate to the story.

Having a teacher read a favourite story encourages active listening, exchange of ideas, and understanding of the important parts of a story and the joy that it brings. Children's language grows through continual exposure to rich language experiences. Adults who engage in asking open-ended questions, repeating new vocabulary, drawing attention to the sounds of language, and being an articulate role model add to this development.

The sheltered space at Langara Child Development Centre, Vancouver, allows natural light to shine through.

SHELTERED ZONE

For Additional Photos

A good outdoor environment should have spaces that are sheltered from rain, wind, snow, and too much sun. The overhang of a roof, canopies, the underside of a high deck, leafy trees, and lawn umbrellas allow children to be outside more often.

An inventive sheltered space at Brooklyn Botanical Gardens, New York

ADULT ZONE

The outdoor spaces of a centre can be designed to offer opportunities for rest, relaxation, and activity to a wide audience—families, older children, and the community. "The more the community at large can utilize the daycare facilities, the more it will value and support them" (Olds, 2001, p. 430).

For Additional Photos

Simon Fraser Child Care Centre

University of British Columbia Child Care Services

Outdoor play spaces also need to enhance the ability of teachers to teach, nurture, facilitate play, supervise, and clean up. A site should offer shade and shelter, places to sit and work with small groups of children, practical storage to support set-up and take-down, and clear sightlines. Place adult perches in the areas where the most supervision is desired. Adults often congregate on playgrounds. Discourage this by having seating scattered throughout the playscape. Remember that sometimes children just need a lap to sit on.

Eco-exercise has become very popular, with year-round outdoor gyms popping up in playgrounds and parks. From coast to coast you can

Brooklyn Botanical Gardens

This adult playspace is adjacent to a children's playscape in Las Palmas, Canary Islands.

find 160 GreenGyms with air skiers, elliptical walkers, and rowing machines:

http://www.greengym.ca/locationmap.html

Including adult play equipment near the children's play space may encourage families to get involved in a more active lifestyle and model this for children.

VANDALISM

Unfortunately, vandalism is a universal common problem, and there is no way to vandal-proof an outdoor area. But there are some steps that can be taken to make the site somewhat vandal resistant:

- Place areas with benches and tables in view of the building.
- Mount signage on sturdy posts. Even if the sign is broken or defaced, the most difficult part to install will have remained in the ground.
- Repair vandalized areas promptly. Replacing signs or replanting quickly has been shown to decrease future vandalism.
- Consider security lighting for particularly vulnerable areas.
- Develop the site slowly; a massive overnight change in the school grounds attracts attention and sets up an appealing challenge to vandals. A project and features that emerge over time are more likely to be viewed as just part of the landscape.
- The most frequently mentioned antidote for minimizing schoolyard vandalism is student and community involvement as the area is developed. Involve many students from a variety of grade levels in the planning and establishment of elements on the school site. Encouraging neighbourhood involvement on work days and special events

is also very positive. The more people that have a positive interest in your project, the more eyes that will be watching your site. Stories abound of how vandalism was stopped or greatly reduced once the neighbourhood was invited to view the space as theirs also. If vandalism does occur, it should be treated as a crime and reported to the proper authorities. Letting students see that damaged property, including plantings, is viewed as a crime can be a valuable learning experience in itself.[*] (Broda, 2007, p. 45)

- Create a sign at the gate to tell the history of the playscape; perhaps when people understand the work and care that has gone into creating it, they may be more inclined to care for it. Add a bulletin board with centre updates to help to make a connection.

Inside LOOK

An Imaginative Strategy to Prevent Vandalism

A boy who shared a Chicago community garden with other children complained that when his vegetables were nearly ripe, someone would pick them before he had a chance to enjoy the harvest himself. His teacher had an idea—instead of growing vegetables with colours everyone recognizes, why not grow some vegetables with unusual colours? Then, other children would either be afraid to pick them for fear of the vegetables being poisonous, or else they would be unable to tell when the vegetables were really ripe. So, with the help of his teacher, here's what the boy decided to grow: Golden Beets, Purple-Podded Beans, Purple Headed Cauliflower, White Cucumbers, Red Leaf Lettuce, Black Bell Peppers, Blue Potatoes, Black Radishes, White Tomatoes, and Yellow Watermelons. (Fell, 1989, p. 55)

Inside LOOK

For Additional Photos

McCleary Park

In 2009 volunteers from ING DIRECT rebuilt McCleary Park in partnership with Bienenstock Natural Playgrounds and the City of Toronto. This collaborative project turned a derelict playground into a vibrant community resource. An old elm tree was cut down and used to make furniture and continues to be the centre of attraction in this playspace.

This slide is built into the existing environment.

This diseased tree that was cut down was incorporated into the playscape.

(continued)

Balancing experiences were incorporated into the environment.

The tree was also used to create seating.

Inside LOOK

Franklin's Garden, Toronto Island

Franklin's Children's Garden is inspired by the celebrated series of books written by Paulette Bourgeois. It is "an interactive garden for kids and families on Centre Island in Toronto. The garden is divided into six sections where children can enjoy gardening, storytelling, and visits with seven child-accessible sculptures from the Franklin the Turtle series" (Parks, Recreation and Forestry, 2012).

This section of Franklin's Children's Garden will bring free storytelling and performing arts outdoors to children in a unique amphitheatre setting. This innovative early literacy program will introduce children to reading through the art of storytelling from spring to fall each year.

Chess and checkers are possible here.

An amphitheatre was incorporated into the garden.

Children help to plant a garden every year.

For Additional Photos

Rockefeller Playground, Battery Park, New York City

New York City has a rich history of providing playgrounds, which play an essential role in the vitality of urban neighbourhoods. Today there are more than 1,000 playgrounds in the city. A new initiative by Mayor Bloomberg is "to ensure that all New Yorkers live within a 10-minute walk of a park or playground. To meet this goal, he has selected 259 schoolyards to open by 2013" (City of New York, 2012).

Rockefeller Playground is filled with elaborate, whimsical sculptures that would clearly engage children's imagination—and adults' as well!

Lynn Wilson

Creative sculptures are incorporated into this playspace.

Lynn Wilson

Playful sculptures for children to explore.

Lynn Wilson

Chess or checkers among playful creatures

For Additional Photos

Inside LOOK

Sherbourne Common

This playspace is located in an innovative water treatment project and is part of Toronto's waterfront revitalization plan. This area of the city, once an industrial park, is now an exciting destination for children and their families. (Waterfront Toronto, 2011)

An inventive approach to play spaces for children in the heart of the city

A playful structure

Inside LOOK

Whistler, British Columbia, Olympic Playground

Three world-class, accessible playgrounds were built in Vancouver, Whistler, and Richmond, venue cities for the 2010 Olympic and Paralympic Winter Games. The playground at Whistler was built to be accessible for all children and designed by Shane's Inspiration (this organization's mission is to create accessible playgrounds for children of all abilities).

An inventive playhouse is created from natural materials.

For Additional Photos

Children's artwork: Jana

Jana Theis

Chapter 6

GREENING OUTDOOR PLAYSCAPES

Power of One   SEVERN CULLIS-SUZUKI

Severn Cullis-Suzuki

Photo by Kevin Van Passen © Copyright The Globe and Mail Inc.

Severn Cullis-Suzuki was born in Vancouver in 1979 and is the daughter of author Tara Elizabeth Cullis and renowned Canadian environmental activist David Suzuki. A budding activist from an early age, she is perhaps best known for the speech she delivered at the age of 12 at the Earth Summit in Rio de Janeiro on behalf of children everywhere. The video has since become a viral hit, known as *The Girl Who Silenced the World for 5 Minutes*. Watch this video at

http://www.youtube.com/watch?v=xPx5r35Aymc

With many awards and accolades given to her, perhaps one of the most notable is the United Nations Environment Programme's Global 500 Roll of Honour. An author, television personality and environmental speaker and activist, Severn lives in Haida Gwaii where she and her husband are raising their children and learning the Haida language. "She hopes her pursuit of traditional and scientific knowledge and dedication to using her voice will help her promote a culture of diversity, sustainability and joy" (Speakers' Spotlight, n.d.).

OUTCOMES:

1. To analyze the benefits of outdoor green environments for children and adults.

2. To compare a variety of influences on garden design.

3. To examine the elements that contribute to successful natural playscapes.

Perhaps the best way to begin this chapter is to ask you to view a YouTube video at

 http://www.ted.com/talks/john_hardy_my_green_school_dream.html

This is a magical story of a very special green school environment!

A WORLD VIEW

> "Nature should be considered a critical variable in the design of all childhood habitats, including homes, childcare centers, schools, places of worship, and neighborhoods, and in the many other community places where children go with family and friends: botanical gardens, museums, city parks, etc."
>
> **—Robin Moore, Natural Learning Initiative, North Carolina State University**

Wherever young children and their families are found are obvious settings for establishing healthy habits and promoting change. Greening is a growing international movement that focuses primarily on the design, use, and culture of outdoor

Experimental Kindergarten, Suzhou, China

spaces, with a view to improving the quality of children's play and learning experiences.

Schools around the world have embraced the notion of school ground greening and are transforming hard, barren expanses of turf and asphalt into places that include a diversity of natural and built elements, such as shelters, rock amphitheaters, trees, shrubs, wildflower meadows, ponds, grassy berms and food gardens. School ground greening is particularly prominent in Canada, Australia, the United Kingdom, the United States, Scandinavia, New Zealand and South Africa. (Dyment & Bell, 2007, p. 2)

THE VALUE OF GREENING PLAYSCAPES

Greening playscapes is an optimistic activity; planting requires patience and an investment in the future. There is no question that green spaces can connect children with the natural world, help them understand where their food comes from, and teach them a wide range of skills—every area of the curriculum can be addressed in this space! When creating a garden, the child's whole body is involved; it is a sensory and physical approach to building their skills. Fine and gross motor movements are required as they dig through difficult clay soil and plant tiny seeds. Their cognitive skills are evident as they decide what is a weed and what is a keeper.

> Picking flowers takes skill and practice: pull too hard and the roots come up, cut too high up and there is no stem to put in the vase. Some flowers can be broken off; some need to be cut with scissors. When the children harvest vegetables, they must use just the right amount of pressure in removing the desired part of the plant to avoid damaging the remaining part.[*] (Starbuck, Olthof, & Midden, 2002, p. 2)

Green playscapes provide a perfect opportunity to learn about nature through direct experiences and experimentation. Water play gives the children insight into land forms and erosion; gardens provide practical lessons about the food we eat and countless opportunities to problem solve. Harvesting and cooking can also become integral parts of the program.

In their study of 41 playgrounds in North Carolina, Hestenes, Shim, and DeBord (2007) found that on playgrounds with more natural elements,

[*]Starbuck, S., Olthof, M., Midden, K. 2002. *Hollyhocks and Honeybees Garden Projects for Young Children*. Redleaf Press. p. 2.

Margaret Atwood and Victory Gardens

Victory Gardens became popular during the 1940s as these gardens provided support for the war effort. People helped by planting in their backyards and in vacant lots in cities and towns. Margaret Atwood, Canadian author, recalls her involvement with Victory Gardens. "When I was small, people had Victory Gardens. This was during the Second World War, and the idea was that if people grew their own vegetables, then the food produced by the farmers would be freed up for use by the army. There was another strong motivator: rationing was in effect for things you were unlikely to be able to grow yourself, such as sugar, butter, milk, tea, cheese and meat, so the more you could grow, the better you would eat, and the better the soldiers would eat, too. Thus, by digging and hoeing and weeding and watering, you too could help win the war. … Many people gave up their gardens after the war. My parents kept on with theirs, because they said fresh food tasted better."[*] (Houghton, 2003, pp. 13–16)

Children's Garden, Hillcrest Public School, Bathurst Street, 1917

William James Photographer, City of Toronto Archives. Fonds 1244, Item 8212

[*]Houghton, E. 2003. *A Breath Of Fresh Air Celebrating Nature and School Gardens*. The Learnxs Foundation & Sumach Press, Toronto District School Board. pp. 13–16. © E. Houghton.

For Additional Photos

children displayed less functional (using the materials in simple, repetitive ways) and more constructive (building, hypothesizing, goal oriented) play.

IMPACT OF NATURE ON CHILDREN

"To forget how to dig the earth and to tend the soil is to forget ourselves."

—**Mahatma Gandhi (quoted in Sinclair, 2005, p. 144)**

The *Green Heart Education* website summarizes the following benefits of involvement with nature:

- Students learn focus and patience, cooperation, teamwork and social skills.

- They gain self-confidence and a sense of "capableness" along with new skills and knowledge in food growing—soon-to-be-vital for the 21st century.

- Garden-based teaching addresses different learning styles and intelligences; our non-readers can blossom in the garden!

- Achievement scores improve because learning is more relevant and hands-on.

- Students become more fit and healthy as they spend more time active in the outdoors and start choosing healthy foods over junk food.

- The schoolyard is diversified and beautified

- Graffiti and vandalism decrease because students respect what they feel some ownership in.[*]

Many of those involved in school-ground greening especially value a longer-term advantage for children: a heightened awareness and understanding of the needs of healthy ecosystems to support human life and well-being.

[*]The Value of School Gardens © GreenHeart Education. http://www.greenhearted.org/school-gardens.html.

Trees provide opportunities to see nature up close and from a different perspective.

There is no question that gardens are living laboratories; they are constantly changing and provide many hands-on opportunities for discovery and experimentation. There is a place for every area of the curriculum in a garden. The garden can also bring the school and the community closer together, and can be a source of pride for both.

Gardening also teaches the important lessons of failure: what to do next time and what not to do. As we prepare children for the real world, it is important to allow them to fail and to learn from their failures.

INFLUENCES ON GARDEN DESIGN
ZEN GARDENS

Zen is not a dogmatic religion or philosophy, but simply a practice. The garden is the perfect setting in which to practice Zen. It presents lessons in patience, compassion, and acceptance—all aspects of the Zen viewpoint. It teaches awareness, simplicity, nonattachment, non-resistance, our interdependence and interconnectedness with all life, and present-moment living. It gives us the opportunity to lose ourselves in mindful, attentive work. (Ray, 1996, p. 2)

Zen Buddhism has existed in Japan since the tenth century and slowly evolved as Japanese priests returned from China, not only with new religious ideas but also impressions of various art forms. Over time, artists began to experiment in more diverse fields such as garden-making, which they originally based on what they had seen in China. Using the raw materials of rocks and sand, they made "paintings" to create an evocative impression of a landscape, every rock being carefully selected and meticulously placed to represent specific features. These *karesansui* or "dry landscape" gardens were, and are, primarily works of art and gardens second.[†] (Rawlings, 1998, p. 160)

FENG SHUI GARDENS

Feng Shui is a term of two Chinese words: feng (wind) and shui (water). Feng Shui is rooted in Taoism, a religion whose followers acknowledge the power of nature and seek to live in harmony with it. Ch'i is a term used to describe the life force of the entire universe. Everything

Given the pace at which the growing world population is consuming global resources and depleting the earth's ecological services (air, water, the ozone layer, forests) there is an urgent need to examine the effects of human activity on both living and non-living systems. Adding an ecological outlook to learning in a garden allows children to see new connections between their own experiences and the world outside the school.[*] (Evergreen, 2003, p. 29)

Most school gardens are inspired by a wish to see children spend more fulfilling time outside, working co-operatively together, adding beauty, life and colour to their surroundings, learning to care for living things, making a connection with nature and the soil. And within these broader aspirations, each garden takes on a special personality of its own: gardens are as individual as their creators, their spaces and the purposes they are designed to fulfill.[**] (Houghton, 2003, p. 23)

[*]Evergreen. 2004. *Small Wonders: Designing Vibrant, Natural Landscapes For Early Childhood*. Learning Grounds Tool Shed Series. p. 29.

[**]Houghton, E. 2003. *A Breath Of Fresh Air Celebrating Nature and School Gardens*. The Learnxs Foundation & Sumach Press, Toronto District School Board. p. 23. © E. Houghton.

[†]Rawlings, R. 1998. *Healing Gardens*. Weidenfeld & Nicholson, London. The Orion Publishing Group, London. p. 160.

around us, in the earth, water and heavens, has an energy with the potential to affect us.* (Rawlings, 1998, p. 39)

The Chinese have long known that physical surroundings affect every aspect of our lives and believe that there is a distinct relationship between success in life and good feng shui.

The Chinese use feng shui, the art of placement, to determine the location and alignment of their gardens, as well as the rocks, pools, and pavilions within them. Harmony and balance are critical to feng shui in the garden. Materials are chosen for their dramatic impact, and colour is used to stimulate the flow of *chi*. Plants such as

ornamental grasses are chosen for their ability to "catch the wind." Careful selection of furniture, ornaments, and containers enhances the environment. Water is an important element, and provides soothing sounds.

DESIGNING THE FIVE ELEMENTS IN YOUR LANDSCAPE

Fire: The centre back area (Fame)

Earth: The centre area (Health)

Metal: The centre right area (Children)

Water: The centre front area (Career)

Wood: The centre left area (Family). (Feng Shui Humber Nurseries, n.d.)

*Rawlings, R. 1998. *Healing Gardens*. Weidenfeld & Nicholson, London. The Orion Publishing Group, p. 39.

EXHIBIT 6.1   Ten Things That Help Make a Children's Garden Great

For
Additional
Photos

1. Read kids gardening books to excite the children.
2. Share images or make simple sketches of interesting design ideas: willow arches, beds for year-round digging, sunflower houses, bean pole rooms, bird and butterfly habitats, sand boxes next to veggie beds, Peter Rabbit gardens (based on stories by Beatrix Potter), water play areas next to gardens, seating areas, washing and eating areas, etc.
3. Go to the garden-to-be in the weeks or months before you start and ask what the kids want to do in their garden. Eat? Watch insects? Dig for worms? Pick plants? Draw on their interests to add elements to the garden.
4. Grow sprouts (mung beans and alfalfa are easy) and eat them in winter and spring. This invites kids to start enjoying fresh green snacks, which can sometimes take a little time. Then grow a few seedlings to transplant to the garden; **kale has simple-to-grow seeds**.
5. Soil test using a biology count. Mark off a 30 cm square per child or every two children. Have the children count how many worms they find per 30 cm square (in the top 115 cm of soil). If there are between 5 and 30 worms, you're likely to have soil that will grow a great garden.
6. Choose 5–10 relatively easy to grow vegetables and fruits along with some herbs For young toddlers, you'll need to consider toxicity of plants too. Some ideas:

   Greens: leaf lettuce, romaine, chard, kale, arugula, spinach
   Taste: cherry tomatoes (the rest of the plant is toxic), peas, strawberries, carrots
   Shade and beauty: runner beans
   Herbs: chives, basil, parsley, oregano, mint
   Fall plants: garlic and kale
   Companion plants: marigolds, nasturtiums, chives
   Children also love pickling cucumbers, and zucchinis make a great show. Raspberries are great too (and perennial), but they are prickly, so they must be planted away from busy areas.

7. Make seed balls with your greens seeds. Toss these into the garden-to-be early in the season and let them emerge as they will. Recipe: 5 parts dry clay, 3 parts worm compost, .25 part seeds. You can buy kits for making these too.
8. Lay stepping stone pathways around the emergent greens and your garden will start to take shape. Try following a natural pattern for pathway inspiration, like a leaf's veins or a spider web.

(continued)

9. Plant your transplants in and around the new greens to shade them as the sun gets hotter. Plant herbs and companion plants between and around the fruit and vegetables for protection from insects.

10. Help the kids make "fairy homes" around as many of the transplants as possible. Provide natural materials such as pine cones, moss, coconut fibre mulch, wood rounds (ask an arborist for help), pebbles, jute twine, etc. Help the kids connect each fairy home into a larger fairy garden with fairy paths, hammocks, tables and chairs, water-catchers (wells), flags, etc.[*]

A fairy garden

[*]©Jane Hayes. www.gardenjane.com.

Contributed by: Jane Hayes. Jane Hayes (www.gardenjane.com) was instrumental in a project at Casa Loma Child Care Centre and many of her ideas listed above came to fruition in this reclaimed planting bed on the George Brown College campus.

COLOUR IN THE PLAYSCAPE

For Additional Photos

There is no question that colour influences our perception of the world around us.

Emotionally we have strong responses to different colors. Some of them, based on our personal experiences, are individual to us, but in general terms certain colors evoke similar responses in all of us. Individual colours can affect us physically too. Exposure to red, for example, increases blood pressure, heart rate, rate of breathing and muscular activity. While red stimulates and excites, blue has the opposite effect. It lowers blood pressure, calms the heart rate and reduces tension. (Search, 2002, p. 75)

We want to provide a riot of colour in the playscape for young children.

For continuous colour, plants that retain their leaves, such as evergreens, during the winter months are very effective in the garden.

WATER IN THE PLAYSCAPE

The urge to seek water is one of the deepest human drives. Whenever children step outdoors, they seem to have an extrasensory ability to find water in any form—alley puddles, gutter streams, ditches, ponds teeming with tadpoles. Being near water reduces a person's heart rate, respiration and blood pressure. Water's soothing presence makes thoughts seem clearer, children sweeter, responsibilities lighter. In addition to its calming influence, water seems to heighten the senses. (Dannenmaier, 1998, p. 52)

Keeping safety in mind, water in a container, fountain, pond, or cascading feature adds life, movement, and a new dimension to any children's garden. The use of water, especially during hot weather, can cool and excite. Sprinklers to run through, babies sitting in wading pools, splashing, and using a hose to mix water with sand are all opportunities for hands-on learning. The effect of winter weather on water should also be observed, touched, built with, measured, and recorded.

When plants in the garden need water, try using the *bucket method*. A large empty container with two 0.5 cm holes drilled in the bottom will allow for a slow flow. Place the container

Fox Hollow Child Care Centre, St. Margaret Village, Nova Scotia

Ice holds many mysteries.

Caring for the garden and other plants in the playscape requires watering.

Bottle watering!

at the foot of trees and large plants that require watering. A smaller version for little hands uses a large pop bottle with the bottom cut off and a hole drilled into the cap (or use a special drip applicator). More information is available on the Evergreen website at

http://www.evergreen.ca/docs/res/Planting-Trees-7-Bucket.pdf

GETTING STARTED—GREENING THE PLAYSCAPE

> "Now more than ever we need to remember that we are vitally connected to the earth. This is not some vague romanticism, but a truth to keep in mind and heart as if our lives depended on it. They do."
>
> —Patrick Lima (quoted in Sinclair, 2005, p. 41)

A garden is often one of the first elements to be introduced when considering a connection with nature. No project should begin without Robin Moore's *Plants for Play* (1993).

Young children are most interested in plants that capture their attention through sensory elements, those with interesting or unusual characteristics, and those with funny or unusual names.

Use plants of various sizes and those they can smell, hear, touch, and taste. Consider creating a border with a flowering hedge of perfumed jasmine to delight babies' sense of smell.

Another option may be to border the garden with boxwood as a way to protect the garden from running feet and bicycles. With edging materials, avoid sharp, protruding edges or edges that may be a tripping hazard.

Consider how climate will affect plant choice. Canada is divided into planting regions called *Hardiness Zones* that indicate a range of the average minimum temperature in a given area. How will climate affect your garden and your plant choices? When in doubt, ask at your local nursery or check online.

INVOLVE THE CHILDREN

Although infants are limited in their input for developing a garden, they will respond to things that happen around them. Try installing mobiles, wind chimes, or sculptures with moving parts in your garden to stimulate babies. When appropriate, young children should be active participants; for example, they can draw where things will go, measure, graph

For Additional Photos

Lynn Wilson

Lynn Wilson

Lynn Wilson

Lynn Wilson

A Garden Project by the children at the University of Toronto Child Care Centre on Charles, George Brown College, Toronto

out their project, etc. Also include them in the actual building of the garden and planting beds as much as possible. School-agers will have advanced skills and will provide much more input.

Ask families to donate seed catalogues or gardening magazines and have the children pick out their favourites, pointing out which ones will work in your region. Perhaps the children will pick out vegetables they have never tasted; this would suggest a trip to the local grocery store to have the children try the vegetables before planting. The store trip may also give the children new ideas as they look at the produce available. This is a good opportunity to talk about where the produce comes from and why we cannot grow bananas in Canada, for example.

You may also want to see the apps available at http://www.emmitsburg.net/gardens/articles/adams/2011/apps.htm

to help the children and adults with their gardening. The children will have lots of ideas and this is an opportunity to also discuss access to the plants, perhaps where stepping stones and pathways might be placed. Kits are available to test the soil to determine if the soil needs to be amended. Ground-level gardens may present challenges if the soil is clay based and may need lots of additional nutrients from your compost pile Have the children place the compost material in a watering can or suitable container, add water, stir vigorously, and then to pour it into the soil.

Children created their own pathway in the garden using painted pieces of flagstone.

Making food for the garden

RAISED BEDS

To create a raised bed, you may want to ask for a donation from your local lumber yard. Helping the children decide where the beds should be placed and how they will be built involves many steps: the height of the bed will be critical as it has to fit the children and not be too wide that they can't reach to the other side. Raised beds are particularly important for children in wheelchairs to provide them with easier access to the plants.

> "Bread feeds the body indeed, but flowers feed also the soul."
>
> —**The Koran**

When children plant their garden, they will want to identify those plants that are "theirs." For example, cut mini-blinds or old wooden venetian blinds into short lengths and label them with acrylic paint or waterproof pen (Lovejoy, 1999, p. 4). The children can decorate paint stir sticks donated by a local paint shop or recycle plastic yogurt tops by gluing them onto tongue depressors.

LIVING WALLS

Making use of the vertical elements in a garden is important where space is limited. Living walls are wonderful additions to early learning environments. Many sites have walls or fences that would benefit from a green wall that hides an ugly exterior. The living walls keep the building warmer in the colder months and cooler in the summer, reducing energy costs. Vertical walls planted inside also have a calming effect as well as reducing noise pollution (Alini, 2011, p. 36). While many of these projects are very expensive, simple adaptations can be made by attaching wooden boxes or planting trays to the walls.

COMPOSTING

Composting turns waste into a resource and vermicomposting helps children (and adults) overcome any fear of worms. The best part is the worms do most of the work! You can purchase a commercial worm bin (red wiggler worms are best) or make one of your own. For information on composting look at the Compost Council of Canada at

http://www.compost.org

For bigger projects, a rototiller may be needed, which will provide an exciting opportunity for the

Raised beds at Howard Park Public School, Toronto

These beds can be wheeled about; Evergreen Brick Works.

Royal Botanical Gardens

children to see a new piece of machinery at work—and it beats digging large areas by hand.

MONEY MATTERS

Planting also becomes a money lesson. Show the children how much money you have to spend or how much fundraising will be necessary to plant the garden and other greening elements of the play space. A good strategy is to give the children a variety of catalogues of outdoor materials so that the children can see the real cost of creating a new play space.

ALLERGIES AND NATURAL ENVIRONMENTS

Pollen is one of man's most well-known natural allergens; the body's reaction to it may result in hay fever or asthma. Problems can occur at any time of year, but especially spring (tree pollen), early summer (grass pollen) and autumn (weed pollen and fungal spores). Through careful selection of species, floating pollen levels can be reduced considerably. Avoid ornamental grasses when in flower, pinks, daisies, thistles, dahlias, marigolds. Although it may limit others' enjoyment of your garden, it is also wise to avoid highly scented flowers, as strong perfumes may trigger allergic reactions in some people.[*] (Rawlings, 1998, p. 33)

---

[*]Rawlings, R. 1998. *Healing Gardens*. Weidenfeld & Nicholson, London. The Orion Publishing Group, London. p. 33.

Search (2002) suggests that "all wind pollinated plants should be avoided because they produce vast quantities of pollen" (p. 163).

CAUTION

It is important to teach the children never to taste any part of a wild or cultivated plant unless an adult says it's okay to eat. Discuss with children that some plants are important as food; others are poisonous and the two can be difficult to tell apart.

PLANTS FOR TOUCHING

There is so much textural variety in the plant world—from furry to smooth to prickly. Help children understand that there are many reasons plants have different textures; for example, succulent plants store water, prickly plants are unappealing to hungry insects and animals, and furry leaves protect from extremes of hot and cold weather. Encourage the children to use all of their body parts when touching the plants. Touch trees to discover their different barks. Hug them while you are at it!

For Additional Photos

Some favourite tactile plants are Jerusalem sage, silver sage, lamb's ear, yucca plants with their coarse spikes, and hens and chicks—a wonderful succulent. Also explore seed pods, thistle, burrs, poppy capsules, and milkweed pods.

Lynn Wilson

*Trees can be cared for in many different ways.
This one at Runnymede Public School has a
knitted sweater!*

PLANTS THAT MAKE NOISE

Creating a garden that appeals to all of our senses
should include plants that appeal to our auditory sense.
Plants such as paper birch make wonderful noises as
their leaves rub together. Bladder senna has pods that
rattle, and ornamental grasses and money plants provide soothing sounds as the wind rustles through them.

> Love-in-a-mist has bright blue flowers that create
> seed heads that rattle when shaken. Corn is
> another plant that is fun to watch grow and
> listen to as well! For many centuries, Chinese
> scholars planted large-leafed plants beneath their
> windows, in order to emphasize the pattering
> sound of rain.[*] (Rawlings, 1998, p. 13)

FRAGRANT PLANTS

Plants produce scent for two reasons. Flower scent
attracts animal pollinators, while aromatic foliage,
bark and roots repel hungry predators. Fragrance
is unnecessary for flowers pollinated by birds (who
have no sense of smell) or by the wind. Some plants
also produce scent only when pollination is likely.
That scent can have strong psychological effects
has long been recognized by the perfume industry
and the power of pheromones to attract is well
established in animal behaviour. Lavender is one of
the best loved of the fragrant aromatic shrubs that
originate from the Mediterranean area. Romans
used lavender to scent linen and also in bathing;
indeed, its name may derive from the Latin verb
lavare *to wash*.[**] (Minter, 1993, pp. 104–109)

Other fragrant plants and herbs include shrub roses,
viburnam, lilacs, sage, basil, rosemary, peppermint,

For Additional Photos

Lynn Wilson

An herb garden at the Toronto Botanical Gardens

[*]Rawlings, R. 1998. *Healing Gardens*. Weidenfeld & Nicholson,
London. The Orion Publishing Group, London. p. 13.

[**]From *The Healing Garden: A Practical For Emotional Well Being*
by *Sue Minter*. Published by *Eden Project Books*. Reprinted by
Permission of The Random House Group Limited.

Lynn Wilson

Milkweed pods

Lilacs

geranium, juniper, basil, jasmine, and mint. Some plants' scents are timed: the four o'clock plant opens late in the day (around 4 o'clock) with fragrant flowers, and the curry plant gives off a spicy aroma when the weather is hot, Look for unusual plants with interesting scents: the chocolate cosmos gives off a chocolate scent, and *Melianthus major* has blue leaves that smell like peanut butter!

Our sense of smell may well transport us back to our grandparent's garden because our nasal receptors extend directly into the area of the brain most intimately associated with memory. The sense of smell is related to age—it fades as you get older; pigmentation—dark-haired individuals have a more sensitive nose; type of scent and extinction—the way your nasal receptors turn off after intense stimulation.

PLANTS THAT HELP TO CREATE BARRIERS

For Additional Photos

Abelia, weigela, viburnum, photinia, and willow are good shrub barriers but can still be seen through. Grasses such as pampas, fountain, and feather reed are all tall and provide a beautiful wall that bends in the wind. Thorny plants such as flowering quince, rose bushes, and barberry can also be used as a fence, or boxwood plants as well.

GOOD GARDEN CHOICES FOR PLANTING

For Additional Photos

Before you buy, get expert advice about suitable plants for your garden given your climate, soil, and sun exposure. You will also want to choose some plants that grow quickly since young children are anxious to see the results of their efforts. Fast-growing seeds such as radish, carrots, chard, arugula, etc., are good picks but plants that have already germinated provide a head start.

Native plants are generally low maintenance, drought tolerant, and generally free of insect and disease problems. They also attract a wide range of native pollinators such as honey bees, hummingbirds, and butterflies. The preservation of native plant species is important; the more native plants we plant in our gardens, the more we help to protect and preserve them for future generations. To learn more about native plants, contact the North American Native Plant Society at

http://www.nanps.org

Another good resource is the Evergreen website at

http://nativeplants.evergreen.ca

For Additional Reading

"Well-arranged plants can become playhouses, hideouts, castles, planets and far-off places. Your plantings also become wildlife habitats saying "Welcome" to birds, chipmunks, butterflies and fuzzy caterpillars" (Keeler, 2008, p. 260).

Fence gardening

A see-through bag allows the children to watch these kernels grow!

Picking beans at the Allegro Child Care Centre, Halifax, Nova Scotia

Harvesting sunflower seeds at the Allegro Child Care Centre, Halifax, Nova Scotia

GREAT FLOWER PERFORMERS

Children love bright colours and these flowers and leaves are sure to excite the children as they watch them grow: cosmos (they have large seeds for little hands), daisies, snapdragons, pansies, nasturtiums (you can eat them if they haven't been sprayed), sweet peas, hollyhocks, sweet William (they are biennial [grow every two years]), zinnias, Chinese lanterns, money plants, bleeding hearts, verbena, balloon flowers, and marigolds (Dannenmaier, 2008, p. 155).

SUNFLOWER

Sunflowers are one of children's favourite plants; they especially appreciate the flowers' fast growth. The largest grow so tall that they soon tower over the children. In contrast, some varieties are only inches tall. There are more than 80 different varieties of sunflowers, and some are perennial (reappear every year). Planting several varieties of different heights is a great way to teach small, medium, large, and very large! Sunflowers come in many different colours and the seeds are good for humans and birds. They are also a great way to introduce the Sunflower paintings of Vincent van Gogh.

For Additional Photos

VINES

Use vines to cover an ugly wall or fence; try cup and saucer vine or trumpet vine. Discover the different ways vines climb, including twining or using tendrils or thorns.

For Additional Photos

VEGETABLES

> "To get the best results you must talk to your vegetables."
>
> **—Prince Charles (quoted in Ray, 1996, p. 126)**

Vegetables are great fun to grow; many germinate quite quickly and are ready for eating within weeks. Many vegetable have an incredible range of colours, shapes, and sizes. Gourds are also a children's favourite; perhaps you can enter the largest pumpkin contest in your area! Consider growing ghost pumpkins, which are white!

For Additional Photos

- Sugar snap peas, great for planting along garden fences early in the season

- Lettuce, spinach, and other leafy greens, with new seeds planted every two weeks for continued harvest (another early season one)
- Radishes grow quickly and are ready to eat in a month (plant early in the season and they won't get too spicy)
- Carrots grow quickly, too, though the seeds are quite tiny and hard to handle (try carrot seed tape)
- Potatoes, planted early, could be ready for harvest before the summer break (just cut seed potatoes with an eye in each piece and bury)
- Green beans, bush or pole, are great raw or cooked
- Cherry tomatoes and tomatillos are fun for kids—make some salsa together (shhhh, secret tip for school and community gardens: to discourage two-legged garden marauders, choose a tomato variety that is orange when ripe; fewer uninvited visitors will take them, thinking they're not yet ripe)
- Pumpkins take more space and won't be ready until fall, but are perfect for teaching patience
- Broccoli is not known as a favourite of children—until they've grown their own (buy starter plants to speed this one up)
- Sunflowers—okay, not a vegetable, but in the fall, your students can dry and eat the seeds, or leave the flower heads in the garden as a treat for birds
- Oriental greens, because they germinate and grow so rapidly in cooler weather.[*]

For information on vegetable gardens go to

 http://www.vesey.com

TOUGH PLANTS

Lamb's ears, cotoneaster, woolly thyme, sandwort, snow-in-summer, periwinkle are all plants that stand up to a lot of abuse and can be planted near pathways or other high-traffic areas.

PLANTS THAT HEAL

For Additional Photos

Through the centuries we have used herbs for many things—food, flavouring, medicines, dyes, cosmetics, scent, and, in some instances, magic.

People have enjoyed their wonderful scents in both fresh and dried form, and soothing teas have been popular for hundreds of years. Historically, growing herbs wasn't a hobby; it was necessary for survival. Herbs are versatile, easy to grow, benefit other plants (repel pests and attract beneficial insects), and add flavour to food. (Davis, Cutler, Fisher, & DeJohn, 2011, p. 8)

The World Wide Fund for Nature estimated that 85% of drugs are in some way linked to a plant source. The reduction in the variety of plants as some species become extinct threatens to limit the discovery of possible future medicines. Several of our most important drugs are derived from tropical rainforest plants. The current loss of rainforest on a massive scale wipes out species before there has been a chance to screen them for medicinal value. Conservation in the tropics and respect for the knowledge of indigenous peoples in the use of herbal medicines is such a key concern.[**] (Minter, 1993, p. 24)

Mint is a wonderful addition to any garden given the varieties and the way that it quickly spreads throughout the garden. Dill is not only a beautiful plant with its furry foliage, but also has a unique and powerful scent.

BULBS

Tulips grow wild in desert-like areas of Turkey and Siberia. When an Austrian traveler saw tulips growing in the gardens of a Turkish sultan in the 1500s, he was so impressed that he took tulip bulbs home to the Emperor of Austria for planting in the Imperial Gardens. When the emperor's gardener moved to Holland, he took tulip bulbs with him. Soon, nearly everyone in Holland with a garden wanted to grow them. The Dutch people export tulips all over the world. (Fell, 1989, p. 37)

Lynn Wilson

There are hundreds of different bulbs to be planted.

---

[*]The Value of School Gardens, 2012: © GreenHeart Education. http://www.greenhearted.org.

[**]From *The Healing Garden: A Practical For Emotional Well Being* by *Sue Minter*. Published by *Eden Project Books*. Reprinted by Permission of The Random House Group Limited.

Bulbs are wonderful spring surprises, but plant plenty since squirrels seem to like some of them more than we do! An extensive list of flowering bulbs in North America—from garden variety to rare and unusual—can be found at

 http://www.gardenimport.com

ANNUALS

For Additional Photos

Most annuals will have to be replanted every spring, but they guarantee a continuous display of beautiful and often fragrant flowers from planting until frost. Even this can be delayed since plants in containers can be moved or otherwise protected much more easily than in a typical garden. Most nurseries have a large selection of superb annuals for sun, shade, or both in a wide range of colours.

Annuals suitable for containers and ground planting include impatiens, begonias, petunias, marigolds, sweet alyssum, portulaca, lobelia, celosia, ageratum, scaveola, snapdragons, verbena, zinnias, nasturtiums, and geraniums (including many scented and cascading varieties).

Pansies can be planted in very early spring for a great show of colour before the gardening season starts; fall mums are a traditional favourite for autumn. For fragrance, consider sweet alyssum, geranium, and heliotrope.

Annual vines are ideal for creating privacy and provide a lot of colour in a limited space. They also help create an ambience by covering walls and barriers. Think about cup and saucer vine, and scarlet runner beans. Perennial vines are excellent for screening and for brilliant fall colour. Boston ivy is self-clinging and doesn't need a trellis; it has a beautiful red colour in the fall.

PERENNIALS

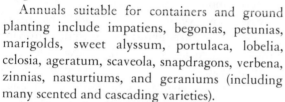
For Additional Photos

Perennials do not have to be planted every year so may save money over the long term even though they may be more expensive initially. Plants such as ferns and hostas have beautiful foliage and do well especially in shaded areas. As they grow, they can be divided every two or three years, which will also help to fill out the garden.

PLANTS FOR ALL SEASONS

For Additional Photos

The children will be outside all year round so consider all four seasons when planning your playspace. Think about plants that burst into

Scarecrow at Fox Hollow, St. Margaret's Village, Nova Scotia

Lynn Wilson

blossom in the spring (fruit trees, forsythia bushes, and tulip bulbs). Think about vegetable and flower gardens in the summer. Think about the harvest in the fall (apples, squash, and pumpkins). Think about plantings for autumn colour (burning bush shrubs and trees whose leaves explode into color such as oak or aspen). Think about trees for winter that have interesting bark, branch shapes, and trunks when the leaves fall, evergreen needles (and piney smells), or bright safe berries that last all winter. You may want to include a scarecrow for fun as well as to keep hungry critters away!

CONTAINER GARDENING

For Additional Photos

People have planted in containers for many centuries. There are a huge variety of plants to choose from, including many bred specifically for container growing because of the rapidity with which plants dry out in containers.

When selecting containers, consider weight when planted, portability, durability, size, colour, and design. Even plastic pails can be used as containers for centres where money is a concern. Clay pots chip and break easily and will crack if the soil is not removed and the pot turned over for the winter. Wall bags made of strong plastic are very versatile and can be hung almost anywhere.

Adequate drainage is vital to the health of plants and most containers have drainage holes. If not, drill holes and include 2–3 cm of broken clay or gravel at the bottom of the container. Adding a small amount of charcoal will prevent the soil from turning sour. Soil prepared specifically for containers often contain moisture-retentive crystals

A shoe bag—a great way to plant up!

Wall bags, Evergreen Brick Works

containers, which can dry very quickly in the heat of the summer sun. Consider having rain barrels to capture runoff for watering plants.

Fruits and vegetables can readily be grown in containers throughout the summer growing season, and many herbs easily grow indoors in containers all year. Tomatoes are popular and easy to grow. Other salad ingredients, such as lettuce, radishes, onions, cucumbers, peppers, and carrots are also easily grown in containers. Beets, beans,

There are many ways to garden!

that absorb water and increase dramatically in size. Do not use these; the crystals are not to be eaten. Instead, add mulch to the top of the container to help retain water. Water is critical for plants in

This rain barrel provides much-needed water; Casa Loma Child Care Centre.

Ryerson Public School

Almost anything can be used as a planter.

and peas also do well. Strawberries are ideal for containers and require relatively little space. A wide variety of strawberry jars and planters exist primarily for this purpose. Blueberries need very acidic well-drained soil and are ideal for container gardening.

When the playspace is covered in asphalt and presents challenges for planting, even containers such as recycling bins work perfectly!

Reuse clear plastic juice bottles by cutting off the bottoms and using them to cover seedlings or new plants during frost warnings. Later, invert the bottles and nail them to a fence for a new container.

ROOFTOP GARDEN

Many child care centres, particularly those in urban environments, find their playspace on a rooftop. Like the Vancouver child care centres mentioned

previously in Chapter 4, a rooftop can become not only an environmentally friendly space but also a beautiful and engaging one. Many rooftops will receive full sunlight if not shaded by other tall buildings, which ensures that many plants will thrive there. Plants and trees will help absorb heat and their roots will collect storm water runoff. Extensive plantings will help to keep the building itself warmer in winter and cooler in summer, providing energy efficiency.

BUTTERFLIES AND BIRDS IN THE GARDEN

For Additional Photos

A butterfly garden is a wonderful addition to any outdoor playscape. Choose a space that receives at least six hours of sunlight daily so plants will thrive; ensure that the spot is sheltered so winds will not disturb the plants and butterflies. Butterflies are attracted to abundant flowers; however, they prefer flowers whose nectar is readily available and/or whose flowers grow in clusters, so choose plants such as bee balm, butterfly bush, lilies, asters, coneflowers, black-eyed Susans, milkweed, yarrow, and thistles. Contact your local garden centre to determine your region's most appropriate plants for butterflies. Butterflies love heat so add gravel paths and flat rocks to provide places for them to rest and prepare for flight. Also provide some water; perhaps in an inverted garbage lid or a shallow dish dug into the ground. Change the water regularly to prevent mosquitoes from laying eggs there.

You can also purchase butterfly larvae from the Boreal Northwest Catalogue at

http://boreal.com

A butterfly garden at Riverdale Farm

GREENING OUTDOOR PLAYSCAPES

There are many resources to help us learn more about birds.

A bird project at Esther Exton Child Care Centre

Other live specimens such as frogs are also available at this site.

Birds can help rid your garden of insects and pests. Birds love the seeds of black-eyed Susans, coneflowers, coreopsis, cosmos, feverfew, scabiosa, and sunflowers, as well as berry-bearing shrubs. Fruits also attract birds—plant barberries, blueberries, crabapples, currants, grapes, serviceberries, etc. When harvesting, we can leave some

fruit behind specifically for the birds over the winter months.

Young children are fascinated by hummingbirds, which are the only birds able to fly backwards and straight up and down, as well as hover. Buy special feeders to attract them, and cluster several for best results. Hummingbirds are attracted to "hot" colours such as red, orange, and yellow so choose these colours in annuals, trumpet vines, and flowering shrubs and trees. More information is available about hummingbirds at

http://www.hummingbirds.net

Water is one of the most important elements to provide for birds in the winter. By planting the appropriate native host and nectar plants and providing water sources and other habitat features, you can turn your school grounds into a National Wildlife Federation certified School-yards Habitat site. NWF's Schoolyard Habitats program can provide resources, training and curriculum support to participating schools, institutions, and community groups. For more information, visit

http://www.nwf.org/schoolyardhabitats

GROUND COVERS

Ground covers are known for being both decorative and garden problem solvers. Some thrive in shade or where lawns don't grow; others are ideal for preventing soil erosion on banks. Nothing beats a lawn but many centres find it difficult to maintain, especially in the spring when the ground is soft and malleable, and little feet can destroy it very quickly.

Brooklyn Botanical Gardens

TREES AND THE NEED FOR SHADE

> "Holding down soil, shading the earth and cooling its surface, absorbing rainwater and gradually re-releasing moisture, softening the sweep of winds, trees are a major climate regulator in our country and on our planet ... The importance of maintaining our green canopy cannot be overemphasized. Climate moderation is perhaps the most essential—and the least recognized—role of our trees."[*]
>
> —Henry Kock, Interpretive Horticulturalist, Guelph Arboretum (quoted in Houghton, 2003, p. 106)

For Additional Photos

Trees provide summer shade, buffer cold winter winds and reduce energy costs; [sic] reduce water runoff and soil erosion, filter dust, block noise and provide habitat and shelter for songbirds and other urban wildlife. In addition, they renew our oxygen and add moisture to the air through transpiration. Within our depleted ozone layer, they block close to 60 percent of the sun's rays. Trees also filter air pollution, taking in such noxious gases as sulphur dioxide, nitrogen dioxide, ground-level ozone, carbon monoxide and microscopic particles that contribute to smog.[*] (Houghton, 2003, p. 106)

Playgrounds are often devoid of shade; trees and other vegetation are often not planted in order to maximize the play space but shade is a critical element in the design of any playscape. Trees are a wonderful way to dramatically change the nature of the environment. Research has found that vandalism drops directly in proportion to the number of trees in the neighbourhood (Bienenstalk, 2011).

When choosing trees, "a good strategy is to look at the trees that are the oldest in your community. They have withstood the test of time, their immune systems have persevered in warding off diseases and tolerated extreme climate and air pollution" (Evergreen, 2004, pp. 108–109).

Think about tree variety, shape, colour, and texture. Each tree's overall shape and growth will determine whether it will fit into your playspace. You might opt for one that is weeping or upright

and columnar, or have a round head or spreading horizontal branches or contorted stems (Fairfax, 1999). Think about planting trees in clusters to create nooks and crannies for the children rather than planting in a straight line. Also consider replenishing a native species that is threatened in your community. "Site manager Sandee Sharpe of *Forest Valley Outdoor School* shares this piece of wisdom with her students: 'Everybody should plant a tree that they will never sit under! It will just be there for somebody else'" (Houghton, 2003, p. 109).[**]

Evergreen trees provide a very different habitat from deciduous trees, and a year-round green backdrop for those in northern climates. Consider

Lynn Wilson

Trees can also become display places for artwork that older children might create for the enjoyment of the babies in the centre.

Lynn Wilson

Even dead trees provide play opportunities; University of British Columbia Child Care Services.

---

[*]Houghton, E. 2003. *A Breath Of Fresh Air Celebrating Nature and School Gardens.* The Learnxs Foundation & Sumach Press, Toronto District School Board. p. 106. © E. Houghton.

[**]ibid., p. 109.

planting evergreens in a cluster to provide the best protection for wildlife. Songbirds, owls, squirrels, and raccoons will use these trees. Leave dead and dying logs, stumps, and leaves to provide habitat for interesting critters!

For Additional Photos

ORNAMENTS IN THE GARDEN

Consider adding whimsy to your garden by purchasing items or having the children make them.

Evergreen Brick Works

Humble Administrator's Garden, Suzhou, China

Lynn Wilson

Lynn Wilson

> "Ecological Literacy is about the survival of the ecosphere and everything in it ... The ecologically literate person of the 21st century will be considered as the responsible, lifelong learner who strives to improve the human condition and the environment within the context of self, human groups, the biosphere and the ecosphere."
>
> **—Michael Pollan (1991, p. 5)**

ALL THINGS TOXIC
PESTICIDES

Children may be particularly sensitive to the cancer-causing and other adverse effects of pesticides, and accumulate a large percentage of their lifetime health risk during childhood. Pesticides, fungicides, insecticides, herbicides, and rodenticides are composed of dangerous chemicals with fatal and far-reaching effects on the Earth (Lovejoy, 2003). Young children are at a greater risk of exposure to pesticides because their internal organs are still developing, they spend more time playing outside, are more likely to play at ground level, put their hands in their mouths more often, and may not wash their hands consistently.

Several recent studies in various parts of the United States found that nearly 85% of schools were treated with pesticides, with no notification or vacancy requirement prior to spraying. Some of the pesticides used have the potential to cause short-term or long-term health effects, including vomiting, diarrhoea, convulsions, headaches, skin irritations, liver damage, neurological problems, and behavioural and emotional disturbances (The World Health Organization, n.d.). Pesticides can "drift" from far lands or golf courses to nearby properties and they can also be tracked indoors on shoes and stroller wheels. Green spaces where children play should be free of pesticides. (CPCHE, 2010)

PLANTS

It is important for educators to learn which plants are poisonous, and which are not. Your regional Poison Control Centre, and local library, are reliable sources of information. *The Canadian Poisonous Plants Information System* website

http://www.cbif.gc.ca/pls/pp/poison

is also a helpful resource. If there is any doubt, always assume a plant is highly toxic. Teach children never

to eat nonfood plants (either indoors or outdoors). Prepare for emergencies—be aware of the Poison Control Centre in your community and have the contact information posted in the centre. If directed to your local hospital, take the plant or part of it with you (Humber Nursery, 2011).

EXTENDING THE GROWING SEASON

Children at Winchester, Rose, and Gabrielle-Roy public schools put up hoop houses made of telephone wire, hula hoops and thick clear plastic to extend the growing season. See pictures of their efforts at

http://www.kidsgrowing.ca/wiki/wiki.php

DOCUMENTING YOUR GARDEN

Track your school garden's growth through photos, student artwork, poems, and a journal. Create and display a calendar of gardening activities: planting dates, special events, volunteer schedules, etc.

Keep your garden in the spotlight by sharing photos, accomplishments, and milestones in the school newsletter and on bulletin boards, and by holding harvest celebrations. Let your local media know about your successes. Older children can create a garden journal; take photos of the planting and various stages of development; write up what each plant needs (i.e., full sun, shade); date planted; when harvested and the days of growth; observations of the process; whether planted in rows or hills; pests that bothered the plant and steps taken to prevent pest damage; colour, size, and weight of harvested plant, etc.

ACCOMMODATIONS

A half wine barrel and window boxes for children in wheelchairs are generally the right height for easy access when planting and growing in containers.

For people who see limited numbers of colours, composition and contrast become key. Many people who are colour-blind in the most common ways can see a single shade of blue or yellow, plus black and white most vividly. Colours like red and green are visible, but often look alike or lack subtleties in tone and for many people greens can take on kind of a muddy appearance. White shows up with boldness against most types of foliage as do yellows and blues. (North Coast Gardening, 2010)

Walkways with contrasting textures will provide cues for entry into another play area. Clearly defining garden boundaries with lumber or bricks is helpful for children who are visually impaired. Growing plants with interesting textures, scents, and colour variations provides a sensory experience for all children.

> Planting herbs that when crushed release aromas as well as fruit trees, jasmine, lemon blossoms etc. add an important element to the garden for those who are visually impaired. Plan also for texture, plants with furry leaves, grasses, curly edges etc. Add a bird bath or bird feeders that will lure birds to the garden. The children will be able to hear the bird calls. The partially sighted can often see tools and pots that are painted yellow. This is why international warning signs are painted in yellow because they can be seen in reduced light and visibility. Braille printers will print out the names of plants onto plastic self-adhesive tape which can be applied. Steps can be replaced with shallow ramps and you can indicate changes in level by using a change of paving texture that is significant enough to be felt through shoes. The blind need to feel free to touch safely and explore. Plant in groups that are large enough to withstand a little damage.* (Minter, 1993, p. 116)

A trickling fountain, the rustle of trees or clumping bamboo, and birds foraging all contribute

---

*From *The Healing Garden: A Practical For Emotional Well Being* by *Sue Minter*. Published by *Eden Project Books*. Reprinted by Permission of The Random House Group Limited.

to a sense of life in the garden. Remember that every human experiences colour differently so ask questions and listen to the children's descriptions of what they see.

CRITTERS IN THE GARDEN

For Additional Photos

Many home remedies exist for insects that may invade your garden. Water and soap sprays are very effective and the children will be keen to volunteer to apply this treatment. Pairing certain plants can sometimes help to keep pests away. Marigolds are said to prevent both flying insects and those in the soil when planted near other plants. Local garden centres can provide specific advice about companion plants.

It is also possible to use insects to get rid of unwanted insects. Ladybugs will eat aphids and are attracted to your garden if you plant Queen Anne's lace, cosmos, daisy, fennel, butterfly weed, nasturtium, marigold, goldenrod, etc. Ladybugs can be purchased from garden centres and kept in the refrigerator to keep them dormant until you are ready to use them. They are most active at night, feeding and laying eggs that will hatch within a week. First water the foliage of the infested plants, then sprinkle a few ladybugs on the soil beneath the plants. You can release some ladybugs every day or two over a

---

Inside LOOK

The Benefits of a Garden

Wriggly worms, purple potatoes and ladybugs were but a few of the discoveries that were found in our Children's Garden at Casa Loma Child Care Centre. In our first year, our garden provided us with many opportunities for learning, not only for the children but for the staff as well. The look of awe and surprise when the children uncovered their first worm, or when they harvested their first tomato or dug up their first purple potato, made it very clear how far removed many of our children were from the natural world. The garden gave us so many wonderful hands-on learning opportunities that helped our children develop a clearer understanding of and respect for insects and worms and the role they played in our garden. From the worm composting bin we set up in our room, to the ladybugs we released in the garden as a natural method of pest control, to the food we prepared with the harvested vegetables, the garden provided us with endless learning opportunities. Our garden also had the unexpected benefit of providing many children the opportunity to work off busy energy as they happily did the heavy work of filling up watering cans and walked back and forth to ensure all the plants received enough water. And last but not least the garden also promoted parent involvement, as each and every day many of the children excitedly and proudly would take their parents by the hand and lead them to the garden to share some new discovery that they had made.

Contributed by: Laura de Vries (RECE) Casa Loma Child Care Centre, George Brown College

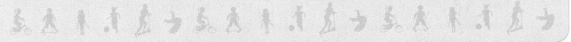

one-week period to ensure good coverage. Green lacewings also have great appetites for other insects.

To take action to minimize the need for insect repellents.

- Remove any stagnant/standing water to prevent mosquitoes from breeding.
- When serving sweet foods such as juices and fruits outdoors, keep children's hands clean and clean up spills quickly to avoid attracting stinging insects.

Releasing ladybugs

The Bug Hotel, Allegro Child Care Centre, Halifax, Nova Scotia

- Keep garbage containers and compost bins tightly sealed and away from play areas. **(CPCHE, 2010)**

GARDEN ALLIES

There are also many critters in the garden that are fun to find and learn more about. Bees are amazing creatures and critical to the pollination of plants. The bees that visit our gardens are all females—the worker bees—and the ones that sting! These bees will sting only when they are afraid, and they die afterward. The male bees, or drones, stay back in the hive to be with the queen. Teach the children to move slowly around the bees; if you have a child who is allergic to bees be sure not to plant flowers or shrubs that attract bees (Starbuck, Olthof, & Midden, 2002).

Spiders are not only good for garden predators; they are fascinating subjects for study. Their intricately designed webs are marvels of geometry, and their ability to wrap their prey with silk before feasting makes them especially engaging to young children. Some spiders are poisonous while others like daddy longlegs are not. Handle spiders with care. Identifying poisonous and non-poisonous spiders will be a good research project for interested older children. Frogs and toads are great eaters and will help to keep down the insect and slug population in your garden. Most snakes are also welcome visitors but again, some

TABLE 6.1	Critters in Our Gardens
CREATURE	**BENEFITS**
Dragonflies	Eat midges, mites and mosquitoes
Earthworms	Create passageways that carry air and moisture to plants roots. Their waste contains valuable plant nutrients.
Frogs and toads	Eat cutworms, larvae, maggots, mosquitoes, and slugs
Ground beetles	Munch on cutworms, maggots, slugs, and snails at night
Ladybugs	Eat aphids, fleas, and other microscopic bad insects
Praying mantises	Eat aphids, some caterpillars and whiteflies
Spiders	Regularly crave pest larvae and insect eggs

Source: Richardson, 1998, p. 92

are poisonous so you will have to know the particulars of your own area.

For information on natural insect control consult

 http://www.naturalinsectcontrol.com and http://www.omafra.gov.on.ca/IPM/english

EATING THE GARDEN

"Living with awareness of oneness with all aspects of life—including each other and food—lies at the heart of enlightened eating and the mystery of food's ability to nourish both body and soul. By approaching food meditatively and with loving intention, we may go beyond the level of thought and intuit the sacred connection between Mother Earth, food and humankind."

—Deborah Kesten, *Feeding the Body, Nourishing the Soul* (quoted in Sinclair, 2005, p. 28)

For Additional Photos

Gardening allows children to make the connection between the earth and the food they eat. They see the transformation from a single seed that they nurture and care for to the plant that they harvest and eat.

Magnifying glasses allow for a close-up look!

This cook is using food grown in the garden for the children's lunches.

Organic gardening and farming methods affect our health, economic systems, and environment. Get your older children to think about the impact their gardening choices can have on the earth and how those choices can affect the health of future generations. (Richardson, 1998, p. 44)

There are so many ways to prepare the harvest. It is also an opportunity to really examine the fruits of their labour.

Simple recipes such as cream cheese and chives are best for younger children while school-agers are ready for more complex instructions and can create delicious treats such as butters with herbs, herb mayonnaise, mint tea, oils, vinegars, soup served in a pumpkin tureen, jams, cold cucumber soup, pea soup, squash soup, tomato salads, etc. They can work with the centre's cook or interested family member.

Visiting local markets at harvest time may also expose the children to new and interesting fruits and vegetables.

HARVESTING HERBS

Herbs can be enjoyed year round by preserving them when they are in full bloom.

The herbs that dry best are thyme, rosemary, bay, marjoram and sage. Pick herbs on a dry morning when the dew has evaporated and choose growth that is in bud but has not yet produced flowers. You can hang them up to dry in a warm, airy place out of direct sunlight or lay them on a tray covered with muslin for a few days until they are dry but retain their greenness. When the herbs are dry, wrap them whole in paper and store in a drawer or a dry but dark larder. You can also crumble them up to save space, discard the

EXHIBIT 6.2   Twenty-Five Cookbooks for Children

1. **I Can Cook: How-to-Cook Activity Projects for the Very Young** by Sarah Maxwell
2. **Hey Kids! You're Cooking Now! A Global Awareness Cooking Adventure** by Dianne Pratt
3. **Chicken Soup for the Soul: Kids in the Kitchen: Tasty Recipes and Fun Activities for Budding Chefs** by Jack Canfield
4. **Real Cooking for Kids: Inside Out Spaghetti, Lucky Duck and More Recipes for the Junior Chef** by Rob Seideman
5. **Super Snacks** by Bobbie Kalman
6. **The Usborne Children's Cookbook** by Rebecca Gilpin
7. **The International Cook Book for Kids** by Mathew Locricchio
8. **Cooking in a Can: More Campfire Recipes for Kids** by Katherine White
9. **Cooking Art: Easy Edible Art for Young Children** by Mary Ann Kohl
10. **The Children's Kitchen Garden** by Georgeanne & Ethel Brennan
11. **The Children's Baking Book** by Denise Smart
12. **Healthy Lunchboxes for Kids** by Amanda Grant
13. **The Toddler Cookbook** by Annabel Karmel
14. **Cook It Together** by Annabel Karmel
15. **Kids' Fun and Healthy Cookbook** by Nicola Graimes
16. **The Kids Cook Book: Recipes from Around the World** by McRae Books
17. **The Kids Multicultural Cook Book: Food and Fun Around the World** by Deanna Cook
18. **Little Monsters Cookbook** by Zac Williams
19. **The Science Chef: 100 Fun Food Experiments and Recipes for Kids** by Joan D'Amico
20. **Kids Around the World Cook! The Best Foods and Recipes From Many Lands** by Arlette Braman
21. **Kids' First Cookbook: Delicious Nutritious Treats to Make Yourself** by American Cancer Society
22. **Children's Quick and Easy Cookbook** by Angela Wilkes
23. **Kitchen for Kids: 100 Amazing Recipes Your Children Can Really Make** by Jennifer Low
24. **The Star Wars Cook Book II: Darth Malt and More Galactic Recipes** by Frankie Fankeny
25. **What's in the Garden?** by Marianne Berkes & Cris Arbo

---

woodier stems and then bottle them. Keep the bottles in a dark place as light will destroy the flavour of the herbs. Another way of preserving herbs is to freeze them. This is a particularly good method for parsley, fennel and dill which do not dry well. Tarragon sprigs also freeze well. When freezing large-leaved basil, pick individual leaves and freeze them in small freezer bags. If you have a large ice-making compartment, you can produce a ready supply of herb ice-cubes by chopping the herbs, adding a little water and freezing the mixtures.* (Minter, 1993, p. 78)

CHOOSING HEALTHY SEEDS FOR NEXT YEAR

To decide what plant seeds to select, look at the whole plant and consider the following characteristics:

- **Colour**—select seeds from plants with healthy, vibrant colour

- **Earliness**—save seeds from plants that produce fruits or vegetables earlier than others

- **Drought resistance**—plants that require little water or that can weather spells of dry weather

- **Disease resistance**—choose seeds from plants that hold up under certain diseases and still produce a healthy harvest

- **Hardiness**—save seeds from plants that hold up under changing weather condition, including high winds, arid heat and chilly nights

- **Insect resistance**—save seeds from plants that have developed a resistance to insects

- **Lateness to bolt**—many early spring plants go to seed once the warm weather arrives. Look for early spring plants that can still grow in the heat without bolting quickly

- **Uniformity**—look for uniform qualities that you want to encourage and are worth saving

- **Vigor**—examine the plants from top to bottom and save the best

- **Flavour**—save seeds from the plants that taste the best

*From *The Healing Garden: A Practical For Emotional Well Being* by *Sue Minter*. Published by *Eden Project Books*. Reprinted by Permission of The Random House Group Limited.

- **Productivity**—save seeds from the most prolific producers
- **Shape**—many children will not eat fruit with bumps, ridges, dips and scars. Save seeds that produce fruits or vegetables that have pleasing shapes
- **Storage ability**—save seeds from plants that store better over the winter

Before storing them, seeds must be dried since moisture will rot the seeds and render them useless. Once they have been thoroughly dried, store the seeds in a moisture proof, airtight container. Store the seeds in a freezer or refrigerator or a very cool place. Label the containers.* (Richardson, 1998, p. 145)

TOOLS AND THEIR STORAGE

For Additional Photos

It is important for children to have the opportunity to use real tools. Many manufacturers now make child-size tools that the children will enjoy using; see Lee Valley Tools at

www http://www.leevalley.ca

*Reprinted with permission from *Gardening with Children* by Beth Richardson, published by The Taunton Press, Inc. (www.taunton.com).

Lynn Wilson

Child-size tools help children engage more fully in a gardening experience.

Store tools in an accessible manner; if you use a shed, keep it secured.

Sharon Lovejoy (2003, pp. 4–11) has wonderful ideas for organization, caring for tools and plants and clean up:

- To remove salt residue from crusty pots and to clean dirty tools, scrub with a mixture of 1/3 white vinegar, 1/3 rubbing alcohol, and 1/3 water.

Inside LOOK

Gardens That Inspire

There are many gardens worldwide that would inspire any educator. Michigan's *4H Children's Garden* at Michigan State University in East Lansing has 60 theme gardens, making it among the most creative American children's playscapes. It has a dinosaur garden, an Alice in Wonderland Maze, a Jack and the Beanstalk garden with giant plants, and a Peter Rabbit garden. *George Washington's River Farm* in Alexandria, Virginia, has 10 children's demonstration gardens including an alphabet garden with wooden letters with A for aster to Z for zinnia. *Veronica's Maze* in Parham Park, England, is an engaging garden space.

Inside LOOK

Veggie Village, Royal Botanical Gardens, Burlington, Ontario

Visitors to the gardens can sign a "100 Mile Veggie Pledge" agreeing to use one locally grown ingredient in one meal per week for a year.

For Additional Photos

- Worn out toothbrushes make great scrubbers for small cleanup tasks.

- Oil jobs—fill a used lotion or hand soap dispenser bottle with mineral oil. Squirt the oil onto metal tools every time you use them, or any time you need to remove sticky sap, grime or sawdust. Then wipe tools with fine steel wool.

- Attach a soap dish with soap and a nail brush near your water source.

- Use old serving pieces as digging and transplanting tools.

- [Use] wire whisks or an old egg beater to whip up potions and brews.

- Use clothes pins and paper clips when harvesting herbs, garlic, onions, flowers, use pins to sort and clip them into bunches

- Give new life to mateless or holey old socks. Cut the foot off and slip the uppers over your wrists to protect your arms from small cuts and your shirts from dirt and damage. They're especially good when you're working around berries and roses.

- Store a roll of string inside an upside-down terra-cotta pot and pull the string end through the hole.

- Hang a role of Velcro tape on a nail. Use the Velcro for quick and easy adjustable tie-ups of vines, shrubs, and veggies.

- Collect flat river stones and use them to name the plants with markers.* (Lovejoy, 2003, pp. 4–11)

BRINGING THE OUTSIDE INSIDE

There are many opportunities to bring the materials found or grown outside into the playroom to provide children with another opportunity to explore in greater depth. Plants inside the playroom also benefit those who work and play there. Creating large sand areas in the playroom also extends the play. Outdoor projects can be celebrated both outdoors and indoors!

For Additional Photos

Lynn Wilson

A sunny window is all that is needed for an indoor garden.

---

*Excerpted from *Trowel and Error: Over 700 Shortcuts, Tips and Remedies for the Gardener*. © 2003 by Sharon Lovejoy. Workman Publishing, New York. pp. 4–11. Used by permission of Workman Publishing Co., Inc., New York. All Rights Reserved.

Inside LOOK

School Community Garden Success Stories

Winchester School Community Garden is one of *Green Thumbs, Growing Kids'* most successful school gardening projects. What began as a composting program that involved staff and families is now a full blown garden with peas, beans, tomatoes, potatoes, salad greens, herbs and much more growing in a space once used for portable classrooms. The children harvest and eat their produce with a fresh Salad Bar two days a week. Students who participate in the Garden Club at the school are responsible for all aspects of maintaining the garden. Over the summer months, Green Thumbs Growing Kids runs special programs for local children and their families and encourages youth groups to help with the maintenance of the garden while learning more about horticultural skills.

In June 2012, Dr. Roberta Bondar, Astronaut, Scientist, and leader in Environmental Education spoke at the launch of *Imagine a Garden in Every School* project at Rose Avenue Public School in Toronto.

(continued)

© Green Thumbs Growing Kids http//www.kidsgrowing.ca

Winchester School Community Garden

Across Ontario, thousands of students, teachers and community members are doing great work to create school food gardens that connect children and youth with nature and fresh food. The goal of Imagine a Garden in Every School is to link these groups together to share resources, ideas, experiences and stories (successes and roadblocks) as well as resources and information that will make it easier for people across Ontario to start and maintain school food gardens.

Inside LOOK

Ossington/Old Orchard Public School

In the mid-1980s, a group of parents approached school principal Ted Curry with an ambitious vision: concerned about the lack of green space available at their children's school, they proposed a transformation of the vast, feature-less expanse of pavement that stretched between Ossington and Old Orchard Public Schools. Curry, whose background included experience in outdoor education as principal of the Island Public School, joined in the parents' early exploratory conversations on school-ground greening, and assisted in taking their inquiries to the area superintendent and, eventually, to the Board. The Board granted its approval to the proposed relandscaping project on condition that the school community itself raise all the funds. The Board also obtained the assistance of the Learnxs Foundation to sponsor the project. The parents, two of whom were landscape architects, formed a gardening committee and set to work. "Once they got the okay, they just ran with it; their enthusiasm was infectious," recalled Curry. "They had all the ideas, sought a phenomenal number of grants, made plans, got contacts and donations, and did it in phases. It took two to three years. With the asphalt surface removed, the ambitious and complex plan slowly became a reality. The central portion of the former pavement was made into a grassy playing field. The slopes of the school's ravine setting, once the banks of Toronto's now buried Garrison Creek, were partly naturalized with native plants and partly terraced to provide a series of garden plots for the students. An orchard was planted to honour the site's farming-community roots, trees were added to provide shade and variety, and the students wove twig baskets around the trunks to protect the tree through their early years. An "aviary" of shrubs was planted along one edge to provide food, shelter and habitat for birds and butterflies. As one of the first major gardening projects in Toronto, Ossington's success has inspired many other schools. A key component of the Ossington parents' vision was to make the garden an integral part of the school community. "'They involved the staff, so that every classroom would have a plot," Curry noted. The Garden Committee has its own fund, holds an annual bake sale, popcorn days and a "vine sale" in the school corridor, where paper vine leaves can be purchased for a dollar each by garden supporters. At regular school-funding events, the committee sells garden mugs and T-shirts that feature its logo of nesting birds. (Houghton, 2003, pp. 31–33)

For Additional Photos

William Quesner

Children's artwork: William

Chapter 7

THE ROLE OF THE EDUCATOR

OUTCOMES:

1. Examine the ways in which educators can support play in outdoor playscapes.
2. Discuss the value of emergent curriculum.
3. Discuss the barriers for educators in the use of outdoor play.
4. Evaluate strategies for educators in providing positive outdoor experiences.

PLAY AND THE ROLE OF THE EDUCATOR

In her book *The Sense of Wonder* (1956), Rachel Carson wrote, "If a child is to keep alive his inborn sense of wonder … he needs the companionship of at least one adult who can share it, rediscovering with him the joy, excitement and mystery of the world we live in" (p. 45).

Play is the context in which children make sense of the world. In a play-based curriculum, adults participate in play, guiding children's planning, decision making and communication, and extending children's exploration with narrative, novelty, and challenges. Because we know that play-based curriculum encourages learning through interaction with objects, people, and information, adults engage in meaningful interaction with children that includes appropriate reinforcement for children's achievements; questions that promote thought, expanded thinking, and problem solving; and conversations that include child-led narratives. Adults enter play and may model new actions to extend play and challenge the child.

> Without continuous hands-on experience, it is impossible for children to acquire a deep intuitive understanding of the natural world that is the foundation of sustainable development.… A critical aspect of the present-day crisis in education is that children are becoming separated from daily experience of the natural world, especially in larger cities. (Moore & Wong, 1997, p. 5)

But simply providing time outside is not enough. The quality of the provision and its accessibility also needs to be carefully considered.

> Children need to be exploring and manipulating their environment every day. If children only get periodic experience of something it is unlikely they will move on in their acquisition of skills; they will spend time simply retreading old skills which is pointless and they are more likely to have accidents.* (Bilton, 2010, p. 33)

Wasserman (1992) states that

> play allows children to make discoveries that go far beyond the realm of what we adults think is important to know … with play, we teachers can have it all: the development of knowledge,

---

*Bilton, H. 2010. *Outdoor Learning In The Early Years. Management And Innovation*. Routledge Taylor And Francis Group. p. 33.

Inside LOOK

Adam Bienenstock

Adam Bienenstock is an award-winning consultant on design, construction, policy, risk and regulatory process for connecting children to nature in our cities.

Contact with nature should NOT be considered a "tool" for ECEs to use to engage children. Connection to nature must be woven into the fabric of everything we do as educators because it is fundamental to optimal child development. Tokenism is not good enough. It is our job as educators of young children to provide them with the best pedagogical approach to maximize their advancement while in our care. There is already ample research to prove that engagement with the natural world is the best possible single intervention to positively affect every area of child development. When contact with nature is made a part of growing up, test scores go up for physical and mental health, motor skills, emotional and social well-being, and yes, IQ scores increase as well. We are hard-wired for this on an evolutionary scale. If you are an ECE, you are obligated to make nature core to your children's experience. The good news is that this works on grown-ups too. According to the research, you will be a happier, healthier, smarter, more effective teacher in the process. See http://www.naturalplaygrounds.ca

of a spirit of inquiry, of creativity, of conceptual understanding—all contributing to the true empowerment of children. (p. 133)

EMERGENT CURRICULUM

Emergent curriculum supports learning and development while respecting children's interests and choices. Emergent curriculum provides early childhood education with a framework to integrate knowledge about development and learning with specific information about individual children, their interests, temperaments, family values, and backgrounds (Gestwicki, 2007). Emergent curriculum provides the framework for child-centred, play-based curriculum to avoid the pitfalls of over structured and laissez faire approaches. Adults' plans respond to children's behaviour, emerging skills, and interests with achievable challenges. Adults' plans are open-ended, flexible, and responsive to children. Both adults and children are decision makers in the content and direction of curriculum. Adults observe and interpret children's behaviour, following the child's lead by observing his or her play, interests, strengths, and needs. Then adults interpret their observations and plan for learning and development. Adults identify the child's developmental and learning skills and plan strategies to support these in play-based curriculum. In this way, the content of play serves learning and development. These plans remain open to change and to new directions that may not have been part of the initial plan. While emergent curriculum is not always predictable, it has a structure that comes from the adults' knowledge and responses to children (Gestwicki, 2007). Emergent curriculum includes connections across curriculum from one area to another and one day to another. Emergent curriculum is created week by week and day by day rather than adults mapping out curriculum content months in advance or creating themes that hijack children's lead. Emergent curriculum focuses attention on curriculum that is personally meaningful to children because the child's construction of meaning is key to learning and motivation.

Emergent curriculum begins with observation of the children's play and the developmental tasks children are practising. Observation continues as the adult provides the environment, provokes interest, sustains children's play themes, enriches and extends play, and provides children with opportunities to represent the learning experience (Curtis & Carter, 1996). Adults also document their observations of the children's play, meaning-making, and learning. Children have opportunities to represent what they know. Adults provide an environment designed with the open-ended materials that enable all children to enter at their own level and discover what interests them. Adults spark interest by focusing attention with novel materials and strategies connected to children's learning and development. Adults sustain children's explorations with collections of related materials that provide the opportunity for children to make connections, create patterns, engage in repeated practice of skills, problem solve and explore in their own way.

Observing children, planning for children's learning and development, and negotiating curriculum content with children are all elements of emergent curriculum. These and the processes of emergent curriculum—observing, providing, sustaining, enriching, documenting, and representing—ensure that curriculum happens!

Inside LOOK

Using an Emergent Curriculum Approach

When I went to Teachers' College many years ago, we all learned how to develop a theme-based approach to curriculum. Over the years, by using an emergent curriculum approach instead, I found that teaching became much more meaningful to me. Instead of me planning a years' worth of themes in advance for approval from my supervisor, the children in my kindergarten program now lead the play. The difference to me as a teacher has been powerful: I am excited about learning alongside the children, and I really am seeing learning come alive.

For children in a school setting, the curriculum may be more structured, yet the benefits of outdoor experiences are highlighted in early years' curriculum as outlined in many Inside Look boxes throughout this text.

EDUCATORS' PERSPECTIVE ON OUTDOOR PLAY—WHAT THE RESEARCH SAYS

"We need a teacher who is sometimes the director, sometimes the set designer, sometimes the curtain and the backdrop, & sometimes the prompter, who dispenses the paints & who is even the audience—the audience who watches, sometimes claps, sometimes remains silent, full of emotion."

—Loris Malaguzzi (quoted in Rinaldi, 2006, p. 73)

Ruth Wilson (1984) argues that based on our evolutionary history we are naturally motivated to associate with other living things. Elizabeth Nisbet and her colleagues (2011) at Carleton University in Ottawa measured people's "nature relatedness." Nature relatedness encompasses a person's appreciation for and understanding of our interconnectedness to all living things. She and her colleagues found that nature relatedness was associated with happiness, autonomy, and personal growth in adults. People who related to nature reported having a sense of purpose in life and were more accepting of themselves. Nisbet and her colleagues argue that perhaps having an appreciation for nature helps us to understand how all life is interconnected and reminds us of our own vitality and purpose.

Susan Herrington (2008) presents the results of a study of early childhood educators' evaluations of the outdoor play space at their child care centres. They were asked what aspects were successful or unsuccessful, and what they would change about their outdoor play space if they could.

Outdoor play spaces with plants had significantly more positive responses, averaging 11 positive responses versus four for spaces without plants. Coding and analysis of interview notes found that 79 percent wanted more sensory stimuli, 64 percent wanted more space, and 57 percent desired more challenging equipment, suggesting

that these are important features in outdoor play spaces for young children. In addition, many participants identified an excess of concrete and asphalt which tended to create a hard cold place that was very loud and often lacking in colour. (Herrington, 2008, pp. 64–87)

Teachers' interactions will be influenced by the quality of the outdoor environment. DeBord et al. (2005) found that teacher behaviours more frequently supported and facilitated children's experiences on the playground when they worked in higher quality outdoor environments. Environmental psychology also offers evidence that greener, more beautiful landscapes favourably affect both children and teachers: stress fades, social interactions increase, and ability to think creatively increases. There is also greater opportunity for hands-on learning about nature and the creation of a sense of place, a place to call their own.

The impact of increased environmental professional development education was also felt by teachers who demonstrated more enthusiasm and greater engagement in their teaching (Strickland & Dempsey, 2009). They learned new subject material and were more willing to pursue new teaching methods. Studies suggest that there are significant changes in practitioners' attitudes and abilities after participating in specialized studies in outdoor play; practitioners posed more in-depth questions, extended opportunities for the child's knowledge base to be enhanced, and provided encouragement to the total group of children. Practitioners who are comfortable with outdoor play generally exhibit more smiling and positive contact with the children and offer more types of play experiences and time for outdoor play (ibid., 2009).

Most research on how nature experience can improve learning has been conducted with young people. But nature-smart education appears to work for everyone involved, including the teachers. A Canadian study showed that greening school grounds not only improved academic performance of students; it also lowered exposure to toxins and increased teachers' enthusiasm for being teachers, in part due to fewer classroom discipline problems.* (Louv, 2011, p. 29)

In a study of child care centres in London, Ontario, Tucker (2010) conducted research to gain insight into the barriers and facilitators to physical

---

*From THE NATURE PRINCIPLE by Richard Louv. © 2011 by Richard Louv. Reprinted by permission of Algonquin Books of Chapel Hill. p. 29.

activity at child care centres and the thoughts of the teachers. She found that barriers to engaging-preschoolers in physical activity included

- inadequate equipment—more money for materials needed
- insufficient space
- weather (dressing and undressing is time consuming)
- daycare policies (eliminating field trips, swimming, etc.)
- safety
- need for more workshops, specialty staff and resource manuals. (ibid.)

In some situations, staff complain that it just takes too long to set up the outdoor environment, which speaks to a badly designed playspace where storage is not easily accessible.

> The majority of early years staff are female but unfortunately outdoors is not a natural environment for many of them. They are, more often than not, keener to be involved in sedentary activities, which usually take place indoors. As a general rule, men tend to do the heavy, active, manual work, which usually takes place outdoors, and football and other sports activities are usually followed by men. It is therefore not only important that staff use the outdoors effectively but also work with children to challenge sex stereotypes and thereby help to challenge these gender-conforming attitudes. (Bilton, 2008, p. 93)

> Studies indicate that while adults may be responsive to and interactive with children in indoor settings, their interactions with children tend to be noticeably different while outdoors. While outdoors, teachers use more negative controls, are more sedentary and engage in less verbal interactions with children. (Bilton, 2008, p. 36)

Unfortunately, it is not uncommon for teachers to text on the playground or huddle together to talk rather than engage the children.

The reasons teachers don't want to spend time outdoors vary from

> "It is too cold, wet, windy, slippery for the children" to "it takes too much time to get ready and parents don't like their children wet, cold or dirty." More often than not it is the educators not the children who don't want to be out in all weathers. Educators who have a positive attitude to being out outdoors [sic] will not only enjoy the experience themselves, but will foster a sense of pleasure in the children as they explore and play together. (*One World for Children*, 2010)

Meaningful interactions happen in the outdoor playscape.

Remember: all that is required for the adults and the children to enjoy the outdoors in all kinds of weather is appropriate clothing! There is no such thing as bad weather, only bad clothing!

Rachel Carson (1956) noted in her book, *The Sense of Wonder* how feelings are more important than facts when introducing children to nature. She wrote, "I sincerely believe that for the child, and for the parent or teacher seeking to guide him, it is not half so important to know as to feel" (p. 45). Even though many of us work intimately with children, we can lose touch with the world through the eyes of the child. A practical strategy is to get down on the ground and look at the world from a child's perspective; what do you see, what do you hear, what can you feel? Try remembering outdoor experiences that you had as a child that were meaningful and significant to you. How can you try to recreate those experiences for the children you are working with? Whitebread (2000) argues that the best teachers use a repertoire of various styles and strategies, it is not the strategies they use which make the difference, but the skill with which they use them. At the centre, early childhood professionals should focus on encouraging gross motor activity during outdoor and whenever possible during indoor playtime. Taking the children into the community and using the outdoor resources available is an important learning opportunity. Dowda et al. (2004) found that children who attended daycares that participated in more field trips and had more college-educated teachers had children who participated in more active physical play (Tucker, 2008).

> "There is little that gives children greater pleasure than when a grown-up lets himself down to their level, renounces his oppressive superiority and plays with them as an equal."
>
> —Sigmund Freud

Young children who develop secure attachments to their teachers are less likely to engage in unregulated anger and behavior problems. They are also more likely to exhibit positive emotions in the school setting. A warm, close relationship between child and teacher, then, can positively influence young children's emerging emotional competence (Shields et al., 2001).

Ingrid Crowther

Relationships are key.

As educators, we have a unique responsibility to encourage not only the children but also their families in engaging in an active lifestyle. Encouragement can take the form of educational programs for parents related to physical activity, or changes to the centre's daily programming to foster more appropriate levels of physical activity. (Ogden et al., 1997)

Inside LOOK

An Environmental Parable

Marsha Yamamoto, former instruction leader of Toronto's *Environmental Education Department*, believes in the power of storytelling as a teaching tool. "I think any time you add a story to a lesson, people remember things better," she commented as she offered an environmental parable for teachers.

We're like a little schoolhouse in the middle of a forest. And what we've done is give our students all the skills and strategies for cognitive learning and for working together co-operatively. We've given them Math strategies for problem solving and writing skills to know how to read and write and become critical thinkers. But we haven't taught them about the environment they live in. We've closed all the windows and drawn the curtains and said, "It doesn't matter that this little schoolhouse is situated in the middle of this great forest. We don't want the kids to go outside. We have so much to teach in here." And meanwhile one corner of the forest has started to burn, while we continue to work in the same way, with a "business as usual" mentality. We never open the curtains. We never look outside. We never see the forest. It's one thing to do all this cognitive work, fostering the Math and Language skills and ways in which children can work together, but let's also learn about the very environment in which we live. There's a twofold reason for students going out into the environment rather than staying inside this small, enclosed schoolhouse. One is that they can explore, connect with and apply their skills and knowledge to the very mystery and majesty of the forest we are living in. The other is that the forest is beginning to burn, and it's no longer a choice about taking the kids out: we need to take them out in that forest now and help them learn how to do something about it.* (Houghton, 2003, p. 122)

---

*Houghton, E. 2003. *A Breath Of Fresh Air Celebrating Nature and School Gardens*. The Learnxs Foundation & Sumach Press, Toronto District School Board. p. 122. © E. Houghton.

ROLE OF THE MANAGER/ PRINCIPAL

> "Leadership is not so much about technique and methods as it is about opening the heart. Leadership is about inspiration—of oneself and of others."
>
> —Lance Secretan

Early childhood programs benefit from skilled management and leadership. The role of the manager has changed from traditional "sage on the stage" to non-traditional "guide on the side." The manager is the keystone to carrying the program's visions, purpose and philosophy forward. He or she can bring clarity or confusion, calm or chaos, stability or fragility to the daily lives of children, their families and the staff team. (Bertrand, 2008, pp. 214–215)

A leader is a person to whom others turn to for direction, inspiration, moral authority and support; someone we trust to guide us towards a shared future and the ability to "paint" an inspiring picture of what the outdoor space may become. A positive organizational climate, which includes opportunities for caregivers to be involved in decision making, creates a coherent administrative framework to support caregivers in centres. With any new initiative, some teachers will embrace change while others will adopt a wait and see approach. The good manager will empower staff at all levels to display leadership and involve and engage team members in building the vision. He or she should also encourage staff to voice their beliefs and acknowledge others' passions and contributions, being respectful of different beliefs and approaches.

A philosophy statement is where it all begins. Bringing all staff, families, and volunteers together to discuss the goals and procedures for the outdoor environment is an important beginning. See Chapter 4 in the discussion about the design of the outdoor space the many questions and answers about how the playscape should be created will help to support the development of a philosophy statement. Most importantly, the manager must "model the way" and be actively and visibly involved, speaking openly and passionately about the outdoor space and how it will make a real difference in the lives of not only the children and their families but also the educators. There are many practical plans that need to be in place and the manager, in collaboration with staff, will establish schedules and program plans for outdoor play that meets the needs, strengths, and interests of the children and eliminates large groups of children outside at any given time. This will guarantee that appropriate staffing is in place to ensure a safe outdoor playscape and that "hot spots" are carefully supervised. The manager will also be responsible for overseeing that all safety precautions are taken to ensure the safety of the children by carrying out daily checks of the play equipment and looking for exposed or projecting elements; deteriorating wood, broken or missing railings, steps, or swing seats; warping, pinching actions (seesaws); loose or uncapped bolts; metal slides in the direct sun; exposed or damaged concrete footings; improperly anchored equipment, poor drainage (standing water); and elements in need of repair. The manager will ensure that items are replaced or repaired when required.

Seasonal maintenance is also important. Although the manager and educators will instruct the children on the safe use of each piece of outdoor equipment, all adults will need to be constantly alert to playground hazards, reporting and repairing them as soon as possible.

Another consideration for managers and educators is the environment in which the early childhood program is located. Many will be located in a school setting, which requires a real collaborative connection between all players. Often school outdoor environments do not lend themselves to young children so renovations and community involvement will be critical in transforming these playscapes so that they are appropriate for both younger and older children. This is an opportunity for all stakeholders to come together to build partnerships as well as redesign the physical environment. Collaboration will ensure that guidelines and rules for behaviour on the playscape are consistent across all programs and that an enthusiastic and informed approach to outdoor experiences is shared. This is a wonderful opportunity for dedicated teamwork in supporting positive experiences for all children.

ENGAGING EDUCATORS

> "Our image of children no longer considers them as isolated and egocentric, does not only see them as engaged in action with objects, does not emphasize only the cognitive aspects, does not belittle feelings or what is not logical and does not consider with ambiguity the role of the reflective domain. Instead our image of the child is rich in potential, strong, powerful, competent and, most of all, connected to adults and children."
>
> —Loris Malaguzzi

BEING OPEN TO CHANGE

In the foreword to Jim Greenman's book—*Caring Spaces, Learning Places*—Reggio Emilia educator Lella Gandini states

> We have all experienced how even a small improvement in a learning space can reverberate in positive ways, but we have also learned that one cannot stop there. It is the value that we attribute to the potentials of children and our respect for their learning as individuals and as groups that can truly create a shift in our teaching, transforming us from being "only" teachers to being true listeners and learners. It is then that the space we create will be affected in a powerful way.[*] (Greenman, 2007, p. vii)

BE BRAVE

Educators' attitudes, understanding and commitment, comfort, confidence, and competence are all crucial aspects of successful outdoor experiences. In Canada, our "difficult" climate actually provides a wonderfully rich and dynamic environment for exploration, play, and discussion. But one of the most underutilized areas of early learning environments is the outdoor playscape in winter. Winter provides enormous opportunities to explore, experiment, and engage in meaningful play yet not all educators will have had an extensive background in outdoor play experiences in Canada. Many will come from climates where snow was unheard of. Despite our varying experiences we have an obligation to provide a positive outdoor learning environment for young children in all seasons. For many, this will be an opportunity to learn alongside the children. During the colder months children are often restricted to playing indoors at home, so it is essential that they are provided with plenty of opportunities for outdoor play when they are in their early learning environments. We need to start by generating the positive kind of thinking that sees rain and snow as resources rather than a hindrance!

Anja Geelen is the creator, editor, and author of the *Little Eyes on Nature Blog*

http://eyesonnature.blogspot.com

She is also the principal of Tawa Montessori Preschool, a small preschool in Wellington, and Little Earth Montessori Kapiti, a new enviro Montessori preschool in Kapiti, both in Aotearoa (New Zealand). She makes a valuable contribution about the role of the teacher in outdoor environments.

> Many a times I have been talking to teachers who are disheartened with their outdoor environment but fear that a change into a more natural environment may not work. And so they refrain from making changes, withholding the children in their care from experiencing the touch of grass under their feet, the scent of lavender up their noses or the sound of tui [a bird] in their ears. Changing your outdoor environment into a naturalized outdoor classroom can be an enormous leap of faith. You cannot necessarily see the outcome of your work, it will take time before the peaceful, serene, outdoor nature classroom reveals itself. Just like children need to see, feel, touch, smell, and hear in order to understand, so will the teacher have to experience the sense of wonder and awe before they can be sure of their decision to put away the traditional substitutes in their outdoor environment. An outdoor environment, full of rubber matting and plastic toys interferes with the pleasure and joys of natural objects like logs, rocks and sand. Visit outdoor classrooms, natural environments and nature playscapes. Talk to teachers who have made the transition, the ones whose love of children and nature is apparent in every action, the ones who share the sense of wonder when watching a worm digging the earth.[**] (Little Eyes On Nature, 2011)

---

[*](Greenman, J. 2007. *Caring Spaces, Learning Places Children's Environments That Work*. Exchange Press Inc. p. vii.

[**]© Tawa Montessori

BE A ROLE MODEL

> "Unless someone like you cares a whole awful lot, Nothing is going to get better. It's not."
>
> —Dr. Seuss

The teacher's interactions with the children are critical. There are new strategies to learn, new expectations required and old approaches to let go of. The teacher should be a facilitator—a person who makes things happen for children! You must be a role model of interest and curiosity. Your enthusiasm is absolutely essential if you want the children to respond in a positive way. Being not only enthusiastic but having that sense of wonder that Rachel Carson spoke so eloquently about is essential. Chawla (2007) states that

> as children gradually become attentive to the interests of their role model, a caregiver who demonstrated environmental stewardship (e.g. enjoyment of nature, concern for the land as a limited resource, disapproval of harmful behaviour) guided children's interests towards environmentalism and satisfied the children's need for emotional support to confidently explore nature. (p. 148)

> Children have an inborn drive to explore their world, but they learn attitudes about it from the people around them—whether something is "yucky" or interesting, for example. If the important adults in their lives love to be outside and look with awe at interesting animals and plants, children will learn the importance of respecting nature. Rather than teaching children specific facts about nature at this stage, we should be encouraging their natural curiosity. (Miller, 1999, p. 195)

Talk about your experiences in the out of doors; what excited you as a child? Talk about how these experiences made you feel and what you learned. As you delight in these stories, the children will also want to share theirs. Look for those teachable moments that have a significant impact on the children. Talking to children about taking care of the Earth is far less effective than demonstrating simple ways of expressing care. So be prepared to practise what you preach; for example, if you get involved in the community for environmental events, share this with the children; if you believe that litter has a negative impact on the environment, make sure that you have recycling bins in the room; if you believe that all living things

This teacher actively engages the children, and they invite her into their play.

need to be protected, then show the children how gentle they need to be with critters you encounter in the outdoor environment. You may want to talk about how you overcame your fear of spiders when you got to know more about how they survive in nature and the intricate webs they weave. When things don't go well—for example, when vandalism occurs—share your optimism with the children and begin again. Be willing to search for

Experimentation is an important element in outdoor play.

answers; you won't know all there is to know but you can encourage the children to be researchers. Provide an abundance of books, Internet resources, gardening magazines, seed catalogues, DVDs, and other appropriate resource materials. Take the children to local experts who can help them solve their problems. The children will learn naturally when they are excited and committed to finding the answers to their questions. Let the children lead the way, even when you know they are heading in the "wrong" direction. This is part of the process of exploration. Scientific concepts are learned in the out of doors; trying to understand why a leaf has white spots and is turning brown, why the rabbits keep eating the lettuce, and why the squirrels love to dig up their bulbs are all part of the magic of discovery for young children.

Many factors play a role in the development of a child's ecological self: where she lives, the socioeconomic status of her family, her cultural background and ethnic group values, age, educational experiences, etc. As teachers, we can make a significant contribution to the development of a child's ecological identity. It is critical to encourage children to use their senses as young naturalists by noticing and describing the characteristics, behaviours, and needs of living things in their natural environments. Model this by making these experiences nonthreatening by being patient, accepting divergent comments and answers, and allowing children to control the timing and tempo of the experience, for example, by

- Turning over rocks and logs to look for animals
- Handling plants and animals with great care and respect
- Wondering aloud if you will see bugs or worms in the same places you found them last time
- Looking closely at plants and commenting on interesting features
- Considering why a plant may not be thriving
- Asking children to comment on changes they see in the plants
- Comparing one plant to another or one bug to another
- Engaging in recycling and appropriate disposal of garbage.

Inside LOOK

The Wonders of Nature

I carefully wrapped my fingers around a mess of sticks, mud and grass and lowered my treasure to the viewing height of my young audience. "It's a nest!" one participant exclaimed proudly. As I leaned the cup-shaped structure toward more eager faces to display the construction inside, another student queried, "What's a nest?" Her wonder and bewilderment opened my eyes to see, as Wendell Berry observed, that many of our children no longer directly experience "reading the great book of Nature."

I'm privileged to work with a TDSB teaching and learning community that also believes that direct experiences in the outdoors are essential for young children to learn to read the book of Nature.

Through no-mow zones, beautiful gardens, and outdoor education opportunities, TDSB teachers and school communities are giving our students opportunities to explore, experiment, discover, and play in rich and diverse outdoor settings.

The benefits for our young students are immediately apparent. Schoolyards have become a setting for asking questions and uncovering answers through discovery and guided inquiry. Students are finding more interesting places for dramatic and active play. Teachers are using their outdoor classrooms to engage students in hands-on learning activities about how nature works and how we depend on its resources. And after one young student said to me, "Miss, I know what those leaf bumps are, they've got insects inside. I've been studying these trees longer than you," I knew she had indeed been reading the great book of Nature.

Pam Miller, Instructional Leader, Sustainability Office

ENCOURAGE A POSITIVE SELF CONCEPT AND SELF-ESTEEM

A major goal in our work with young children is to promote a positive self concept, to enhance their self-esteem, and provide outdoor experiences that help every child be successful in their own right. We need to provide genuine praise and encouragement as children attempt difficult and challenging experiences by supporting their skill development over time. By providing a safe and nonthreatening environment, we encourage children to try. By providing structured and nonstructured experiences and ensuring fun rather than competition, children will feel secure in your care.

Rinaldi (2000) points out that each child creates her own meaning but is truly supported to do so when peers and adults validate her competence. The development of a self-concept that is strong, outgoing, and confident becomes part of this meaning making when the child is surrounded by warm reciprocal relationships.

KNOW HOW TO PLAY

Children will always learn more from what we do than what we say. Wilson (2008, p. 43) says that

> children watch us for information about what is valued, sacred and important in life. The attitudes and values that children see reflected in the lives of their parents and teachers tend to be the attitudes and values they'll carry with them throughout life. The adult's own sense of wonder—more than his or her scientific knowledge—is what will ignite and sustain a child's love of nature. Teachers should guard against taking leadership away from the children or influencing the children to follow their lead rather than initiating or creating for themselves.

Teachers should understand exactly why they are engaging in the children's play and how their involvement will scaffold the experience. Less is always best! Let the children lead the play.

When children are frustrated by their projects or with each other, teachers should be on hand to provide support, encouragement, and encourage a problem-solving approach that comes during a discussion with the children rather than the teacher solving the problem for them. Be prepared for a child who does not want to participate. He or she may need more time to observe and gradually enter into play or not. It is important to recognize the nature of each individual child in our group—the eager beavers and the shy and withdrawn. When

the play becomes objectionable—for example, racist comments or negative stereotypes are evident in the children's play—the teacher should engage in the play in a more appropriate manner. Educators will exercise their judgment about when and how to intervene to prevent harm to children without unnecessarily disrupting their play. Skilled educators often act as confidants when children are troubled or unhappy. For many children, they become significant adults, offering alternative role models, and different ideas from those they might encounter at home or school. These relationships may be particularly important for older children whose home lives and social contact are restricted by poverty and deprivation (National Playing Fields Association, 2000). "With infants, the primary component of the environment is an alert, available adult who enjoys being outdoors and doesn't feel babies have to be protected totally from the world around" (Gestwicki, 2011, p. 103).

With very young children, model only as a last resort; instead mimic the infant's or toddler's

Know how to play.

Ingrid Crowther

Body Art Extravaganza

I feel incredibly lucky to have a playground with lots of natural resources; it's large and surrounded by trees. I often use the playground as an outdoor classroom, an extension of the curriculum that's happening inside. We had spent the morning inside making a hand print mural. When it was time to transition outside the children were still focused on covering the whole mural paper. We decided to take it outside and finish the hard work we had started. One of my most memorable moments was what happened next, an activity we later described as *Body Art Extravaganza*. It started with a simple bump from another child who was holding a paint brush. This evolved into body art painting, we then added shaving cream and a hose. Having such a large outdoor space allowed the children to explore where there were very few limitations. It was amazing how different children responded. Some of the children spent time making predictions and testing their theories as they mixed colours all over their bodies. Other children worked together to paint on each other. This brought on a different dynamic within the group as individuals who didn't often engage each other were working together toward a common goal. Children who didn't want to participate in the hand painting inside suddenly were painting their legs and faces. Another child who didn't want to participate assigned himself the role of the hose holder, creating his own space where he could spray children off so they could start over and over again! Adding full-length mirrors so children were able to see their transformations made this experience incredibly meaningful.

Body Art Extravaganza!

Kelly Antram

actions, using appropriate language to describe the process and celebrate his or her accomplishments. Supporting children with special needs in their play is critical. Young children who struggle with motor coordination can benefit from your physical support of the activities they are naturally curious about.

FIRST BE AN OBSERVER AND THEN A PLANNER

Observation is critical to the educator's ability to plan. Assessing the learning of each individual child is required if effective and relevant learning is to take place both inside and outside.

> When outdoor play is seen as a vital part of early years education, it is more likely to be well planned, well organized, well provided for and

developmentally appropriate. The role of the adult in the preparation for play, their interaction during play and the assessment of and for learning as a result of play is absolutely crucial. Just as we would not expect children to learn and develop effectively in an unplanned indoor classroom, we cannot expect that mere exposure to the outdoor environment will be enough to support effective learning. (Harriman, 2010, pp. 50–51)

Observe what each child enjoys doing, what playspaces are used, what zones and for how long, type of equipment and materials, will the child try new things with the equipment, what materials and equipment does the child avoid, what type of play child is engaged in; for example, Parten's Social Play levels—unoccupied behavior, onlooker, solitary independent play, parallel activity, associative play, cooperative or organized play or Similansky's

Cognitive Play Levels—functional play, constructive play, dramatic play, sociodramatic play, games with rules, in what situations does the child initiate play, who does the child like to play with, how are conflicts resolved, when is there a need for an adult to encourage a child, risk taking, problem solving, etc.?

Early learning practitioners scan play episodes to determine when and how to intervene in child's play so that it is a positive experience for children. Observation will provide insight into individual, cultural and social needs of the children.

> This observation is crucial for informing the next stage of planning and all adults must be given time to give feedback and contribute to the planning. The most effective planners are those settings that have built in time specifically for this. The same time each week or the same 20 minutes each day is by far the most effective. Some settings find this difficult to organize but more and more are now realizing the importance of it and are reorganizing their days to accommodate it. (Durant, 2007, p. 6)

> Making and expressing choices, plans and decisions is fundamental to a child's developing sense of competence and equality. As daily planners and decision-makers, children acquire increased confidence in interacting with peers and adults. They come to see themselves as respected partners in shaping many of the ongoing events in their world. (Hohmann & Weikart, 1995, p. 381)

When planning experiences for the children, it is critical that we consider the developmental level of the children we are working with:

- Why are we engaging in this experience?
- What are the developmental goals?
- What concepts are being taught?

- What will the children learn?
- Will it be meaningful to them?

When interacting with the children we understand that they move from concrete to abstract understanding, which is why hands-on experiences are the most effective. Therefore, at times, it is important that children play in a "prepared environment." The areas should be equipped or arranged to accommodate desired forms of play including tools and building materials for constructive play, water and containers for water play, art materials for art activities, etc.

Cullen (1993) found that

> the longer the outdoor play period, the better the quality of play, especially creative play, and that the more complex forms of cooperative play were facilitated by the staff. She concludes that the reason for this is simple. The longer the children spent outside the more the staff had to plan for. The more staff had to plan for, the more effort they put into the plans and so the more interesting the range of activities. (p. 10)

A PLANNING GUIDE

Draw your outdoor playspace and use this as a basis for a planning guide. In many centres, a planning sheet is required so that families can see what experiences will be taking place. Some centres have two plans, one for indoor activities and one for outdoor. Other centres plan a more integrated approach and have one planning guide for both indoor and outdoor play.

The same energy that goes into planning for the indoor space should be extended to the outdoor environment every day. Creating a schedule that shares

Interesting setups engage the children.

This centre posts its outdoor play schedule and is available for families' comments and contributions.

the responsibility for the early morning set-up and takedown among all staff provides opportunities for everyone to share their expertise. This also provides an opportunity for staff to share their ideas in a more collaborative format. The environment should be set up before the children go outside and taken down at the end of the day when necessary; however, whenever possible and when children request it, leave their structures and play materials intact so that they can begin again another day.

Explain the choices to the children before they go outside. Helping the children begin their outdoor play is an important role of the educator. Stories with unfinished endings can be a great catalyst for energizing and inspiring the children. The most important incentive is that the environment has been set up in a way that it "takes the children's breath away." Based on the children's play experiences the day before, on the children's indoor interests, or the continuation of a project, the outdoor playscape should reflect the teacher's observations of the children's pursuits. In the beginning, there are so many wonderful things to do that some children will need time to decide, while others will rush to an area.

Good planning prevents large groups of children on the same piece of equipment; it is better to encourage turn taking or redirect the children. Setting up many interesting experiences outside will alleviate large groups of children in any one location

Organize and place tools and materials so children have easy access and can return them independently. Then provide time for real discovery and exploration.

Extension activities such as a field trip, sharing an interesting book or reference material, or visits from community experts motivate children to continue their explorations in new ways, providing new information and connecting their work to their lives outside the school.

PROVIDE MEANINGFUL RESOURCES, LOOSE PARTS

It's hard to imagine an early childhood staff that feels it has enough resources. Whether they operate for profit or not, whether large or small, nearly all programs feel they can't get closer to their dreams without additional resources. Programs always need more money, more time, and more staff. They also need more vision. And as programs grow and refine their visions, they will uncover resources they never imagined. Sometimes there are resources right under our noses that we haven't

---

Inside LOOK

Exploration

Children flourish outdoors. Their curiosity leads them to smell a flower, poke in the dirt, consider the spider and her web, gaze at clouds and ask, "Why?" Early childhood educators are in the enviable position of being able to reconstruct previous perspectives of outdoor play, playgrounds, and outdoor learning experiences. A shift is occurring from purchasing shiny, colourful climbing structures, and cute little play houses to planning natural play spaces with trees, gardens, and water sources for children to explore and learn from. We know that many children do not have consistent access to outdoor play that allows for exploration and learning. Now, early childhood educators are developing their skills and interests in ensuring quality learning experiences, through play, when children are outside. Urban planners are focusing on playgrounds that foster play for all children and include natural elements. We are making changes that will positively affect children's development. The outdoor play space is a vital learning environment and is as significant to a child's development as the classroom environment. Outdoor play can foster an understanding of nature, assist children's views of themselves as members of the natural world, provide opportunities to develop social interactions with peers, and offer a place to develop confidence in skills. Planning for the outdoor learning environment is essential to providing a comprehensive curriculum.

Sally Kotsopolous Program Co-ordinator, Humber College Institute of Teaching and Learning

tapped: ideas to inspire us, models to visit, expertise from other fields, stories and relationships to nourish our souls. While it's true we need more money, money alone isn't what's holding us back. We need to transform our thinking about resources and expand the field of vision we work with. (Curtis & Carter, 2003 p. 203)

Think of thrift stores, garage sales, dollar stores, and hardware stores. Buy or collect baskets, trays, bowls, dishes and cutting boards, nuts, bolts, pulleys, napkin rings, scarves, fabric, jewellery, plastic containers, and book cases.

IMPLEMENT THE PROJECT APPROACH

The history of the project approach is well documented and this method is widely used in the field of early childhood. Leaders in North America are Sylvia Chard and Lillian Katz who have developed training and an insightful website

www www http://www.projectapproach.org

This approach to young children's learning is most closely associated with emergent curriculum and Reggio-inspired curriculum, both of which emphasize developing and planning curriculum in response to children's interests and concerns. Unlike more traditional approaches to curriculum, which involved lesson plans with some type of "hook" intended to get children's attention, emergent curriculum and Reggio-inspired curriculum start by exploring what is engaging and meaningful to children.* (Redleaf, 2010, p. 1)

Many educators have learned about these methods and some will have adapted and used parts of each philosophical approach in a way that best suits their learning environment. A project may be defined as an in-depth investigation of a real-world topic worthy of children's attention and effort. This approach allows for children to become immersed in a topic that is of great interest to them. This may engage the children for as little as one week or several months, depending on the children's interest and enthusiasm. This integrated approach allows for all areas of the curriculum to be explored. The project can be carried out by a full group or by small groups of children. A central principle of the project approach is that learning is based on prior learning. The children are actively involved in determining what they already know and what

else they want to know about the topic. The "What We Know" and "What We Want to Know" webs are tools to support the development of the project. First, the ECE discusses the topic with the children to find out their experiences and what they already know. This is done by brainstorming the children's experience, knowledge, and ideas, and representing them in a topic web in words and pictures.

Educators help children make decisions about the direction of the study, the ways in which the group will research the topic, and gathering representation materials that will demonstrate and highlight the topic. The role of the teacher is first and foremost that of a learner alongside the children. The teacher also is a teacher-researcher, a resource, and guide as he or she lends expertise to children (Edwards et al., 1993).

Once the concepts are clearly stated as to what the children are learning, it becomes easier to evaluate progress throughout the project.

Next, the children develop questions to answer through investigation, and document the questions on webs or lists. Projects provide a means to integrate learning between home, community, and early childhood environments. Like all good curricula, projects build on parents' unique knowledge of their children and support reciprocal home and centre learning. The two-way exchange of ideas and learning opportunities related to the project promote the achievement of many outcomes. Projects are carried out in the context of the community and its resources. For example, when children are engaged in an in-depth investigation of how plants grow, they may visit a local nursery and gain firsthand knowledge that they take back to their home and early childhood environment for use in their own gardens.

Recording the information that the children have collected can be done in many ways—collecting real objects, drawing pictures, writing notes, making audiovisual representations, taking photos, building models, etc. Parents and other community experts are asked to contribute knowledge and artifacts that will promote the children's learning. Children are encouraged to seek new sources of information through this process. The ECE displays the documentations and children's representations to promote awareness of the outcomes of the children's investigations. Finally, a culminating event is organized through which the children share with others what they have learned.

The project approach enables children to grow in their literacy, numeracy, and problem-solving

---

*Hey Kids! Out the Door, Let's Explore! By Rhoda Redleaf. ©Readleaf Press (2010).

FIGURE 7.1 Teacher's Web on the Garden Project

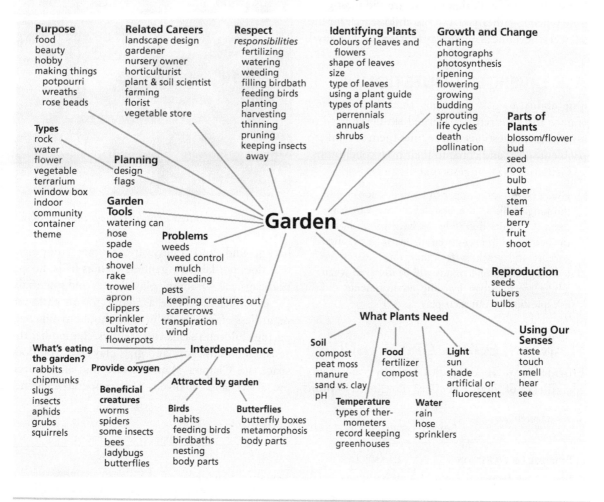

Purpose
food
beauty
hobby
making things
  potpourri
  wreaths
  rose beads

Types
rock
water
flower
vegetable
terrarium
window box
indoor
community
container
theme

Planning
design
flags

Garden Tools
watering can
hose
spade
hoe
shovel
rake
trowel
apron
clippers
sprinkler
cultivator
flowerpots

Related Careers
landscape design
gardener
nursery owner
horticulturist
plant & soil scientist
farming
florist
vegetable store

Problems
weeds
  weed control
  mulch
  weeding
pests
  keeping creatures out
  scarecrows
transpiration
wind

What's eating the garden?
rabbits
chipmunks
slugs
insects
aphids
grubs
squirrels

Provide oxygen

Beneficial creatures
worms
spiders
some insects
bees
ladybugs
butterflies

Respect
responsibilities
fertilizing
watering
weeding
filling birdbath
feeding birds
planting
harvesting
thinning
pruning
keeping insects
  away

Interdependence

Attracted by garden

Birds
habits
feeding birds
birdbaths
nesting
body parts

Butterflies
butterfly boxes
metamorphosis
body parts

Garden

What Plants Need

Soil
compost
peat moss
manure
sand vs. clay
pH

Temperature
types of ther-
  mometers
record keeping
greenhouses

Food
fertilizer
compost

Water
rain
hose
sprinklers

Identifying Plants
colours of leaves and
  flowers
shape of leaves
size
type of leaves
using a plant guide
types of plants
  perrenials
  annuals
  shrubs

Light
sun
shade
artificial or
  fluorescent

Growth and Change
charting
photographs
photosynthesis
ripening
flowering
growing
budding
sprouting
life cycles
death
pollination

Parts of Plants
blossom/flower
bud
seed
root
bulb
tuber
stem
leaf
berry
fruit
shoot

Reproduction
seeds
tubers
bulbs

Using Our Senses
taste
touch
smell
hear
see

Source: Sara Starbuck and Marla DeWerff Olthoff, 1996 from *Hollyhocks and Honeybees: Garden Projects for Young Children*, 2002. Redleaf Press.

skills in real-life contexts. Children are engaged in dramatic play, art, construction and other forms of representation. Projects, like good stories, have a beginning, a middle, and an end. This structure helps the early childhood educator to organize the progression of activities according to the development of children's interests and personal involvement with the topic of investigation. The teacher's role is to deepen the children's understandings by asking probing questions, encouraging children to represent their experiences, and creating opportunities for discussion and reflection.

ENCOURAGE DISCUSSION

Children should not be interrupted in their play unless they want to talk, and conversations should be about what they are doing and thinking. Wilson (2008) states that

in addition to identifying and responding to children's interests and fears, teacher should also pay close attention to their discoveries and experiences. As children share what they discover and/or experience, their understanding of what it means deepens. This is especially true if the teacher shows a sincere interest and encourages the children to think about the why, hows, and what ifs. Questions are meant to provoke thought, to challenge perceptions, to have children question their ideas and concepts. As teachers our role is to ask questions that are more than a right or wrong response. We want to encourage divergence [sic] therefore, open-ended questions represent one of the best ways to do this. An open ended question allows for many different answers—there's not just a "right" or "wrong" answer. Open-ended questions help children problem-solve and think creatively. They also foster close observation, further conversation, and inquiry." (p. 41)

There may be many situations where you do not know the answer. Perhaps these are the most genuine when together you and the child search for the answers; never be afraid to say that you don't know!

ASK DIVERGENT QUESTIONS

Our ability to ask questions that stimulate and engage the children is a learned skill. We need to ask children questions that require them to think, to problem solve, and come to their own conclusions.

Gellens (2007) suggests that

> giving children the opportunity to develop critical thinking skills is the best legacy we can leave them … adults don't always have to teach, but can simply allow children to learn. Too often parents and teachers feel they must direct the learning. Children's minds will be involved when adults create active learning environments and ask questions about their play. (p. 41)

PLAN FOR EQUAL OPPORTUNITIES

Provide equal opportunities for physical activity regardless of age, gender, language, ethnic

Ingrid Crowther

Questions help children develop critical thinking skills.

background, and ability. Incorporate equipment that does not label by gender, such as balls, hoops, beanbags, etc. Dramatic play clothes and materials, for example, should be available for all children, regardless of gender. Educators should avoid comparing children's skills and abilities. Remember the research on how boys and girls play in the outdoor space (see Chapter 3) and ensure that all children are active and involved. Use cooperative games

TABLE 7.1	Seven Types of Divergent Questions
PURPOSE OF QUESTION	**EXAMPLES**
Instigating discovery	What kind of environment do earthworms prefer?
	How do the leaves of different flowers look different?
	Why are there holes in the leaves of our beans?
	Why is the tomato lying on the ground with a bite out of it?
Eliciting predictions	What do you predict will happen if we don't water this plant?
	What do you predict will happen if we plant the sunflower in the shade?
Probing for understanding	Why do you think this marigold is taller than that marigold?
	Why do you think that plant died?
Promoting reasoning	Why do you think the worms crawled under the damp paper towel?
	What evidence do you have to support that?
	What conclusions can you draw from that?
Serving as a catalyst	What could we do to keep the birds from eating the berries?
	What could we do to keep the soil from drying out so quickly?
Encouraging creative thinking	What would happen if the stores stopped selling vegetables?
	What would happen if plants never stopped growing?
Reflecting on feelings	What was it like sitting inside the sunflower house?
	How did you feel when you found the big pumpkin in the garden?
	What was the best part of watching the ants working in the garden?

Source: Starbuck, S., Olthof, M., Midden, K. 2002. *Hollyhocks and Honeybees Garden Projects for Young Children*. Redleaf Press. p. 18

that do not exclude anyone or ask anyone to sit out for part of the game (e.g., tag, musical chairs). Terry Orlick's (1978) work on cooperative sports and games is a must-read for those working with older children. His philosophy is that in cooperative games, everybody cooperates, everybody wins, and nobody loses. Children play *with* one another rather than *against* one another. These games eliminate the fear of failure and the feeling of failure.

BE PREPARED FOR DIFFICULT SITUATIONS

> Nature can be cruel—it is, after all, about survival of the fittest. Don't hide this from children. They will see signs of predation—a bloody clump of bird's feathers, a diving beetle sucking the life out of a tadpole, or a much-loved dog proudly dropping a dead rabbit at their feet. Help them to understand that each species has to find its own way to survive. (Danks & Schofield, 2005, p. 19)

We must also be vigilant in that we do not overwhelm young children with dire news about the destruction of the environment. Helping children to be knowledgeable about things that are relevant in their lives, in their backyards, and in their community is far more developmentally appropriate. When we do this, we lay the foundation for future environmental leaders.

BE A PHOTOGRAPHER

There is no question that a picture is worth a thousand words and this is never more apparent than when young children are involved. Perhaps one of the most effective books on this topic is *Picture Science, Using Digital Photography to Teach Young Children* by Carla Neumann Hinds (2007). In her introduction she states

> We live in a visual world. Photography has become a part of everyday life, and no matter where we are or what we do, photographic images surround us ... Photography is also a powerful teaching and learning tool ... You don't need to be a professional photographer to bring digital photography into your classroom. In fact, everyone can use the camera—students and teachers alike. Using a digital camera offers you unlimited opportunities to create personalized learning materials for your classroom and to enhance your teaching. ... using photography in the early childhood classroom isn't just about taking pictures: it involves using the camera to make ideas visible, to communicate and collaborate with each other, and to help children explore and understand their world. ... The camera can be a great tool for collecting data, and you can use the images you create to promote observation, recall information, analyze data, demonstrate conclusions and reflect on the process of learning.[*]

There is no question that the use of photos helps children understand in a more concrete way abstract concepts and ideas, particularly for those who are in the early-reading stages of development. The excitement of capturing a moment in the playscape is always exciting and it is so much more powerful than any picture in a book or magazine. The camera also provides a lens through which the children can view objects over time (perhaps spring flowers emerging from the ground or the arrival and thaw of a snowfall), and allows children the opportunity to revisit their ideas repeatedly. Photography provides an opportunity for children to expand their language skills as they discuss their images with each other. This is particularly helpful for children who are English language learners.

Because you may be setting the stage for a lifelong love of photography, bring in books of famous photographers such as Ansel Adams, Paul Weston, Alfred Steiglitz, Brian Adams, and Annie Liebowitz to share with the children.

Digital photography can play a significant role in helping students to develop inquiry skills and there is no better place than the outdoors. You and your students can use photographs in countless ways:

- Gather information on a field trip or outdoor exploration by taking pictures of objects that can't be taken back to the classroom
- Document change over time or cause and effect by taking pictures for days, weeks, months or hours
- Classify information by sorting pictures into different categories
- Create matching games and puzzles to encourage observation
- Document children's observations with photographs
- Use photographs to discuss what happened during an exploration and why
- Use photographs in charts and other displays to demonstrate children's conclusions

---

[*]Neumann Hinds, C. 2007. *Picture Science Using Digital Photography to Teach Young Children*. Redleaf Press. Introduction.

- Help children sequence the steps they took in carrying out their investigation
- Use photographs to spark discussion and to let children reflect on their learning process
- Include photographs in a portfolio to illustrate specific skills the children demonstrated or struggled with during their inquiry
- Create books or presentation about the project to show to parents and the community.* (Neumann Hinds, 2007, p. 6)

When children are able to see the photos they have taken, it is exciting to watch them begin to analyze what they see. Conversations begin; they share visual cues and ask new questions. A skillful teacher will ask open-ended questions and encourage creative thought.

REPRESENTATION AND DOCUMENTING CHILDREN'S LEARNING

Representation is an internal process in which children construct mental symbols to stand for actual objects, people, and events. Through representation, experience and knowledge are clarified, integrated, and shared (Homann & Weikart, 1995).

> Documentation serves three key functions, to provide children with a concrete and visible memory of what they have said and done, using images and words to serve as a jumping off point to explore previous understandings and to co-construct revisited understandings of the topics investigated. Children become even more interested, curious, and confident as they contemplate the meaning of what they have achieved. Secondly, [they] give educators an insight into the children's learning processes, their understanding and misunderstandings of everyday institutions, objects and events. In this sense, documentation becomes a tool for research, and a spur to continuous improvement and renewal. Thirdly, [they] provide parents and the public with detailed information about what happens in the schools as a means of eliciting their reactions and support. In turn, children learn that their parents feel at home in the school, at ease with the teachers. (Bennett & Leonarduzzi, 2004, p. 15)

Documentation is the process of recording and reporting on children's learning through multiple media. Documenting children's learning can take a variety of forms such as individual profiles, anecdotal

*Source: Neumann Hinds, C. 2007. *Picture Science Using Digital Photography to Teach Young Children*. Redleaf Press. p. 6.

Documentation is an opportunity to share with families.

Lynn Wilson

notes, tape recordings, videotaping, photos, samples of children's writings, journals, narratives for display, bulletin boards, paintings, class murals, sculptures, etc. Its purpose is to create a visual record that makes children's learning evident. It informs viewers of the learning processes children went through in their play and the meaning it had for them. Documentation is a valuable tool that teachers can use to record and communicate to the children, to families, and to colleagues. Documenting what the children have seen and representing their ideas will help them to reflect on their experiences and deepen their understanding. Art materials provide opportunities for two- and three-dimensional representation and an opportunity for the children to draw what they are interested in. Many children may want to use journals to record their progress, or they can create a large book that reflects the whole group's experience. Use photographs to track projects from beginning to the end, and incorporate graphs, poems, songs, recipes, children's artwork and comments. Then bind the book and place it in the book centre for all to read.

These documentation panels are wonderful opportunities for the children to share with their families their learning. When panels are displayed in the playrooms and entranceways, it creates a powerful message that the children's work is valued. It also helps families deepen their understanding of how their children make sense of the world, and provides an opportunity for discussion and a chance for children and teachers to interact with families in a meaningful way.

SUPPORT PROSOCIAL BEHAVIOUR

Living requires that we develop identity and a strong sense of self but we also need to understand others. Living in harmony, acting cooperatively, and negotiating with others requires that we take another's perspective and assert ourselves. As children mature, they acquire the experience that contributes to growth in their sense of self and the abilities involved in being social. Adults play a central role in scaffolding the development of the child's social and emotional development.

> The goal of development is that a strong sense of self is balanced with the ability to consider others, their ideas and feelings. Empathy is broadened when children share experiences, relate and respect each other in the context of caring secure relationships with adults. Children can sometimes unleash powerful feelings, in themselves or in their companions, through their play. The process often has valuable cathartic or therapeutic effects but can also be disturbing. Children are entitled to expect that adults involved in play provision will understand and be responsive to cues that they may be in need of comfort or reassurance as a result of their play. (National Play Fields Association, 2000, p. 8)

Vygotsky (1978) argues that in play, children have to show great self-control; children cannot just act on impulse, they have to bow to the rules of the game—whatever they may be—because play is social and involves others. If you want to stay "in" you have to "play the game."

> Pellegrini (2005) concurs with this and argues that children have a vested interest while playing with peers to stay "in" but through the play learn difficult and demanding strategies to co-operate, compromise and inhibit aggression. So without realising it children learn to do these things, or if they do not, they find they can be isolated.* (Bilton, 2010, p. 49)

Emotionally competent children know how to vary their behavior to correspond with the thoughts, feelings and situations of those around

Courtesy of Richmond Adelaide Child Care Centre

Connections are forever being made.

them. They are also less likely to be involved in angry disputes with peers and more likely to use constructive strategies in response to potentially conflicting situations. They are also more likely to be popular with their peers than other children. The lack of emotional competence, on the other hand, tends to promote "spiraling difficulties" in children's ability to interact and from relationships with others. (Denham, 2001, pp. 23–45)

Compelling research demonstrates that positive outdoor playspaces promote more cooperative play and more civil behaviour: "The relationship between the design of school grounds and children's behaviour

---

*Bilton, H. 2010. *Outdoor Learning In The Early Years. Management And Innovation*. Routledge Taylor And Francis Group. p. 49.

The change in his behavior was significant as the new playground emerged. There were sheltered places where he could go when he felt overwhelmed, gardening, art experiences, and physical play. But perhaps the most important element for him was our animals. When one of the chicks fell into the pond, he was the first to rescue him. We celebrated his hero status! As time went on, this child—who had developed empathy for the animals—transferred this empathy to the other children in the program. While other supporting factors were in place for this child, I strongly believe that we would never have had the progress we have seen today without this wonderful natural outdoor playground.

seems clear: playgrounds become much more peaceful and harmonious when play spaces are diversified" (Evans, 2001, p. 28). Interesting playscapes are the answer when boredom results in aggressive behaviour.

Improvements can be even more dramatic if students are involved in the process of greening (planning, design, fundraising, implementation, maintenance). A mounting body of evidence likewise indicates that green settings generally may help to promote increased concentration, attentional functioning ,and self-discipline. Research indicates that children with Attention Deficit Hyperactivity Disorder and others who are reluctant learners respond positively in the outdoor environment, and are more able to focus and concentrate when they are not confined to a desk (Faber-Taylor et al., 2001). The positive relationship between physical activity and academic success has been repeatedly demonstrated (Etnier et al., 1997, Symons et al., 1997, Lieberman and Hoody, 1998). This success supports all areas of development including children's social and emotional connections to others.

Here are some suggestions for assisting children in resolving conflicts or challenges:

- Match expectations to the developmental level of the children and what might be happening on that particular day; be flexible.
- Encourage independence, trust, autonomy, and positive social interaction by being a positive role model.
- Have you created a culture of empathy and caring for each other?
- Discuss feelings; label the children's emotions.
- Encourage the behavior you want to see.
- Be watchful of challenging children and catch them doing things "right"; celebrate their efforts and break the cycle of negative feedback.

- Explain the consequences of behaviour in a nonthreatening manner.
- Enforce limits consistently.
- Advise children of upcoming changes in activities for those who find transitions difficult.
- Anticipate behaviour and provide alternatives using positive directions.
- Encourage the children to create rules for the outdoor space.
- Break tasks into smaller steps when necessary to give the child a sense of accomplishment.
- Bring yourself into the space where the conflict is occurring. Often just your presence will be enough for the children to redirect themselves on their own. This is called your *arc of influence*.
- State expectations clearly.
- Provide ways for children to express their emotions constructively.
- Have them listen carefully to each other when describing the conflict.
- Encourage brainstorming of possible solutions.
- Have the children pick one alternative and come back and evaluate how well it worked.

BE MORE THAN A POLICE OFFICER

In an increasingly litigious society, the role of adults in "policing" playgrounds has been encouraged, but this is not the role they should play. Instead, teachers and caregivers should continue to support and encourage children during outdoor play just as they do during indoor time. … a playground must not only be child-friendly but also adult-friendly. The outdoor play space should enable adults to safely observe and playfully interact with the children in their care so that they can fully capture naturally occurring teachable moments as they happen. Young children's outside play is not a time for adults to relax. ... Adult assistance, modeling, and support are offered rather than instruction and control.* (Theemes, 1999, p. 67)

ENGAGE IN SELF-REFLECTION

Part of being a reflective professional is to continually examine our profession, and its practices and standards, and to question the status quo. Refection is a characteristic of effective educators. It helps us gain better perspective, insight, and understanding, and helps us feel more confident and professional in our work with children and their families. The process of self-evaluation is a valuable tool to ensure that centres are evaluating their impact when providing outdoor experiences designed to improve the achievements, successes, and quality of children's learning.

While it's true that there are barriers outside of ourselves, perhaps the biggest barrier is a person's internal feeling of powerlessness. It's easy to forget that you do have a tremendous amount of power in your program, starting with your attitudes, the organizational climate you create, the physical space you design, and the materials you present to the children. You have control over these things. They communicate your values and intentions and in turn, shape how you feel and behave while in the space. (Curtis & Carter, 1996, p. 194)

*Theemes, T. 1999. *Let's Go Outside: Designing the Early Childhood Playground*. High Scope Press, Ypsilanti, Michigan. p. 67.

It is important to remember that, like children, teachers also need opportunities to engage in new experiences. This renewed interest in the outdoors will inspire the children with whom they work.

DOCUMENT·YOURSELF

Educators may also find documenting their own observations in a journal helpful; it provides

- **A valuable tool for developing critical reflection**
- **A record of significant learning experiences that have taken place**
- **A place to record important information about a project that the teacher may wish to discuss with others**
- **A reminder of important elements of the project if a topic arises with another group of children at a later date**
- **An opportunity to record children's comments about their outdoor play experiences that might be included in presentations at workshops or in newsletters at the centre**
- **A foundation for professional development**

A detailed garden journal may also be a helpful resource. This journal allows you to keep specific information about individual plants, what worked and what didn't. ... Take photos and/or make sketches of the plants for a further reminder and add them to the diary. Another option might be to take an extra wall calendar, take it apart and laminate the page for each month. Attach it along with a Magic Marker on a string near the outdoor work area. The more accessible it is, the more you'll use it. For each month, record daily weather and rainfall, and note when seeds sprout, pests appear, bushes bloom and vegetables ripen. (Lovejoy, 1999, p. 4)

ENGAGE IN PROFESSIONAL DEVELOPMENT AND ADVOCATE FOR CHANGE

Initial teacher education and continuing professional development have a key role in equipping educators with the appropriate skills necessary to deliver high-quality outdoor learning and to build on their confidence. We have the responsibility of ensuring that teachers in training value the place of outdoor learning in the curriculum. There is a great deal of support available online and we should be aware of how those sites can support professional development. "Teachers secured in their personal development are more likely to be responsive to both children and parents in terms of their cultural and individual needs" (Wilson, 2010, p. 125). "The impact of increased environmental education was felt by teachers who demonstrated more enthusiasm and greater engagement in their teaching. They learned new subject material and were more willing to pursue new teaching methods" (Broda, 2007, p. 19). It is also important that educators have the skills, confidence, and permission to make necessary changes to improve their outdoor space.

Teacher training in outdoor, play-based education is quickly becoming one of the great challenges in teacher education. There is widespread recognition that educators in schools, early learning environments, and community centres should be integrating more outdoor learning into their programs, yet few college and university faculty are adequately prepared in this area. Faculty often have the same fear and trepidation about the outdoors as do their students; asking them to teach outdoors brings these to the fore. But the benefits of outdoor play are tremendous, so much so that faculty are finding innovative ways to learn how to

Inside LOOK

Consult the Experts

There are many resources and some guiding strategies to help teacher educators inform professional learning in outdoor play-based education. Rachel Carson's ideas in using children's inherent sense of wonder for the natural world are a great starting point. Introducing Richard Louv's work helps remind teachers of the importance of getting young children outside to learn, in order to counter what he calls nature deficit disorder. And David Sobel's concept of play in place-based education is a useful tool for highlighting the power of place for all educators—getting children outside classrooms to learn in, about, and for their own communities.

   Natural Curiosity: Building Children's Understanding of the World Through Environmental Inquiry by Lorraine Chiarotto, 2011 is a resource that provides an overview of teaching strategies for outdoor and environmental learning specifically for K–6 educators, and provides solid advice for teacher training in this area as well. It promotes inquiry-based learning as a key strategy, letting children's questions and ideas direct the experience, and using play to explore them; similarly in-service training should focus on teacher's questions, perceptions, and knowledge as a starting point. Experiential learning is also central for both types of learners; as many teachers weren't exposed to this approach in their own formative years, teachers need to participate in play-based, hands-on learning before they can implement it with their own students. Most importantly, teacher training needs to take place outside, explicitly modelling what learning looks like outside the confines of the four walls of the classroom. Just like their students, teachers need opportunities to discover firsthand the joys, challenges, and exciting moments of outdoor, play-based teaching and learning in natural and built environments; once they have experienced these, they are more likely to implement this with their own learners in future.

Contributed by: Dr. Hilary Inwood, OISE, University of Toronto

make outdoor play experiences safe and enriching experiences for all.

Encourage nature-based child-friendly spaces in your own community. Educate parents, grandparents, and other educators about the benefits of outdoor play. Lobby governments, give workshops on the power of outdoor play, and support local greening projects—look for ways to make this issue an important one in your own community. When visiting your doctor, let him or her know about physicians who are now prescribing time in nature to encourage a more active, healthy stress-free lifestyle. Work with architects, builders, and community planners by building new partnerships to bring the resources of the private sector together with public agencies.

It is important for teachers to support each other and this is especially true for new teachers. New graduates are more likely to be successful when they are mentored by gifted teachers who are committed to outdoor education. A mentoring approach helps create a stable and strong early childhood environment. The strength in individual talents and expertise is combined for the greater

Inside LOOK

Changing Attitudes

I attended an Outdoor Play Workshop and I came back to my centre determined to get us all outside. We teach in the north and so the conditions are cold and windy for a great part of the winter months. We would often say it was too cold to go outside because really we didn't want to go out! But having been given so many incredible resources and ideas for outdoor play in the winter, I was really excited about sharing these with my colleagues. At first, there were only a few enthusiasts. However, when other teachers were able to see the incredible learning that was taking place with the children, everyone became involved. This has changed our whole approach to outdoor play, not just in the winter but all year round! It was the best workshop I ever attended.

Inside LOOK

Manitoba Nature Summit

The Manitoba Nature Summit was founded in 2008 by a small group of Early Childhood Educators who also professed an eagerness for sharing their love of the outdoors with other ECEs. The group was concerned with the lack of outdoor play that was happening in ECE programs and, after many conversations, determined that perhaps the people providing ECE might be lacking an understanding of what it means to be outside, or what to do outside with children. The idea for a Summit, a meeting of the minds, was developed and the first-ever Manitoba Nature Summit was held in September 2010. Adults who work with children were invited to explore and experience an outdoor extravaganza of activities, all with the mindset that these were things that could be done with children. After the first Summit's success, the second Summit was held September 2012. It reinforced the sense that being outside with children is not only good for them but also good for those who work in early learning and child care.

Contributed by: Ruth Lindsey-Armstrong, ECE Instructor, Red River College of Applied Arts, Science & Technology, Winnipeg Manitoba

good. It is also important for teachers to link with other teachers in a variety of different programs in their community, sharing their ideas and expertise. These collaborative ventures allow teachers to grow and expand their teaching repertoire.

INVOLVE FAMILIES

Given the diversity of many of our early learning environments, teachers need to be able to adapt to ensure an inclusive and welcoming environment. It is difficult to fully understand how worldviews and cultures influence children, because they are woven through every aspect of the learning process. There is a great deal for teachers to learn. It is worthwhile to be patient. For example, in Aboriginal communities, Elders place much hope in the education system and in teachers' abilities to help Aboriginal children.

> Aboriginal communities have high standards for their children's education. They not only want their children to do well, they want quality learning opportunities for their community. The time teachers spend getting to know the students and their patterns of learning provides the foundation for a strong learning relationship. In the holistic worldviews of Aboriginal communities, a teacher is teaching not only the child who comes to school but also the child who is a member of a family, a community and a culture. It is important to learn about each student as an individual. (Alberta Education, n.d., pp. 30–31)

> "When you take the time to talk to students, remember: the first moments are sacred; they involve the honouring of the dignity of each life that you meet. Take the time to listen with your heart."
>
> **—Anonymous Aboriginal teacher**

Many families are unsure of how to participate and contribute to their early childhood environment but families have much to offer! Try surveying families or, on a home visit, find out their interests, hobbies, or special training that may be helpful to green your play space. Many family members, young and old, will have skills and talents, contacts in the community, experience in locating and writing grants to improve the outdoor space, and gardening experience. Many may be very enthusiastic about supporting outdoor experiences.

> Some families may have a particular reverence for nature or certain animals; some families may discourage children from handling insects or other creatures; and others may come from cultures where children are expected to listen, not to question. Individual children may have had interesting and or problematic experiences with living things that are important for teachers to know. Some children may have pets or have had farm experiences. Others may have helped with a garden or have plants at home. Still others may have had a bad experience being bitten by a dog or stung by a bee. Some may also have allergies that may impact on their outdoor experiences. Families can provide teachers with important clues about such experiences as well as which living things intrigue their children, what questions they have and what strategies you might use to support children's learning. (Chalufour & Worth, 2003, pp. 8–9)

Being thoughtful about cultural influences and interacting with families in a respectful way increases the chance of their involvement.

In order to help families understand the value and benefits of outdoor play, educators need to provide families with information on what children are learning in the outdoor environment. Email or send a letter to families or post a notice or a documentation panel that they will see when picking up children to let them know about the learning that is taking place in the outdoor environment as well as what they might do with their children at home to reinforce and expand that learning.

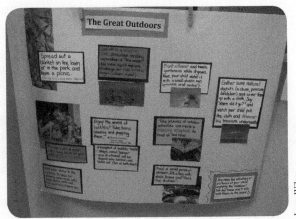

Encourage families to play an active role in the centre and in their community.

A garden party

provides an opportunity for families to stay and participate in the children's experiences. Celebrate outdoors as well as indoors!

INVOLVE THE COMMUNITY

A schoolyard is a school's "external environment," whether large or small, beautiful or unsightly, actively used or completely abandoned. Whatever its condition, a schoolyard is an indicator of the health of the surrounding community, and each has a powerful impact on the other. An unimproved or degraded schoolyard sends a negative message about the school and the neighborhood in which it is situated. A dynamic and active schoolyard adds to the vibrancy of both. (Broda, 2007, p. 29)

Invite families to the school so they can experience firsthand the importance of the outdoor environment and its learning potential. As families participate in a hands-on gardening experience, link this activity to the many skills that the children will be learning. The gardening experience is also another opportunity to discuss ways in which they can support children's explorations at home and in the community. Let families know that their participation is welcome and needed and that you are interested in having them share their expertise as well as their concerns. Many family members will have skills and talents that they would love to share—encourage active engagement in your early learning environment. Being outside at the beginning and end of the day

Children learn in their homes, communities, and early childhood settings, so promoting continuity of learning is essential to early childhood curriculum. What children learn at home and how they learn at home are essential elements of early childhood programs. A healthy community is a healthy place for children and families. It is important to work with stakeholders, partners from public health and sports and recreation organizations, local businesses, architects, landscapers, horticulturalists, government, and school boards to access healthy living opportunities for everyone. Working together to ensure effective and coordinated efforts will enhance the quality of life for all concerned. Visit the *Ontario Physical and Health Education Association* (OPHEA) website for

Inside LOOK

The Importance of Communication

… the space can, through documentation, communicate what children and teachers are doing and learning, what changes and growth are taking place, and what relationships are developing. The communication through teachers' journals, letters to parents, and photographs with transcriptions of children's words also offers occasions to know and understand. This can form a sense of continuity for the families who miss so much of what is happening during their absence at work. It is a way to give a voice to children and their teachers and simultaneously to invite the parents to become part of the community that is being created. (Lella Gandini in Greenman, J. 2007. *Caring Spaces, Learning Places Children's Environments That Work*. Exchange Press Inc. p. vii) excellent strategies for creating healthy schools and communities:

 http://www.ophea.net/healthy-schools-communities

A website that is an inspiration for community development and promoting goodwill among neighbours is

 http://www.myhrm.ca

The design, preparation, planting, and maintenance of a school garden offers many opportunities for community building. Transforming a portion of a school yard from a grass, dirt, or asphalt space into a living and blooming landscape is a complex project, one that involves a broad range of skills and many willing participants. Consider local garden clubs that may have members who would be happy to provide guidance and support. Local nurseries and hardware stores may be willing to support your plans for a magical outdoor playscape. Use their expertise, particularly regarding plant selection.

TAKE LOTS OF FIELD TRIPS

Programs are enhanced when the playscape reflects the resources and interests that are unique to your area and families. The optimum learning environment is one that integrates the playroom with the home and the community. Therefore, field trips can be rich learning opportunities when they are relevant to the children's interests and meaningful to the children's particular stage of development.

Walks with babies and toddlers, whether on foot or in a stroller, are tremendous opportunities for children to learn about the world around them.

Riverdale Farm, a farm in the city; Toronto.

Join in when celebrations occur in your community.

Point out the fire engines, walk by construction sites, stop at fountains, and touch the flowers in the gardens to engage young children. The world has much to offer. By visiting farms where the children can actively participate, or natural spaces and parks, educators can provide a connection to the community and expand the children's understanding of outdoor environments. As children develop questions that can be answered by a trip to a community location, make sure that you do your homework. Travel in advance to the site and decide on the safest and most efficient route. Family members may be great contacts for this so include them in your planning. Talk to the people you will be visiting and be clear about your expectations for the visit, length of time that is appropriate for the age group, etc. Low adult-to-child ratios are always the most effective. Often trips are organized when resources or materials are needed—the local hardware shop, the nursery, the garden club, parks, flower shops, and sometimes just a walk in the neighbourhood to observe what others have done

Beaches Boardwalk, Toronto

in their gardens. Bringing along clipboards, paper, markers, coloured pencils, etc., if the children will be documenting what they see. A camera will be essential for documenting this experience, perhaps by digital photos and/or a video.

For many children who leave child care at an early age feeling safe in their community and knowing where to go if they are worried or afraid when they are home alone is very important. We can support this when we are on walks and field trips.

Things to remember when preparing for a field trip:

1. CHOOSING THE TRIP

- Consider the interests and developmental levels of the children in the group.
- Are there appropriate activities to involve the children?
- Has at least one staff person visited the site ahead of time?
- Speak to staff at the site and discuss the purpose of the visit.
- Is the environment safe?
- What will you need to bring to enhance the experience (e.g., magnifying glasses)?
- Will you be bringing back anything to the centre (e.g., specimens)? If so what do you need to bring?
- Will the children be collecting and what resources will they need to do this?
- Are there any difficulties presented by transportation to the site?

2. PREPARING THE FAMILIES

- Invite family members to accompany their child.
- Give the families advance notice of the trip verbally and in written form.
- Before the trip, explain how the children will be transported and what activities they will engage in during the trip.
- Have families sign to authorize their child's participation in the trip.

3. PREPARING THE CHILDREN

- Discuss all safety issues with the children in advance including safe travel behaviour.
- Prepare children through the curriculum for where they are going and what they might see.
- Encourage children to discuss what to expect on the trip, as well as involve them in problem solving regarding safety and emergency situations.
- Will the children be drawing or taking photographs?

4. FOLLOWING UP

- What were the children's observations of this field trip?
- Record their observations on chart paper.
- How will the children represent this experience?
- Discuss photos or videos taken.
- Create a documentation panel to share with the children and families.
- What visitors to the centre might complement this experience?
- What books, DVDs, etc., can add to this experience?
- Can the children replicate this experience in their own environment?

Inside LOOK

Fleming Public School—Communities Growing Together

Some gardening efforts start more simply. Grade Five teacher Irene Hodges and Grade Eight teacher Judy Thorne felt strongly that involving parents in an effort to beautify their "plain" school would reinforce a feeling of ownership in the school. They invited parents, some with little English, to join their children in planting 1,500 tulip bulbs purchased with the proceeds of a student penny drive. Despite a downpour of rain on the Saturday appointed for planting, eager students, teachers, and a large number of parents worked together cheerfully to get all the bulbs into the ground.

(continued)

The next spring when beautiful tulips started opening up and you saw this glorious amount of colour … we were just so proud of ourselves. We could do anything now! Exchanges sometimes translated from or into English by children, flew back and forth between neighbours and teachers, with inquiries and answers about where bulbs might be found and the best way to plant them in home gardens. Gardening in the front of the school had become a form of conversation with the surrounding community, which would lead, the following year, to a more ambitious kind of gardening project behind the school.[*] (Houghton, 2003, p. 34)

Before

After

[*]Houghton, E. 2003. A Breath Of Fresh Air Celebrating Nature and School *Gardens*. The Learnxs Foundation & Sumach Press, Toronto District School Board. p. 34. © E. Houghton.

Inside LOOK

Thorncliffe Park Public School—Communities Growing Together

Thorncliffe Park Public School is Canada's largest elementary school (K–5) located in east-central Toronto situated in a community of towering apartment buildings. … There are three courtyard gardens here. Vivian Gault, a Grade 2 teacher and head of the Garden Committee used her love of soil to instill in her students an eagerness for learning about all growing things. She convinced her 80 year old father to come to volunteer with weeding and maintenance and to get the children involved in planting. Vivian's father and a friend began to come regularly to work with the students in the courtyards. Gault felt that the bond forged between the seniors and the children became one of the most precious aspects of their mutual gardening experience. "They've learned the wonderful lesson that's so dear to my heart, the connection with these two seniors. In fact, some of my former students, now in or finished with high school, come back and know my dad by name. Five or six or seven years down the road they remember him: 'Oh, remember when you did this with my class, wasn't that fun!" Children who are recent immigrants to Canada often have their first encounters with soil in the Thorncliffe Park gardens. Some have never seen a root before. Gault described their reaction: "You can tell when a girl with a long shalwar kameez, which is the clothing of many of the children of our school and a hijab around her head never had a chance to put a trowel in her hand before, or a rake, or to put her feet on a hoe or a pitchfork trying to get the soil turned over. Her look of absolute sheer pleasure shows that this is the first time she's ever done it." The three courtyards of Thorncliffe Park offer special places of beauty and solace to many in the busy school community. "We have many children in our school with special needs, and the gardens are a perfect place to take them. We have autistic children. We have dyslexic children. We have hearing impaired children. And you can see these children with their educational assistants going out, just getting a breath, looking at beauty, learning and finding literally, a breath of fresh air." (Houghton, 2003, pp. 37–38)

TABLE 7.2	An Outdoor Scavenger Hunt

Find someone who works outdoors.	Can you see a black car?
Find a seed pod.	Find a flower and draw it.
Find a tiny, smooth, and round pebble.	How does the wind sound?
Find a red leaf.	How many people can you hear?
Find something prickly.	Find a feather.
Find something fuzzy.	Find a white rock.
Find something soft.	Find a stop sign.
Find a pine cone.	Smell a pine tree.
Lie down and look up at the sky—what do you see?	Feel the bark of a tree and tell me about it.
Listen for the music of a songbird.	Can you find an insect?
Listen for a barking dog.	Wear a pair of old socks over your shoes and see what you collect.
Look for a kitten.	What machines can you hear?

A scavenger hunt can also be created for winter weather. Look for your breath, bird feeders, squirrel nests, bird nests, icicles, ice puddles, pinecones, dried leaves, evergreens, dried berries, animal tracks, snow people, birds, snow banks, a spot to make a snow angel, a place to build a fort, make a snow ball, etc.

"We need love to make us human. And we can best love and be loved when we have strong families, communities, and surrounding ecosystems. We also need to recognize that there are great mysteries in our lives we can never understand. We need to have sacred places, wildernesses we treasure because they feed our spirit. These are the values that all people can agree on. The challenge is to create societies and ways of life based on those needs. Enjoy your discoveries. Open your eyes, mind and heart to the beauty of the world. Then you can help make it a better place for yourself and all the other children who will inherit it."

—**David Suzuki and Kathy Vanderlinden**
(1999, p. 7)

Fenna Robertson

Children's artwork: Fenna

Chapter 8

LOOSE PARTS AND MATERIALS

"I'm not a do-gooder. I'm a doer who has figured out that hands-on, eyeball to eyeball making a difference is a way to live a very full life. Be selfish, go help someone."

—*Bobby Sager*

Team Sager Hope Ball

Team Sager Films

Bobby Sager is the author of *The Power of the Invisible Sun* (2009) a book about the power of hope, thankfulness, and his approach to making a difference. The book features the remarkable photographs that Bobby has taken of children he met in war-torn areas such as Afghanistan, Rwanda, Pakistan, and Palestine. Chronicle Books wrote about his book:

In war-torn countries around the world, philanthropist and photographer Bobby Sager has discovered the transcendent power of hope through the eyes of children. Despite unthinkable violence and destruction, his portraits reveal joy, innocence, and strength.

Bobby joined forces with the musician Sting and inventor Tim Jahnigen to develop something quite extraordinary and revolutionary: an indestructible soccer ball.

While a soccer ball may seem a small thing to most, an indestructible soccer ball will come to represent an incredible and elevated sense of durability, longevity, possibility, hope. Put simply, these

balls won't let them down—and are the entry point to learning critical life skills through play—discipline, teamwork, citizenship, knowing how to give constructive feedback, and being a supportive friend.

Every child needs to earn a ball—with their partner organization—by setting goals around team dynamics and sportsmanship. This will make the receipt of the ball—and trading in of their old, beaten up balls—that much more powerful.

For more information go to

http://www.teamsager.org

OUTCOMES:

1. Discuss the benefits of loose parts in the development of children's play.

2. Review a variety of loose parts appropriate for different age groups.

3. Evaluate the criteria for selection of toys and materials for the outdoor space.

4. Analyze the value of prop boxes, collections, porta paks, and story boxes in enhancing the outdoor play experience.

OUTDOOR PLAY MATERIALS
LOOSE PARTS

"A creative playspace without loose materials simply isn't one."

—Polly Hill

Four important reasons why we incorporate loose parts into play environments include:

- Loose parts encourage children to create their play options within the environment
- Loose parts expand the play options which increase the variability of the play and the potential for active movement
- Loose parts support the child's developmental level, as each child will use the loose parts in ways that are age-appropriate and reflective of their interest
- Loose parts stimulate children in their play, thus increasing appropriate play behaviors. (Dempsey & Strickland, 1999, p. 153)

The outdoor environment provides children with a rich array of flexible manipulatives, yet today's parents are inundated with ads about the latest gadget or electronic device designed to improve their children's cognitive abilities. Marketing is geared to the youngest of our children as consumers, who then pressure parents to provide the latest electronic toy. Often these toys provide very little novelty and have one use only. In contrast, architect Simon Nicholson's theory of loose parts is powerful in its simplicity. In *How Not to Cheat Children: The Theory of Loose Parts* (1971) he states that

all children love to interact with variables, such as materials and shapes; smells and other physical phenomena, such as electricity, magnetism and gravity; media such as gases and fluids; sounds, music and motion; chemical interactions, cooking and fire; and other people, and animals, plants, words, concepts and ideas. With all these things all children love to play, experiment, discover and invent, and have fun." Familiar "leftovers" from everyday life—used tools, kitchen utensils, accessories and gadgets—provide children with a sense of real life. They can move them, build with them, stack, arrange, tear down, and rearrange them, use them as props for imaginative play, create their own structures and incorporate them into their games. (p. 30)

In short, every major form of play uses loose parts.

For Additional Photos

"In any environment, both the degree of inventiveness and creativity and the possibility of discovery are directly proportional to the number and kind of variables in it. Most environments that do not work do not do so because they do not meet the "loose parts" requirement."

—Simon Nicholson

Kritchevsky and Prescott (1977) also support Nicholson's work, stating that the more complex an environment, the greater its potential to keep children continuously interested. If children are expected to play in an area for any length of time, high complexity seems virtually essential. Loose material is the only type of play equipment shown to have equal appeal to children across all age and grade levels. Robin Moore points out, in support of Nicholson,

Water play when you control the hose is the best fun!

that "kids really get to know the environment if they can dig it, beat it, swat it, lift it, push it, join it, combine different things with it." (Moore, 2010)

Therefore, loose parts are materials that can be used together, combined, collected, sorted, separated or pulled apart, lined up, dumped, etc. Natural materials such as rocks, leaves, sand, water, as well as toys, building systems, dolls, figures, clothing, scarves, hats, coats, shoes, boxes, paper, and playing cards will all add depth to the children's play. Loose parts are almost everything but worksheets. Consider the play value of a large set of blocks of varying shapes and sizes: when children play with blocks they discover the relationship between and among solid shapes. Children discover that two large blocks make a tower the same size as four smaller blocks. They make decisions about how they'll put blocks together and which block to use next; they estimate, measure, and use mathematical problem solving.

It is important to keep the playscape fresh and interesting by rotating materials or adding new props to expand the children's play. This is easy to do when you consider the vast variety of simple, inexpensive and recyclable materials that can inspire explorations and develop specific skills and concepts.

Families are perfect partners in trying to gather loose parts for our work with young children. They are often more than happy to provide meaningful materials for the children to explore. Consider sending home an interesting flyer listing many of the items below. This list is not inclusive but just seeing the items that can be incorporated into the children's play should "sprout" all kinds of ideas to support the children's learning. Together, families and teachers can create amazing collections!

TABLE 8.1   Start Collecting!

Acorns	Basters	Brooms	Can opener
Airplanes	Beads	Brown paper bags	Candles
Aluminium foil	Berry baskets	Bubble mixture	Cans—all kinds
Appliances	Bingo chips	Buckets	Canteens
Baby bottles	Binoculars	Bug catchers	Canvas
Baby clothes	Bird seed	Burlap	Cardboard boxes
Back pack	Blankets	Butterfly nets	Carpet
Balance beams	Blocks	Buttons	Castanets
Balls	Board games	Cable and cable spool:	CDs
Bamboo/bamboo mats	Books	Caftans	Chalk
Bandages	Bottle caps	Cake pans	Chopsticks
Bandanas	Bottles	Calculator	Cigar boxes
Barometer	Bowls	Calendars	Clay
Barrels	Boxes—all sizes	Camera	Clocks
Baskets	Branches	Camping gear	Cloth/rugs

(continued)

TABLE 8.1   Start Collecting! (continued)

Clothes hangers	Flower pots	Little People	Pool floaties
Clothespins	Food colouring	Locks and keys	Popsicle™ sticks
Coffee pots	Footballs	Lunch boxes	Postcards
Colourful junk mail	Fossils	Magnets	Prisms
Compass	Frying pans	Magnifying glasses	Puppets
Cooking stove	Funnels	Mail	PVC tubing
Corks	Gardening tools	Makeup brushes	Quilts
Cables	Gems	Maps	Radios
Crates	Geoboards	Marbles	Rattles
Cups	Gift wrap	Measure tapes	Recipes
Cushions	Gloves	Milk cartons	Recorders
Cylinders	Glue	Mirrors	Ribbons
Decks of cards	Glue sticks	Mittens	Rings
Detergent bottles	Gourds	Money	Roller blades
Diapers	Greeting cards	Mosquito net	Ropes
Dish cloths	Hats	Moss	Rulers
Dish tubs	Hinges	Moulds	Sacks
Dixie cups	Hoops	Muffin tins	Salt & pepper shakers
Doilies	Hoses	Musical instruments	Saran wrap
Dolls	Hour glass	Neck ties	Sawdust
Door mat	Ice cream scoops	Newspapers/magazines	Sawhorses
Dowelling	Ice cube trays	Nylons	Scales
Dress up clothes	Ice shapes	Oil pastels	Scarves
Ear muffs	Jacks	Old bicycle tires	Scoops
Earrings	Jars	Packaged seeds	Scooters
Easel	Kettle	Paper and paint	Scuba gear
Eating utensil	Key pads	Paper clips	Shells
Egg beaters	Keys	Paper rolls	Shoe boxes
Elastics	Kites	Parachute	Shoe laces
Electrical cables	Knapsacks	Pens/pencils	Shovels
Embroidery hoops	Koosh balls	Picnic baskets	Sifters
Envelopes	Lace	Pie plates	Sleds
Evergreen branches	Lantern	Pieces of screening	Snowshoes
Eye droppers	Laces	Pillows	Soccer ball
Fabric dyes	Lacrosse equipment	Pipe cleaners	Spatulas
Fans	Ladders	Pitchers	Sponges
Feathers	Ladles	Pizza pans	Spoons
File folders	Lamp	Place mats	Squirt bottles
Fire pit	Laundry baskets	Plastic Easter eggs	Steering wheels
First aid kit	Leaves	Plastic tubing	Stethoscope
Flags	Light-sensitive paper	Plastic water slide	Sticks

(continued)

| TABLE 8.1 | Start Collecting! (continued) |

Stones	Telescope	Variety of brushes	Wigs
Strainers	Tennis balls	Velvet	Wind chimes
Straws	Tent	Volleyball	Wind mills
String	Tents	Waffle maker	Wind socks
Strollers	Thermometer	Wagon	Wipes
Stumps	Thimbles	Walkie talkies	Wire
Sun glasses	Three-hole punch	Wallets	Wood planks
Sundial	Tiles	Wallpaper books	Woodworking bench
Table cloth	Timers	Washcloths	Worm garden
Takeout containers	Toboggans	Waste basket	Wrenches
Tambourines	Tool belt	Water	Yarn
Tandoor	Tool box	Water balloons	Yogurt containers
Tape	Tools	Water pumps	Zippers
Tape recorder	Towels	Waterproof aprons	Zip-top bags
Tarps	Traffic signs	Wax	Zither
Tea pot	Trowels	Wax paper	Zoo animals
Tea strainers	Tunnels	Wheelbarrows	
Telephone books	Ukulele	Whistles	
Telephones	Umbrellas	Wiffle balls	

MATERIAL SELECTION

Toys and games have been unearthed from the sites of ancient civilizations and were made from natural materials such as rocks, sticks, and clay. While the toy industry is a multi-billion dollar industry worldwide and there are unlimited numbers of toys and materials available for purchase, children still find pleasure in the most simple materials—rocks, sticks, and clay! Toys vary from simple and inexpensive to very complex and expensive. The choice of materials for outdoor play will vary based on the needs, interests, and budget of the centre as well as the suitability of the materials. Purchases should support the children's physical, social, emotional, and cognitive development embedded in a play-based environment. Purchased materials should also support the children's development of their imagination and stimulate enquiring minds.

The materials we provide send powerful messages to the children in our care; for example, toys that promote violence send messages that aggressive play is acceptable, providing plastic junk food in the dramatic play centre contributes to acceptance of unhealthy food choices, a growing concern. Toys that also lure children to television characters or other media toys may also raise concerns.

Exploring and discovering

Lynn Wilson

SAFETY

As educators we know that we never use any materials that could be harmful if touched, eaten, chewed, or could cause any type of adverse reaction. All materials should be carefully screened by educators to ensure their compliance with government safety standards. Consider the durability of the toy, kind of paint used, size of detachable parts, presence of sharp edges, and the ease of cleaning and disinfecting. It is imperative to always read the labels of new materials to ensure that they meet all regulations and safety standards. Look carefully for small parts warnings such as a choking hazard and the recommended age for use. Use a toilet paper roll or choke tube to test the size of loose parts. Small toy parts—such as Lego building blocks, dice, beads, etc.,— that can fit inside a choke-test cylinder or no-choke testing tube, which measures (3.25 cm wide by 5.6 cm long), and simulates the size and shape of a young child's throat are potential hazards. It is also important to consider all of the expected uses of the material while realizing that children may have their own unsafe way of using the toy.

Check toys and materials regularly for broken parts, deterioration, defects, etc., and supervise the play carefully, ensuring for example, that toys are not left where another child may trip. We must always be vigilant. All toys manufactured in Canada must comply with the rules and regulations of the *Hazardous Products Act*, which is administered by the Health Canada Product Safety Bureau. A copy of the act can be obtained through the nearest Product Safety Bureau office (Health Canada, 2003). The Canadian Toy Testing Council is a nonprofit organization that tests toys to help consumers make good toy purchases.

 http://www.toy_testing.org

Then Health Canada Consumer Product Safety is another organization that supports safe purchases.

 http://www.hc-sc.gc.ca/cps-spc/advisories-avis/info-ind/requirements-conditionseng.php

TOXICITY

Toxicity is an important consideration; for example, older toys and some materials may contain lead, mercury, cadmium, arsenic, and bromine. Recent concerns surrounding toxic chemicals in children's toys have focused on phthalates, a group of chemical compounds typically added to plastics to increase their softness and flexibility, and bisphenol A (BPA), a building block for polycarbonate plastic that is used in common plastic products such as shatter-resistant baby bottles and in the linings of food and beverage cans. In 2011, new Canadian regulations were put in place to ensure products that are imported, sold, or advertised in Canada do not present a risk of phthalate exposure to children and infants. Teachers can become advocates by contacting companies to ensure that the materials they are planning to order are safe

and alerting them to the fact that educators are aware and want to ensure the safety of the children in their care.

A powerful CBC documentary called "Forever Plastic" will give you greater insight into the concerns about the use of plastics. See

http://www.cbc.ca/documentaries/doczone/2009/foreverplastic

ASK THE CHILDREN

Depending on the age group of your children, let them help select toys and materials. Provide catalogues and visit local stores to discuss the cost of the materials to create a great budgeting opportunity and perhaps the seeds of a fundraiser! Older children will be influenced by exposure to television, peer pressure, store displays, etc., and will have strong points of views on purchases. Many toy departments are categorized by gender, with blue toys for boys and pink for girl. This is a great opportunity to examine and reject gender stereotypes. We should also be aware that popular toys may also be ones that promote violence and aggressive behaviour; while these should be discouraged, they provide a wonderful opportunity for debate.

AGE APPROPRIATENESS

We must be aware of the developmental appropriateness of a material or a piece of equipment. Most toys have suggested ages for use; this information is based on the developers' understanding of the child's chronological age, physical size, skill level, and maturity, which can be used as a guideline. However, labelling is not intended to be a substitute for appropriate adult supervision and proper use and care of the toy since children will vary in their skill and maturity levels (Health Canada, 2003).

SKILL DEVELOPMENT

It is important that we also consider the developmental needs of the children using the materials and the skills that will be developed through their use. We know that the biggest impact will be when a variety of senses are used in its manipulation. It is also important to consider whether adult intervention is required or whether the child can manage/manipulate on his or her own. Balance promoting physical, emotional, cognitive, language, and creative development through your toy selection. Balls of all sizes, riding toys, bean bags, etc., support the development of motor skills; cognitive skills are reinforced when children explore magnetic toys, construction sets, cause–and–effect toys; emotional development is explored when children re-enact what they know—family living—through dramatic play props and materials, as well as objects that they are familiar with—pots, pans, telephones, kitchen utensils, etc. Materials and toys provide an opportunity for children to learn new skills that reflect real-life experiences—enjoyment, frustration, challenge, success, and failure.

SENSORY MATERIALS

Materials that allow children to explore and express their feelings are an important element of outdoor play. Providing materials such as paint, crayons, markers, clay, Play-Doh™, goop, etc., allows for creative expression and the development of their fine motor skills. Rattles, drums, recorders, tambourines, and other musical instruments provide opportunities that encourage rhythm and movement. A blanket created from a variety of textures for infants to lie on, toys or other materials that support visual experiences such as hanging mobiles from the trees or providing kitchen utensils for the children to create their snack, enhances their outdoor experiences.

For toddlers, the world is a fascinating place!

Lynn Wilson

REAL OBJECTS

There is no question that children prefer real objects rather than plastic replicas. High levels of frustration are often experienced when this happens. Children want to imitate the people they see in their lives and the tools that they use—pots, pans, bowls, spatulas, cash registers, briefcases, telephones, screwdrivers, etc.

> Important learning takes place when providing materials for infants and toddlers who may be exploring an object for the first time. Brio, the famous maker of wooden railroad sets, produces some fine, brightly coloured, sturdy trowels, shovels, garden rakes and hoes, in addition to a small functional wheelbarrow.* (Richardson, 1998, p. 78)

Lee Valley also provides child-size tools.

MANIPULATIVES

Manipulatives include materials such as Duplo, Lego, Bristle Blocks, Puzzles, nesting boxes, pegs and pegboards, beads for stringing, lotto games, sewing cards, Unifix Cubes, acorns, pine cones, bread tags, buttons, corks, keys, Geoboards, and Board Games, for example. All of these materials support the development of the concepts of size, shape, classification, sorting, grouping, seriation, patterning, and one-to-one correspondence. These skills are reflected in the universal play theme of ordering and creating relationships between objects, exploring the reciprocity of objects as they are placed and arranged and rearranged. Physically, the manipulation of these materials supports the development of both gross and fine motor skills and the practice of eye–hand coordination and visual discrimination. When using these manipulatives the children are often interacting, learning how to co-operate with each other, and completing tasks successfully by trying out new ideas and taking risks.

OPEN/CLOSED

Open toys and materials—such as clay, blocks, Lego, construction toys, a large cardboard box, etc.,—challenge the children's imagination, have no correct outcome, and are the most valuable loose parts. Another example of open-ended materials is Tree Blocks (building blocks made entirely from reclaimed trees). See

http//:www.treeblocks.com

---

*Reprinted with permission from *Gardening with Children* by Beth Richardson, published by The Taunton Press, Inc. (www.taunton.com).

These materials allow children to create their own toys. Closed materials involve a right answer or a finished product: puzzles, Montessori materials, etc.

ACTIVE/PASSIVE

Providing a wide range of materials for the children to choose from allows them to move to toys that reflect their interest at any given time. High-energy toys that support gross motor experiences such as balls, ropes, tether balls, bicycles, wagons, skates, etc., may give way to more passive materials such as books, blankets, and dolls as their mood and interest changes.

VERSATILITY AND INVENTIVENESS

Some materials are more attractive to children because of their versatility; when toys can be combined with other toys, they encourage more complex play. While there are many inventive electronic toys and video games, there is a growing concern about the use of these materials and sedentary behaviour.

QUANTITY

Preferred items should be available in enough quantity for children to share, to maximize their explorations, and to provide opportunities for choice. This is very important for younger children who will all want the same item at the same time and are still developing their concept of sharing. Providing duplicates of popular toys when possible minimizes this frustration and encourages social peer-to-peer interaction!

DURABILITY

Toys and materials must be durable; those created for home use may not be appropriate for the type of use in a group setting. All purchases will need careful consideration especially when working with infants and toddlers who will mouth everything.

SOCIAL CONNECTIONS AND CULTURAL CONSIDERATIONS

Some toys and materials work best in combination with other children; for example, dramatic play materials, blocks, team games, etc. Toys often provide a bridge between the child and the adult and nothing is more important than a meaningful connection as a toy is explored together with the child leading the play. Toys that are reflective of the child's outdoor environment can make his or her play more meaningful. Toy bears, foxes, or whales could be used in communities where these animals are part of the habitat. In an urban setting the program might have a collection of toy squirrels, birds, dog, and cats with the other animals. The playground equipment should incorporate the landscape of the community rather than simply replicate a city playground. In a fishing community, an old boat becomes an excellent piece of playground equipment. A teepee or tent can provide a space for children to get away for some quiet time and also begin to understand what it was like to live in this environment (Our Children, Our Ways, 2000).

ADAPTABILITY

Funding is an issue in most child care environments so select play materials, such as open-ended materials, that are adaptable for a variety of different uses. A skillful teacher can attract the children to these materials with interesting set-ups. Teachers, too, need to be adaptable and should also be open to children moving materials from one area of the play space to the other as their play develops and expands. Choosing materials that can be adapted also will be important when providing accommodation for children with special needs.

CLEANLINESS AND AESTHETIC APPEAL

Teachers will need to balance the play potential of a piece of equipment or toy with the need to keep it clean. While plastic materials are easier to clean, they often do not have the same aesthetic impact that more natural materials demonstrate. How often materials will need to be cleaned is a reflection of the age and the vulnerability of the children. Ask yourself whether the colour, size, and shape add or detract from the overall aesthetic appeal. Think about whether or not this purchase will add to the "visual clutter" of the outdoor playscape or whether it will be a welcome addition. The Reggio Emilia approach to using natural materials has inspired many centres to create more calm and inviting playscapes.

View the video at

http://imaginationplayground.com

to see an incredible playground—Imagination Park, South Street Seaport, New York City—designed by David Rockwell. View the loose parts in Rockwell's *Imagination Playground in a Box* and the impact it has on children's creative play.

CONNECTION TO FAMILIES AND THE COMMUNITY

> "When this generation of grandparents disappears, the chance to collect precious memories about games they played and toys they made will disappear with them."
>
> —Renzo Laporta and Jean-Pierre Rossie (2010)

This quote reminds us of the expertise that exists in our communities. Do you make use of these Elders who have so much to share? Do the materials that you are considering reflect the families and the community in which you live? Avoid all toys that send negative messages about racial, ethnic, or cultural groups, or those that reinforce gender stereotypes. To encourage interactions between parents and their children, encourage a toy swap among the families. It is a good way to reuse materials.

COST

Centres must balance expenditures on play materials with their durability to ensure a long life in the play space. An expensive object will not necessarily be long lasting. Make wise investments in materials that will stand up to constant use. Also consider free materials when families or community members donate "beautiful junk" to the centre. Often, donated objects such as kitchen utensils, clothing, old telephones, etc., will provide hours of constructive play. As they move on to others centres or school, some families leave behind a "memory" present—a valuable addition to play materials.

TAKING ACTION

There are times when toys or equipment are produced that create a great deal of controversy. When this happens, it is a great opportunity for teachers to get involved, perhaps by hosting a meeting of families to consider appropriate action to advocate for healthier community outdoor play environments.

PROP AND LOOSE PARTS BOXES

Very little money, but plenty of imagination and cheap and free resources are often the best way of improving the space quickly. Boxes are the answer!

Loose parts boxes contain more open-ended materials while prop boxes often have a dramatic play element to them. Stored outside in a secure location, boxes are ideal way to organize materials for easy access by both educators and children. Boxes should be durable—Tupperware containers for example, suitcases, hat boxes, back packs—and well labelled. If the boxes are used among different age groups, it might be the responsibility of the users to add one new thing to the box after their use; that way the boxes are always growing. Boxes can be created for any age group from infants to school-agers. There are so many ideas for prop boxes—the list is limited only by your imagination. Always consider the safety of the children and the age appropriateness of the box.

Below are specific examples. Include storybooks in the box to encourage early literacy when the children's interest is high.

 Ball Box—ping-pong balls, rubber sponge balls, tennis balls, beach balls, soccer balls, footballs, soft balls, Koosh balls, balls that light up when squeezed, red/white and blue balls, textured balls, balls with numbers, balls with shapes on the outside, etc.

For Additional Reading

Play-Doh™ Box—play clay (wrap tightly), plastic place mats, cookie cutters, ice-pop sticks, tongue depressors, rolling pins, plastic knives, plastic scissors, scissors with different cutting blades, garlic press, plastic pizza cutter, wire mesh, sieve, muffin tins, small animals, vehicles, etc.

For Additional Reading

Going on a Picnic Box—blanket, chair, picnic basket, colourful cups and dishes, food, napkins, lemonade, sunscreen, vacuum bottle, coolers, beach umbrella, inner tubes, air mattress, beach towels, sunglasses, straw hats, beach ball, and teddy bears for a Teddy Bear Picnic!

For Additional Reading

Mini Beasts Box—Bugs/insect/worms, bug catchers, magnifying lenses, trowels, grass, terrarium, fish bowl, shoebox, canning jar, butterfly net, spoons, clipboard, pencil, paper, collection of laminated bug photos.

For Additional Reading

Hospital Box—doctor's uniform, nurse's uniform, smocks, disposable plastic gloves, bandages, stethoscope, watch, sling, masks, caps, shoe covers, doctor's bag, blankets, pillows, clipboard, notepaper, pencil, telephone, cotton balls, swabs, hot-water bottle, dolls, eye chart (Toronto's Sick Children's Hospital does not recommend the use of syringes or medicine bottles).

 Gardener's/Florist Box—shovels, trowel, rakes, gardening gloves, watering cans, spray water bottles, flower pots, potting soil, seed packets, baskets, aprons, cash register, gardening magazines, ribbon, wrapping paper, tape, vases, silk/real flowers, order book, wheelbarrow, pieces of hose, spray nozzles.

 Magic Box—different simple tricks in drawstring bags with pictorial instructions, magic hat, wand, cape, stuffed bunny, deck of cards, string, handkerchief, black velvet cloth, dice, balls, coins, crystal.

Writer's Box—markers, calligraphy pens, thin markers, fancy pencils, pencil sharpener, erasers, pencil crayons, crayons, charcoal, oil pastels, ballpoint pens, stapler, staples, clipboard, stickers, coloured paper, index cards, tag board, graph paper, chart paper, blank booklets, envelopes, chalkboards, eraser, chalk, magic slates, magnetic board, hole punch, paper clips, paper fasteners, pencil boxes, Chinese brushes for calligraphy, stamps, stamp pads, rulers, scissors.

 Painter's Box—rollers, brushes, sponges, paint trays, scrapers, wallpaper, sandpaper, tape measure, drop sheet, empty paint tins, buckets, painter's cap, paint chips.

 Sewing/Weaver's Box—wool, string, twine, clothes pins, clothing line, netting, strips of crepe paper, plastic strips, ribbons, raffia, rickrack, lace, tape measure, needlepoint screening, wood for a frame, hoops, blunt embroidery needles, thread, fabric, crochet hooks, knitting needles, scissors, buttons, beads, leather, grasses, twigs, leaves, bark.

 Treasure Box—rocks, nuggets (paint small rocks gold), coloured stones, coins, marbles, old jewellery, chest keys, pirate hat, eye patch, black boots, bandanas, scarves, stuffed parrot, belts

Go to http://www.leehansen.com/printables/masks/pirate-hat-craft-sheet.pdf for a pirate hat pattern.

 Mud Pie Box—boots, raincoats, mud, water, pie plates, cake tins, moulds, spoons, muffin tins, juice cans with edges taped, empty milk cartons, bowls, tea pot, tea cups, grass, clover, pine needles, small berries, flower petals, dandelions, crushed dry leaves, twigs, wood shavings, sand, green leaves, moss, seaweed, corn silk, straw, hay, crab grass, chickweed, pencil sharpenings, seashells, rocks.

 Travel Box—suitcases, travel brochures, maps, posters, old airline tickets, passports, old phone cards, beach hats, towels, beach balls, plastic sunglasses, terry robes, sandals, paper, pencils, camera, sun hats, sunscreen, small travel kit—shampoo bottles, toothbrushes, toothpaste, brush, comb, sunscreen, pretend money, postcards, travel magazines, fins, snorkels, beach umbrella.

 Camping Box—tents (more than one for visiting), blankets, logs, red-orange cellophane for recreating flames, sleeping bags, pillow cases, backpack, cooler, cereal boxes, granola bar boxes, trail mix, frying pan, pots, vacuum bottle, plates, cups, cutlery, spatula, tongs, marshmallows, lanterns, fishing rod, blue tarp (for a "lake"), folding chairs, camera, swimsuits, flashlight, maps, binoculars, sunglasses, mosquito net, stuffed animals.

 Pizza Box—unused pizza boxes (ask neighbourhood pizza parlours for donations), stove/oven, round cardboard pizza circles for the children to decorate (access to arts and crafts area), toppings made from felt, pizza cutter, order pad, cash register, pretend money, telephone, apron, chef's hat, table, cutlery, table cloth, menu—wouldn't it be so much more meaningful if the children could be making real pizzas!

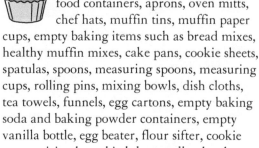

Baking Box—play dough, empty food containers, aprons, oven mitts, chef hats, muffin tins, muffin paper cups, empty baking items such as bread mixes, healthy muffin mixes, cake pans, cookie sheets, spatulas, spoons, measuring spoons, measuring cups, rolling pins, mixing bowls, dish cloths, tea towels, funnels, egg cartons, empty baking soda and baking powder containers, empty vanilla bottle, egg beater, flour sifter, cookie cutters, icing bags, birthday candles, bottle opener, cookbooks, timer, cash register.

For Additional Reading

Mystery Suitcase—a suitcase, trunk, or interesting container can hold all kinds of objects that would appeal to young children—feathers, keys, scarves, bells of all kinds, wind chimes, feather duster, sunglasses, goggles, cameras, binoculars, kaleidoscopes, large make-up brushes. The suitcase can be filled with related items or just interesting materials. Babies will respond when they see the suitcase and know that something fun is inside. A trip to the dollar store may help you decide what to put in the suitcase.

For Additional Reading

COLLECTIONS

Baskets, bags, small suitcases, and shoeboxes are perfect storage for a wide range of collections that the children can take outside. Fill the containers with bottle tops, shells, yogurt pots, plastic containers, keys, wheeled vehicles, purses, hats, musical instruments, cookie cutters, juice bottles baseball cards, autographs, coins, decals, dolls, flags, plastic insects, kites, marbles, music boxes, puppets, postcards, rocks, autographs, bottle caps, etc.

Inside **LOOK**

Creating Prop Boxes

I attended a workshop on prop boxes and couldn't wait to start organizing our existing materials into prop boxes. My enthusiasm was infectious so all of the teachers agreed to spend an evening going through all of our toys and materials. It was a great way to clean out all of our cupboards and we were surprised at all we found buried away on shelves and in corners. And so began the great Prop Box Experience. We now have an incredible collection of prop boxes, all well labelled and filled with interesting and unusual materials. We held a fundraiser to supplement our boxes and our families were incredibly generous when asked to donate materials they had at home. We are now more able to respond to the children's interests and the boxes have helped us expand and extend their play. Each teacher has made a commitment that every time he or she takes out a prop box, he or she will add one item to the box so the boxes are forever growing!

Inside **LOOK**

Fascination with Keys

In my kindergarten field placement, my faculty gave us a collection assignment. We were to create a collection that was appropriate for the age group we were working with and based on the children's interests.

The caretaker in the centre had been opening a jammed cupboard when the key broke in the lock. The children were incredibly interested in how the key broke and, more importantly, how the cupboard would be opened! That night I looked all over my house, called all my friends, and collected over 30 keys. I brought the keys in. The enthusiasm for the collection was incredible. Several children tried many of the keys in the matching cupboard to see if they would fit, others sorted the keys by colour, some took all the old keys and put

(continued)

them in a pile, and others made up stories about what type of castle the key would open. The conversation was rich and inventive. As a follow-up experience, I created a lock board with eight different types of locks with eight matching keys. The children spent hours opening and closing the locks. When my faculty was talking to us about how important collections were, I thought I understood what she meant but it wasn't until I saw this idea in action that I realized the power of it. I am now working in the field and you should see my collections!

PORTA PAKS

These simple portable bags are positive additions to the outdoor environment. Teacher made activities can be enclosed in a large Ziploc bag and when possible laminated for durability. They can be placed within easy reach at the doorway to the outside and the children can take one out, sit under a tree by themselves or with friends and complete the challenges inside.

STORY BOXES

Story boxes can be created from a story that is one of the children's favourites. Craft a wide range of activities related to the story, place each one inside zip top bags or interesting containers and store them in the box. The children should be able to identify the story by the decorations or drawings on the outside of the box. The children can take it outside, complete the activities, as well as read the story either on their own or with friends.

For Additional Photos

Lynn Wilson

Colour-matching game

Lynn Wilson

Puzzles made from magazines and tongue depressors!

Lynn Wilson

A fish-matching game

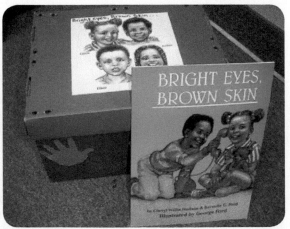

Lynn Wilson

Bright Eyes, Brown Skin *story box*

Handa's Surprise story box

STORAGE

For Additional Photos

In most centres, storage is a major issue—there is never enough of it! A thoughtful organized approach to the toys and materials is essential. Since we know that the most valuable creative materials are those with which the children can interact, digging machines, wind machines, waterwheels, and clothesline pulleys and a wide range of loose parts, etc., should be accessible and easy for the children to locate and return. Double doors on the storage shed will make access easier. The shed should be durable, easy to maintain, well ventilated, and vermin- and water proof. Be sure the shed can be locked and will withstand vandals.

Locate the shed in a convenient spot that will not impede supervision of the children. If children and/ or teachers always must carry everything from the classroom out to the playscape, it is doubtful that a wide range of play activities will be accommodated.

Quick and easy storage

A storage shed in the garden at the Copper House

Proper organization makes everyone's job easier.

Easy access

Ideally, a centre will have several storage locations with each well labelled. For example, keep the wheeled vehicles close to the bike paths; sand and water play equipment, garden tools, and pet supplies near the environmental zone; construction materials and carpentry tools near the cognitive/construction zone; and art supplies near the water source.

Arrange hooks and shelves to accommodate the type of equipment being stored. This will make it easy for the children to locate, remove, and return the materials. Storage containers located throughout the play space allow a "help yourself" approach and empower the children in their play choices.

Lovejoy (2003) proposes an interesting storage idea:

> Attach a series of terra cotta pots horizontally to a tall vertical post. These pots can contain art materials, gardening tools etc. Round brown clay tiles that are about a foot long that are used for drainage are perfect for storing small items. Bury them upright into the ground at varying heights and they can become holders for a variety of any items. They can also be used for spot planting.* (Lovejoy, 2003, p. 138)

Also "mounting mailboxes on walls, fences and posts throughout the playspace provide[s] storage for tools, twine, gloves, seed packets, labels and perhaps even a first aid kit" (Lovejoy, 2003, p. 142).**

END-OF-THE-DAY ROUTINES

For many children, putting away at the end of the day is a frustrating experience since the adult's and the child's concept of time may be very different. Children will want to keep things in place so they can return to the play the next morning. In some sites that may be possible but in others things must be put away. In these situations, suggest that children draw what they have done or take photographs that can be brought out with them the next day to remind them of their work.

---

*Excerpted from *Trowel and Error: Over 700 Shortcuts, Tips and Remedies for the Gardener* © 2003 by Sharon Lovejoy. Workman Publishing, New York. Used by permission of Workman Publishing Co., Inc., New York. All Rights Reserved.

**Ibid., p. 142.

Children's artwork: Mia

Courtesy of Mia Perketa

CURRICULUM EXPERIENCES FOR PLAY ZONES

> "Imagine a classroom with sky for a ceiling and earth for a floor. A room without walls or desks, where young scientists explore the world of bugs; mathematicians measure rainfall; budding writers record their observations; and actors rehearse on a natural stage."*
>
> —Herbert W. Broda (2007, p. 27)

Curriculum is an organized system of intentions and plans to promote children's development and learning. Curriculum is every learning experience in an early childhood setting including planned experiences and activities that spontaneously emerge from children's play and interactions. Play-based curriculum is a selection of activities organized to facilitate movement, activity, choice, autonomy, communication, and social interaction (Bennett, 2004). Play is children's method of learning, and knowledge and skills become meaningful when used in play. Tools for learning are practised and concepts become understood. All elements of learning and development are explored and practised in play. The whole child is unified and supported in play-based curriculum.

Creating curriculum requires knowledge and many skills. We know that learning progresses from simple to complex; therefore, educators plan developmentally appropriate curriculum that adds a new variable only after the children have mastered the variables already present. We plan opportunities for children's hands-on manipulation with real, concrete objects as their learning progresses from concrete to abstract. As educators, we must plan repeated practice to ensure motivation and the child's active engagement.

In this chapter you will find hundreds of ideas organized by the zones discussed in Chapter 5 *(environmental, physical/active, social/dramatic, cognitive/construction, art, and quiet/communication)* to help you support and facilitate children's learning. The approach here is multidisciplinary and in any zone, you will find activities that engage children's diverse learning styles and interests through visual, oral, and kinesthetic means as well as inquiry-based learning that provide opportunities for children to direct and lead the

play. Early childhood curriculum is a life shared between adults and children. Emergent curriculum emphasizes that plans for children evolve from the daily life of children and adults in early childhood settings, not pre-set recipes. Plans are necessary to prepare programs that respond to children's needs and skill development based on the insightful observations of the educator. While the ideas presented will provide you with a wide range of experiences, it is hoped that you will see not just the idea, but the face of a child in your care—an opportunity to expand and build on that individual child's observed interest. This is not meant to be a prescriptive approach to learning but rather an opportunity to engage and scaffold what is already happening in your outdoor environments. Not all of the activities may be appropriate for the age group or be of interest to the children who you are teaching but hopefully many of these experiences can be adapted in meaningful ways. *While at times we may guide activities, this must not take the place of creative play where the children set their own agenda and choose their own open-ended materials.*

"Unpredictability is a feature of the environment. Daily planning can never predict children's sudden excitement at the appearance of a rainbow or a noisy police helicopter overhead. Unpredictable events are often the most exciting and engaging events for children as well as many adults" (Garrick, 2009, p. 81).

This collection of experiences is an invitation to you as an educator to participate in a shift in attitude and a true understanding of the long-term benefits of innovative outdoor play experiences. As you move forward, it is critical that you review the processes of emergent curriculum to ensure that your planned materials/experiences support a play-based, child-centred, child-led approach.

GUIDING PRINCIPLES FOR OUTDOOR EXPERIENCES
PROTECT THE NATURAL WORLD

- Treat all natural things—animals, plants, soil and water with care and respect

- Keep any animals you're working with safe. Handle them gently and be sure that they have food, water and air. When you are finished, put them back where you found them.

- Get permission before you collect any plants. Be careful not to disturb the area around them

---

*Broda, H.W. 2007. *Schoolyard-Enhanced Learning: Using the Outdoors as an Instructional Tool, K-8*. Stenhouse Publishers, p. 27.

- Whenever you are doing an activity outdoors, create as little disturbance to the area as possible

- Whenever possible, recycle or reuse materials—such as paper and water—that you have used in your activity. (Suzuki & Vanderlinder, 1999, p. 11)

IDEAS FOR OUTDOOR PLAY

One way to focus on meaningful experiences is to look for special days to celebrate throughout the year with a link to planned or spontaneous curriculum:

February—Heart Month

February 2—World Wetlands Day

March—Nutrition Month

March 22—World Day of Water

April 7—World Health Day

Third week of April—International TV Turnoff Week

April 22—Earth Day

May 3—International Migratory Bird Day

May 10—International Day for Physical Activity/Move for Health Day

May 15—International Day of Families

May 22—International Day for Biological Diversity

June 5—World Environment Day

June 8—World Oceans Day

June 15—Nature Play Day, The Child and Nature Alliance of Canada

June 17—World Day to Combat Desertification And Drought

June 21—National Aboriginal Day

June 29—International Mud Day

August 9—International Day of the World's Indigenous People

September—Clean Up the World Campaign

September 8—International Literacy Day

Third Saturday in September—Ocean Conservancy International Coastal Clean-Up

Third Sunday in September—Terry Fox Run

September 26—World Wide Day of Play

First week of October—International Walk to School Week

First Monday of October—United Nations World Habitat Day

October 16—World Food Day

October—National Family Week

October 24—International Day of Climate Action

November 6—International Day for Preventing the Exploitation of the Environment in War and Armed Conflict

November 20—National Child Day

December 5—World Soil Day

December 10—Human Rights Day

December 11—International Mountain Day

ENVIRONMENTAL ZONE

For Additional Reading

1. **Earth Day:** Earth Day is celebrated every year on April 22 and is a worldwide movement to appreciate and celebrate the planet on which we live. Have a birthday party for the Earth. Older children might enjoy celebrating Earth Day by creating a T-shirt with their own symbol or logo celebrating Earth Day! White T-shirts for this project can be purchased inexpensively or families may be able to provide one for their child. Use markers designed specifically for cloth. Earth Day is a perfect opportunity to discuss the three Rs: reduce, reuse, and recycle!

2. **Earth Day Planting:** One centre holds a barbecue every Earth Day and invites families to bring a plant to be planted in the centre's garden. Another centre had a parent who was a landscape architect create a planting map for the centre. Each plant was identified by name with the cost and families signed up to purchase their favourite plant. On the Saturday closest to Earth Day, all of the families arrived at the centre and the local garden centre delivered all of the plants at a discount. This was a great cooperative effort that involved families, teachers, and children! Children still come back to the centre with their families to visit their family plant.

3. **Mother Earth:** Aboriginal people in Canada share a reverence, appreciation, and respect for nature. They also recognize that everything in nature is connected in a circle of life. Contact your local Friendship Centre or other Aboriginal organization and ask if an Elder would come to speak to the children and share stories about Mother Earth. Attending a pow-wow is another learning opportunity. June 21 is National Aboriginal Day in Canada.

For Additional Reading

4. **Tummy Time and Grass:** Take the time with young children to really see the common things in our environment that we sometimes take for granted. Watch an infant putting his or her feet on the grass for the first time, how does the baby react? Encourage tummy time

A pow-wow in Orillia, Ontario

Lynn Wilson

to really feel the grass, smell it, put your cheek on it. Explore!

For Additional Reading

5. **Why Is Grass Green?**

   Place a sheet of white construction paper on the grass. Step on the paper and twist your foot into the grass. Lift the paper and examine it. What do you see? Grass and other plants are green because they contain a pigment called chlorophyll. Plants make food from carbon dioxide, water and sunlight through the process of photosynthesis. Without chlorophyll, this process would not take place. (Potter, J. 1995. *Nature In A Nutshell For Kids*. Jossey-Bass. p. 36)

   Photosynthesis results in plants emitting oxygen as part of the air we breathe.

6. **Think Green:** Find as many green things as you can outside. This is another opportunity to talk about photosynthesis in plants.

7. **Grassy Noises:** Make a loud and squeaky noise by making a whistle from a wide blade of grass. Stretch the grass with both hands between the tops and bottoms of your thumbs and blow across the blade of grass. This may take some practice for little hands!

8. **Furry Sculptures:** Collect a large handful of burdock burrs and let the children experiment with these sticky creations (a way to discuss Velcro!)

9. **Cycles:** Find something that is part of a cycle. For example, plant-bud-flower-seed-plant; egg-larva-pupa-adult-egg; egg-tadpole-frog-egg.

For
Additional
Reading

10. **Babies:** Look at young plants and animals (include all of the animal groups: mammals, invertebrates, birds, amphibians, reptiles, fish, etc.). Visit with the animal babies in the outdoor playground at your centre or a nearby one that has infants. What are the babies able to do and what have they yet to achieve?

11. **Be a Detective:** Really examine a plant. Where does your plant live, in the sun or the shade? Trace, draw, or make a rubbing of the leaf. What shape is it? What colour is it? Are both sides of the leaf the same? Are all the leaves on the plant the same? What does the edge of the leaf look and feel like? Are there flowers on your plant? If so, what colour are they? How many petals does it have? What's in the centre of the flower? Does the flower have a fragrance? What shape is the stem? Squeeze it, what happens? What does the root system look like? Is there any insect damage? Draw or take a picture of your plant.

12. **Why Are Trees Important?**

Ask the children to think about all the ways in which trees are important to us. What does the tree offer to living things—shade, shelter, food, transportation? What creatures might use it? Which animals use a tree's branches? Which animals use a tree trunk? Which animals use a tree's leaves? Think about all the ways that trees differ from one another. Consider their height and width, their bark, their leaves, their branches. How many different types of trees can you find in your area?* (Ward, 2008, p. 16)

13. **Spectacular Trees:** Forsythia, lilacs and tulip magnolia trees are spectacular spring additions to any playground. Check out early spring bloomers in your neighbourhood and consider planting them in your own playscape. Check out this website for some spectacular trees:

 http://conservationreport.com/2010/10/17/nature-a-sampling-of-the-most-spectacular-trees-in-the-world

14. **Dwarf Trees:** A dwarf tree is just right for children. Dwarf trees take up very little space, some will bear fruit within a year or two of planting and the fruit will be easy for the children to reach; others, like this Japanese maple, will provide interesting colour.

15. **Tree Touch:** Touch the tree; how does the bark feel? Do all trees feel the same? Explain that the bark is the skin of a tree and it has many layers and tissues. As the trunk of the tree grows in width, the outer tissues lose their supply of nutrients and water. These outer tissues separate from the inner layer and become rough.

16. **Healing Trees:**

How do trees heal themselves? Examine trees to find one that has a wound and examine what has happened. Weather conditions, fires, people and animals all wound trees. It first leaks sap from the wound opening. In most cases, a callus quickly forms at the edges to keep the sap from oozing out. Cells in the cambium or growth tissue begin to multiply and grow inward. If the edges are jagged, the opening may never close completely.** (Potter, 1995, p. 91)

17. **Maple Tree Candy:** During the spring if a sugar bush is not available you can take boiling maple syrup outside and pour it onto a flat surface of snow. This is a boiling substance so the teacher should complete this part of the task. You can place an PopsicleTM stick into the warm mass and watch it harden into a delicious treat! If you are lucky, you might have a sugar maple tree in your own playscape and you can harvest your own syrup.

For
Additional
Reading

18. **Tree Stumps:** Examine a tree stump and look at the rings. The distance between the rings indicates weather conditions and the time in the tree's life. The rings are widest at the beginning when the tree was first growing and very close together in a very dry season. Counting the rings will tell you how old the tree is. Estimate before you count.

19. **Roll Over:** Moving old logs unearths many types of critters.

*From *I Love Dirt!*, by Jennifer Ward, © 2008 by Jennifer Ward. Reprinted by arrangement with Shambhala Publications Inc., Boston, MA. www.shambhala.com. p. 16.

**Potter, J. 1995. *Nature In A Nutshell For Kids*. Jossey-Bass. p. 91.

Lynn Wilson

Many critters can be found under logs.

Anna Azimi/Shutterstock

A wish tree

20. **A Tree Tells a Tale:**

Wood chips at the base and a gaping hole in the trunk mean a *woodpecker* has been spearing insect larvae with its long tongue or building a nest; *Snowshoe hares* gnaw small bites from the bark of woody plants; discarded pinecones that are picked clean of seeds mean a *red squirrel* lives nearby; a tightly packed leaf and twig nest as big as a bicycle tire is usually the summer home to squirrels[;] they often winter inside hollow tree limbs lined with leaves and moss; if large pieces of bark, entire twigs and succulent buds have been chiselled from a tree, a *porcupine* has dined; missing bark and gouged wood ribbed with teeth marks tell you a hungry *moose* has made a meal of a young tree; deep claw marks on tree trunks are *black bears'* way of saying "I'm big and I'm nearby, [sic] it could be hibernating under that tree; poop like pellets at the base of a tree may mean a *great horned owl* is roosting there. They eat small animals and birds whole and then regurgitate fuzzy pellets of indigestible feathers, bones and fur!* (Drake & Love, 1998, p. 63)

---

*Drake, J. & Love, A. 1998. *The Kids Cottage Games Book*. Kids Can Press. p. 63.

21. **Wish Tree:** Having children record their wishes on a wish tree provides an opportunity to talk about how we may make the world a better place. Yoko Ono shares that when she was a child, she would go to her temple and write her wish on a thin piece of paper and tie it to a tree branch. The wish tree has been part of many of her exhibits around the world. The photo below is a wish tree in Washington, D.C.

22. **Commemorate a Special Event:** Plant a tree or build a garden to commemorate a special event or a moment in the life of the centre. Plant a memory tree, one the children can return to as they grow older. If space and funds allow, have each child plant his or her own memory tree.

For Additional Reading

23. **Plant a Tree:** In many communities, seedlings of young trees are made available for planting and, in some cases, at no charge. Encourage each child to plant his or her seedling with his or her family. In some cases, all the seedlings might be planted at the centre itself since in many child care and school locations, adequate shading is a challenge! There are many ways to measure, graph, photograph, and record the growth of each child's tree.

For Additional Reading

24. **What Could Be Wrong?** Look carefully at the trees over the season. What's happening to this tree? The leaves have changed, and are covered in spots. Is it sick? Be a detective. Use books and the Internet to see what's happening. Try taking a leaf to a local nursery and ask an expert when you just can't find the answer.

Lynn Wilson

A sick tree?

25. **Leaf Maze:** When raking leaves in the fall, see if the children can create a maze for their friends to find their way through (National Wildlife Federation, 2010)

26. **Leaf Spelling:** Rake leaves into names or initials (National Wildlife Federation, 2010).

27. **Leaf Gathering:** Have the children collect leaves for activities or just for the fun of collecting. Toddlers love to collect and dump!

28. **Leaf Piles:** Rake leaves into giant piles and encourage the children to jump in, throw the leaves up in the air, or make leaf angels instead of snow angels!

29. **Leaf Catching:** On a windy day make leaf catchers out of lightweight recyclable plastic bags and try to catch the leaves before they hit the ground!

30. **Sweep Netting:**

    Sweeping a large net or a pillowcase through long grass is the most effective way to catch the invertebrates hiding among the stems—beetles, bugs and flies. The net should be lightweight, with a large opening, and used very gently so as not to harm them. Don't forget to return the creatures to the area where they were caught. (Danks & Scholfield, 2005, p. 72)

31. **Habitats for Animals and People:** Discuss with the children if they think basic survival needs—food, water, air, shelter, and a place to raise their young—are the same for people

and animals. List these elements and ask the children where they think humans get these things. This provides an opportunity to explore where air, water, food, etc., come from. It may also be interesting to talk about animals vs. people's homes. Some children may wish to draw their ideas.

32. **Looking for Homes:** Children can look for homes for animals and insects—nests, burrows, dens, hiding places, and tree holes.

33. **Animal Habitats:** Use a variety of magazines such as *Ranger Rick, Your Big Backyard, National Geographic* and other nature magazines to cut out pictures of replicated animals, insects, birds, etc., and laminate them for longer use. Discuss the different types of habitats animals need to survive and have the children decide if the animal in the picture belongs in a meadow, forest, grassland, desert, ocean, lake, river, or wetland. This can be a graphing exercise if the children are interested.

34. **Animal Fables:**

    Explain what fables are and share some examples of fables that include animals who speak. Encourage children to create their own fables using animals they observed during the walks." Younger children may enjoy using finger puppets to create their own puppet show (*Hey Kids! Out the Door, Let's Explore!* By Rhoda Redleaf (2010). pg.1). "Some First Nation children played with puppets that they wore on their hands or fingers. These puppets were made by stuffing animal hair into hides that formed the shape of the puppet. (McCue, 2006, p. 42)

35. **Be in the Community:** It is important that children have opportunities to explore the world around them, either on day trips, or on overnight or several-day excursions depending on their age. Many children recount these trips as some of their most significant childhood memories. Ideas for visiting in the community include aquariums, appliance repair shops, artists' studios, beaches, boat yards, camping shops, computer offices, construction sites, a court house, factories, farms, forests, government offices, greenhouses, hospitals,

museums, music stores, orchards, a police station, a radio station, a railroad yard, a restaurant kitchen, ships, theatres, zoos, and many more! Festivals and local celebrations are also opportunities to connect children to their communities. Also consider camping, ecology trips, and hikes.

36. Community Connection: Gardens are everywhere! Where can you walk in your community—parks, nurseries, beaches, open spaces, gardens? What can you see, dandelions in sidewalk cracks, buds opening in the spring, cool spaces in the summer because of a canopy of trees, a field of wild flowers, moss growing on rocks? Bring along a magnifying glass for a close-up look. What other interesting sculptures have people added to their gardens? Take photos, graph, and pick the favourites.

37. Statues in the Community: These children often passed a war monument on their way to community trips. They asked why it was there and the teacher, not knowing, took the children to the statue—a teachable moment for everyone! There are many such opportunities in our communities.

A war memorial

38. A Cemetery Visit: For older children, much of our local history is "stored" in our cemeteries. Children's own personal experiences or the death of a loved playroom animal which may spark questions about death and dying. They may talk about funeral traditions in their own culture. They may ask why children died so young when they look at death dates on the tomb stones. Are any famous people buried here? Approach with sensitivity and an understanding of the children's ability to manage a difficult topic.

39. A Generous Gift: Many communities have senior residences and they may appreciate a bouquet of flowers or fruits and vegetables from the children's garden. You may be surprised at how this simple gesture may start a wonderful relationship between the children and the elders in their community.

40. Decorate the Neighbourhood: Take a wagon for a walk and collect a variety of stones and bring them back to the centre. Use chalk or paint to decorate them, load them back up again and decorate the neighbourhood with the new and beautiful stones. Glow-in-the-dark chalk is a new and fun idea to try out!

41. Nature Walks: Label big baskets, sturdy brown bags, sand pails, zip-top bags, etc., labeled with the children's names and collect items during your walk. Examine the items on your return; how do they smell? Do they change when immersed in water? Encourage sorting and classifying of items based on the children's own observations of the collection—big, small, pretty, ugly, smooth edges, jagged edges, ones I want to take home, etc. Graph the results.

42. Socks for Your Shoes: Pull on some socks over your shoes and go for a walk. Visit an interesting forest, a park or a field. Take off your socks and check them out with a magnifying

Lynn Wilson

glass. Do you see some seeds that have hitched a ride with your socks? Put your socks into a plastic bag and give them a little water. Put the bag in the sun and watch what happens. Try planting your sock—what happens?

43. **Sticky Walk:** Form a piece of cardboard into a circle to create a bracelet. Place a strip of double-sided tape, sticky side up around the circle. Take the children on a nature walk and find out what they have collected on their bracelet when they get back.

44. **Shoelace Walk:** Take along a shoelace on a nature walk and determine how many objects can be strung on a shoelace.

45. **Water Walk:** If you live near the water, there are so many things to explore and discover. Collect rocks worn smooth by water; look for driftwood, shells, beach glass, and interesting rocks; then paint them. Take along a picnic and have a great water day!

For Additional Reading

46. **Shells:** Shells have incredible properties for exploration and discovery. Try looking at them with a magnifying glass.

47. **Beach Glass:** Often children will find beautiful pieces of glass that have been worn smooth by the waves at the beach. You can demonstrate by having an adult collect small pieces of glass and place them in a jar of water. Shake away!

Lynn Wilson

A water day at Lake Ontario

This will take some time and can be done over several weeks where the children take turns shaking the jar.

48. **Summer Treasure Baskets:** For programs that close over the summer months you might consider sending each child home with a treasure basket. Over the summer months the children can fill their baskets with reminders of their summer holidays and bring their baskets back to be shared in the fall.

49. **Bird Sounds:** Find a local birding book and pick three or four of the most common birds in your area. (Your local library should be able to help and may have a CD with bird sounds.) Help the children find the birds using binoculars when possible and try to match the bird with its song.

For Additional Reading

50. **Bird Tracking:** Keep track of the different kinds of birds that come to the bird feeders. How often do they come? Which birds are timid, which ones are bold? Do they come on their own or with other birds? Are you quick enough to take some photos? Robert Bateman's book on *Backyard Birds* is spectacular!

51. **Nesting Ball:** In the spring, collect a variety of bits and pieces such as yarn, ribbon, strong, lint from the clothes dryer—anything a bird could use to create a nest. Place all the items in a mesh onion bag and hang where the children can see it and birds will have access. If you use very colourful items, you may see them reappear in a bird's nest.

52. **Caring for Birds:** Set up a bird bath or build birdhouses and feeding trays that can be kept stocked with seeds all year round on the playground. Children can also make their own bird feeders with some help—perhaps from a local birding expert. This will also be an opportunity to see how often squirrels steal the birds' food—not to mention nighttime visitors such as raccoons!

53. **Gourd Nests:** When gourds or pumpkins are harvested, keep some to create bird nests by halving them and filling with bird seed or

carving out windows and doors and placing bird seed inside. Hang these creations in a spot where the children can see what happens.

54. **Peanut Heart Feeder:**

    Unshelled peanuts (if no one has a nut allergy) can be pierced and threaded on wire to create a bird feeder. The wire can be moulded into a heart shape. The peanuts can be pierced with a wooden skewer then threaded onto the wire. Twist the ends of the wire together to form the heart. Tie the bird treat to a tree. (Woram & Cox, 2002, p. 98)

55. **Bird Bath Made Easy:** Take a plastic flower pot and turn it upside down. Take a plastic bowl big enough to cover the top of the pot and glue. Presto, an inexpensive bird bath!

56. **Pebble Birdbath:**

    Use a broad, shallow terracotta pot saucer and a collection of natural polished pebbles. The children can paint the saucer then arrange the collection of pebbles in the bottom of the saucer and glue them down using a waterproof adhesive. You can add grout over the pebbles and the entire base of the saucer. Use a damp sponge to smooth the surface and keep the tops of the pebbles visible. (Woram & Cox, 2002, p. 74)

57. **Bird Beaks:**

    Pay close attention to beaks. Do all bird beaks look the same? There are different types of beaks and each serves a specific purpose. Short beaks are seed beaks, perfect for cracking nuts and seeds open. Long and narrow beaks may be used to sip nectar, whereas sharp and pointy beaks may be used for tapping trees and eating bugs. Hooked beaks are used for hunting animals, such as mice and rabbits.* (Ward, 2008, p. 26)

For Additional Reading

58. **Bird Feet:** Bird feet or claws are important in many ways. They help birds catch, hold, and eat their food; swim, walk, climb, and

---

*From *I Love Dirt!*, by Jennifer Ward, © 2008 by Jennifer Ward. Reprinted by arrangement with Shambhala Publications Inc., Boston, MA. www.shambhala.com. p. 26.

Lynn Wilson

To whom do these belong?

perch; they also help to protect them from their enemies. Some have sharp talons and some have webbed feet. Try focusing on bird feet when you are bird watching and look for prints on the ground or the snow.

For Additional Reading

59. **Bird Feathers:** It is not unusual to find bird feathers. See if the children can match the feathers to the bird they belong to. Look at feathers carefully and gently pull apart the web of the feather. Look for tiny barbules that project from the barbs. Use magnifying glasses to help. Feathers also insulate and waterproof a bird's body. Find out more!

60. **Bird Eggs:** Collect a variety of different eggs—chicken, goose, duck, turkey, guinea hen eggs—that are available from local farmers or stores and compare their size, colour, weight, etc. Use the Internet to find out more about different types of eggs; for example, the ostrich egg is the largest in the world. What else can you find out about eggs?

61. **Bird Food Tree:** Create a food tree for the birds—hang popcorn, cranberries, dried fruits, pretzels, pinecones covered in peanut butter (not in summer; the peanut butter can spoil and make the birds sick) and rolled in seeds, etc., from the branches.

62. **Sunflower Seeds:** These can be eaten by older children but are labour intensive to shell. You may want to take the head of the plant and put

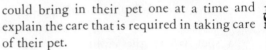
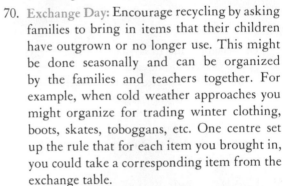

it in a place where birds can access it easily and watch them eat as well.

63. Hummingbirds: Dissolve one part sugar to three parts hot water. Add beet juice since hummingbirds are attracted to the colour red. Pour into a hummingbird feeder and hang from a tree branch.

64. Squirrels and Chipmunks: These critters are often easy to spot and fun to watch. See how clever the squirrels are at eating the birds' food. Watch how chipmunks can fill their cheeks with lots of food.

65. Teeth: Have the children look at their teeth in the mirror and count them. Show the children a picture of beaver teeth. Talk about how animals that eat plants have flat teeth and animals that eat meat have sharp teeth. Animals that eat both have sharp teeth in the front and flat teeth in the back. You may also want to relate this to dinosaurs, children's favourites (Garrett & Thomas, 2005).

66. Tails: Many creatures have tails that help them survive: some use them to brush away flies and biting insects; other are used for balance, to signal a warning, for grasping tree branches; some birds use them to manoeuvre in flight; fish use them to move. Talk about tails!

67. Snakecrow: Cut an old black or green hose into three-foot sections. Paint the hose with snakeskin patterns. Hang the hose in fruit trees to scare squirrels, raccoons, and birds away from the fruit (Lovejoy, 2003, p. 17).

68. Caring for Others: In many countries, children care for animals year round. Developing positive relationships with pets can enhance a child's self-esteem and confidence and develops empathy.

69. Pets: If allergies are not a problem, it might be fun to have a Pet Day where the children can bring in their pets. If this seems too difficult to manage at one event, perhaps children could bring in their pet one at a time and explain the care that is required in taking care of their pet.

70. Exchange Day: Encourage recycling by asking families to bring in items that their children have outgrown or no longer use. This might be done seasonally and can be organized by the families and teachers together. For example, when cold weather approaches you might organize for trading winter clothing, boots, skates, toboggans, etc. One centre set up the rule that for each item you brought in, you could take a corresponding item from the exchange table.

71. Litter:

Use 2 empty jam jars, damp soil, a thin slice of apple, a square of aluminum foil, a small piece of a plastic bag and a large sheet of paper. Half fill the jam jars with soil and put the slice of apple in one and the foil and plastic in another. Cover them with soil and leave the jars in a warm place. After a week, empty the contents of both jars onto the paper. You will see that the apple is beginning to shrivel up and decay but the foil and plastic look like new. This shows that tiny organisms in the soil break down natural waste, but litter made from metal and plastic does not decompose easily. It can stay in the environment for a long time, harming generations of wildlife. (Bramwell, Burnie, Dicks & Few, 2009, p. 25)

72. At the Beach:

In a beach bag, include a wide range of items and have the children decide if the items would be found at the beach—include shells, picnic items, sun hats, snorkelling masks, pails, shovels, sunglasses, garbage, plastic bags, broken glass, etc. Discuss the importance of keeping the beach safe for everyone. Plastic dumped in the oceans kills one million seabirds and 100,000 marine mammals and turtles every year. (Bramwell, Burnie, Dicks & Few, 2009, p. 49)

This can be expanded to discuss litter in our communities.

73. **Recycling Bottles:**

    Read the story, *The Adventures of the Plastic Bottle: A Story About Recycling* by Alison Inches. This diary of a plastic bottle as it goes on a journey from the refinery to the manufacturing line to the store and finally to a recycling plant where it emerges into its new life as a fleece jacket! Talk about landfills and why we need to recycle. Have a recycled jacket on hand for exploration. What other items have been recycled in such positive ways? (Charner, 2010, p. 26)

74. **Preserve the Beauty:** Encourage the children to throw away their trash in appropriate receptacles. Encourage recycling; on a community walk look for the different ways recycling is collected in your community and the symbols associated with this process. Teachers can lead by example.

75. **Natural Recycling:** You need one red pepper cut in half and a clear zip-top bag. Leave the pepper uncovered for a few hours, giving microscopic mould spores in the air a chance to land on the soft inner surface of the pepper. Place the pepper inside the bag and seal it. Leave the bag in a warm place. Look at the pepper every day and note how its appearance changes. After about two weeks, the pepper will start to shrivel and grow patches of gray or green mould, a type of fungus. This shows that when a plant dies, the remains are quickly broken down by fungi, bacteria, and other tiny organisms. In nature, this rotting process returns all the plant's nutrients to the soil (Bramwell, Burnie, Dicks & Few, p. 83).

76. **Sort and Classify for Recycling:** Use real objects or create a variety of flash cards using pictures from magazines, plastic, metal, and paper items along with items that cannot be recycled such as puppies, people, etc. Can the children identify which recycling bin each items should go in? An extension of this experience might be a visit to a local grocery store to look for items that can be recycled (Charner, 2010).

For Additional Reading

77. **Lunch!** For children who bring their own lunch to the centre, discuss how lunch boxes can be more sensitive to the environment. How can we make a litter-free lunch?

78. **Find It:** Take photos of places in the outdoor play space and laminate them. Initially the children can look for the exact objects; when they become more proficient, take photos from different angles or have the children find a "treasure" somewhere near the photo.

79. **Where Do I Live?** Mount a city map on the bulletin board and have the children mark with a push pin where their home is.

80. **Mapping:** Some of the older children may be interested in creating a simple map of their community on paper and then in a 3D format using boxes and tubes, etc. Have children observe the types of homes they see, where cars park, the parks, fire stations, hospitals, bakery, child care centres, schools, etc.

81. **Mapping with Technology:** Older children will be interested in using GPS systems to locate familiar landmarks and even their own homes with Google Earth. It's also a great way to take a new and interesting look at your centre.

For Additional Reading

82. **Rock Discoveries:**

    Walk slowly and look carefully for a sharp rock, a flat rock, a bumpy rock, a crumbly rock, a rough rock, a smooth rock, a shiny rock, a dull rock, a rock with speckles, a rock with stripes, a multi-coloured rock, a rock with only one colour. How many of these can you find? You might prepare a checklist for older children. What happens when you put your rocks in water? How are their textures different?*

    Talk about scientists who study rocks—geologists.

83. **Making Soil:**

    Rub two rocks together over a piece of white paper. Examine the dusty substance with a microscope. Soil is made up of plant and

---

*From I Love Dirt!, by Jennifer Ward, © 2008 by Jennifer Ward. Reprinted by arrangement with Shambhala Publications Inc., Boston, MA. www.shambhala.com. p. 67.

For Additional Reading

animal debris and of tiny pieces of rock. Sometimes rocks are broken by ocean waves or by river and creek water washing over them. Sometimes the wind blows across rocks, loosening the top layers. Sun and rain slowly cause rocks to crumble."* (Potter, 1995, p. 24)

84. **Soil Discoveries:**

Put soil into a mason or clear jar. Fill the jar with water and give it a good shake. Then put the jar down and see what happens. You will discover that the largest soil particles will settle on the bottom, finer soil will come next and in the water you will see a layer of fibrous pieces. This is called humus. On the surface of the water you will find bits and pieces of stems, leaves, seeds or broken roots that have not yet decomposed. (Fell, 1989, p. 13)

Try this experiment with a variety of different soil types and discuss what happens.

85. **Dirt Friends:** Dig up a couple of capfuls of dirt. Dump them onto a piece of white paper and use a magnifying glass to examine the dirt to see what insects, plants, or rocks the children can find. Then use a small sifter to sift dirt through and really get a good look at all the little creatures. The soil is loaded with microorganisms; it's alive!

For Additional Reading

86. **Tools of the Trade:** It is important that children use real gardening tools rather than plastic replicas. Tools that children should be familiar with and taught to use safely are rakes, watering cans, hoes, spades, trowels, wheelbarrows, old serving spoons, spray bottles, gloves, hats, and sunscreen.

For Additional Reading

87. **Tool Storage:** Store tools within easy reach of the children to allow for independent play.

88. **Watering Cans:** Collect old watering cans at garage sales or ask families for donations. Group them all together for a wonderful visual impact. Hang them so the children can easily reach them. Use them for watering or fill with soil to use as planters.

89. **Juice Bottle Watering:** For new trees or plants that need consistent watering, take a bucket or plastic juice bottle and cut off the bottom. Special

*Potter, J. 1995. *Nature In A Nutshell For Kids*. Jossey-Bass. p. 24.

drip spouts are available or you can drill a few holes into the bottle cap. Fill with water and this slow drip will ensure that the plant receives enough water to ensure maximum growth.

90. **Marking Plantings:** The children can decorate wooden paint stir sticks to identify their plant.

91. **Signing the Garden:** When planting more than one type of garden, have the children can create their own signs for their gardens. Experts in the deaf community may also be able to come and teach the children signs for outdoor experiences.

92. **Garden Clubs:** Connect with experts! Invite enthusiastic gardeners in your community to come and speak to the children. Ask if they will help with garden projects at your centre?

93. **Community Gardens:** Is there a possibility of a community garden where people come together to plant in an area in the community? The children could have a section of the garden to plant. Perhaps there is a plot of land that is not well cared for; could the children "take over" the space and improve its appearance with their planting efforts?

94. **Cheat Mother Nature:**

You don't get enough sunlight for veggies anywhere? Don't despair. Artificial aids might help. Mirrors placed in strategic spots in gardens can direct a lot of sun to areas where it's lacking. So can panels of gatorboard or plywood covered in inexpensive kitchen foil. (Day, 2010, p. 15)

For Additional Reading

95. **Dream Garden:** When it's still cold and icy outside, create a dream garden. Have the children cut out and make their own dream gardens, using old gardening magazines, seed books, etc.

96. **Funny-Name Garden:** Some children will enjoy creating a Funny-Name Garden by planting only plants with unusual or funny names—bleeding hearts, Japanese blood grass, snake weed, spider wort, lamb's ear, elephant ears, Joe pye weed, cattails, cat nip, Jenny green teeth, just to name a few!

97. **Weird Garden:** There are unusual fruits and vegetables that will provide great opportunities for comparison and contrast if planted

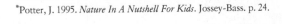

beside the "ordinary" types. Try red brussels sprouts, sweet corn "Indian Summer" (white, red, purple, and yellow), golden raspberries, Chioggia beets, "One Ball" zucchini, "Crystal Lemon" cucumber, Borlotti beans, "Tigerella" tomatoes, and "Maxim" strawberry. Ask your local nurseries for other ideas that will work in your zone.

98. **Really Huge Garden:** Check out seed catalogues and use the expertise of your local garden centre to have the children pick out seeds or plants that will grow to be giants—pumpkins, long carrots, muskmelons, jumbo cabbage, cucumber, giant flowers, etc.

99. **Huge Garden:** Use seeds and cuttings from plants donated by parents, the local nursery, etc. Try asking for donations from seed companies. Let the children decide what to plant and where—they will learn by trial and error. Plant fruits and vegetables and have a special harvest meal made from the children's efforts. Pick flowers when in bloom and bring them inside for the lunch table.

100. **Little Garden:** Every space can have a garden, no matter how small. There are many types of small seedling trays that allow for the sprouting of seeds. If cost allows, the experience becomes more meaningful if each child has his or her own tray. Some quick-to-grow seeds are marigold, candytuft, cornflower, nasturtium (leaves and seedpods can be eaten), poppies, and mallow. Most of these germinate in one to three weeks and can then be transplanted.

101. **Teeny, Tiny Garden:** Wash a cardboard egg carton, and fill with soil. Plant seeds in each hole, and water carefully. When the seedlings are about 2.5 cm tall, carefully cut the sections apart, and plant the carton sections in the ground. Watch what happens to the carton as it slowly disintegrates. This is a great activity if you want to get a jump start on your spring planting!

102. **Fence Garden:** Using a clear plastic cup to hold seeds so children can see the seeds sprouting.

A fence garden!

103. **Granny/Grandmère/Oma/Nonna/Bubbe/Oba-chan/Halmoni Garden:** Grandparents from many cultures will have other favourites they would like to plant. The harvest will provide a great opportunity to eat a variety of foods that may be new to some of the children but also will give the children an opportunity to talk about their favourite food! Older children may also want to do some research by finding out how people of different cultures plan their gardens. They might go on a tour of the neighbourhood to look at different gardens and what is planted in them. They might take along clipboards and sketch what they see. If grandparents are not available, try a seniors residence in your community.

For Additional Reading

104. **Fairy Garden:** There are many wonderful books about fairies. Read these stories to the children and then plan and plant a fairy garden. You may also want to read *Fairy Houses Everywhere!* by Barry and Tracy Kane and add some homes for your fairies. Draw a big circle and create a trench around it. Plant large grasses in the trench, leaving a doorway. The grass will grow and provide a private space for the children. Plant in the middle of the circle and include items such as leaves, wood chips, rocks, pinecones, sticks, little bells or chimes, and anything that is safe and could be used for fairy dust!

For Additional Reading

105. Zen Gardens: Each child could have his her own Zen Garden if materials allow. This is a great opportunity to discuss gardens from a wide range of cultures and the influences that make them special.

106. A Cactus Garden: Provide the children with a variety of succulents that survive warm in areas with little water. This provides an opportunity to talk about deserts. Have the children feel the plants carefully—how do they feel? How are they different from other plants they might have seen?

107. Mystery Garden: Take a variety of seeds and mix them together. Plant and wait for the results.

108. Bonsai Garden: Bonsai gardens are a Japanese art form using miniature trees grown in containers. Is there an expert in your community?

For Additional Reading

109. Pizza Garden: Choose herbs and plants that will be a welcome addition to a homemade pizza. You could make the garden in a circle shape just like a pizza. Divide each section and add plum tomatoes, peppers, onions, parsley, oregano, garlic, basil, etc. In the photo on this page, children plant a Pizza Garden in containers with clients and volunteers at the *Centre for Addiction and Mental Health* in Toronto.

110. Salsa Garden: Plant onions, garlic, tomatoes, chili peppers, green peppers, coriander and plant marigolds close by to keep the bugs away. Harvest, chop, and eat!

111. Garden Salad Basket: Find a large wicker basket and line it with plastic. Add soil and compost, and plant a variety of lettuce seeds or seedlings. Plant oak leaf lettuce, Boston lettuce, ruby red, spinach, arugula, mustard, etc.

112. Dye Garden: Include plants that can be used to make dyes, such as

    Marigolds, Coreopsis, Zinnia, Cosmos, Dahlias, Tansy, Indigo, and Blackberries. Children may choose to dye cloth, but can also make paints out of the plants in this

Lynn Wilson

Clients and children plant a Pizza Garden.

garden.* (Starbuck, Olthof, & Midden, 2002, p. 47)

Aboriginal peoples used spinach or moss to dye material green, onion skins and sunflowers for yellow, and beets for red. Wild berries are another good source of colours.

113. Alphabet Garden: Find a flower or vegetable for every letter of the alphabet and plant it—for example A is for aster, B is for balloon flower—Z is for zinnia! *The Hayes Valley Farm*, an urban farming project in San Francisco, has posted many photos of its alphabet garden and lists plants for planting from A to Z! See

For Additional Reading

http://www.flickr.com/photos/edibleoffice/sets/72157624454856630

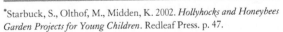

114. Popcorn Garden: Fill a pie plate with potting soil and plant the kernels.

---

*Starbuck, S., Olthof, M., Midden, K. 2002. *Hollyhocks and Honeybees Garden Projects for Young Children*. Redleaf Press. p. 47.

115. **Barefoot Garden:** Plant a variety of different types of grasses and allow only bare feet in the garden (check the regularly to ensure its safety).

116. **A Rainbow Garden:** Create a bed in the shape of a rainbow and have the children decide where plants of the same colour should go. Find a book that explains how rainbows appear to enhance this experience.

117. **An Organic Garden:** *Ann Lovejoy's Organic Garden Design School* is an excellent book for those who want to start an organic garden.

118. **Plant an Herb Garden:** There are many fragrant and interesting herbs to plant. A visit to a local nursery will help you decide which ones to plant.

119. **Bulbs-Only Garden:** For a great spring showing, plants bulbs in the fall.

120. **Sunflower Garden:** Organize a picnic lunch to be eaten under giant sunflowers. Encourage the children to imagine what it would be like to be very small. Think Gulliver's Travels!

121. **Water Garden:** Which plants grow in water? If there is a nursery or lily pond in your area, take the children to see it, or show a video clip of a water garden. Create your own water garden in an old aquarium or waterproof container and plant water plants, or use a large pot with a small pump to create a water feature. Your water feature is sure to lure frogs and toads to come and play!

122. **Tire Gardens:** Fill the centre of a tire with soil and plant. This creates a perfect boundary for very young children.

123. **Tall Tire Gardens:** Pile tires on top of each other at varying heights to raise the level of the beds closer to the children's eye level. Use a strong glue to ensure they won't topple over. Empty tires can also be used as targets for tossing bean bags.

124. **Tea Garden:** Plant peppermint, lavender, lemon verbena, harvest rose hips, bergamont, marjoram, chamomile, jasmine, coriander, thyme, rosemary, or violets. Purchase small gauze tea bags and make your own special teas for fundraising.

125. **Peter Rabbit Garden:** Reading Beatrix Potter's books may inspire the children to plant a garden that they think Peter would love to visit.

126. **Salad Garden:** Plant everything you need for a salad—radishes, beets, edible carrot leaf, lettuce, cucumber, cherry tomatoes, scallions, and spinach!

127. **Rock Garden:** Create a rock pile; place the largest rocks at the bottom with the smaller ones on top. After each layer, add a layer of soil and press down. Try planting sweet alyssum, portulaca, thyme, lavender, etc.

For Additional Reading

128. **Mould Garden:** Use a jar lid, and place bread, a piece of fruit, or a tomato in the lid and leave for several weeks. What happens? Use magnifying glasses to see the changes that take place. Children may want to draw a picture of the results.

129. **Perfume Garden:** Plant fragrant roses, lavender, lemon thyme, sage, lemon balm, geraniums, sweet alyssum, lemon verbena, viburnum, peonies, phlox, lilies, marigolds, sweet woodruff, basil, rosemary.

For Additional Reading

130. **Name Garden:** Look through seed catalogues and gardening magazines, or visit a local nursery to find plants that have names of the children in the group and plant them in a special name garden. Try Jack-in-the-Pulpit, Johnny jump up, sweet William, rowan, basil, sage, heather, hyacinth, iris, lily, rose, violet, etc.

131. **Moss Garden:** First Nations people used moss inside a "moss bag" within a cradleboard to serve the same purpose as the modern diaper. Moss was also used as gauze for cuts and wounds. Watch moss grow: spread a layer of glue on a wooden disc or piece of bark and sprinkle sand on the glue. Shake off the excess. Add moss collected by the children, twigs, pinecones, acorns, etc., and let dry out of direct sunlight for several days. With a spray bottle, spray the moss to

keep it moist. Your garden will grow as long as it is sprayed and kept out of sunlight (Our Children, Our Ways, 2000).

132. **Hanging Colander Garden:** Use an old colander to make a your own planter.

You need 4 S hooks, lengths of small link chain, and an old colander. Using a bag of sphagnum moss and a bag of soilless mix. Put both of them in separate pails and add enough water to moisten them. Let them sit for a few hours. Squeeze out any excess water from the moss and line the colander with it. Add the soilless mix and plant away. Attach all the chains together on a large S hook and hang it up.* (Morris, 2000, p. 119)

133. **Bagel Garden:** Martha Schwartz in Boston created a most unique and engaging bagel garden. A clipped boxwood hedge bordered the garden and enclosed 96 lacquered bagels laid out in a grid pattern on a ground of purple gravel. The Bagel Garden appeared on the January 1980 cover of Landscape Architecture magazine and created quite a stir among landscape architects.

134. **School Peace Gardens:**

 http://www.ihtec.org/PrimaryPages/ISPGHome. html

The International School Peace Gardens began in 1994 as a United Nations 50th- anniversary program to nurture global peace through

Courtesy of Martha Schwartz Partners

The Bagel Garden

*Morris, K. 2000. *The Kids Can Press Jumbo Book of Gardening*. Kids Can Press. p. 119.

education. There are now peace gardens around the world. The garden symbolizes each school's commitment to peace—peace in the school community, peace in the global community, and peace with nature. The website will provide you with photos and ideas about creating your own peace garden.

"Before we can achieve a peaceful world, we must first imagine one."

On August 6, 1945, an atom bomb was dropped on the city of Hiroshima in Japan. Japan has set aside August 6 as a day to wish for world peace. Many people around the world share in this celebration. The story book *Sadako and the Thousand Paper Cranes* by Eleanor Coerr is a powerful book to read at this time. See

http://rosella.apana.org.au/~mlb/cranes/ reslink4.htm#Gardens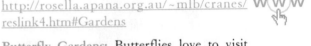

135. **Butterfly Gardens:** Butterflies love to visit certain plants for sweet nectar, and they are attracted to flowers by both colour and scent. Some favourites are butterfly bush, marigolds, zinnias, asters, borage, nasturtium, milkweed, sedum, cosmos, black-eyed Susan, bee balm, phlox, snapdragons, and Joe-Pye weed. Plant in a sunny spot. Butterflies like flowers of one colour and those with a strong, sweet smell. Ask your local nursery for advice on the best picks for your neighbourhood. Most butterflies spend their time in the sun so the best time to look for butterflies is on a warm, sunny day without much wind. Binoculars will help you get a close-up look.

136. **Butterfly Concentration Game:** Find pictures on the Internet of butterflies that are common in your area. Print two copies of each in colour. Laminate them and have younger children match them. Older children can play a concentration game, with the number of cards reflective of the children's skill level.

For Additional Reading

137. **Butterfly Life Cycle:** Talk to the children about the life cycle of butterflies—the egg grows and develops, the caterpillar's job

is to eat, the chrysalis is where the caterpillar changes form, and finally the butterfly emerges. This provides a great opportunity for creative movement.

138. Butterfly Migration: About 13 species of North American butterflies migrate north in early spring and south in late summer. The Monarch can migrate 4,500 km from eastern Canada to its wintering sites in Mexico. Each year hundreds of millions of butterflies make their way across North America. Ask the children what they already know about animals that migrate—whales, songbirds, zebras, caribou, etc. Ask the children what threats they think these animals face on their migrations (www.nwf.org). Older children may consider participating in a tagging project; find more information at

 http://www.monarchwatch.org/tagmig/tag.htm

139. Terrarium: Put gravel or small stones at the bottom of small jars and place a thin layer of soil on top. Plant some small plants into the soil. Put the jar outside but not in direct sunlight. Keep the lid on the jar and watch how the "rain" builds up on the top of the lid and falls back to keep the plants well watered. This is the beginning of understanding the water cycle.

140. Instant Pond: Dig a shallow, wide hole, place an upside-down trash can lid inside, and bury it up to the rim. Layer the inside of the lid with pebbles and fill it with water (Lovejoy, 2003, p. 12).*

For Additional Reading

141. Flowers—Encourage children to discuss how we use flowers in our home, in medicine, for gifts, in art, and in ceremonies in religious centres, etc.

142. Wildflower Window Panels:

Remove the backing from contact paper and press wildflowers onto it. Press the paper's

Lynn Wilson

A see-through garden

sticky side directly onto a window. The light will shine through and the colours last a surprisingly long time. Coloured leaves also make a beautiful panel. Try coloured tissue paper and coloured cellophane for variety. (Miller, 1999, p. 197)

143. Plexiglas Viewers: Place flowers, seeds, etc., between two sheets of Plexiglas. This allows the children to see both sides of the specimen. Hang the viewers on a fence, or in a window. In the photo on this page, the children used clear plastic folders and hung them on the fence with their treasures inside.

144. Flower Photos: Take pictures of the flowers in your playspace, laminate them, and then see if the children can match the picture with the real flower. You can also print off two of each picture and have the children play a matching game or a concentration game. For a longer activity, take pictures in your community and take a walk to find the match.

145. Deadheading: Help children understand that when flowers fade, cutting off the flower provides the plant with the energy to send out more blossoms.

146. Drying Flowers: Pick flowers when the outside air is dry and pick those that have just begun to open. Hang the flowers upside down from hooks in a dark place for about 10 days.

*Excerpted from *Trowel and Error: Over 700 Shortcuts, Tips and Remedies for the Gardener* © 2003 by Sharon Lovejoy. Workman Publishing, New York. Used by permission of Workman Publishing Co., Inc., New York. All Rights Reserved p. 12.

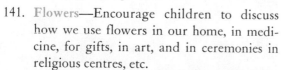

147. **Pansies:** Pansies are often one of the first plants to be successfully planted in the spring. Look carefully at a variety of pansies; do they look like they have faces? Press them between pages of a book and use them when dried for art projects or to glue to fancy note paper. Edible flowers make wonderful decorations for food projects—paint pansy flowers (that have never been sprayed with pesticides) with egg white then sprinkle on fine sugar and leave them to dry!

148. **The First Flower of Spring:** When the first flower pokes through the earth, hold a flower celebration.

For Additional Reading

149. **Spring Hunt:** Search for signs of spring. Look for new growth, feel the difference in the air, pay attention to returning birds, and animals awakening.

150. **Dandelions:** One of the first signs of spring is dandelions popping up everywhere. They make great bouquets for the lunch table and, if they aren't picked, a fluffy round seed head forms. Watch the seeds float to the ground like little parachutes. An old tale says that after one blow, the number of seeds left is the time of day or the number of children you will have! Other people believe that your wish will come true if you blow all the seeds off the stem.

For Additional Reading

151. **Dandelion—Flower or Weed?** Dandelions open in the morning and close at night. People spend a lot of time weeding dandelions out of their lawns and gardens but every part of the plant is useful. It can be used for salads and tea, medicine for digestive disorders, vitamins and minerals, and dye. Collect dandelions that have not been sprayed with pesticides and make dandelion tea.

152. **Do You Like Butter?** Hold a dandelion or a buttercup under the chin of a friend. If the colour reflected is strong, that person is supposed to like butter!

153. **When Space Is Limited:** Container gardening is a possibility even in the smallest outdoor playspaces. What interesting containers can you find?

154. **Pot Towers:** Stack a series of pots, each one sitting inside another. Leave a rim within each pot in which to plant trailing vines.

155. **Interesting Containers:** Plants can be planted in a variety of different containers. Have the children create a list of unusual containers and plant away—old boots, sneakers, tea cups, baskets, watering cans, pots, coconut shells, etc. The children can decorate containers by gluing twine or yarn around the edges, and painting with acrylic paint. Encourage recycling by having children plant in food cans or cereal boxes.

156. **Hats:** Collect old hats for a new type of planting container. Turn the hats upside down, line with plastic, add soil, and plant.

157. **Strawberry Surprise:** This family created a clever planter for their strawberries and brought it to a garden celebration at their centre.

A strawberry garden

158. **Three Sisters:** Indigenous people believed that the Three Sisters of life—corn, bean, and squash—symbolized that interdependence was critical to life itself. Corn, the tallest, provides support for the climbing bean, and squash leaves keep out the weeds and conserve moisture for all three plants. Eating all three will be a great treat for the children. When the corn is ready, the children will enjoy peeling off the husks and stripping the silk—a great opportunity to talk about different textures. Eat it and enjoy!

159. **Corn Tasting:** Go corn picking if possible and compare the different types of corn. Also try canned corn, creamed corn, and frozen corn and decide which is the tastiest.

160. **Corn Husk Dolls:** Dry corn husks in a cool dark space and when you are ready to make the dolls, soak the husks in warm water for a short period of time. Let the children experiment with raffia to create a head and body. You might provide accessories for the doll such as wool, crepe paper, googly eyes, ribbon, or other items from the art zone. To provide more colourful versions, try dying the husks by adding food colouring as they are soaking in warm water.

For Additional Reading

161. **Scarecrow:** Create an interesting scarecrow to protect your garden by stuffing old clothes. A pillow case or pantyhose makes a good head. You might make an edible scarecrow by adding plants in pockets.

162. **Herbs for Infants/Toddlers:** Herbs such as mint, basil, dill, oregano, and young thyme are safe for infants and toddlers to explore without the worry of something harmful going into their mouths.

163. **Herb Bouquet:** Collect herbs such as thyme, sage, rosemary, and mint into a bouquet. Wrap the stems with aluminum foil and poke the wrapped stems through a doily. Tie with a ribbon.

164. **Herb Identification:** As the children become more familiar with the herbs from their garden, play a guessing game with them. Blindfold the children and ask if they can identify the herb just by smell and touch.

165. **Medicines:** You may want to discuss with older children how medicines are made from flowers and herbs such as alfalfa, horsetail, plantain, red clover, St. John's wort, dandelion, yarrow, etc.

166. **Plant Fast Growers:** Plant flowers and vegetables that are fast growers or are impressive when grown—corn, sunflowers, radishes, or pumpkins. Track on a calendar the planting date and the growth of the plants. The laminated calendar can also be a reminder of when to water, weed, etc.

167. **Planting Fun:** Tulip, onions, garlic, and potatoes are fun to plant, and they are large and easy to handle. Cutting potato "eyes" to plant, or planting seeding onions and garlic is visually more immediate to young children.

168. **Celery and Mums:** Help children understand that tubes within plants transport nutrients. Water, nutrients, sugars, and gases travel to where the plants need them the most. Trim the ends off celery and white mums and place in glasses of water that have been coloured with a variety of different food colourings. Watch what happens overnight!

169. **Carrot Tops:** Take the carrots grown in the garden, eat all the way up to the greens, but leave the green curly tops. Plant these tops and wait and watch for a week. Beet, turnip and pineapple tops can be used as well.

For Additional Reading

170. **Sweet Potato Tops:** Poke three toothpicks around the "waist" of a sweet potato. Suspend the sweet potato on the toothpicks in a glass of water, half in and half out. Add water occasionally to keep the same water level. Soon a vine will begin to grow; watch for a lilac-coloured sweet potato flower.

171. **Fiddleheads:** The name alone will create curiosity. This spring delicacy is fun to look at and more fun to eat. Enjoy!

172. **Fruit Pots:** Discover the differences in a variety of citrus fruits—Blood oranges, navel oranges, Meyer lemons, pink and yellow grapefruit, etc. The children can touch and smell the fruits then compare the aromas, note the differences in the rinds, and use a

variety of juicers to taste the differences in the juices. You might show pictures or go on the Internet with older children and find out where these fruits grow. Some children think they just come from the supermarket! When finished, use the rinds, fill with soil, and insert new plants or seeds. These can be planted directly into the soil where they will disintegrate. Different types of melons can also be used as plant holders in the same way.

For Additional Reading

173. Upside Down? What happens if you hang a plant upside down from a tree or hook from a container that will keep the soil from falling out? Make predictions. (The stems will reach for the sun.)

174. Which Seeds Do I Pick? Larger seeds— such as radishes, peas, beets and spinach—are easier for little hands to plant. Seeds for lettuce and carrots are so tiny that they must be scatter planted (using the thumb and forefinger to gently sprinkle on the soil). As these grow, thin them out to grow the healthiest plants.

175. Bird Seed: Examine bird seed carefully. Cut open some of the seeds and look inside. This is a good way of demonstrating that different kinds of seeds grow into different kinds of plants. Plant some bird seed and watch for growth in usually three to five days. For more visual impact, plant in a glass jar filled with moist paper towels.

176. The Wonder of Seeds: There are so many different kinds of seeds; some grow in plants after the flower has faded, some are hidden inside fruit, some grow inside pods, others grow inside their own spiny cases. Collect a variety of different types of seeds and examine Each.

177. Interesting Seeds: Eat an orange and/or a lemon. Keep the pits, let them dry for a day or two, then plant them. Put a few Popsicle™ sticks around the edge of the pot and cover with clear plastic. Keep the soil moist and then watch the plants grow.

178. All Kinds of Seeds:

At the end of their life, plants produce and release their seeds to grow in new places. What seeds look and feel like tell us about how the seeds get away from their parent plants. Seeds that are blown away by the wind are often tiny, or, if larger, have hair-like parachutes or wings to keep them up in the air. Can you find some of those? Seeds with sticky or spiked sides attach themselves to animals that brush past. They eventually fall off and, with luck, start to grow. Can you find some of those? Seeds inside a soft fruit or vegetable are eaten by animals, then pass through their digestive system and end up in animal droppings, ready to grow. (Kindersley, 2010, pp. 76–77)

179. Seed Game from Ghana: Ensure that none of the children has a nut allergy. Collect 24 round seeds or nuts such as hazelnuts, walnuts, or acorns. Two players face each other, each behind their own row of 12 nuts. To begin, one player rolls one of her nuts toward her opponent's row. If her nut hits one of his, she takes it and her turn continues; but if her nut does not hit one of his, he takes the one she rolled and his turn begins. Players alternate turns. The object is to get the most nuts in a preset number of turns.

180. Seed Party: Cut fruits and remove the seeds. Observe the children's discussions about their similarities and differences. Talk about seeds that are eaten and those that are not. Place the seeds in zip-top bags and label them. A fun matching game can be created with pictures of the fruit and matching seeds (Brown, 2004).

181. Seed Book: Children who like to record their observations may be interested in creating a seed book. They can use pictures from seed catalogues, glue seeds to their pages, or press flowers for their book. They can record their thoughts as well.

182. Seed Balls: For 15 children, use 2500 mL cups of clay from a craft store, 1500 mL of compost, and 125 g–250 g of seeds and mix together. Use native seeds. See

http://www.evergreen.ca

Start with the dry ingredients first and then slowly add the water until the soil is moist but not sticky. Roll into balls that are about 2.5 cm in diameter. Toss the balls into the garden and be sure to water them regularly. Record which seeds grow from the balls.

183. **Bean Seed in a Jar:** Fill a glass jar with wet paper towels and place lima beans (great because they are so big) and place the jar in a sunny spot and see what happens. What happens if you plant the seed upside down?

For Additional Reading

184. **Weight Lifting Seeds:** Seeds are powerful; plant a bean then cover it with a coin—will it grow and push the coin out of the way?

For Additional Reading

185. **Jack and the Beanstalk:** Recreate this story with the children and collect a variety of beans—green ones, purple ones, and red ones—and plant them. What happens?

186. **Sprouts:** Sprouts are seeds that have just begun to germinate so they grow very quickly. There are lots of varieties: snow peas, alfalfa, chickpea, mung beans, lentils, azuki beans, green peas, mustard, watercress, etc.

187. **Interesting Fruits:** Think of all of the interesting fruits from faraway places that we have access to. Explore as many as you can find; for example, star fruit, dragon fruit, rambutan, jackfruit, passion fruit, lychee, mangosteen, kumquat, and durian. Some children may be familiar with these and anxious to share their opinions. Find out more about these fruits using the Internet.

188. **Interesting Vegetables:** Have the children tried plantain, okra, artichokes, kohlrabi, bok choy, brussel sprouts, asparagus, or tomatillos? A trip to the market may be in order. Bring back a variety of vegetables to try. The children may also be surprised at the original shape of vegetables they usually see only cut up!

189. **Poison Ivy/Poison Oak:** If you live in a forested area that might contain poison ivy or poison oak, it is a positive way to begin to discuss the different types of plants in a forest. Point out that some plants are not people friendly and touching the leaves may result in a serious rash. Even the smoke from burning any part of these plants can give you a rash. Show the plant in situ or using a picture. Other plants can be dangerous; for example, azalea, daffodils, foxglove,

holly, etc. Robin Moore's book *Plants for Play* outlines many plants that are not appropriate for children's playscapes.

190. **Maple Keys:** Crack large maple keys in half and spread the pieces. Place the shape across your nose—you have a maple nose! You can also throw maple keys into the air to watch them spin like a helicopter!

191. **Milkweed Pods:** Milkweed plants have seed pods. If you split the pods before they are ripe you will see scales that look like fish scales. However, when fully ripe, they are full of fluffy white down. Blow these seeds away! You are helping to start a new plant! Some people believe that if you catch one of these seeds you can make a wish, blow it away, and it will come true.

192. **Pussy Willows:** Pussy willows are one of the first signs of spring. Feel how soft they are. Try making a flower arrangement with them and watch what happens over time. (The soft gray turns yellow as they mature.)

193. **Ms. Egghead:** Cut the top off an egg shell and fill the shell with soil. Sprinkle with grass seed and decorate the shell "face." Put the eggs into an egg carton and place in the sun. What happens? Does your Ms. Egghead need a haircut? How long did it take? Graph the results.

194. **Mr. Potato Head:** Scrub a potato and cut off the top. Make a face with bits of carrots, green peppers, mushrooms, etc. Where the white of the potato is exposed, sprinkle with grass seed or sprouts, and in two or three days the potato will have "hair."

195. **Garden Maze:** To demonstrate how plants seek out light, cut a hole in one end of a shoe box, glue two pieces of cardboard upright with holes in them to create a maze for a bean seedling. Plant a seed in a pot and place it at the opposite end of the box. Cover the box and allow light to enter only through the end hole. What happens?

196. **Plants Need Light:**

On a sunny day, find a blooming crocus and look at the petals carefully. Cover the flower with a shoe box for 5 minutes. Remove the box and look at the petals. What happened to them? All plants and flowers react to sunlight, but with some the reaction is more obvious. Crocus flowers are very sensitive to light. You can also see the crocus close its petals later in the day when the sun goes down.[*] (Potter, 1995, p. 10)

197. **Pickle in a Bottle:** Place a tiny cucumber that is still growing on the vine inside a small glass jar. Set the jar on the soil so it can continue to grow. Cover the bottle with a few leaves to protect it from direct sunlight. The bottle acts like a greenhouse and soon the cucumber will fill the bottle.

198. **Collecting Acorns:** In the early fall oak trees provide many acorns (the seeds of new oak trees). Examine them carefully; you may need a hammer to open one up to see what is inside.

199. **Acorn Finger Puppets:** Use acorn tops as hats for your fingers. Use a skinny marker to make a face on your finger. Presto! A new kind of puppet!

200. **Spinners and Knockers:** You can create great games by using acorns and/or chestnuts. Use acorns like tops for spinning. They also can be used like marbles to knock others out of a drawn circle. Drill chestnuts and insert a string to bang against another. The winner is the one with the chestnut still intact. (Some people say putting the chestnut in the freezer improves your chances). Supervise very carefully to avoid aggressive play.

201. **Pinecones:** Talk about how evergreen trees produce their seeds in cones. When the cone opens its scales, the seeds are released. Collect as many different pinecones as you can find and compare their size, shape, colour, etc. Older children may want to match evergreen leaves with the corresponding pinecones.

202. **Pinecones and Water:**

    Collect pine cones. Put some of the pine cones in water and leave others dry. The wet pinecones' scales will start to close after a few minutes. Pinecones rely on the force of the wind to blow their seeds to a spot where they can grow.

Therefore, the seeds must be light and as dry as possible. During rainstorms, the pinecones act as little umbrellas to keep the seeds dry. When the pinecone dries, it opens again.[**] (Potter, 1995, p. 7)

203. **Composting:**

    You can make your own composter by using a large plastic garbage pail with a lid. Cut out the bottom of the pail and using a hammer and a nail, make three parallel circles of holes around the top, middle and bottom of the pail. Place the composter in a sunny spot away from any walls so that air can circulate. Start with a layer of soil, add a layer of material that is fresh and green, add a layer that is dead, dry and brown and keep alternating brown and green layers. Keep the lid on your composter. Your compost is ready when it looks dark brown and smells like earth. Don't add fish, meat, bones, dairy products or kitty litter. They create a smelly mess and attract rodents and raccoons.[†] (Morris, 2000, p. 15)

For Additional Reading

204. **Worm Farm:** Worms are invertebrates and there are more than 3,000 varieties in the world. Worms breathe through their skin and don't have eyes but they are very sensitive to vibrations and light and dark. They eat soil and organic matter, making the soil "richer." Introduce the children to worms by creating a worm farm. Stack three or four crates or bins made of plastic, wood, or any other lightweight, waterproof material after drilling holes in them. The worms live in the bins and simply wriggle up from the lowest bin into the one above, where they can eat fresh fruit, vegetable, and other scraps that might otherwise go to waste. These scraps become the worm castings that make such good fertilizer.

For Additional Reading

205. **Exploring Worms:** Encourage the children to interact with worms by handling them carefully and returning them to the earth.

206. **Entomologists:** Explain to the children that entomologists are scientists who study insects. Create a bug catcher by using a large

---

[**]Ibid., p. 7.

[†]Morris, K. 2000. *The Kids Can Press Jumbo Book of Gardening*. Kids Can Press. p. 15.

---

[*]Potter, J. 1995. Nature In A Nutshell For Kids. Jossey-Bass. p. 10.

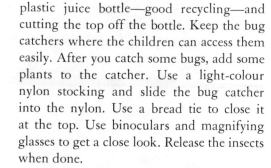

plastic juice bottle—good recycling—and cutting the top off the bottle. Keep the bug catchers where the children can access them easily. After you catch some bugs, add some plants to the catcher. Use a light-colour nylon stocking and slide the bug catcher into the nylon. Use a bread tie to close it at the top. Use binoculars and magnifying glasses to get a close look. Release the insects when done.

207. **Stakeout:** Stake out an area with long concrete nails and string, or toss hula hoops into the playground. Have the children explore their space and concentrate on what they find—ants, caterpillars, spiders, beetles, etc. Using a magnifying glass adds another element to this experience. Caution the children to be gentle and not disturb the creatures or their homes.

208. **Camouflage:** Hide objects where they blend in with the protective covering of the environment. After the children discover the objects, discuss how some animals have skin coverings that hide them from their enemies. Ask the children to find a spot where they blend in. Try collecting a variety of natural items and give the children a collection of different colours of construction paper and have them place them where they "hide" best.

209. **Ants, Ants, and More Ants:** One of the easiest critters to study outdoors is ants because they are so plentiful. Use magnifying glasses to study ants and the ways that they move. Ants use their antennae to smell with. If you are having trouble finding them, leave a variety of tiny bits of foods that the children think ants might like outside overnight. What happens in the morning? Were other insects attracted to the food? What else do the children want to learn about ants? Make Ants on a Log—celery, peanut butter (if no allergies in the group, or use cream cheese) and place "ant raisins" along the celery! Yum!

210. **Ladybugs:** Ladybugs are wonderful additions to any garden because they love to eat pests that can be harmful to plants. You can buy ladybugs from many nurseries. Be gentle with them; they are tiny!

211. **Spiders:** Spiders are arachnids and have four pairs of legs, no antennae or wings, and two body segments. Though many species have multiple eyes, most spiders do not see well. They use sensory feelers directly in front of their mouths to feel and handle their prey. All spiders use silk and spin it from spinnerets at the rear of their abdomen. Look for spiders on the playground and examine them closely.

212. **Spider Fog Walk:** Nothing is more impressive than finding spider webs on a foggy day. The moisture in the fog settles on spider webs making them sparkle when the sun shines through them—wow!

213. **Spider Webs:** Find a spider web and carefully sprinkle talcum powder on it. Gently lift the web with black construction paper until it is free and secured on the paper. Spray with adhesive. Look for webs that are different. Do different spiders make different webs? Do all spiders spin webs to catch their food? Find books to explain how spiders make this sticky substance in their bodies (Brown, 2004).

214. **What Tangled Webs We Weave:** Watch a spider weave its web. Can you find a spider sending out a trail of silk (a dragline) and floating in the wind?

215. **Little Miss Muffet:** Read the nursery rhyme to the children and talk about whether or not we should be afraid of spiders. Then imagine a similar poem that the spider might have written about Miss Muffet sitting down beside him (Garrett & Thomas, 2005).

216. **Anansi the Spider:** There are many stories that are popular in Jamaica that are written about Anansi, a mischievous character who is always getting into trouble.

217. **Grasshoppers:** Grasshoppers are easily caught and observed by children. They appear in the late spring and early summer when they hatch from eggs laid the previous fall. They

are built for jumping with their long hind legs, and many species use their wings to keep them in the air longer. Listen to the sounds they make by rubbing their wings together or by grinding their mandibles. Their life cycle is an interesting one. Check out their compound eyes! Make sure to release the grasshoppers after your investigations.

218. **Terrarium/Ant Palace:** Make a terrarium or an ant's palace from a variety of materials—plastic bottles, sand, etc.

219. **Insect Nets:** Make an insect net out of an onion or plastic bag.

220. **Bees! Be Careful:** Bees are amazing pollinators and need two things to do well—nectar, which is loaded with sugar and is their main source of energy, and pollen, which provides a balanced diet of protein and fat. To attract bees, you need a range of plants with flowers that bloom through the whole season—native plants, herbs, and perennials. Local nurseries will be able to help you with your selection. We need bees! They come to the flowers to get nectar and when they land they get covered in pollen. The bees and other insects carry the pollen from one plant to another, allowing the plant to make its seeds.

For Additional Reading

221. **Bee Keeper:** If you are lucky, a bee keeper may be willing to explain his or her craft to the children.

222. **Blindfold Discoveries:** Have children pick a partner for this experience. Have one child blindfolded with the other child taking him or her on a sensory walk around the play-space. What things can the blindfolded child identify by touch, smell, sounds, etc.? Have the children take turns. They may want to draw a picture of the things they experienced on their walk.

223. **Touch Your Surroundings:** Encourage the children to touch their surroundings—feel soft moss, rough bark, and smooth stones. Help them develop their vocabulary.

224. **Texture Boards:** Create a texture board using natural materials for the children to explore.

Bees!

Lynn Wilson

225. **Texture Walk:** Take a walk in the neighbourhood and look at all the different flower textures.

226. **Identifying Leaves by Texture:** Children can compare the texture of a wide range of leaves collected on one of their nature walks. Children can do this with their eyes open and then try to match pairs of the same leaves with their eyes closed.

227. **Time Tracking:** Fill a large yogurt container with artifacts that are important to the children in the centre. Bury it on the grounds of the school. Open it sometime later depending on the age group. Have the children blindfolded to see if they can recall the items just by touch.

228. **Stethoscope:** Take a stethoscope outside and listen to noises. Children are often amazed to hear sounds that come out of the ground, the sidewalk, and even trees and rocks.

229. **Can You Hear It?** You need two children to try out this experiment. Try dropping

a metal ball bearing on a coffee tin turned upside down. Ask one of the children to move away slowly and to stop when he or she can't hear the sound any longer. Have the children change positions and try again.

230. Guessing Games: Describe an object or a critter on the playground and see if the children can guess what it is; for example, "I have blue feathers and I have a loud voice" (a blue jay). If the children become familiar with bird songs, they might be able to imitate them. They may also describe objects in the environment that make sounds—chimes, car noises, etc.

231. Aromas: Aromas can stimulate mental alertness and memory. Peppermint, basil, cinnamon, rosemary, and lemon are believed to enhance alertness. Lavender, orange, and chamomile alleviate stress. Crush the leaves of herbs and smell! Have the children experiment with these, creating a graph of their favourites and least favourites. You could create a potpourri of interesting smells for a great little gift.

232. Smelly Walk: Animals use their noses to find food. Bring a few food items outside for the children to identify by smell. Take a walk to a pizzeria, a bakery, flower shop, laundromat, book store, cheese shop, or community garden. Notice other smells (for example, the air after a rainfall, someone cutting grass or cutting down a tree, a new asphalt road being laid, etc.).

233. Bat a Sock: Make smelly socks filled with herbs, lavender, orange peel, pinecones, etc., that can be batted by babies. As the sock is batted, the aroma is enhanced.

234. Smell Floral Fragrances: Have the children smell a variety of floral fragrances in diverse forms—candles, perfumes, shampoos, potpourri, incense, air fresheners—and have them attempt to match the scents to the flowers that produce them.

For Additional Reading

235. Bringing Plants Inside: A plant in the playroom raises the oxygen level and reduces the pollutants in the air. There are also wonderful opportunities for exploring the plants when nature is brought inside.

236. Water: Water play fascinates children; it moves, it changes the colour of sand, it can be manipulated, it drips, it makes noises, it can be dammed up, it can be channelled along the ground, it is essential for life, and much more.

For Additional Reading

237. Swimming: Of all the recreational sports that children are involved in, not knowing how to swim can be life threatening. If there are swim programs in your area, get involved. Take the children to local swimming pools, wading pools, or splash pads if they are available to help children feel comfortable in the water. If not, invite a water safety instructor to your centre to do some preventive education. It could save a life!

238. Water Play: Pour it, wash dollies with it, use it in squirt bottles to "paint" the fence, make puddles, and splash.

239. More Water Play: For some children, returning on Monday from a weekend at home may be a difficult transition. Water play can be a calming experience.

240. Squirt Bottles: Nothing is more fun than using squirt bottles on plants, walls, equipment, and all each other. Supervise closely!

241. Slip Sliding Away: A sheet of plastic, a slight incline, and some running water is all you need for water fun!

242. Running Water: The sound of running water is soothing. Can you create a path for the water from your tap, angling the water with stones and pebbles toward the sand area? Use tubes, plumbing pipes, clear hose pieces, bamboo, and wood to help the children create water pathways.

243. Sensory Experiences with Water: How does the water at the centre taste? Does it taste the same as your water at home? How does the water at the centre smell? How can we make water taste and smell different (add lemon, etc). What does water look like? What other things look like water? How does water feel

to your hands, in your month? How does water sound when we pour it?

244. **What's in My Water?** Collect water samples from a variety of sources in your community (don't forget muddy puddles). Use a filter and a large jar to strain your water samples. Compare the colour, appearance, and smell of the water before and after filtering. This is an opportunity to talk about water filtration plants and the processes to keep our water safe to drink.

245. **Bubble Fun:** Children can create their own bubble wands from pipe cleaners, hangers, etc. Chasing bubbles is always an enjoyable event no matter the child's age. Provide each child with a cup of bubble mix. Straws in the bubble mixture gives children an opportunity to understand that pushing air through the straw produces bubbles (add glycerine for stronger bubbles). Children can also see the different colours as the light shines through the bubbles. Give this a try in winter; what happens to the bubbles?

246. **Paper and Water:** What happens when you add shredded paper to a plastic swimming pool filled with water?

247. **Catching Bubbles:** What happens when the children catch bubbles on construction paper? Talk about why the popped bubble leaves a wet circle.

For Additional Reading

Ingrid Crowther

Bubbles

248. **Soaps:** Use a variety of soaps in water and see which one foams up the fastest and which soap smells the best. Use a fizzy water "bomb"; many of these are available with a variety of fragrances or flower petals, and are very dramatic.

249. **Washing Our Clothes:** A great way to help children learn about evaporation is to have them collect clothes from the house centre and encourage them to wash the clothes. Adding soap changes the whole experience, and rinsing is great fun. The children can hang the clothes on a clothes line outside; have them monitor the drying process.

250. **Car Wash:** This is a great opportunity to engage the children in caring for their bikes as well as watching what happens when soap and water are mixed. Lots of other things often get washed in the process! Consider writing the words "Wet" and "Dry" in chalk on the ground and cordon off a specific area for this activity.

251. **Wash Windows:** After a storm, or when the windows are dirty, encourage the children to wash them clean.

252. **Rainy Day Art:** Watercolours are good for pastel colour and washes. The children can paint their pictures and then put them outside in the rain to see what happens. You can also sprinkle on salt while the picture is still wet; when the salt dries, it will sparkle.

Lynn Wilson

Fun with paper in the pool

253. Rain Walk: Encourage the children to use all their senses to enjoy a walk in the rain. What happens to the flowers, trees, leaves, animals when it rains? What does the sky look like? How does it feel when the raindrops land on your hands and your face? How does the air smell? Can you see a rainbow? Can you hear the birds? Take off shoes and walk in the grass; how does it feel?

254. Acid Rain:

Place white chalk in a plastic cup and pour in … 5 ml of white vinegar. Chalk is made of limestone. Limestone is a rock that reacts to the acid in vinegar. When you poured the vinegar on the chalk, it gave off a gas, which you saw as lots of bubbles. Acid rain contains a very weak acid that it collects from polluted air. When acid rain falls on limestone, some of the rock is eaten away. Acid rain can also poison our lakes, rivers, and streams.[*] (Potter, 1995, p. 6)

255. Rain Water:

Place a coffee filter over the mouth of a plastic cup. Put a rubber band around the filter to keep it in place. Make a small dent in the middle of the filter. Place the cup in the rain to collect the water. After the rain, remove and examine the filter. What do you see? Most likely you will see some small dark particles that the rain collected on its way to earth. These dirt and dust particles are sometimes harmful.[**] (Potter, 1995, p. 31)

256. Water in the Air: Wet a paper towel for each child. Discuss how it feels and how we use these to soak up spills. What happens to it if we leave it outside? How do the paper towels dry? Discuss evaporation. A similar experiment can be done by putting two saucers outside with a measured amount of water in each. Place one in the sun and one in the shade. Water evaporates faster when it is heated.

For Additional Reading

257. Making Rainbows: Take a garden hose and spray water up into the air on a sunny day.

Keep the sun at your back. Can you see the rainbow? What colours can you see? The order of colours is red, orange, yellow, green, blue, indigo, and violet.

258. Rainy Day Fun:

On a rainy day splash about in puddles then draw a chalk line around the puddles. What happens to the puddles? Add food colouring, glitter or bubbles to puddles and investigate. Have raindrop races on window panes. If it is really raining, construct a canal system and float some boats. (Harriman, 2010, p. 40)

259. Puddle Fun: Don't forget to look at the surface of the puddle. Can you see your face? Touch the puddle; what happens? Can you float things in the puddles? What things can you toss into the puddle to make a splash? What makes the biggest splash?

For Additional Reading

260. Mud: Ride through the mud and compare tracks left by tricycles, wagons, scooters, etc. Do the same with shoes that the children can

© Little Eyes On Nature. Tawa Montessori School

Can there ever be enough mud?!

[*]Potter, J. 1995. *Nature In A Nutshell For Kids*. Jossey-Bass. p. 6.
[**]Ibid., p. 31.

Dinosaurs and mud!

easily slip into, oversized boots, and have them stomp on long rolls of butcher block paper. Be careful—the mud will be slippery! June 29 is International Mud Day!

261. Mud, Mud, and More Mud: Nothing provides a more complex sensory experience than exploring mud.

262. Mud Pies: Mud is squishy and it is great to investigate. Squish it, push it, splash it. What shapes can you make? What designs can you make if you transfer mud to paper? What things can you add to your creation?

263. Toilets—How Do They Work? Take the back of the toilet off and let the children see the way the toilet actually works. This provides an opportunity to discuss low-flow toilets and how putting a heavy object in the tank will reduce the amount of water used.

264. Where Does Water Hide? Squeeze an orange, bite a tomato, rub a leaf in your hands, cut a cactus pad, check a covered dish of soil after several days.

265. How Is Water Used Outside? Do a community walk and record where you find water.

266. Absorbing Water: On plastic trays, one for each child, place a variety of absorbent and nonabsorbent items on the ground. Each child gets a paper towel for his or her tray. Have the children pour a small amount of water on their paper towel and discuss absorption. Invite the children to experiment with the variety of items and encourage them to make a picture graph of the items they used. Extend this discussion to materials we use for rain coats. How do birds and animals keep dry in the rain?

267. A Touch Trick: You need three bowls, one with very warm tap water, one with ice water and one with water at room temperature. Arrange the bowls so that the one with water at room temperature is in the middle. Place one hand in the very warm water and the other in ice water for about 1 minute. Then place both hands in the water at room temperature. What do you feel in each hand? The hand in the ice water feels hot in the water at room temperature. The hand that was in very warm water felt cold in the room temperature. This is known as sensory adaptation. Your senses were trying to figure out what to feel. Your sense receptors need time to get used to the change.* (Potter, 1995, p. 112)

268. Mixing: Using transparent plastic tubing and two corks to fit the ends, have the children hold the tube in a U shape and pour water into the tube. Take two colours of food colouring and place each colour into one end of the tube and add the corks. Move the tube up and down to mix the colours.

269. Making Waves: Place large combs in a large water container for the children to make waves.

270. Water Experiments: See how different materials settle in water. Fill a clear container half full with gravel, sand, and dirt. Add water until the container is nearly full. Put on the lid and shake. Let it settle and have the children predict then describe what happens.

271. Water Changes: Oil and water don't mix. Have the children pretend there has been an oil spill. How will the children clean up the water? Encourage inventive problem solving. Blow across the top of the water and oil; what happens to the oil if there is a storm? Use a feather and drag it through the oil; talk about the impact on birds and marine animals.

For Additional Reading

---

*Potter, J. 1995. *Nature In A Nutshell For Kids*. Jossey-Bass. p. 112.

272. **Water Orchestra:** Fill several glasses with different levels of water and have the children experiment to make various sounds.

273. **Sink and Float:** Conduct sink and float experiments and graph the results.

274. **Walnuts and Water:** Create walnut boats by cutting a walnut in half. Eat the nut then put a small amount of play dough at the bottom of the shell to hold a straw in place. Glue or tape a sail to the straw. These make great boats to be sailed on the playground waterways.

275. **Underwater Viewer:** Make a viewer with a paper cup (or milk carton) with the bottom cut out, some clear plastic wrap and a rubber band.

276. **Tap, Tap, Tap:** Try tapping a variety of objects underwater; for example, metal spoons, toy cars, two cups (water carries sound better than air)

277. **Clean Water:** At *Kew Beach Public School* in Toronto, for Earth Day each child painted his or her own wooden fish and displayed them along the fence of the school. This reminded the community of the importance of clean water for all creatures.

278. **Keeping the Ocean Clean:** Ocean Conservancy's International Coastal Cleanup has become the world's largest volunteer effort for ocean health. Nearly nine million volunteers from 152 countries and locations have cleaned 66 million kilograms of garbage from the shores of lakes, streams, rivers, and the ocean on just one day each year. Visit the website and plan to participate with children and their families on the third Saturday of September. See

http://www.oceanconservancy.org/our-work/marine-debris/international-coastal-cleanup-11.html

279. **Water on Earth:** Show the children a globe and have them explore where they find water—rivers, lakes, streams, oceans, seas, etc. What is used to represent water on the globe? What do other colours on the globe represent?

280. **Where on Earth?** After the globe exploration (see above), discuss who lives in water, on land, and in the air. This is a great opportunity for a graphing exercise!

281. **What Is Chalk?:** Chalk is made up of the remains of tiny sea creatures that lived during the Cretaceous period. They were so small that you would need a microscope to see them. Over millions of years, their shells formed into thick layers on the sea bottom. Chalk is used as an ingredient in cosmetics, toothpaste, cement, and fertilizer. But chalk is best known as a writing tool. Gather coloured chalk, dark construction paper, and 1 cup of water. Dip the chalk into water and draw on the paper. The chalk will look waxy like pastels or sticky crayons. Once dry, it won't brush away easily.

282. **Chalk and Leaves:** Try a different media by using chalk to draw on leaves!

283. **Chalk Walls:** Make shapes and targets on the walls and throw bean bags or balls at them. Water balloons are great fun on a hot day. Can the children aim and hit their mark?

284. **Loose Parts:** Remember the importance of using a wide range of loose parts in the playground during the winter months. When children are actively engaged in their environment and properly dressed, they won't want to come back inside no matter how cold the weather. Have appropriate clothing available so children can really experience the weather—sliding on slippery days and experiencing strong winds and sleet.

Lynn Wilson

A fish fence!

285. **Winter Language:** Think of all the words that are connected to winter and encourage their use and understanding—chilly, freeze, frigid, frost, frostbite, wind chill, temperature, ice, snow, hail, sleet, ice, cold, etc.

286. **Snow Angels:** Have children lie down and spread their wings. Hop out of the angel and decorate with natural items, make faces, add clothing, etc.

287. **Snow People:** Build away!

288. **Snow Families:** Create a snow family and dress them up with clothes from the child care, natural objects, etc. Make an edible snow family by placing items that birds will love to eat! Try blindfolding the children to "pin the nose" on the snowperson with a carrot!

289. **Snow Person:** Build a snow person when packing snow is at its best. You may want to watch *Frosty the Snowman* or sing the Frosty song!

290. **Alien Snow Creatures:** Tell a silly story about aliens landing on the earth. Create alien snow creatures! Add spray bottles of paint, and odds and ends from the art centre and create away. This works best if the snow is packing snow.

291. **Snow Snake:** When you have good packing snow, make a number of snowballs and line them up like a snake. The children can decorate the face with items found in nature and they may be interested in spraying the snake with watered-down food colouring (Bienenstock, n.d., p. 34).

292. **Snowball Hurdles:** Have the children build a snow wall and see if they can jump over the snow hurdle.

293. **Snow Fort:** Build a snow fort by rolling large snowballs for the base and continue until you have a ring. Don't forget to leave a doorway! Add as many layers as you can lift. On the outside, pack snow into the holes. Now you are ready to snuggle inside. Add blankets, dishes, pots, and pans, and have fun!

294. **Straw Forts:** Create "straw bale play spaces such as mazes, play houses and forts which can be soaked to make them freeze hard and [can be] packed with snow" (School Grounds Transformation, n.d.).

295. **Snow Castles:** Create a snow castle by using sand pails and sand toys; provide a variety of other containers for added interest. Add additional props as the children request them. Cut old Christmas tree branches for trees.

296. **Feeding Birds in Winter:** Fill pie plates with water and bird seed, freeze, and hang near a window. Roll a pinecone in peanut butter and then roll in bird seed; hang outside. Be careful putting out bread for birds. If it goes mouldy, it can make the birds sick.

297. **Winter Feeding:** Try placing some peanuts in the snow and the next day observe what has happened. Let the children try to guess who visited their playspace overnight. Avoid if peanut allergies are an issue.

298. **Hibernation:** Who stays around in winter and who hibernates? Answers will depend on the area in which you live. Do your research.

299. **Outside Breath:**

    Your lungs are warm, so when you breathe out, your lungs push out warm, moist air. The cold air outside cannot hold as much moisture as warm air, so the moisture in your breath condenses into tiny droplets as it becomes colder. You can see these tiny droplets floating in the air.[*] (Potter, 1995, p. 36)

300. **Extreme Winter Weather:** Children can learn why we experience extreme weather in the winter months by reading and talking to weather experts.

301. **What to Wear?** What types of clothing are worn by people in the north who experience extreme cold? How do they protect themselves? Use the Internet to help you.

302. **Winter Clothing:** Older children might enjoy making mitts and headbands out of felt. This is a great way to support fine motor skills. The children can trace their hands on two pieces of felt, making the wrist area

---

[*]Potter, J. 1995. *Nature In A Nutshell For Kids*. Jossey-Bass. p. 36.

wider so they can fit their hand inside. Pin the two sides together so the children can practise a blanket stitch around their mitten. Headbands can be made with a piece of felt long enough to go around their head. After attaching Velcro to both ends, decorate the headbands (Drake & Love, 1996).

303. Knitting: Knitting a scarf to keep warm may take some time for beginners but if you have an experienced knitter in your community it may be a great volunteer opportunity. Visiting a wool store is an experience in itself!

304. Taking Temperatures: Try taking temperatures in several locations in the playspace. Ask the children why they think the temperature is different in some spots.

305. Taking Snow Temperatures:

Using two thermometers place one into the top of a snow bank and the other well into the snow bank. Leave them for about 10 minutes and record the results. The one deepest into the snow will register a warmer temperature than the one on top. Snow acts as a blanket to insulate and warm the ground. Animals burrow into the snow to keep warm during the winter.* (Potter, 1995, p. 120)

306. Touch Walk: Go for a touch walk and see which things feel colder—the railing or the wooden door, the tree trunk or an icicle, etc., and discuss why.

307. Icy Fingers: Fill disposable gloves with water and add food colouring if desired. Put them in the freezer. When they are frozen take them outside and place in a spot where the children will see them. What happens? The icy fingers can also be used inside in the water table.

308. Ice Cube Melt: Place ice cubes in zip-top bags and place them on a variety of different coloured construction paper. Watch which ones melt first and relate this to the colour of clothing people may want to wear in summer or winter. Try putting one bag of ice in the sun and one in the shade. Which one melts faster?

309. Ice Shapes: Make a variety of ice shapes by freezing water in different containers. Embed objects, toys, etc., in the containers. Use milk cartons, ice cream, or a variety of plastic containers or muffin tins to create various shapes and sizes. The children can make frozen villages. Add food colouring for a different look.

310. Ice and Markers: Place ice blocks in an area where the sun is most prominent. The children can draw on the ice with markers and observe what happens. The ice palette soon becomes clear for the next artist.

311. Ice Painting: Sprinkle dry tempera paint on paper. The children can use ice cubes to blend the dry paint, or try an icicle. Ice cubes can be frozen with Popsicle™ sticks in the centre to make handling the ice more comfortable for the children, or use Popsicle™ makers. If you anticipate that this might be too messy, the same experience can be carried out in an aluminum pie plate or on a food tray. Add food colouring to the ice cubes for a more complex experience.

312. Slippery Ice: Freeze a variety of ice shapes and challenge the children to move the ice pieces from one part of the tray to another using tongs!

313. Icy Races: Find an area of ice that is flat and conducive to racing cars and trucks along an icy path. Estimate which ones the children think will travel the farthest. Discuss why this happens or why it doesn't. You can also graph the results.

314. What Slides On Ice?

Does everything slide on ice? Experiment with sliding several objects on ice. Do leaves slide on ice? Does a mitten slide on ice? Do sticks slide on ice? What about small stones? Then ask the children to share characteristics of things that do and do not slide on ice.** (Redleaf, 2010, p. 17)

315. Spray Painting: Mix spray bottles with a variety of different colours and encourage the children to paint the snow, paper hanging from the fence, a piece of acrylic, etc.

---

*Potter, J. 1995. *Nature In A Nutshell For Kids*. Jossey-Bass. p. 120.

**Hey Kids! Out the Door, Let's Explore!* By Rhoda Redleaf (2010). pg. 17.

316. **Hammer Walk:** When ice is present, taking a hammer or a wooden mallet to ice "puddles" is an interesting experience for the children to engage in. Supervise carefully!

317. **No More Salt:** De-icing salt filters down into the soil, which injures plant roots and can kill them. Complete NPK (nitrogen, phosphorous, and potassium) garden fertilizer can be used as a de-icer near landscaping instead. Potassium melts the ice and phosphorus is slip-proof (Lovejoy, 2003, p. 105). Or, try using dirt or ashes from the fireplace; they won't melt the ice but will provide traction.

318. **Driving in Winter:** Stamp out some roads in the snow and bring out the wheeled vehicles. Add road signs and little people. Talk about the challenges of driving on the roads in winter.

319. **Snow Hopscotch:** Draw lines for hopscotch in the snow with food colouring and hop away!

320. **Tic-Tac-Toe:** Stamp out the frame for the game and play it in the snow. Use two colours of waterproof bean bags as markers.

321. **Snow Maze:** Stamp out a large square or circle, or be even more creative and create vertical and horizontal lines inside the shape. Play tag, but you can't step outside of the rows that have been created.

322. **Footprint Chase:** This type of tag requires the chasing child to step into the snow footprints of the person running away.

323. **Snow Tracks:** When a newfallen snow has happened, look very carefully for animal tracks. You might need a field guide to help you discover who has been playing in your playscape! Trackers can determine the type of animal, size, and direction in which they were travelling. This is a skill necessary for survival for many Aboriginal people.

324. **Funny Walks:** Try out a variety of walking styles in the snow—toes in, toes out, one foot in front of another, backwards, sideways,

running steps, across slippery ice, in deep snow, ice skating, on snowshoes, etc.

325. **Snowshoes:** Child size snowshoes are available. Give them a try! You can make your own from heavy-duty cardboard cut into oval shapes. Poke two holes around the child's foot and secure with twine! They won't last long but the children will enjoy the experience. Aboriginal people made their snowshoes from spruce and rawhide thongs.

326. **Snow Goggles:** Aboriginal people who lived in the northern part of Canada invented goggles. They made them out of ivory, bone, and antlers to prevent snow blindness. Children may want to try to make their own snow goggles.

327. **Winter Sport Activities:** While not every child will have access to skis, having a few sets at the centre so children can take turns using them can be fun. What other activities happen in winter? Snowboarding, riding on skidoos, ski jumping, cross-country skiing, kite skiing, snowshoeing, ice fishing, Polar Bear swim, curling, hockey, broom ball, tobogganing, ice sailing, luge, dog sledding, skating, and speed skating!

328. **Find a Good Hill:** Slide like penguins, move like a seal, etc. Use cafeteria trays for make-shift toboggans or an old plastic baby bath tub—punch a hole in the front and attach a rope. The Mi'kmaq people of eastern Canada made the toboggan from bark and animal skins. By the 1600 they were made of thin boards curved at the front, ideal for hauling game, moving camp, and travel.

329. **Winter Olympics:** Depending on the age of the children, create a Winter Olympics with flags and activity stations around the playspace. Ask for family volunteers to help out at the Olympics. Try games like broom ball, a snow discus throwing contest, sled races, curling, etc.

330. **Ice Skating:** If you have the space and the time to get it ready, nothing is more fun than skating on your own ice rink. You might

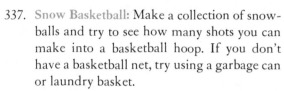
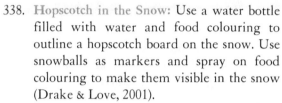

have a skate exchange or encourage donations at your centre to make sure that everyone has skates and can participate. Begin by shovelling snow into the area that you want to use after removing any hazardous materials. You will need to create a snow boarder or use lumber if available to contain the water. Then the stomping begins as the children tamp down the snow. Wait until the temperature is well below freezing and flood the rink with water over several days. Now you are ready to go. Keep the snow shovelled off the rink and repair any cracks or chips with water.

331. **Little Ice Rinks:** Fill several edge baking sheets with water. Let freeze. Remove from the tray so the children now have an ice rink of their own. Add little people, cars, trucks, etc.

332. **Snow Golf:** Take cleaned empty tuna cans and embed them in the snow around the play yard. You can make flags and number the "holes." Plastic golf clubs are available or try a second-hand sports store and cut the clubs down to the children's size. Supervise carefully! This works in warmer weather as well!

333. **Winter Bowling:** Fill the bottom of large juice bottles with sand, and set them up in a triangle. For bowling balls, use different size rubber balls depending on the children's skill level. The bowling alley can be as long as you think the children can manage. Mark the end with food colouring. You may need to stomp down the alley for a smoother delivery.

334. **Target Practice:** Use large coffee cans, plastic containers, etc., arranged in a pyramid. The children can throw snowballs to see how many containers they can knock down.

335. **Pinecone Toss:** How many pinecones can you throw into the hula hoop peeking out of the snow?

336. **Snow Soccer:** Set up the boundaries for your game and a goal at each end. Divide into two teams and play away. Hot chocolate at the end of the game is a good way to celebrate!

337. **Snow Basketball:** Make a collection of snowballs and try to see how many shots you can make into a basketball hoop. If you don't have a basketball net, try using a garbage can or laundry basket.

338. **Hopscotch in the Snow:** Use a water bottle filled with water and food colouring to outline a hopscotch board on the snow. Use snowballs as markers and spray on food colouring to make them visible in the snow (Drake & Love, 2001).

339. **Parachute Fun:** Put cotton balls (snow balls) on the parachute and see how many the children can keep on the parachute. You can also use real snow balls; what happens to them?

340. **Freeze Tag:** Run until you are caught. Freeze in place like a statue. You can be released only when someone else "frees" you by touching you.

341. **Winter Camping:** Set up a tent and all the camping gear you can find. Place logs in a circle and fill with red and yellow tissue paper for a fire. See the Camping Prop Box in Chapter 8 for more ideas.

342. **Winter Picnic:** Make a winter picnic table out of snow and cover it with a plastic table cloth. Pack up some delicious treats in a picnic basket and enjoy a winter lunch! Eat lots of warm things—stew, soup, chili, hot chocolate, etc.

343. **Beach Party:** Bring out all the warm items you have associated with summer: swimming pool, towels, sun umbrella, props such as sun block bottles, leis from the dollar store, etc. Have a beach lunch outside on a beach blanket!

344. **Winter Solstice:** December 21 is the shortest day of the year in the Northern Hemisphere. Track how sunlight changes over the next few months. Many of the religious holy days celebrated by people around the world are linked in some way to the winter solstice in the Northern Hemisphere. The term "solstice" means "sun stands still." Celebrate winter solstice with a winter potluck feast.

For Additional Reading

345. **Lunar New Year:** Create a wonderful dragon with boxes and material and do a dragon dance!

346. **Mitten Match:** Use a tub with a variety of mittens inside and see if the children can find the match. Do you have enough to make patterns?

347. **Pop, Pop, Pop:** Take a variety of plastic juice bottles, fill with water, and leave outside overnight. Make predictions then discuss what did happen.

348. **Snow Shovels:** Don't have enough snow shovels for all the children? Try using a plastic dust pan—just the right size and height for little hands.

349. **Winter City:** Fill a wide variety of plastic containers with ice and freeze overnight. Add food colouring for extra fun. Remove and let the children create a city of their own. Add props—wheeled vehicles, Little People, wood, material, etc.!

350. **Snow Blocks:** Encourage the children to build with snow blocks, which provide many of the same opportunities and challenges that indoor blocks do.

351. **Snow Jewels:** Freeze yogurt containers with water and food colouring and you have frosty blocks! These children called them snow jewels.

352. **Scavenger Hunt:** Hide fun items throughout the playground and hand out shovels for the children to find the treasures. You can also give the children a plastic zip-top bag with a treasure inside. Have them create a trail through the snow, bury their bag, and retrace their steps. When the children have returned to the starting point, have them follow another child's path to find that treasure.

353. **Plants in Winter:** Many plants lose their leaves in the winter and only their stems are exposed. The plants are dormant—saving all their energy until spring—and will grow again when it gets warmer. Other plants do die but their seeds will grow into new plants next year. Bulb plants stay safely

Lynn Wilson

Making snow jewels

Lynn Wilson

Creating a jewelled pathway

underground until it is spring again. Other plants, such as evergreens, stay green all winter long because they have needle-like leaves that can withstand the cold. They provide insulation and protection for many critters. Older children can record the life of plants and trees through all the seasons. This is a great photo opportunity!

354. Glitter Snowflakes: Have the children sketch different kinds of snowflakes using dark paper and chalk. Apply glue to the lines drawn, then sprinkle with glitter (Garrett & Thomas, 2005).

For Additional Reading

355. Freeze a Snowflake: Freeze black paper or black velvet, take it outside, and catch some snowflakes. Use magnifying glasses to examine each snowflake carefully. Ice crystals join together when falling from the sky to create a snowflake. No two are ever alike.

356. Sand in Winter: The children will continue to enjoy sand play even during the coldest weather.

357. Ice Cups: Freeze juice in a cup and encourage the children to try and eat their juice cups without their hands!

358. Frozen in the Pan: Take the children on a nature walk, collecting outdoor treasures in a pie plate. When you return, fill the pie plate with water, add a loop of yarn at the top and leave outside overnight. Next morning, remove the pie plate and hang the frozen collage outside. What happens when the sun shines through?

360. Watch Me Melt: Have the children create their own snowperson on a cookie sheet and decorate it with natural objects, yarn, extra clothing, etc. Bring the snowperson inside and watch what happens. Estimate how long it will take for it to melt.

361. Measure Up: Have the children fill a bucket with snow. Take it inside and see what happens when it melts. Does the snow or the melted water take up more space?

362. Bringing Snow Inside: Bring in bucketloads of snow to fill the indoor water table. Provide mittens and lots of interesting props to help explore the medium. Food colouring can be added to extend this experience. This can also be done outside.

PHYSICAL/ACTIVE MOTOR ZONE

Ingram Publishing/Thinkstock

Before introducing any challenges with play equipment, the children will need time to explore and experiment on their own. Remember the importance of noncompetitive experiences for young children!

363. **Asphalt Games:** Pictures and patterns on the surface of the playground can stimulate imaginative games and physical involvement. Try chalk and let the children come up with their own asphalt games.

364. **Street Games:** A DVD called *New York Street Games* is a great resource for older children. It includes an instruction book and is available at Amazon.com. Educators looking for new ideas will find this useful!

365. **Sticky Popcorn:** "The children begin this game by "popping" (jumping or hopping) as individual pieces of sticky popcorn searching for other sticky pieces. When one piece comes in contact with another, they stick together until everyone ends up as one big popcorn ball" (Orlick, 1978, p. 20).

366. **Action Boxes:** Cover small boxes with paper. Attach a picture of a movement on each side of the cube such as walking, running, rolling, jumping, and crawling. The children throw or roll the cubes and perform the movement.

367. **Magazine Pictures for Action:** Cut pictures from various sports magazines, etc., laminate them, and place them in a gym bag. Invite the children to take turns picking a picture from the bag, holding it up, and having the other children replicate the movement. Another option is to have the child who is picking the action picture to not show it to the children but to replicate the action him- or herself. The other children copy when they have figured it out. Show the picture at the end.

368. **How Many Ways Can We Move?:** Show the children a sheet of chart paper and read the question: *How Many Ways Can We Move?* Ask the group if they can think of 20 different ways they can move their bodies and write down their suggestions numbering them from 1 to 20. Encourage them to consider what they can do while they are standing, then sitting—not to forget their fingers, head, mouth, and eyes! Use a camera to take photos of their movements. These can be collected and made into a book for the book centre. (Sams et al., 2006). Or laminate the photos and use them as flash cards with children taking turns to be the "leader" on the playground. To simplify the activity for younger children, use fewer cards.

369. **Movement Words:** To encourage novel ways of moving, gather interested children and give them word clues—move in slow motion, with one foot and one hand on the ground, with no feet touching the floor, in a swirling motion, through thick fog, as if they were in a blender, as if their feet were tied, as if the floor were made of glue, as if the floor were made of hot sand, like a kangaroo, like a monster, silently, as if being chased, like a log rolling down a bumpy hill, or through a tiny, tight doorway (from Catherine Barry).

370. **Target Practice:** Target games are common among children of all cultures. Acorns, walnuts, pinecones, seed pods, etc., make wonderful natural materials for target and throwing games. Ask families to share their childhood games.

371. **Croquet—England, Bocce—Italy, Boules/ Petanque—France:** All are fun games. If the centre doesn't have its own set of balls and equipment, perhaps a family might be able to loan one. These games are played in different countries so invite a community expert to explain how these games are played.

372. **Games from Around the World:** There are so many international games that it would be impossible to list them all. Try the following websites for a comprehensive overview of games to include in your program:

http://edis.ifas.ufl.edu/pdffiles/4h/4h05500.pdf, http://library.thinkquest.org/J0110166, and

http://www.topics-mag.com/edition11/games-section.htm

373. **Run, Run as Fast as You Can:** Fun games that focus on basic motor skills and agility are What Time Is It, Mr. Wolf?, Simon Says, Red Light, Green Light, Frozen Tag, etc.

374. **Lawn Bowling:** Many communities have are lawn bowling clubs. Take a field trip to see how the game is played and scored; perhaps set up something similar back at the centre.

375. **Frisbee Fun:** The Frisbie Baking Company in Bridgeport, Connecticut, made pies that were sold to many New England colleges. College students soon discovered that the empty pie tins could be tossed and caught. Ultimate Frisbee was invented in New Jersey and is a recognized sport that is a cross between football, soccer, and basketball. The latest invention is Frisbee golf, with professional playing courses and associations. A collection of Frisbees will provide hours of fun if you have the space! Try them out on a really windy day for different results.

376. **Jacks:** An age-old game but if you don't know how to play it, watch this video:

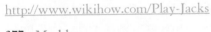 http://www.wikihow.com/Play-Jacks

377. **Marbles:**

When you play marbles, you "play for keeps." That's marble talk for winning any marble you hit and losing your own when you miss. Draw a circle about 1 metre in diameter in the dirt. Each player places an equal number of marbles inside the ring. Players take turns shooting at the marbles from outside the ring. If you knock a marble out of the ring, you keep it and shoot again from where your shooter stopped. Your turn ends when you fail to knock any marbles out or your shooter stops inside the ring. Any shooters inside the ring remain there for others to shoot at. The game ends when all the marbles have been shot out of the circle.* (Drake & Love, 1998, p. 64)

378. **Hopscotch Around the World:** As well as using numbers in the squares, try adding colours, shapes, letters, children's names,

etc., for something new! Hopscotch is played around the world and this website will show you how to create a wide range of different types of this experience. Visit

http://library.thinkquest.org/J0110166/hopscotch.htm

379. **In-Line Skating:** With the proper safety equipment, in-line skating can be a great experience for older children.

380. **Racquet Match:** Have a collection of different types of racquets—paddleball, squash, tennis, badminton, etc. Let the children experiment with them then see if the children can match a photo of a person using the racquet with the racquet itself.

381. **Lacrosse:** Lacrosse is an Aboriginal game and a popular team sport that uses a hard ball and a stick with a net at the end. Find many Native games and resources for teachers at

http://www.ainc-inac.gc.ca/ach/lr/ks/index-eng.asp

382. **Baseball:** There are many ways to play baseball so that all children can be more actively involved. T-ball, where the ball sits on a holding stick, is an easy target for most young children to hit. Children in wheelchairs can play if the surface of the play area is suitable.

383. **Juggling:**

Begin to learn to juggle using bean bags. Start with one then move on to more. Hold one ball in your dominant hand, throw it up in an arch and catch it with your other hand. Pass the ball back to your dominant hand and keep practicing. Next reverse your throw, it will take longer to perfect this move. Now try two balls. Hold one ball in the fingertips of each hand. Toss the ball from your dominant hand up in an arch toward your other hand. When this ball reaches the top of the arch, toss the ball from your other hand toward your dominant hand, below the arch of the first ball. Catch the balls and practice, practice, practice. **(Drake & Love, 1998, pp. 42–43).

---

*Drake, J. & Love, A. 1998. *The Kids Cottage Games Book*. Kids Can Press. p. 64.

**Ibid., pp. 42–43.

For Additional Reading

Aboriginal children usually juggle small balls made of animal skins stuffed with animal hair or moss.

384. **Straw Poking:** Provide a colander and thin drinking straws in the sand box. Invert the colander and watch the toddlers explore the container itself. Then add the straws so they may try to poke the straws through the holes. A great eye–hand coordination, cause-and-effect experience for toddlers (Redleaf, 2009).

385. **Toe Pick-Up:** On a warm day have the children take off their socks and shoes and provide them with a variety of small objects such as marbles, pebbles, a piece of Lego, etc., and see if they can pick these objects up with their toes.

386. **Knot Tying:** Many sailors use a wide range of knots for a variety of reasons. Is there a sailor who can visit and teach the children this skill?

387. **Outdoor Mazes:** Teachers often set up obstacle courses for children to manoeuvre through. Once the children are engaged in this experience, encourage them to create courses for each other using materials outside. The children might also be interested in drawing a maze out of chalk or coloured tape and trying to find their way out. For older children, use chalk to add numbers and letters to the area inside hoops—invite the children to hop to number 3, skip to letter B, jump to number 7, etc.

388. **Athletic Heroes:** Help the children to research information about athletes whom they are interested in. There may be a great deal of interest during the Olympics or the Tour de France (bicycling), for example. Find out about the athletes' training regime.

389. **Police Department:** Do the local police department do safety talks on bicycle safety and/or bicycle safety checks? Invite the officers in and have a Bike Rodeo! Invite families to come as well!

390. **Traffic Lights:** Make traffic lights by covering a milk carton with black construction paper and placing red, yellow, and green circles on the light. Attach to a stick and place in the ground. Construction paper signs also make good temporary traffic signs.

391. **Hobby Horses:** Use long wrapping paper tubes to make a homemade hobby horse. Convert a paper bag into the head: draw the eyes, ears, mouth, and nose on the bag and attach yarn for the mane. Stuff with newspaper. Insert the tube into the bag and tie with string or clear packing tape. Attach more wool for reins.

392. **Toys for Babies:** Have the interested older children make a pull toy for younger children in the program. Toilet roll tubes or paper towel rolls can be "punched" and colourful yarn used to tie them together. They can be painted and decorated in a safe way and can be used as wall decorations when the children are not playing with them.

393. **Tic-Tac-Toe:** Create a huge playing field with chalk, coloured tape, or string. Mark Xs and Os using rocks, seed pods, sea shells, driftwood, etc.

394. **Edible Tic-Tac-Toe:** Use bread sticks to create a much smaller board and use cucumbers for Os and crossed green beans for Xs. Players get to eat the pieces as the game progresses!

395. **Giant Checkers:** Make a large board with chalk on the pavement. Use lids or plastic plates for checkers. Try painting them!

396. **Clothes Pins in the Bottle:** This old game can be made more challenging or more simplistic by increasing or decreasing the mouth of the bottle used. Children stand over a milk bottle and see if they can drop clothes pins into the bottle.

397. **Feather Fun:** Give children feathers to blow, balance on plates, or chase.

398. **Pick-Up Sticks:** Create your own pick-up sticks by purchasing wooden skewers and painting the ends of the sticks for different point values. Hold all of the sticks together in one hand and let them fall. Try to retrieve all of the sticks without moving any of the other sticks. Try removing only "your" colours.

399. **Balancing Equipment:** Some playground equipment provides balancing opportunities.

Children may be interested in using a stop watch to see how long they can balance on one foot or how long it takes them to walk along a balance beam.

400. **Balancing Act:** Take a heavy rope and have the children create an interesting pattern with the rope—can they walk along it? When they become skilled at this, give them a tray with a tennis ball on it to carry with them as they move along the rope. What other objects can they find to transport from one end of the rope to the other?

401. **Balancing the Egg:** Balance on a sprinkler hose and give the child a spoon and an egg to transport from one end of the rope to the other.

402. **More Balancing:** Have the children create their own chalk line and see if they can balance on it. Small balance beams (use a 5 cm × 10 cm plank), stepping stones, etc., provide a different experience that supports the development of coordination and body control. You might want to use some log "slices" that can be sanded by the children and numbered. Slices are flat so they provide a great balancing and leaping opportunity while extending the children's learning by asking them to find the number that comes next, before, etc.

403. **Bean Bag Balance:** Give each child a bean bag then call out a part of the body and have the child balance the bean bag on that body part. Start with the children standing still then have them slowly move around while playing.

404. **Ladder Play:** Lay one or more ladders on the ground. Can the children walk rung on rung, on tiptoes or knees, or sideways, backward, etc., along the ladder?

405. **Stilts:** Make stilts with tin cans and twine or by taping blocks to your shoes. How does this change your perspective?

406. **Hand Games and Singing Rhymes:** Children may know many different hand games and rhymes. (Many rhymes are also associated with skipping ropes and balls). Ask the children to share their games and rhymes.

Ladders provide great balancing opportunities.

407. **Ground Hog Day Chase:** In North America, the most famous weather forecaster is the ground hog. If the ground hog can see its shadow on the morning of February 2, there will be six more weeks of winter. If it doesn't see its shadow, spring is on the way. On this special day, play a tag game that involves chasing each other by stepping on each other's shadow. You could also create shadow pictures with a bright light.

408. **Marco Polo:** Ask families to share the games that they played as children. Children may have played Marco Polo in a swimming pool and it can also be played on dry land. One person is "it" and closes his eyes. The other children scatter (create boundaries or "it" will never catch anyone) and "it" calls out "Marco" and the other children respond with "Polo." The child tries to uses his hearing to try to touch the children who are trying to escape. You may want to explain to the children who Marco Polo was.

409. **Runners:** Children who are interested can practise running 50 metres and timing themselves. They can create their own running record and see if they can improve their time. This can turn into an individual graphing exercise.

410. **Yoga:** Yoga is a wonderful way for children to focus on their bodies and often calm themselves. It also teaches them movement,

For Additional Reading

posture, and simple breathing exercises. Ask a local expert to come in and demonstrate. This could be a great end-of-the-day event with families, children, and teachers participating.

411. Slides: Find a great hill that allows for sliding on grass on old cardboard boxes or long plastic sheets in the summer and sliding on cafeteria trays or toboggans in winter!

412. Tire Fun: In many countries playground equipment includes tires as they are plentiful. For tire races, children stand the tires up and roll them around the playground.

413. Tire Painting: Why not try rolling the tires into paint and transferring the tire tracks to butcher block paper rolled out on the playground? Another idea is to paint interesting designs on the tires.

414. Rug Squares: Use carpet squares, one for each child, as paving stones and have the children move in different directions—forward, sideways, or backwards. The children can skip, jog, jump around the area but when a signal is given they sit on a carpet square. Musical squares can also be played; the children race for a square when the music stops Remember, no one gets eliminated in these types of games! Careful that the children don't slip!

415. Bottle Flip Cap: All you need is a handful of bottle caps and a small rubber ball. You place

Lynn Wilson

Tire fun in Jamaica

the bottle caps upside down on the ground, then the children try to flip them over by hitting them with the ball.

416. Ping-Pong Game: This fun game allows the children to think about how much air can be expelled from their lungs at any one time. Place a square board, approximately 60 cm × 60 cm, on several empty planters. With one child at each side of the board, place a ping-pong ball in the middle and ask each child to try to blow the ball off the board and past his or her partner.

417. Water Ping-Pong: Use water guns or spray bottles to see how quickly the children can move a ping-pong ball through a maze or across a finish line.

418. Ball Skills: Use a variety of balls to develop the techniques of aiming, predicting, and estimating by throwing balls into a variety of containers, through hoops, off walls, etc. Use the Ball Prop Box described in Chapter 8.

419. Catch the Ball: To make a scoop for a catching game, use a large soap or water bottle with a handle and cut the top off the container above the handle. Make a small hole at the bottom of the container. Knot one end of a white elastic Thread the elastic through the inside of container, pull through the bottom, and tape the knot on the bottom of the scoop. Take a ping-pong ball, punch a small hole in it, and push the elastic through the ball. Knot at the bottom. The child then tosses the ping-pong ball up and tries to catch the ball in the container. These scoops can be used for catching any type of ball, bean bag, etc.

420. Fleece Balls: Make balls by wrapping wool across and around a cardboard circle with the centre cut out. When enough wool is wrapped, a length of wool is tied around the centre and the loops around the edge of the circle are cut apart.

421. Balls and Cans: Use the cans that tennis balls come in or larger types of cans to catch tennis balls.

422. Ball Wall: Create patterns and targets on the wall with paint.

For Additional Reading

423. **Nylon Stockings:** Tie a knee high sock or nylon stocking with a tennis ball in the toe and bounce it on the ground or against the wall. You can also swing this around and toss it some distance. Have the children estimate how far they think they can throw it. Measure their results.

424. **Ball Maze:** Using outdoor blocks, create a maze. See how many times children must kick the ball to send it through to the end of the maze.

425. **Balloon Bats:** Bend a metal coat hanger into a diamond or circle shape, then twist the hook of the hanger to form a closed handle. Pull a nylon stocking over the hanger and secure it to the handle with masking tape. Bat balloons about! (Safety tip: balloons are safe for young children only if they are wrapped inside a nylon stocking to prevent choking.)

426. **Balloons and Body Parts:** Make up large picture cards showing a variety of body parts. Show the cards to the children one at a time and have them try to keep the balloon in the air using only the designated body part.

427. **Balloon Fun:** Ask the children to try keeping balloons in the air with just their feet. Then try using a wooden spoon or paper towel tube to keep the balloons aloft. Next have the children try walking across a field while trying to balance balloons on their heads (Bennett, 2005).

428. **Water Balloons:** On a hot day, have children toss water balloons back and forth.

429. **Static Electricity:** Supervise carefully! Rub balloons quickly on your hair or a piece of wool. Push the balloon onto the wall. Have the children try placing the balloon on different surfaces. Shut off all the lights, rub the balloons and watch the "spark" jump between the balloons. Talk about "hat head" in the winter when taking off our woolen hats.

430. **Koosh Balls and Paddles:** Bounce a Koosh Ball on a paddle. How many "bumps" can you count? Have the children try bounce the ball off their paddle then turn around and catch it!

431. **Hit or Miss:** Pass a Koosh Ball back and forth with a partner; how long can the children go before someone misses? Try moving closer or further away depending on how skilful you become.

432. **Two-Handed Koosh Bounce:** Instead of using one paddle, try two. Can the children pass it back and forth between the two paddles?

433. **Koosh Badminton:** Play Koosh Ball badminton or volleyball by using the paddle and a net. The children can make up their own rules for this fun game!

434. **Shuttlecock:**

In China, the original game of badminton needed only a homemade shuttlecock (made of cork and feathers) and they hit it back and forth in the air with wood and animal-skin rackets similar to Ping-Pong paddles. People said whoever kept the shuttlecock in the air for the longest would have a long life; and whoever made it fly high would reach heaven.* (Drake & Love, 1998, p. 121)

435. **Hacky Sack:** Use a special Hacky Sack ball (made from cotton or a knitted ball) or a Koosh Ball and see if the children can keep it in the air using only a foot! This is an ancient game played by Koreans called *chae-bi*.

436. **Jumpsy Ropes:** With a simple box of elastics, make several jumpsy ropes for the children to jump over. The children can tie them together to make a rope as long as they like!

437. **Bean Bag Math:** Many bean bags now come numbered or numbers can easily be sewn on. Number buckets for children to throw the matching bean bags into.

438. **Hula Hoops:** Hoops provide many opportunities for young children—How high can they lift the hoop? Hop into, out of, around, over the hoop. Use the hoop to jump with. Roll the hoop and keep it from falling. Can you roll your hoop to a partner? When the music stops, jump into your hoop and make a shape.

---

*Drake, J. & Love, A. 1998. *The Kids Cottage Games Book*. Kids Can Press. p. 121.

439. **Hoop Challenges:** Have a variety of different coloured hoops. You can yell the colour of one of the hoops and the children race to that colour and jump inside (have lots of the same colours). When the children are ready for another challenge say, "Two people in a green hoop" or "Three people in a yellow hoop!" Supervise carefully.

440. **Towel Parachute:** Take old towels and cut a small hole in the middle, just big enough for a tennis ball to fit through. One child holds each end of the towels and tries to move the towel so that the ball will fall through the hole.

441. **Towel Toss:** Encourage two children, holding the ends of a towel, to toss the ball in their towel to another pair of children also holding a towel.

442. **Simple Parachute:** If a store-bought parachute is not available, use a single sheet or old bedspread. The children can use fabric crayons or batik to personalize the sheet.

443. **Ocean Waves:** Shake the parachute up and down. Begin slowly and gradually increase the tempo. Throw a ball into the centre and have the children count how many times they can bounce the ball before it falls out.

444. **More Waves:** Can the children keep several balls from falling off the chute?

445. **Merry-Go-Round:** Children can walk, run, gallop, skip, hop, jump, leap, etc., while moving in a circle with the parachute. Children can alternate levels and directions.

446. **Head and Shoulders:** While holding the parachute and singing, the children can touch the respective body parts in the song "Head and Shoulders."

447. **Name Game:** Eric, Eric what do you say! Hop around the chute today.

448. **Retrieval:** Place bean bags or balls under the chute. When a child's name is called, she tries to gather as many as she can until she is trapped by the chute.

449. **Leaf Fun:** Collect a wide variety of leaves and place them in the centre of the parachute. What happens when it moves up and down?

450. **Connect:** Place a beach ball in the centre of the parachute. Call a child's name and everyone can try to manoeuvre the ball toward that child.

451. **Music and the Parachute:** Collect a wide range of different types of music, such as reggae, classical, jazz, music from a range of different cultures, etc. Record about 20 to 30 seconds of each so that there is a frequent change in tempo and beat. Have the children move the parachute to the music.

452. **Popcorn:** Toss several lightweight balls or a bag of cotton balls into the centre of the chute while the children lift the chute up and down.

Pop, pop, pop your corn,

Pop it big and white.

Popping, popping, popping, popping,

Popping til it's white.

SOCIAL/DRAMATIC PLAY ZONE

Lynn Wilson

453. **Gathering Place:** Children will want to come together in small or large groups for a variety of reasons. Old logs in a circle formation provide an interesting gathering spot.

454. **Home Sweet Home:** There are so many ways to make interesting enclosures, from sunflowers planted in a circle with an opening for the entrance, to willow formed into a globe enclosure, to a teepee shape with runner beans planted at the base (other types of vine-like plants can also be used such as pumpkin, melon, or gourd). Old branches from Christmas trees that are left on the street for disposal are perfect for creating a home away from home!

455. **Suggestion of Other Beings:** Decorating trees may provide opportunities to incorporate folk tales, etc.

456. **Dramatic Play:** Having a wide range of props and materials allows the children to use their imagination. Invite families to add

Imagination at work!

props that can be used in this area; that way you might get a wide range of materials from different cultures such as tablecloths, wall hangings, rugs, scarves, cooking utensils, blankets, etc. Remember, the more variables, the more active the learning! Prop boxes, travelling suitcases, etc., allow you to be organized and ready when the children ask for support!

457. **Driving:** Young children enjoy the experience of being in a wheeled vehicle.

458. **Camping:** Many city children do not have the experience of camping in the woods so providing props enables them to imagine this experience.

459. **Sidewalk Café:** Perhaps the interested children could organize a sidewalk café where the other children can come and order food and drinks.

460. **Picnic Outside:** Enjoy having lunch outside rather than eating inside!

461. **Kitchen Play:** For young children, using materials that are common and that they recognize from their home environment is a meaningful opportunity to explore the items' properties. Don't forget to ask families to contribute empty boxes and containers of the foods they eat at home—this will provide you with real variety in a way that is meaningful for the children.

462. **Things with Handles:** For young children, having a collection of containers with handles, such as lunch boxes, baskets, shopping bags, purses, old briefcases, rubber tote boxes, plastic pails, etc., provides great opportunities, especially for toddlers who love to haul things about (Miller, 1999).

463. **Hats, Shoes, and Jewels:** Any collection of wearables will provide hours of fun. The more diverse the collection, the more engaging. It is also an opportunity to provide props and materials from a wide range of cultures.

464. **Costume Party:** Set up the dramatic play area with several interesting bags from local clothing stores filled with open-ended

materials such as fabric pieces, jewellery, ties, belts, scarves, feather boas, crowns, saris, etc. Tell the children they have been invited to a costume party and let the them design their costumes. Access to the art area will help enhance this experience. Take photos when finished and serve a special snack for this gala occasion.

For Additional Reading

465. Surprise Suitcase: Set aside some interesting dramatic play clothes and when the children's interest is waning, bring out the surprise suitcase and watch the fun!

466. Pirate Fun: Whatever the children's interest, try to provide the resources and loose parts to enrich their play—see the Pirate Prop Box.

467. Mirror Fun: Safe, unbreakable mirrors set up in the dramatic play area allow the children to see their reflections. Mirrors are a must!

468. Sunglasses: Collect old sunglasses. Compare, sort, and discuss how sunglasses make the world look different. Take photos of the children.

469. It's Summer, but It's Winter: Have a winter party with all of the winter clothing the children would wear on a cold and blustery day!

470. Object in the Bag: Collect a wide variety of different types of bags. Ask children to pick one object from the bag and tell a story about it. Younger children might talk about how the object is used. A variation on this might be that the first child chooses an object from the bag, starts a story, and passes the bag to the next person, who chooses a new object and continues the story.

471. Group Story-Telling Bag: Each small group receives a bag. The children look inside and decide among themselves what role they each want to play and what their story will be about. Each group presents their story to the other groups.

472. Story-Telling Bag: Give children an empty bag and have them gather a wide variety of props in the outdoor playscape. Bring the bags to a circle and trade bags, or take a bag

Attention-grabbing bags and sand are a wonderful playful combination!

Lynn Wilson

to visit younger children and tell a story with the props.

473. Fun Bags: Have theme bags at the ready to be taken outside. The bags can be rotated and filled with new props and materials.

474. Bags in the Sand Area: Adding a collection of interesting and unusual bags sparks all types of interesting play.

475. Sun Tea: Use a large plastic jar with a lid. Fill the jar with water and add enough tea bags to make a strong brew. Place the jar on a dark surface that will absorb the sun. If the sun is strong, the water will heat up and the tea will steep. Add a few slices of lemon and allow the tea to brew for a few hours—then serve it up!

476. Let's Cook: Line the bottom of a pizza box with tin foil. Place the box in direct sunlight (remind the children not to look directly into the sun) and try cooking something delicious An incredible example of solar power!

474. Build a Clay Oven: A big project with lots of benefits!

475. Edible Flowers and Vegetables: Create a salad of vegetable florets and unsprayed edible flower petals.

476. Step-by-Step Recipes: Have children follow step-by-step visual recipe cards to create something delicious; yogurt with several

layers of different fruits, such as blueberries or strawberries from the garden, for example.

477. Berry Picking: If you have a local pick-your-own farm, take a trip and pick berries for everyone! Failing that, many farmers markets have the pick of the crop.

478. Market Visits: Harvest time is a wonderful opportunity to see a wide range of wonderful crops and fall flowers.

479. Lemonade: Plant a mint garden and add the leaves to lemonade. Try combining various amounts of mint leaves, boiling water, honey, lemon juice, and ice cubes. You might make several variations of this lemonade and have the children arrange them in order from most to least sour.

For Additional Reading

480. Taste Test: Try eating the harvest from the garden and prepare it in a variety of ways. How does freezing or canning change the texture, taste, etc.? How can the children involve themselves in preserving the foods that they have grown—pickles from cucumbers, jams from the fruit, drying the fruit, etc.?

481. Food and Festivals: Older children may be interested in researching the many festivals and celebrations that focus on planting and harvesting around the world.

482. Drying Fruit: Put a variety of fruit slices on a plate—for example, an apple sliced into very thin rounds—and cover with cheesecloth. Place the plate in direct sunlight and bring it inside at the end of the day. Return the fruit to the sunlight the next day after turning over the fruit. What happens over time? Do a taste test—how do fresh and dried fruit differ?

483. Invent a Sandwich or a Salad: With harvest materials from the garden, the children can invent a super sandwich or an incredible salad.

484. Matching Tastes: Using a fruit such as strawberry, have a taste test to see if strawberry jam, strawberry juice, and strawberries fresh from the garden taste the same. How are they similar and how are they different?

485. Create Fancy Oils/Vinegars: All kinds of wonderful tastes can be created by putting herbs into oil and vinegars. This could be a great fundraising idea!

486. Vegetable Peelers: Give the children opportunities to learn how to use a vegetable peeler. Can they remove the skin of an apple all in one go? Can they make curls with carrots and celery? Yum!

487. Stone Soup: Read the famous book *Stone Soup,* and use the vegetables from the garden to create a delicious soup. Provide a variety of crackers and have the children graph the crackers they liked best with their soup.

For Additional Reading

488. Mobiles: Listen to the trees: collect objects that make interesting sounds and hang them from the lower branches of a tree. Try chimes, foil pie plates, bells, eating utensils, recycled objects, etc. This is perfect for nonmobile infants! Create more elaborate sound machines for older children by hanging a rope between two trees or in the corner of a fence. Consider hanging objects such as an old metal tea pot, metal soup spoons, pot lids, old CDs, food tins, etc. Some may need to have a hole drilled for in order to be able to hang them. Fishing line makes an "invisible" wire.

489. Clear Mobiles: Have the children bring in clear containers and fill them with objects they have collected or find in the art centre. Hang them from trees, in windows, etc. Around Christmas time, it is possible to find clear balls for hanging on the Christmas tree. They can be filled with water in different colours, or objects, and also be hung outside.

490. Cookie-Cutter Chimes: Hang a variety of cookie cutters from tree branches to create wonderful sounds.

491. Really Listen: Ask the children to stop and sit or lie on the ground and just listen. What do they hear?

492. Listen to the Sounds: Give each child two Styrofoam cups and cut a hole in the bottom

of each cup large enough for the child to insert one ear. The children now have two amplifiers to increase their hearing. What can they hear? Make a graph of the results—insects, birds, traffic noises? Take pictures of the children wearing their amplifiers!

493. **Sound Games:** Let the children create their own sound game. Take small empty canisters and ask children to fill sets of two with matching objects they have found outside like sand, small pebbles, sticks, etc. Let the children mix them up and find the pairs that match by shaking them.

494. **Musical Fence:** Make a musical fence by hanging pie tins, spoons, a rattle, a collection of keys, brushes, and other objects at the children's level and let them make music.

495. **Music Wall:** Here is an example of how everyday kitchen items can be used to create a music wall.

496. **Hollering Tubes:** Collect things that are fun to holler into or through such as large buckets, longer gift wrap tubes, shorter toilet paper tubes, pieces of plastic pipe, or flexible dryer ducts. Let the children sing or holler through the tubes as you play music (Miller, 1999).

497. **Homemade Instruments:** Use a bread or cake pan and have the children stretch elastics across the pan. What happens? Talk about "good vibrations"! Other ideas include creating shakers by filling coffee cans with beans or small pebbles. Be thoughtful about using food in any creative experience as some families may be offended by wasting a valuable resource. Glue or tape two pie plates together after placing pebbles, metal washers or bolts inside. Encourage the children to use different parts of their hands to make music. Encourage children to make music by holding spoons loosely between the thumb and middle finger and striking their thigh while striking the top of the spoons.

Lynn Wilson

Ordinary kitchen utensils and pots and pans make great sound instruments.

498. **Playground Orchestra:** Create a playground orchestra with drumsticks or sticks. Experiment with different places and ways of striking objects as the children create their orchestra.

499. **Drumming:** Collect and decorate a variety of large tubs such as coffee cans, oatmeal tubs, laundry soap boxes, plastic buckets, cookie tins, and pastry brushes, and create your own orchestra. This is an opportunity to discuss drumming in Aboriginal communities and its sacredness to traditional rituals. An Elder may be willing to come in to demonstrate the significance of drumming to the children.

500. **Music Everywhere:** Play the children's favourite music outside or encourage them to listen to audio stories. The children may

want to create dances; provide scarves, boas, capes, floating fabrics, etc.

501. **Music for Babies:** Even the youngest child will respond to music. Provide safe props for them to explore as the music plays.

For Additional Reading

502. **Sounds for Babies:** Older children may have fun creating interesting objects to put in the trees or on the fence near where the babies and toddlers play. These can be both visual and auditory gifts.

503. **Rap a Tune:** Older children might be interested in creating a rap about the garden, worms, birds, or other critters and wildlife found in the playground.

For Additional Reading

504. **Music from Around the World:** Provide the children with a variety of music from around the world.

505. **Nature's Music:** Many items found in nature can provide sounds for the children's orchestra.

506. **Seed Instruments:** Fill ice cream containers or other plastic containers with large seeds for great sound makers.

507. **Karaoke:** Access to one of these machines will provide hours of fun. All you need is an electrical outlet and children who want to sing!

508. **Megaphones:** Slice the bottom off milk jugs to create megaphones. To experiment further, insert a long wrapping paper tube into the mouth of the jug. What happens to the sound of the children's voices?

509. **Funnel Telephones:** Take 3–4 metres of clear plastic tubing and attach a funnel at each end of the tube. Let one child speak into the funnel while the other listens.

510. **Real Telephones:** Provide lots of different types of used phones (ask families and friends for donations). The children will enjoy pretending to call their parents at work, calling about an emergency in the dramatic play area, calling for a taxi, or texting an important message. They can also pretend to be taking photos on smartphones!

511. **Walkie-Talkies:** Emergency workers often use these handsets in their jobs. The children will enjoy communicating with each other in different parts of the playspace.

512. **Playground Telephones:** Many new equipment companies are adding more interactive opportunities for children. The playground telephone is an example of this!

513. **Tape Recorders/Smart Phones:** These are great vehicles for taping things that happen outside—bird songs, traffic noises, children's songs, discussions, etc. Children can also create their own listening games by asking other children to identify the noises they have taped.

514. **Microphones:** Older children will enjoy being on stage with a microphone lip-syncing to their favourite singing artist.

515. **Video Cameras/Smart Phones:** Video cameras are an expensive acquisition but clearly one that will bring hours of memories and opportunities for recall. Smart phones are more common and will also provide a record to be shared with not only the children but also families.

516. **Bingo:** Create Bingo cards with words or statements about nature for older children, or create laminated cards with real leaves in the squares for younger children to match. The caller will have a matching set of cards to flash to the players.

517. **Sound Bingo:** Record common sounds and create a Bingo card with pictures of the corresponding sounds. Play the recording and have the children use small stones for their Bingo markers.

518. **Fancy Bottles:** For infants and young toddlers, fill a variety of clear plastic bottles such as large juice containers, large water cooler bottles, small water bottles, and shampoo bottles (anything that is clear, has an interesting shape, and will not break) with a variety of appealing natural objects (seashells, rocks, grass, pine needles, etc.), and water and food colouring. Make each bottle different from the others. Add oil; since water and oil don't mix,

this provides a different visual experience. Glue the lids on tightly. These are particularly appealing when exposed to the sun, perhaps hanging from a tree, fence, or piece of outdoor equipment. Older children might enjoy creating some of these for the younger children.

519. First Aid: Many older children benefit from first aid training, a life skill that will give them confidence when dealing with a first aid issue for themselves or their friends. This is particularly relevant to children who are often alone at home after school.

For Additional Reading

COGNITIVE/CONSTRUCTION ZONE

Lynn Wilson

520. **Blocks:** Blocks and lots of them are a necessity for outdoor play experiences. Blocks are one property that can be used in all play zones throughout the playscape and not limited to one particular zone.

521. **How Do Things Work?** Find out how ordinary things work—water, garbage collection, recycling, food, clothing. Ask experts who, what, where, when and why. What are the children interested in knowing more about?

522. **Outdoor Buddies:** Older children can be buddied up with a younger child, much like Reading Buddies. Older children will build on their confidence in support of a new younger friend in exploring natural environments

523. **Baby Shapes:** Infants and toddlers need opportunities to explore their world and the objects in it. Ensure that they have the opportunity to explore the playscape while pointing out interesting shapes for them to view.

524. **Shapes:** The children can use ropes to make shapes on the ground. Can they name the shape they have made? Can they sit inside it? You can extend this experience by playing music; when it stops, name one of the shapes and have the children jump inside it.

525. **Shape Villages:** Have the children create a shape on the ground and then create their own village with a variety of little people, small houses, cars, trucks, etc., or a variety of open-ended building materials that they chose for themselves! You can extend the experience by having them stay inside the shape when they are playing—a practical way to really understand the shape. This experience works both indoors and out.

For Additional Reading

526. **Collections:** Help children create interesting storage boxes for the treasurers they collect along the way. These boxes can be inexpensively purchased at dollar stores. Many of these items can become the foundation of the mathematics program since in order to group objects together the children must first discriminate, reason, analyze, and select in order to formulate groups. Regrouping encourages flexibility of thought and divergent thinking.

Lynn Wilson

This indoor activity of exploring spaces can be transferred to the out-of-doors.

Classification is a basic aspect of life sciences and allows children to organize knowledge.

527. **Sorting Real Objects:** Sorting and classifying collections of objects that are familiar to the children helps them understand things that are the same and things that are different, and materials that possess common properties but are not identical.

528. **Sorting and Classifying Objects:** Through their observations, children are learning to explore, predict, and test information and ideas. Children must discriminate, reason, analyze, and select in order to formulate groups. There are many ways to sort items and this encourages divergent thinking; for example, "These are the ones I want to take home with me"!

529. **Sorting and Classifying Plants:** Older children may have fun classifying plants

according to insect, animal, and bird names—wormwood, dog-tooth violet, cowslip, skunk cabbage, foxglove, cranesbill, etc.

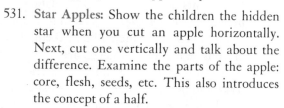

530. **Apple Sorting:** The children can sort apples by a number of properties—colour, size, weight, shape, etc. Eat them when you are done and record the children's favourites. What things are made from apples, and how many can you make or taste with the children? Try apple butter, apple cider, apple jelly, apple pie, and apple crisp.

531. **Star Apples:** Show the children the hidden star when you cut an apple horizontally. Next, cut one vertically and talk about the difference. Examine the parts of the apple: core, flesh, seeds, etc. This also introduces the concept of a half.

532. **Leaf Match:** Matching is the ability to discriminate and is crucial to the development of other mental abilities. Discriminating between letters is also an important aspect of early literacy. Provide a variety of doubles of real leaves and have the children find the matches. Or can they also find the match using coloured-paper leaf shapes?

533. **Matching:** Choose a variety of seeds and see if the children can match the seed with a duplicate then match the seeds with the pictures of the parent plant.

534. **Find the Tree:** Find two leaves from the same trees; press them and laminate them for a nature matching game. The game can be extended by giving a child one of the laminated cards and asking her to find the tree that it belongs to.

535. **Snowflake Math:** Cut out a variety of snowflakes, two of each design. Glue onto black tagboard and laminate them. Now you have a matching game that can be played outside.

536. **Postcard Matching Game:** Buy a collection of postcards with natural outdoor themes, with two of each. Laminate and see if the children can find the match.

537. **Colour Matching:** A trip to the local paint store will supply you with a wide range of colour swatches. Ask each child to pick their favourite colour and try to find a flower or plant in the playscape that matches. The same idea could be carried out on a nature walk in your community or to a local nursery.

538. **Small, Medium, and Large:** Sunflowers grow in all sizes and are perfect for helping children understand the concept of small, medium, and large. Provide lots of opportunities for children to make these comparisons by planting a variety of sunflowers in the garden.

539. **Seriation:** Concepts are best taught when children can manipulate real objects. This begins with the awareness of difference and the ability to compare. Shells, leaves, nuts, branches all provide opportunities for seriation.

540. **Three Bears:** A great way to enjoy the concept of seriation is the story of *Goldilocks and the Three Bears*. Set up the dramatic play area with three bears, three beds, three pillows, three bowls, three chairs, three spoons, etc. Enjoy reading the story together and watch what happens. Have a Teddy Bear Picnic and invite parents and grandparents. Other fun stories include *The Three Billy Goats Gruff* and *The Three Little Pigs*.

541. **More Seriation:** There are many ways to incorporate seriation opportunities into the children's experiences.

These simple spiders provide opportunities for lively discussions and an opportunity to learn more about seriation.

542. **Patterns and Designs:** Look for patterns in nature: circles, lines, triangles, etc., as well as items with unusual markings.

543. **Movement Patterns:** A great way to reinforce the children's understanding of patterns is to have them create movement patterns. For example, an AA, BB, AA pattern might be jump, jump, clap, clap, jump, jump, etc. Using their whole body helps to reinforce the concept.

544. **Treasure Hunt:** Collect small plastic gold coins (or spray paint small rocks gold), inexpensive bead necklaces, small rings, and a treasure chest to reflect a pirate's treasure. Make a treasure map that has familiar markings the children will recognize. The children will search for the treasure and share what is inside. Children can sort and classify the materials based on their properties. With more experience, the children can create their own maps for others.

545. **Another Treasure Hunt:** Take this opportunity to focus on numeracy. Hide, for example, six objects in the playspace and have the children hunt for them until all six have been found. Consider adding a large timer to see how long it takes for the children to find the objects.

546. **Temporal Ordering:** Draw a series of pictures to show the development of a plant from a seed to a mature plant. Have the children tell the story and arrange the pictures in order. This concept conveys a sense of order and a sense of time and its effect. This also calls on the child's memory to order what comes first, second, etc.

547. **Dressing for Outdoors:** Take photos of the children in various stages of getting dressed in their outdoor clothes during the winter for outdoor play and laminate the photos. Have the children order the cards, revealing the fastest and most efficient way of dressing for outside. This supports the concept of temporal ordering.

548. **Common Relations:** Encourage the children's ability to identify and pair items that are usually associated but are not identical. This experience fosters mathematical understanding through one to one correspondence, and fosters diversity since there are many kinds of pairs—hammer and nail, animals and their homes, occupations with appropriate tools, mother and father animals and their babies, etc.

549. **Graphing:** Graphing is a great way to collect and record data and is also a visual way to organize and present information. It presents and clarifies the relationship between groups. When creating graphs, always begin with the children themselves, Graphs with real objects are the most important of these graphing experiences. Take a long roll of butcher block paper and divide it into two sections. Based on the topic you are working on, give the children two choices and have them stand in the appropriate column on the paper—would you like to eat the squash from our garden or our blueberries? These real objects would be the first bars of the graph. As the children become more adept, you can give them more choices to consider. Then move to a picture graph, having a picture, photograph, etc., of the choices the children will need to make—would you like to weed the garden today or water the plants? The children can stand on the paper again or you can transfer these choices to Bristol board for all the children to see. Graphs can represent many things: a chance to decide if we have more or less of something, or record information about the children themselves—how many of you have blue eyes, brown eyes or green eyes? Others can be simple Yes or No responses—did you like the broccoli soup we made today? Finally, symbolic graphs could be introduced after the children are confident with the previous two methods. A symbol is used to represent a real thing or record a vote; for example, using stickers, dots or their names to indicate a choice.

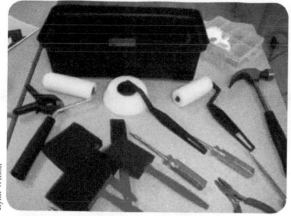

Real

Pictorial

Symbolic

Graphing is fun!

550. **Graphing My Body:** Performance of simple types of body movements can also be graphed.

551. **Graphing Fruits and Vegetables:** Create a graph with pictures of the children's favourite fruits and vegetables.

552. **Shoes, Shoes, and More Shoes:** Create a large graph with characteristics of shoes—laces, buckles, slip-on, Velcro, etc. In circle time or with interested children, have them examine their own shoes for similarities and differences. Ask the children to take off their shoes and place their shoes in the corresponding column on the graph.

553. **Counting:** Have the children estimate how many trucks, buses, bicycles, etc., will pass by their fence at a given time. Graph the results. For younger children you might have a picture of each of the types of transportation you are counting and have them place a block under each picture each time one goes by. You might also count the number of cars by their colour. Increase the difficulty by expanding the number you are counting— remember, simple to complex.

554. **Geoboards:** You can purchase plastic geoboards or make your own following a grid pattern by hammering in nails into a wooden board. Let the children explore the board and the elastics first. Then give the children brown elastics to begin with and trace out pattern

cards for them to copy. You can increase the challenge by giving them more complex pattern cards and using coloured elastics.

555. **Puzzlers:** Break a carrot into three pieces. Can the child put the carrot back together again?

556. **Stone Math:** Use stones and counters to develop math skills.

557. **Wheeled Vehicles:** Create licenses for all the wheeled vehicles in your centre. Attach them to the rear of the bikes, wagons, etc., and identify parking spaces that correspond to their licence. Encourage children to park in their designated spot by matching numbers.

558. **Felt Board Math:** Cut out a variety of flowers and vegetables out of felt along with a flower pot and soil. Use them to encourage the concept of more or less. Plant two tulips and add two yellow daffodils. How many plants do we have? Or plant four tomatoes and pick one, etc. This is even more meaningful when done with real fruits and vegetables!

559. **Big Games Outside:** Many traditional board games can be replicated in a grand scale outside, for example, a giant checkerboard with Frisbee™s for checkers. Many board games develop math skills as children measure, estimate and calculate.

560. **Weather Tools:** Use thermometers to find the temperature, sundials to track the sun

Counting

and estimate time, wind socks to determine wind strength and directions, and rain collectors to determine rainfall. Keep graphs and compare the results.

561. **Simple Rain Gauge:** Use an old juice container with the lid cut off. Place a piece of Play-Doh™ along the inside vertical wall of the container and push a ruler (face out) into the Play-Doh™. Record how much rain falls. Do this during rainy season and make a graph of the results.

562. **Weather Around the World:** As older children become more familiar with daily temperatures, bring in a newspaper and look at the city temperatures around the world. The children might have relatives or friends who live in different cities and they can find out what their weather is like.

563. **Extreme Weather:** Children are often frightened by episodes of extreme weather. It may be helpful if they understand in scientific terms how the tornado or hurricane, etc., comes to be. This is also an opportunity—without frightening the children—to know what safety measures should take place in an emergency.

564. **Air:** Can you see it? Put a crumpled piece of paper into the bottom of a glass. Hold the glass upside down and push it into a bowl of water. Does the paper get wet? Water didn't rush into the glass and the paper stays dry because the glass was already filled with something—air!

565. **Dust on the Windowsill:**

Take two index cards and record the date on the card. Have the children smear each index card with petroleum jelly. Tape one card on the windowsill inside the playroom and other on the outside of the window. Each day for a week, have the children check the cards, look at them under a microscope and record their observations. Discuss what they see and what particles arrived there. (Mayesky, 2012, p. 482)

566. **Air Pollution:** Look at pictures of air pollution and discuss how and why this happens. What can we do to make air in our communities healthier?

Lynn Wilson

The wonders of forced air!

567. **Air:** This child experienced air in a new and interesting way when he stood over a subway grate on a community walk. Teachable moments!

568. **Windsock:** An easy way to make a windsock is to cut off the sleeve from a lightweight long-sleeved shirt. Make a 5 cm wide strip of cardboard into a ring and staple it into place. Poke a hole through the sleeve at the ring, feed a piece of string through the hole and knot it. Tie the other end of the string to a tree limb.

569. **Properties of the Wind:** Chinese ribbons are traditional objects that can be used to dance and twirl. They can also be made by taping crepe paper inside a long wrapping paper tube. For younger children, use a paper towel roll. Playing with these on a windy day enhances the experience. Try adding music! Try tying ribbons around trees or other structures on the playspace. Leave one long tail to flutter in the wind. For younger hands, try using embroidery hoops, canning jar rings, plastic dollar store bracelets, or shower curtain hooks, and tie on fancy ribbons, interesting fabrics, things that sparkle, etc.

570. **Feel the Wind:** On a windy day have the children hide behind different objects to hide from the wind. Where is the best spot and why? Collect pinwheels made from construction paper or flags the children have made from a variety of materials and take them out on windy days to see what happens. Also use bubbles on windy days, and the parachute or wind chimes!

571. **Tin Can Wind Chime:** Make a musical wind chime using an old can and pretty glass beads to catch the light, then hang from a tree. Pierce the tin and attach the beads, strung on fishing line or sturdy string. You can also add bells (Woram & Cox, 2002).

572. **Kite Flying:** The children can make their own kites and experiment with the properties of wind and speed. They may have to problem solve solutions to their flying challenges. In Japan May 5 is *Children's Day* and is celebrated by flying kites.

573. **Photographs:** Have the children take photos on trips or for projects that they initiate. They may want to make a book out of their photos with their own scripted text.

For Additional Reading

Lynn Wilson

There are many things to photograph in a child's environment.

574. **Sun Reflectors:** Use a square of aluminum foil glued on a sturdy square of cardboard to create reflections on a sunny day. Also try using small unbreakable mirrors.

575. **Mirror Games:** All you need is a sunny day and an unbreakable mirror. Have the children draw a maze on the pavement with chalk and see if they can manoeuvre their beam of light through the maze. For older children, make it more challenging: can if they can do this without touching the maze walls?

576. **Hot Walk:** Take a walk about on a hot day, ask the children how the heat affects them. How does the sunlight shining on objects look? How does the heat affect flowers they see? Do their petals and leaves droop or curl under? Why? Can heat be seen rising from the pavement or the hoods of cars? What does it look like? Where else can heat be seen rising? What colour is the sky? Are there clouds in the sky? Does the number of clouds affect the temperature? Can the children tell how hot things might be by looking at them? How?* (Redleaf, 2010, p. 23)

Experiment by touching different objects. Be careful.

577. **Sun and Shade:** Help the children discover that sunlight warms the Earth. Touch different outdoor objects in the sun and in the shade. Which ones are cooler, and which ones are warmer?

578. **Sun and Shade and a Thermometer:** Help children experiment with differences in temperature between sun and shade using a thermometer. Put one pail of water in the shade and one in the sun. Place a thermometer in each. After about an hour, compare the results. Feel the difference by touching the water in each pail.

579. **Sun Experiments:** On a hot day put out a variety of objects that might melt in the sun. Have the children decide which object will melt first, second, or not at all and record the results. Try chocolate, butter, tin foil, stone, etc.

580. **The Sun Is a Heater!** Remove the labels from two cans. Paint the outside of one can black and leave the other as it is. Fill each can with cold water and take the temperature. Leave the cans outside in the sun, and after a few hours, take their temperatures again. Feel the cans! The black can absorbs the sun's energy while the metal surface reflects it; the water in the black can will be warmer.

For Additional Reading

581. **Sun Word Game:** For older children, ask them how many words they can think up that begin with the word "Sun"—Sunday, sunbathe, sunburn, sunflower, sung, sunrise, sunny, sunshine, sunglasses, sunroof, sunspot, sunbeam, etc. (Redleaf, 2009)

582. **I Spy:** Play "I Spy" and use spy glasses made from paper towel tubes.

583. **Binoculars:** Add binoculars to your props— these are always big favourites. They can also be made with two toilet paper rolls taped together to simulate the real thing.

584. **Search and Find:** Place a variety of items— metal and nonmetal, in the sand area and give the children magnets. What do they discover?

585. **Kim's Game:** Place a number of natural outdoor materials on a tray in front of the children. Give them one minute to look and feel all of the objects on the tray. Cover the tray and ask the children to name as many objects as they can. Let the children find new objects to place on the tray and have them play this game with each other. You can also play this game with a group of children, having one child hide under a blanket and another child trying to guess who is missing.

586. **Human Sundial:** Stand in the middle of the playground and have each child take turns drawing his or her outline on the ground. Wait a few hours and do a second shadow standing in the same place as the first outline. What has happened over time?

587. **Shadow Hunt:** Can the children make their shadow disappear? Can they find other shadows of trees or buildings? Can they

---

*Hey Kids! Out the Door, Let's Explore! By Rhoda Redleaf (2010). pg. 23.

make their shadows move? Can they chase each other's shadows?

588. **Science Slides:**

Purchase a plastic sleeve for each child (the best ones are those used for collecting baseball cards that are 3" × 4" [7.5 × 10 cm] and open on one side). Send these home with a note, asking the families to help their child find a nature item and put it in the sleeve to make a "slide." Have the children bring them back in and set them up in the science centre for all the children to explore and discuss. Add magnifying glasses and encourage the children to talk about their slides. (Charner, 2010, p. 81)

589. **Upside-Down Bikes:** How else can bikes be used? What happens when we turn the bike upside down?

590. **Courier Delivery:** Set up a transportation route with landmarks such as a bus stop, garage, car park, and shops. From a central point such as a post office, have a variety of letters and parcels ready to be delivered. Following a simple route map or spoken instruction, encourage the children to deliver mail, either on foot or using a wheeled vehicle, to its destination (Harriman, 2010).

591. **Cause and Effect:** Cause-and-effect experiences are the basis for scientific investigations. They conveys a sense of the individual's ability to be effective, to act on her world, and produce results—to make things happen. The volcano never fails to interest children and is an exciting cause-and-effect experience. Mix baking soda and vinegar and food colouring for dramatic results. Each child should create his or her own volcano. This is most effective when it is done in a big way—try this in the sand pit with a huge mound of sand!

592. **More Cause-and-Effect Ideas:** Other cause-and-effect activities include Jack-in-the-box, windup toys, musical instruments, flashlights in a dark tent, garlic press with Play-Doh™, blowing soap bubbles, listening to their hearts after a good run, hammering nails into boards, floating and sinking objects in water, etc.

593. **Dying—Cause and Effect:**

Aboriginal people used plants in order to dye their clothing. Have the children discuss the colours they think will appear in this dying experience. Have a variety of white cotton fabric and a variety of fruits and vegetables— onions (yellow), oak bark (brown), strawberries, cherries, raspberries (pink), beets (red), red cabbage (purple/blue), spinach (green). This experience will have to be heavily supervised since boiling water is needed for each addition to the pot. Chop the plant material into small pieces with double the amount of water to plant material. Bring to a boil, then simmer for about an hour. Strain and add the cotton fabric to the mixture. For a stronger shade, leave overnight. Use gloves as this will stain your hands! (Alberta Online Encyclopaedia and Edukits, n.d., p. 1)

594. **Cellophane Changes the World:** Stretch cellophane inside an embroidery hoop. Make several hoops with different colours of cellophane. What reaction do you see from the children (Miller 1999)?

595. **Woodworking:** This is a great activity to do outside since it does create a lot of great sounds. Visit your local lumberyard and ask for scraps. Let the staff know it is for the children; you will be amazed at how generous people will be. Help the children learn how to safely use real tools, many of which now come in smaller sizes for little hands. Also provide lots of glue! Provide a variety of measuring tools. Having this set up near the art centre gives the children lots of materials to work with.

596. **Puzzles:** The outdoor play space provides lots of room on the grass or on a table to complete puzzles.

597. **Signing Puzzle:** This is a great opportunity for children to become more familiar with signing.

598. **Puzzles with the Children Themselves:** Glue pictures of the children onto store-bought foam puzzles.

Lynn Wilson

Puzzle fun

Lynn Wilson

I see you!

Lynn Wilson

A Raisin Bran puzzle

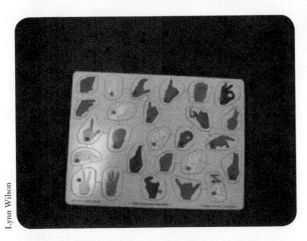

Lynn Wilson

Learning to sign

599. **Inexpensive Puzzles:** Make great puzzles from simple objects like cereal boxes.

600. **Lego/Duplo:** So many skills are involved in Lego/Duplo experiences; give children ample opportunities to explore these materials. Some quick and easy ideas are the following: hold up a shape, then hide it and see if the children can replicate it. Move from simple to complex varying colours and directions. Use a colour spinner and have the children choose Lego only of that colour in their building. With a partner, pick the same six pieces for each person. Sit back to back or behind a wall. One child completes a structure with the six pieces and then explains to the other child how to put the pieces together. If the second child has questions, only yes or no responses are possible. Then compare, did the instructions work?

601. **Dominoes:** A favourite game in many cultures.

Lynn Wilson

Giant dominoes

Lynn Wilson

Card playing

Lynn Wilson

Non-traditional ways of measuring!

For Additional Reading

602. **Card Games:** Children learn many skills while playing card games. Cards were played by Chinese royalty more than 1,000 years ago. The photo is an example of how cards can be used in a variety of ways.

603. **Measure Everything:** Provide the children with interesting materials to use for measuring—metre sticks, measuring tapes, liquid measures, measuring cups, etc.

604. **Fun Ways to Measure:** In this group, the children were interested in dinosaurs so this measuring activity actively engaged them.

605. **Gravity:**

Everything on earth is pulled by gravity. Isaac Newton (1642–1727) developed the concept of gravity after observing an apple falling from a tree. Experiment with objects by throwing

them up in the air and noticing what happens every time. Have a gravity race. Select natural objects of any size, shape or weight for the race. Drop your selected objects from the same height to see which one lands first. Regardless of weight or size, objects dropped from the same height will fall at the same speed unless an object has a large surface that interacts with air. Air gets in the way when leaves and feathers drop, causing them to drift a bit and slowing down their fall.* (Ward, 2008, p. 109)

606. **Weighing Objects:** Use balance scales and weigh scales to compare the weights of rocks, tubs of sand, jugs of water, acorns, pumpkins, shells, pinecones, etc. Have the children record their information on small clipboards.

607. **Pulleys:** Make pulleys using buckets and ropes and fill the buckets with leaves, feathers, water, and rocks to see which weighs more. How creative can the children be when given an open-ended task? Graph the results.

608. **Child-Size Metal Detector:**

Put metal objects such as ball bearings into flowerpots, under bushes and ask children if they can find them all. Support children in this by having numbered cards for the number of objects that have been hidden. (Bilton, 2008, p. 93)

From I Love Dirt!, by Jennifer Ward, © 2008 by Jennifer Ward. Reprinted by arrangement with Shambhala Publications Inc., Boston, MA. www.shambhala.com. p. 109.

609. **Little Things:** Use magnifying glass to find little things—the insides of flowers, spider webs, fly wings, grass, insects, etc.

610. **Rain Sticks:** Rain sticks are used to imitate the sound of rain in an effort to coax rain from the sky. Use bamboo stalks in a variety of lengths and pour in a variety of beans, seeds, and rice. Support the children's discovery of the most effective rain stick and graph the results.

611. **Sifting Sand:** Provide the children with a variety of interesting materials to sift sand—fabric netting, colanders, screening, funnels, strainers, a fly swatter, needlepoint canvas—along with a variety of empty containers to collect the sand. Can the children predict how the sand will blow through the objects? You might graph the results by taking a photo of each of the objects, putting them in a line at the top of graph paper, and having the children record their results.

For Additional Reading

612. **Pumpkins!** Creating a pumpkin patch provides all kinds of ideas for math—estimate and weigh a variety of pumpkins, graph the favourites, count the seeds, estimate distance around the pumpkin then measure with wool or a cloth measuring tape, etc.

613. **My Personal Pumpkin:** This works best when there is a pumpkin for everyone. When the pumpkins are young and green, use a large nail to write the child's name into the rind. Don't go too deep. Point the name to the sun and watch what happens over time. Put some straw mulch under the pumpkins so they won't rot on moist soil. Talk about what the children think will happen.

614. **Estimating Airplanes:** Talk about perspective; watch an airplane in the sky and discuss how little it appears. Then ask the children to estimate how big they think the plane really is. (Have one in mind; an Airbus is different from a Cessna.) Have one child stand where the nose of the plane would be on the ground, then have the children stand where they think the end of the plane would actually be and how far the wings would reach. Have

the distance measured ahead of time. When the children are all in position, have the child at the nose of the plane hold the string and another stretch the string to the plane's actual size. This simple estimating game also can be played with dinosaurs, elephants, buses, etc.

615. **More Estimating:** How much sand do we need to weigh as much as this rock? How many steps to the fence, etc.?

616. **Even More Estimating:** How much string do we need to wrap around this tree? Look at a variety of different trees and estimate the circumference of each. Talk about the differences in the trees, and their bark and leaves.

617. **How Many?** How many small cups of water does it take to fill a large pail or container? Record the results.

618. **Sunlight Predictions:** The children can collect a variety of objects and predict whether or not the sun will shine through them. Create a chart to record the results.

619. **Popcorn Explosion:** Place a coloured sheet on the ground and heat some oil in a frying pan. Add popcorn kernels and plug it in. Have the children estimate where they think the furthest popcorn piece will land. Be careful of spattering; keep a safe distance away from the popper. Have fun eating the results of this experiment.

For Additional Reading

620. **Fliers:** Make and decorate paper airplanes and helicopters and fly them from the climber. Estimate how far the children think their plane will fly, then measure the results. Let the children problem solve adjustments to their fliers.

621. **Car Races:** Using an inclined plank, estimate which cars will go the fastest down this ramp. Discuss why some are slower than others.

622. **Body Tracing:** Have the children trace each other's bodies, guessing each other's vital measurements—distance from elbow to ear, the diameter of the head, length of the foot, distance from knee to the toe, etc. They can use a measuring stick or tape measure to get the actual measurements. Then they

can design clothing and accessories with coloured chalk.

623. **How Many Watermelon Seeds?** Give each child a slice of watermelon and have the children estimate how many seeds they think their piece has. Eat and count.

624. **My Watermelon:** Have the children estimate how much string they will need to go all the way around the watermelon. Is my head as big as a watermelon? Measure to find out. Can they find something outside that they think is larger, smaller, or the same size as the watermelon? Can they find something that is heavier than their watermelon?

For Additional Reading

625. **Paper Boats:** Read the book, *Curious George Rides a Bike* by H.A. Rey. Make the paper boats from newspapers as outlined in the book. If you have a stream in your neighbourhood, have the children estimate which boats will make it to an imaginary finish line first or create your own waterway on your playground.

626. **Build a House:** How many cereal boxes do we need to build a playhouse? All you need is a variety of cereal boxes and wide clear tape! Don't forget to leave a window and a door!

627. **Fire Making:** With older children, create a fire pit with rocks to contain the fire and to prevent any flames from reaching any of the nearby vegetation. Have the children practise laying a variety of different types of fires, such as teepee, basic A, criss-cross, etc. Have them estimate which one will burn the most effectively then try it out. Toast some marshmallows once the fire is established.

628. **Porta Paks:** Porta Paks are a great way for children to conduct simple science experiments, math investigations, and creative ideas outdoors. Store materials for experiments in a large labelled zip-top bag. Simple pictorial instructions are included for the children to follow. Children can take these outside and tidy-up is a breeze since all the materials simply go back into the bag. See Chapter 8 for more Porta Pak ideas.

ART ZONE

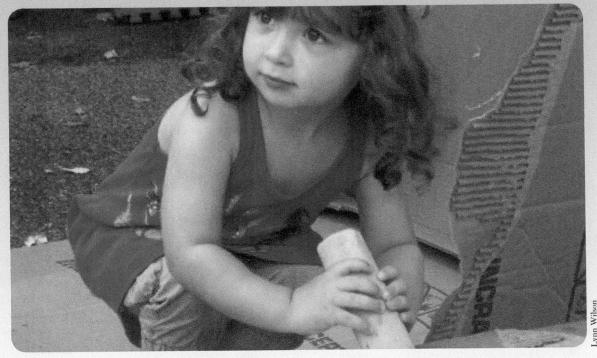

Lynn Wilson

629. **Marking Territory:** A well-designed entrance can have a strong impact on the centre's identity within the local community and helps visitors to feel more welcome. Help the children identify their space by creating signs and totems to let everyone know who "lives" there during the day. Mosaics, murals, and other pieces of art made by children add interest to outdoor areas. This also helps to strengthen the identity of the school and encourages the children to use space for different activities. The photo demonstrates a totem made by cutting Sonotubes into rounds. The children then decorated their own section of the totem.

630. **Inventions:** With a wide range of props and materials, much can be created! See the photo below for more ideas!

631. **Painting Outside:** Use paper on Plexiglas, easels, fences, the ground, or, a fold-down table.

632. **Tools to Mark With:** Use a variety of tools to make it more interesting to paint—house-painting brushes, hair brushes, rollers, paint trays, sponges, combs, cooking utensils, string, yarn, Q-tips, deodorant roll-top bottles, corncobs, corks, old mascara brushes, nail polish brushes, basters, baby bottle brushes, medicine droppers, pot scrubbers, tooth brushes, chalk, chalk dipped in water, crayons tied together, highlighters, calligraphy pens, charcoal sticks, glitter

Winter fun

Ingrid Crowther

pens, coloured glue, stamps and stamp pads, shaving cream, markers, etc. For a more natural approach, use tree branches, feathers, twigs, ferns, leaves, etc.

633. **Paper to Paint On:** Use coloured paper, computer paper, corrugated cardboard, cardboard, chart paper, wrapping paper, waxed paper, parchment paper, newspapers (look for a variety of local papers from different cultural groups), Bristol board, finger-painting paper, butcher paper, etc.

634. **Different Surfaces to Paint On:** Use cloth, tin foil, cellophane, T-shirts, wood, clay, ceiling and floor tiles, paper bags, juice or plastic lids, Plexiglas, screens, old placemats, rocks, bark, sidewalks, comic strips, window shades, venetian blinds, coffee filters, boxes, magazines, wallpaper, paper plates, paper towels, suede, vinyl, canvas, paper rolls,

Lynn Wilson

Creativity at work

Body painting and body prints!

tissue paper, bubble wrap, doilies, or old shower curtains (Abraham, 2005).

635. **Body Painting:** Interested children can paint on themselves with paint, shaving cream, etc. This is a great summer activity when the children are in bathing suits. You may want to look at books that describe how people from many cultures decorate their bodies.

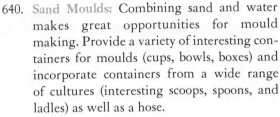

636. **Garden Aprons:** Older children may be able to follow a simple apron pattern to create their own garden aprons from sturdy fabric such as muslin. Plain aprons can also be purchased. Children can apply paint to a variety of leaves and press them into the fabric for a decorative touch or paint directly on the aprons to personalize their own apron.

637. **Body Prints:** After playing with shaving cream, this child is making a body print.

638. **Footprint Art:** After removing their shoes, encourage the children to step in the paint and walk around on a long piece of butcher paper. Supervise carefully as it can get slippery. Use a hose to clean up at the end.

639. **Shoe Prints:** Collect a variety of work shoes, boots, etc. Collect pictures of people who might wear these shoes in their work environment and have the children match the shoes to the pictures. To extend this experience, have the children wear the boots, put them into paint, and walk along a long roll of butcher block paper. The children could also paint their own feet to add another element to this mural.

640. **Sand Moulds:** Combining sand and water makes great opportunities for mould making. Provide a variety of interesting containers for moulds (cups, bowls, boxes) and incorporate containers from a wide range of cultures (interesting scoops, spoons, and ladles) as well as a hose.

641. **Sketching:** Give the children clipboards and graphite pencils, charcoal, etc., and have them sketch their favourite plant or flower, or anything they would like. Take a photo of the flower and post with the drawings.

642. **Sketching Walk:** Talk a walk and bring along sketching materials. What do the children want to sketch?

Examining the budding tree

Artists drawing what they saw.

ART ZONE

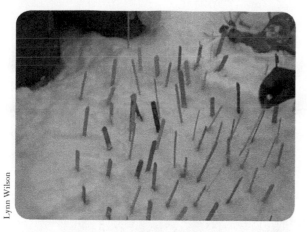

Popsicle™ fun

643. **Snow Art with Popsicle™ Sticks:** The children can paint a variety of Popsicle™ sticks with different colours and designs and create their own masterpieces in the snow.

644. **Marble Painting:** Place large pieces of paper or butcher block paper in a plastic swimming pool. Have the children pour paint into the pool and give them a collection of marbles of all sizes. Roll away, lift and tip the pool, and watch the designs appear. Supervise carefully if doing this with younger children. Hang the papers on the fence to dry for all to see.

645. **Sun Prints:** Pin leaves or place rocks on leaves on top of dark construction paper. Leave them in direct sunlight for about an hour and a silhouette will be left. Sun prints can be made from all kinds of objects.

646. **How Blue Is Blue?:** Bring out a variety of paint colours and have the children mix paints on a piece of acrylic—much like a painter's palette—to get the colours they need. Experimenting should be fun! Encourage them to try to paint the sky on a large sheet of white paper in the colours that they see.

647. **Necklaces:** Children can create necklaces by stringing leaves on a bodkin needle and a thin piece of wool or cord. This can be extended to include an edible necklace—dried apricots, prunes, apples, pretzels, raisins, popcorn, and pumpkin seeds.

648. **Petals and Seed Pictures:** Using a range of materials such as dandelion heads, leaves, stems, sunflower seeds, rose petals, etc., encourage the children to create pictures.

649. **Leaf Painting:** Use leaves for paper and see what happens!

650. **Leaf Tiaras:** Buy some plastic headbands from the dollar store. When the leaves are falling bring a variety of leaves to the art table and have the children create their own magical tiaras with lots of glue! You might want to include other fall items such as acorns, maple keys, etc.

651. **Leaf Printing:** Paint leaves on one side and press them onto a plain table cloth, napkins, butcher block paper, or card stock for some amazing designs. Use a wide range of leaves for the best effect!

652. **Pumpkin Painting:** Paint the pumpkin you grew!

For Additional Reading

An artist at work!

653. Tree Painting: Use nontoxic paint to paint the bark of a tree. This is an opportunity to learn close up about tree bark.

654. Buried Treasure: Bury objects in the sand and have the children "discover" them. For example, hide or create a tropical feel by creating palm trees, blue containers sunk into the sand for lakes, grasses made out of tissue paper, evergreen branches.

655. Sandpaper Art: Place a variety of different types of sandpaper on the art table and let the children explore the different textures of the sandpaper. Place paper on top and let the children make a rubbing of each sandpaper with crayons.

656. Wreath Making: Collect a variety of interesting fall items—acorns, leaves, twigs—and glue them on a Styrofoam ring to create a wreath for the entrance to the playground.

657. Weaving: Using spiders as an inspiration, try weaving using branches from trees, or weaving with wool by winding it around the branches and hanging objects such as pinecones, dried and fresh weeds, seed pods, shells, etc. For a larger project, try tying ropes between two trees and then using wool, string, or twine to weave between them. You may want to decorate the finished product with bells or other sound makers.

658. More Weaving: Try a more structured approach by collecting a variety of materials and weaving them into the fence. Try ribbons, wool, material, paper, feathers, long grasses, leaves, etc.

659. Fence Weaving: Use coloured clothes pins to create patterns on the fence.

660. Museum Visit: A visit to a textile museum may help spark an interest in crafts with older children. A volunteer may be willing to come in and work with the children to encourage knitting, loom weaving, macramé, bead weaving, pottery or ceramics, quilting, etc. Many of these crafts can be hung outside; for example, children may be able to create macramé plant holders.

Watts Towers

661. Beautiful Junk: Simon Rodia was an inspired artist who created the Watts Towers in Los Angeles, California, out of what many people would consider junk. He built the spires over 33 years and used materials such as coloured glass, beach shells, broken tiles, pieces of mirror, and pottery pieces. Many images of the towers can be found on the Internet and may inspire artists in your centre to look at "junk" in a new way!

662. Famous Artists: Visit a local art gallery and look at paintings and sculptures are inspired by nature. Look for artists such as Robert Bateman, John Audubon, Claude Monet, and Vincent Van Gogh. If you are not sure, ask staff at the gallery to help you guide the children. Later, many of the children may be interested in creating their own masterpieces and learning more about the artists they have seen.

663. **Winter Count:** Each year during the winter, the Sioux tribe used to do a "winter count." They thought of all the important things that had happened since last winter and recorded them by drawing pictures to preserve their history. The children may want to try to remember important events in the same way.

664. **Bead Work and Embroidery:**

You might invite an Aboriginal artisan to demonstrate beadwork. First Nations beadwork originated with the art of porcupine quills, dried grass and moose hair embroidery. In many communities, these objects were dyed and sewed or embroidered into tanned animal-hide clothing, footwear, belts, gloves, etc. (McCue, 2006, p. 39)

665. **Flowers:** Do flowers all have the same petals? Are they all the same shape? Are there colour differences? What is different and what is the same about flowers?

666. **Pressing Flowers and Leaves:** Press garden flowers and leaves in a heavy book or phone directory for several weeks. Take them out to create flower pictures, greeting cards, pictures for framing, book marks, etc. Rubber cement works best on these projects. Another approach is to use clear contact paper, peel off the backing and lay it sticky side up on a surface. Have the children lay their flowers and leaves on top then seal with another piece of contact paper. These make great window decorations!

667. **Flower Art:** Ask a local florist to come in and show the children how he or she arranges flowers and the tools used. Using flowers from the garden, and with the florist's support, have the children experiment with their own creations. Also try using dry flowers and small dollar store baskets for a variation on this experience.

668. **Ikebana:** Ikebana is a traditional Japanese art form that uses shape, line, form, and parts of the flower not often seen in floral arrangements such as stems and leaves. It is thought to have come to Japan with Buddhist practices more than 500 years ago.

Invite an expert to explain this art form to the children.

669. **Origami:** Older children may enjoy creating origami boxes, flowers, animals, etc. Have origami paper and a good origami book as a guide, or a volunteer who is educated in this craft!

For Additional Reading

670. **Art from Nature:** Show woodcuts, botanical drawings, and pictures of famous floral paintings such as *Jamaican Flowers* by Frederic E. Church, *One Year the Milkweed* by Arshile Gorky, etc.

For Additional Reading

671. **Plant Mural:** Create a mural with seed packages, tags from plants that identify the species, fruit and vegetable pictures from magazines, and newspaper grocery store advertisements.

For Additional Reading

672. **Potpourris:** Collect leaves and flower petals—rose buds and petals, lavender flowers, geranium, lemon balm, peony, phlox, daylilies, lilac, etc. Place them on a large sheet of paper and allow them to dry (not in direct sunlight). When dry, grind them. Place the collection in a new sock or tightly woven mesh bags, tie, and decorate with ribbons. These can be used for fundraising efforts.

673. **Rubbings:** Go on a "feely walk" and bring along lightweight paper and smooth crayons to record the textures as rubbings. Try leaves, tree bark, sidewalks, bricks, etc. Can the children guess where the rubbings came from? Older children may be interested in exploring in the city looking for brass signs or gravestones. (Cemeteries are interesting places to find out about the history of the community).

For Additional Reading

674. **Rubbing Books:** Children may be interested in creating a book with all of their rubbings. They might order the pages by placing the roughest to the smoothest or vice versa before binding their book.

675. **Making Fossils:** Make a salt dough and then have the children flatten their dough. They can choose from a variety of objects to place in their "fossil"—shells, twigs, cleaned and

boiled chicken bones, etc., then lift off. Let their finds dry. For a quicker process, place them in the oven on low heat.

676. Brick House: Clay soil is best for making bricks but if soil in your centre is sandy, try adding one part flour per four parts of soil. Add water to the soil until the texture is like bread dough. Shape it into a rectangle or place it into a baking pan (greased with petroleum jelly for easy removal) or empty milk carton. Allow the mixture to set, then use a wet table knife to cut various-sized bricks. To make large bricks, add straw, hay, or grass clippings for additional strength. When the bricks have dried, use them to build. For extra fun, you may want to create fossil imprints, using toy dinosaurs or animals.

677. Sand Paintings: Use paper and glue to make sand paintings right in the sand box.

678. Rangoli: Rangoli is a traditional decorative folk art of India. These decorative designs are made on floors of living rooms and courtyards during Hindu festivals and are meant as sacred welcoming areas. Search the Internet or books for the intricate designs and give the children a variety of stones and pebbles to create their own designs.

679. Sand Sculpture: You need a spoon, saucepan, 500 ml of sand, 250 ml of cornstarch, and 250 ml of water. Mix the sand, cornstarch, and water together in a pan. Heat over low heat and keep stirring. Remove when the mixture is thick. Let it cool and begin the sculpting. Let it dry to harden.

680. Sand Inside and Out: Bring sand into the playroom to expand the children's opportunities to engage with sand.

681. Stone Sculptures: Choose rocks of different sizes, shapes, and colours. Have the children pick the rocks that are the most interesting to them. Encourage the children to make rock sculptures. This provides a great opportunity to discuss balance, gravity, tipping point, etc. Some children may want to paint, or add props or other creative materials to their sculptures. The children might want to create a sculpture garden with all their structures strategically placed. Take photos and display the children's creativity.

682. Inukshuk: An Inukshuk is a stone landmark or cairn built by the Inuit and other people of the Arctic region of North America. The Inukshuk was used as a marker for travel routes, fishing places, camps, hunting grounds, or food caches. The children may be interested in using stones to create an Inukshuk to mark their territory. The flag of Nunavut bears the symbol of the Inukshuk.

683. Making Paper: This is an opportunity to help children understand how recycling can be useful and how trees are used in paper production. Have the children tear old newspapers into small pieces and cover with water. Let soak for a least an hour. Use an egg beater or an electric mixer to stir up the paper until it is mushy. Mix in cornstarch and more water if needed. Food colouring can also be added to make coloured paper. Put a screen on a cookie sheet and pour in the pulp mixture. Let it drain briefly. Gently lift out the screen with the new paper on top, cover with paper towels, and press down on the new paper. Let dry overnight and peel off the paper the next day. Experiment with different types of paper—magazines, junk mail, coloured paper—and see which works best.

684. Wrapping Paper: Place leaves on a large piece of newsprint and dab paint from a sponge over the top of the leaves. When the leaves are lifted off, the imprint will be there. The same idea can be done with paint, a small piece of wire mesh ,and a toothbrush. Dip the brush into the paint then rub it over the wire mesh to create a spatter painting over the leaves. When the leaves are removed, a negative image remains.

685. Art from Recyclables: Give each child a plastic bag filled with recyclables such as plastic utensils, paper or Styrofoam

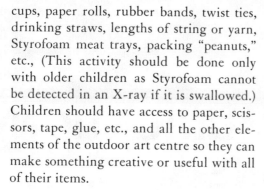

cups, paper rolls, rubber bands, twist ties, drinking straws, lengths of string or yarn, Styrofoam meat trays, packing "peanuts," etc., (This activity should be done only with older children as Styrofoam cannot be detected in an X-ray if it is swallowed.) Children should have access to paper, scissors, tape, glue, etc., and all the other elements of the outdoor art centre so they can make something creative or useful with all of their items.

686. Stamps: Used stamps can be bought in bulk. The children can sort them to find those stamps that represent the outdoors.

687. Friendship Bracelet Box: Create a portable small suitcase with embroidery thread, gimp, safety pins, scissors, measuring tape, an old pillow to work on, and instructions to create friendship bracelets.

688. String Games: String games increase children's creativity and dexterity. Aboriginal string games usually consisted of strings made from animal sinew. There are many books with interesting string games. Check them out!

689. Outdoor Displays: Display the children's artwork outside as a great background for an outdoor garden party for families.

QUIET/COMMUNICATION ZONE

Lynn Wilson

690. **Quiet Space:** Many children are happiest when adults can't see them and they create their own communities with their friends. Provide old sheets that can be painted or batiked and hung over frames to create a hideaway home.

691. **Hiding Places:** We can provide hiding places by providing nooks in the playscape. If we don't, children will move to the farthest reaches of the playscape to find private places for themselves and their friends.

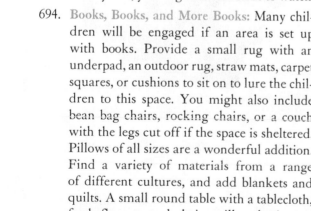

692. **Sky Watch:** Find time for simple things—spread out a blanket and have the children lie on their backs and look for cloud shapes. Over time, help the children identify the different types of clouds. Some of the easiest to identify are Cirrus, the highest clouds made of ice crystals; Stratus clouds, which are low hanging and stretch across the sky; and Cumulus clouds, the fluffy ones and the ones we most often see on clear days!

693. **What's Outside My Window?** Sometimes some of the most interesting things happen outdoors when children are inside looking out. If you have a window ledge that the children can sit at, add paper and pencils, markers, binders, and notebooks and encourage the children to draw or write about what they see. If you add stick-on hummingbird feeders to the window or hang a piece of beef suet in an onion bag at a nearby tree, you might attract birds to watch.

694. **Books, Books, and More Books:** Many children will be engaged if an area is set up with books. Provide a small rug with an underpad, an outdoor rug, straw mats, carpet squares, or cushions to sit on to lure the children to this space. You might also include bean bag chairs, rocking chairs, or a couch with the legs cut off if the space is sheltered. Pillows of all sizes are a wonderful addition. Find a variety of materials from a range of different cultures, and add blankets and quilts. A small round table with a tablecloth, fresh flowers, and chairs will make it very appealing. If the space is under a tree you might add mobiles, kites, or material such as a sari hung loosely to create a softer, cosier space. Tents and parachute enclosures are also ideas for this area. Display books in an appealing manner and, when possible, with the covers showing. Recorded music can also be playing. If you are near an electrical source, tapes and headsets can be used but iPods and iPads can also be utilized without a power source. You might have children and their families record themselves reading a favourite story. A flannel board and puppets might also be included in this area.

695. **Borrow a Book for Outside:** Have kits with books in a protective covering ready to take outside. Place them near the exit to outside.

696. **Infant/Toddler Books:** Photo albums, both big and small, make perfect books for little hands. You can include nature items under plastic pages to make a durable and interesting book for young children.

Story bags

"Old MacDonald Had a Farm"

697. **Clothes Line Stories:** These are a fun way of sequencing a story for the children to organize and tell while practising a variety of different skills.

698. **Puppets Ready to Go:** A shoe storage bag is a great way to organize and make puppets accessible to the children outside.

699. **Puppets:** Children enjoy story telling with puppets, especially those they have created themselves.

700. **Glove Puppets:** Mittens provide opportunities for songs and role playing.

701. **Puppet Theatre:** An puppet theatre is a perfect opportunity for a stage performance. The children may be able to create their own with boards, hammers, fabric, etc.

702. **Blackboard:** Small blackboards, brushes, and a variety of white and coloured chalk may engage many children. You can easily make these with a can of blackboard paint and pieces of plywood cut to size.

703. **Writer's Suitcase:** Small, easy-to-manage suitcases can be filled with all kinds of interesting props and materials to be taken outside as explained in Chapter 8.

704. **Writing Station:** You can also bring all of the above items to a specific writing area set up to encourage print making for many of the other play zones. Items can be organized in small travelling suitcases, baskets with

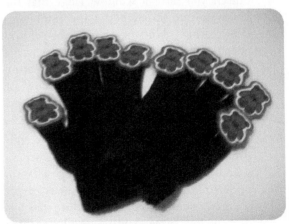

My own puppet tin

Song mittens

handles, etc., for easy transport. Word cards can also be made available for those who would like to use them.

705. **Post Their Stories:** Post the children's written work in outdoors to encourage families to visit the playground to see their children's work.

706. **Clipboards:** Clipboards are great tools for just about every zone of the playspace. Provide them along with markers, coloured pencils, etc., to encourage meaning making. They can be used in dramatic play for creating menus, for following treasure maps, making out tickets—all finds of fun!

707. **Flannel Boards:** Create small flannel boards for individual use and with a variety of flannel pieces, magic can happen! Children can make their own felt characters and many store-bought items can be added to this collection.

708. **Stories Front to Back:** Colour photocopy pages of a story book and laminate them with a piece of Velcro on the back. Ask the children to arrange the story from beginning to end.

709. **Proverbs:** How many proverbs or saying can you come up with that have their roots in nature; for example, "light as a feather," "a rolling stone gathers no moss," "the calm before the storm," "sly as a fox," "can't see the forest for the trees," "every cloud has a silver lining." Can you think of others?

710. **Cookie Sheets:** Cookie sheets or metal stove-top protectors make good magnetic boards. You can also magnetize a flannel board by inserting a piece of thin metal between the backing and flannel. Magnetic strips can be cut and glued to just about any object and used in memory games, sorting and classifying, grouping, etc.

711. **Sign Language:** Helping the children learn to sign is a valuable life skill that enables the children to communicate with deaf people. Many infants in child care centres are now taught simple signs to help them communicate; for example, the sign for "more" at the lunch table. With older children, download the signs for alphabet letters from the Internet and use them to create mystery hunts. Give the children cards with words spelled out in sign and they have to find the location of the treasures by deciphering the letters.

Cookie sheets have many uses.

Lynn Wilson

712. **Dr. Seuss:** March 2 is the birthday of Dr. Seuss. Read *The Lorax* or any of the children's favourites.

713. **Board Games:** Many board games are great fun to play in a quiet secluded spot. Chess, Checkers, Bingo, Backgammon, Boggle, and Candy Land are just a few. Try Twister for a more physical game. There are also several games with an environmental theme such as Arctic Survival, R-Eco, Dominant Species, etc. Older children may enjoy making their own game.

714. **Tic-Tac-Toe/Hangman:** There are several simple paper games that are fun to play. Tic-Tac-Toe is a fun X and O game and Hangman is a great word game for older children.

715. **Dear Diary:** Some older children might enjoy making their own diary and writing in it during outdoor play. Make covers from batik or tie-dyed material.

716. **Pantomime:** Children may enjoy acting out a pantomime of a favourite story.

717. **Charades:** This game can be played in small teams or with two people. One side chooses a book title, song, movie, TV show, etc., and acts it out without speaking. The other side has to guess what is being acted out. You can use a timer to help move the game along. For younger children, use pictures of things to be acted out.

718. **Pictionary:** Divide older children into two small teams. Each person on the team chooses a card with a word such as "flower." The player goes to the easel and draws the picture until someone from his own team guesses it correctly.

Abraham, C. (2005). Curriculum Ideas. Exploring the 5 Senses. Retrieved November 25, 2012, from http://www.child-carelounge.com/diva/LearningFoundationssample-5Senses[1].pdf

Active Healthy Kids Canada. (2012). Is active play extinct? Active Healthy Kids Canada 2012 Report Card on Physical Activity for Children and Youth. Retrieved June 9, 2012, from http://dvqdas9jty7g6.cloudfront.net/reportcards2012/AHKC%202012%20-%20Report%20Card%20Long%20Form%20-%20FINAL.pdf

Alberta Education. (n.d.). Our Words, Our Ways. Retrieved September 24, 2012, from www.education.alberta.ca/media/307116/o03.pdf

Alini, E. (2011, November 7). Green monsters: How designers and botanists are putting a colourful flourish on drab urban landscapes. *Macleans,* Retrieved October 24, 2012, from http://www2.macleans.ca/2011/11/07/green-monsters

Allen, Lady of Hurtwood. (1968). *Planning for Play.* Cambridge, MA: MIT Press.

Baratta-Lorton, M. (1976). *Mathematics Their Way.* Menlo Park, CA: Addison-Wesley Publishing.

Barker, R. (1994). School grounds as a community resource. *Streetwise, 5*(4), 11–16.

Baskin, Y. (1997). *The Work of Nature: How the Diversity of Life Sustains Us.* Washington, DC: Island Press.

Beach, J. & Friendly, M. (2005). Child care centre physical environments. Quality by Design Working Paper. Child Care Resource and Research Unit, University of Toronto. Retrieved September 24, 2012, from http://www.childcarequality.ca/wdocs/QbD_PhysicalEnvironments.pdf

Beaucage, J. (2009). Through the Eyes of a Child. First Nation Children's Environmental Health, Union of Ontario Indians. Retrieved February 9, 2012, from http://www.anishinabek.ca

Bell, J.F., Wilson, J.S., & Liu, G.C. (2008). Neighbourhood greenness and two-year changes in children's body mass index, *American Journal of Preventive Medicine, 35*(6), 547–553.

Bengtsson, A. (1974). *Adventure Playgrounds.* New York: Praeger.

Bennett, J. (2004). Curriculum Issues in National Policy-Making. Keynote address to EECERA Conference, Malta, September 2.

Bennett, J. & Lonarduzzi, S. (2004, March). *Starting Strong. Curricula and Pedagogies in Early Childhood Education and Care. Five Curriculum Outlines.* Directorate for Education, OECD.

Berman, M., Jonides, J., & Kaplan, S. (2008). The Cognitive Benefits of Interacting with Nature. *Psychological Science, 19,* 1207–1212.

Bertrand, J. (2008). *Understanding, Managing, and Leading Early Childhood Programs in Canada.* Toronto: Nelson, Thomson Canada.

Best Start. (2005). Positive Self Image. Retrieved July 8, 2012, from http://www.beststart.org/resources/hlthy_chld_dev/pdf/fact_pros.pdf

Best Start. (2011). What the Research Says About Physical Activity and the Early Years Retrieved July 6, 2012, from http://activeforlife.ca/wp-content/uploads/2012/09/Best_Start-What_the_Research_Says_on_PL.pdf

Bienenstock, A. (n.d.). Resource Book. Connecting Children to Nature Where and When They Play. Retrieved September 21, 2011, from http://www.naturalplaygrounds.ca

Bilton, H. (2002). *Outdoor Play in the Early Years: Management and Innovation,* 2nd ed. London: David Fulton Publishers.

Bilton, H. (2008). *Learning Outdoors: Improving the Quality of Young Children's Play Outdoors.* New York: Routledge.

Bilton, H. (2010). *Outdoor Learning in the Early Years: Management and Innovation,* 3rd ed. New York. Routledge, Taylor and Francis Group.

Biography.com. (2012). Bindi Irwin. Retrieved September 25, 2012, from http://www.biography.com/people/bindi-irwin-241515

Blatchford, P., Baines, E., & Pellegrini, A. (2003). The social context of school playground games: Sex and ethnic differences, and changes over time after entry to junior school. *British Journal of Developmental Psychology, 21*(4), 481–505.

Boise, P. (2010). Go Green Rating Scale. Retrieved September 24, 2012, from http://www.gogreenratingscale.org

Bower, J.K., Hales, D.P., Tate, D.F., Rubin, D.A., Benjamin, S.E., & Ward, D.S. (2008). The childcare environment and children's physical activity. *American Journal of Preventive Medicine, 34*(1), 23–29.

Boyatzis, C. J., Mallis, M., & Leon, I. (1999). Effects of game type on children's gender-based peer preferences: A naturalistic observational study. *Sex Roles, 40,* 93–105.

Bramwell, M., Burnie, D., Dicks, L., & Few, R. (2009). *Planet watch: A young person's guide to protecting our world.* London: Dorling Kindersley.

Brennan, G. & E. (1997). *The Children's Kitchen Garden: A Book of Gardening. Cooking and Learning.* Berkeley, CA: Ten Speed Press.

Broda, H.W. (2007). *Schoolyard-Enhanced Learning Using the Outdoors as an Instructional Tool, K–8.* Markham, ON: Pembroke Publishers.

Brown, Katelyn. (2012, September). Email communication.

Brown, S.E. (2004). *Bubbles, Rainbows, and Worms: Science Experiments for Preschool Children.* Beltsville, MD: Gryphon House.

Brown, S. & Vaughan, C. (2009). *Play: How It Shapes the Brain, Opens the Imagination, and Invigorates the Soul.* New York: Avery.

Bucklin-Sporer, A. & Pringle, R.K. (2011, February). Reconnecting kids to nature: The benefits of school gardens. Retrieved September 24, 2012, from http://www.naturalhomeandgarden.com/community/reconnecting-kids-to-nature-benefits-of-school-gardens.aspx?page=7

Cameron, D. (2009). Play Scotland—Play-Related Quotes. Retrieved October 23, 2012, from http://www.playscotland.org/play-related-quotes

Campbell, D.W. & Eaton, W.O. (1999). Sex differences in the activity level of infants. *Infant and Child Development, 8*(1), 1–17.

Canadian Standards Association. (2008). *Canadian Playground Standards*, 4th ed. Retrieved September 25, 2012, from http://publiccommons.ca/documents/1028

Canadian Wildlife Federation. Get to Know Your Wild Neighbours. (2012). Retrieved January 17, 2012, from http://www.get-to-know.org/contest/canada

Carson, R. 1956. *The Sense of Wonder*. New York: Harper and Row Publishers.

Carson, R. 1962. *Silent Spring*. Boston, New York: Houghton Mifflin Company.

Chalufour, I. & Worth, K. (2003). *Discovering Nature with Young Children*. St. Paul, MN: Redleaf Press.

Charner, K. (2010). *Learn Every Day About Our Green Earth*. Lewisville, NC: Gryphon House.

Chawla, L. (2007). Childhood experiences associated with care for the natural world: a theoretical framework for empirical results. Retrieved March 5, 2012, from http://cye.colorado.edu/cye_journal/abstract.pl?n=1840

Chawla, L., & Hart, R.A. (1995). The roots of environmental concern. *The NAMTA Journal, 20*(1), 148–157.

CHealth. (2012). Asthma in Canada. Retrieved September 25, 2012, from http://chealth.canoe.ca/channel_section_details.asp?text_id=3370&channel_id=2014&relation_id=18604

Cheskey, E. (1994). Habitat restoration: Changing the schoolyard changes behaviour. *Green Teacher, 47*, 11–14.

Cheskey, E. (2001). How schoolyards influence behaviour. In T. Grant and G. Littlejohn (eds), *Greening School Grounds: Creating Habitats for Learning* (pp. 5–9). Gabriola Island, BC: New Society Publishers.

Childcare Design Guidelines. (1993, February 4). City of Vancouver: Land use and development policies and guidelines. Retrieved July 7, 2011, from https://vancouver.ca

Children and Nature Network. (n.d). Retrieved June 6, 2012, from http://www.childrenandnature.org

Cimprich, B. (1993). Development of an intervention to restore attention in cancer patient. *Cancer Nursing, 16*, 83–92.

City of New York, (2012). School yards to playgrounds. Retrieved September 26, 2012, from www.nycgovparks.org/sub_about/planyc/playgrounds.html

Clendaniel, M. (2008, August 14). *Adventure Playgrounds*. Issue 12. Retrieved April 7, 2012, from http://www.good.is/post/adventure-playgrounds

Coffey, A. (2001). Transforming school grounds. In T. Grant and G. Littlejohn (eds), *Greening School Grounds: Creating Habitats for Learning*. Toronto: Green Teacher.

Coffey, A. (2004). *Asking Children, Listening to Children: School Grounds Transformation*. The Ontario Trillium Foundation.

Community Knowledge Centre, Toronto Community Foundation. Not far from the tree. Retrieved September 25, 2012, from http://ckc.tcf.ca/org/not-far-tree_

CPCHE (Canadian Partnership for Children's Health and Environment). (2010). Advancing Environmental Health in Child Care Settings: A Checklist for Child Care Practitioners and Public Health Inspectors. Toronto, ON. Retrieved June 2, 2012 from www.healthyenvironmentforkids.ca

Cragg, S. & Cameron, C. (2006). *Physical Activity of Canadian Youth*. Ottawa: Canadian Fitness and Lifestyle Research Institute.

CSEP. (2012). Canadian Physical Activity Guidelines and Canadian Sedentary Behaviour Guidelines. Retrieved November 19, 2012, from http://www.csep.ca/english/view.asp?x=804

CTV News. (2011, October 26). Take me outside. Retrieved September 25, 2012, from http://takemeoutside.ca/the-run/45-in-the-media/299-ctv-news

Cullen, J. (1993). Preschool children's use and perceptions of outdoor play areas. *Early Child Development and Care, 89*, 45–46.

Curriculum for Excellence Through Outdoor Learning. (2010). Learning and Teaching Scotland. Retrieved April 19, 2012, from http://www.educationscotland.gov.uk

Curtis, D. & Carter, M. (1996). *Reflecting Children's Lives: A Handbook for Planning Child-Centred Curriculum*. St. Paul, MN: Redleaf Press.

Curtis, D. & Carter, M. (2003). *In Designs for Living and Learning—Transforming Early Childhood Environments*. St. Paul, MN: Redleaf Press.

Dale, D., Corbin, C.B., & Dale, K.S. (2000). Restricting opportunities to be active during school time: Do children compensate by increasing physical activity levels after school? *Research Quarterly for Exercise and Sport, 71*(3), 240–248.

Danks, F. & Schofield, J. (2005). *Nature's Playground. Activities, Crafts, and Games to Encourage Children to Get Outdoors*. Chicago: Chicago Review Press.

Dannenmaier, M. (1998). *A Child's Garden: Enriching Outdoor Spaces for Children and Parents*. New York: Simon and Schuster Editions.

Dannenmaier, M. (2008). *A Child's Garden—60 Ideas to Make Any Garden Come Alive for Children*. Portland, OR: Timber Press.

Davis Cutler, K., Fisher, K., DeJohn, S., & the Editors of the National Gardening Association. (2011). *Herb Gardening for Dummies*, 2nd ed. Mississauga, ON: Wiley Publishing.

Day Nurseries Act. Reg. 262ms. 53(4). Retrieved October 23, 2012, from http://www.e-laws.gov.on.ca/html/regs/english/elaws_regs_900262_e.htm

Day, S. (2010). *Incredible Edibles: 43 Fun Things to Grow in the City*. Tonawanda, NY: Firefly Books.

DeBord, K., Hestenes, L.L., Moore, R.C., Cosco, N.G., & McGinnis, J.R. (2005). *POEMS: Preschool Outdoor Environment Measurement Scale*. North Carolina State University, University of North Carolina-Greensboro. Lewisville, and Kaplan Early Learning Company.

Dempsey, J. & E. Strickland. (1999). The whys have it! Why to include loose parts on the playground. *Early Childhood Today, 14*(1), 24–25.

Denham, S.A. (2001). Dealing with feelings: Foundations and consequences of young children's emotional competence. *Early Education and Development, 12*(1), 23–45.

Diamond, A. (2007). *Tools of the Mind*. Vancouver, BC: University of British Columbia.

Dietze, B. & Kashin, D. (2012). *Playing and Learning in Early Childhood Education*. Toronto: Pearson Canada.

Dombro, A.L., Colker, L.J., & Trister Dodge, D. (1997). *The Creative Curriculum for Infants and Toddlers*. Washington, DC: Teaching Strategies.

Dowda, M., Pate, R.R., Trost, S.G., Joao, M., Almeida, C.A., & Sirard, J.R. (2004). Influences of preschool policies and practices on children's physical activity. *Journal of Community Health, 29*(3), 183–196.

Drake, J. & Love, A. (1996). *The Kids Campfire Book.* Toronto: Kids Can Press.

Drake, J. & Love, A. (1998). *The Kids Cottage Games Book.* Toronto: Kids Can Press.

Drake, J. & Love, A. (2001). *The Kids Winter Cottage Book.* Toronto: Kids Can Press.

Durant, S. (2007). *Outdoor Play.* London, UK: Step Forward Publishing.

Dyment, J.E. & Bell, A.C. (2006). Our garden is colour blind, inclusive and warm: Reflections on green school grounds and social inclusion. *International Journal Of Inclusive Education, 1,* 952–962.

Dyment, J.E. and Bell, A.C. (2007). Grounds for Movement: Green School Grounds as Sites for Promoting Physical Activity. Retrieved February 21, 2012, from her. oxfordjournals.org/content/23/6/952.full.pdf

Esbensen, S. (1987). *An Outdoor Classroom.* Ypsilanti, MI: High Scope Press.

Etnier, J.L., Salazar, W., Landers, D.M., et al. (1997). The influence of physical fitness and exercise upon cognitive functioning: A meta-analysis. *Journal of Sport and Exercise Psychology, 19,* 249–277.

Evans, G. (2006). Child development and the physical environment. *Annual Review of Psychology, 57,* 423–451.

Evans, J. (2001). In search of peaceful playgrounds. *Education Research and Perspectives, 28*(1), 15–56.

Evergreen. (2004). *Small Wonders: Designing Vibrant, Natural Landscapes for Early Childhood.* Toronto: Learning Grounds Tool Shed Series.

Evergreen Brick Works. (2012). Retrieved May 12, 2012, from http://ebw.evergreen.ca

Faber Taylor, A. & Kuo, F.E. (2008). Children with attention deficits concentrate better after walk in the park. *Journal of Attention Disorders.* Thousand Oaks, CA: Sage Publications.

Fairfax, K. (1999). *The Tranquil Garden: Creating Peaceful Spaces Outdoors.* New York: Hearst Books.

Fell, D. (1989). *A Kids First Book of Gardening: Growing Plants Indoors and Out.* Philadelphia: Running Press.

Fields in Trust. (2010). Play Scotland—Play-Related Quotes. Retrieved June 1, 2012, from http://www.playscotland. org/play-related-quotes

Flett, C. (1992). *Our Children, Our Ways.* Winnipeg, MN: Red River College.

Forest Schools. (n.d.). A History of Forest Schools. Retrieved April 29, 2012, from http://www.forestschools.com/ history-of-forest-schools.php

Frost, J. (n.d.). The Dissolution of Children's Outdoor Play: Causes and Consequences. Retrieved May 17, 2012, from Frost, J. (1992). *Play and Playscapes.* Albany, NY: Delmar Publishing. http://www.fairplayforchildren.org/ pdf/1291334551.pdf

Frost, J. (2006). Evolution of American playgrounds. Retrieved August 12, 2012, from http://www.scholarpedia.org/ article/Evolution_of_American_Playgrounds

Frost, J. (2012). University of the incarnate word. J.E. & L.E. Mabee Library. Retrieved May 2, 2012, from http://library.uiwtx.edu/frost/joefrost.html

Frost, J.L. & Klein, B.L. (1979). *Children's Play and Playgrounds.* Boston: Allyn & Bacon.

Frost, J. & Talbot, J. (1989). Magical Playscapes. Retrieved July 2, 2012, from http://www.gsa.gov/graphics/pbs/Magical_ Playscapes.pdf

Frumkin, H. (2001). Beyond toxicity: Human health and the natural environment. *American Journal of Preventative Medicine, 20*(3), 232–240.

Gamson Danks, S. (2010). *Asphalt to Ecosystems. Design Ideas for Schoolyard Transformation.* Oakland, CA: New Village Press.

Gamson Danks, S. (2011). Asphalt to ecosystems. Retrieved September 25, 2012, from http://www.asphalt2ecosystems. org/home/about_the_author

Gardner, H. (1999). *Intelligence Reframed: Multiple Intelligences for the 21st Century.* New York: Basic Books.

Garrett, L. & Thomas, H. (2005). *Small Wonders: Nature Education for Young Children.* Quechee, VT: Vermont Institute of Natural Science.

Garrick, R. (2009). *Playing Outdoor in the Early Years,* 2nd ed. New York: Continuum International Publishing Group.

Gellens, S. (2007). *Activities That Build the Young Child's Brain.* Tampa, FL: Early Childhood Association of Florida.

Geneva Foundation for Medical Education and Research. (2010). What is WHO's mandate? Retrieved November 23, 2012, from http://www.gfmer.ch/TMCAM/WHO_ Minelli/P2-3.htm

Gestwicki, C. (2007). *Developmentally appropriate practice: Curriculum and development in early education,* 3rd ed. Independence, KY: Thomson Delmar Learning.

Gestwicki, C. (2011). *Developmentally appropriate practice: Curriculum and development in early education,* 3rd ed. Independence, Toronto: Cengage Learning.

Ginsburg, H., & Opper, S. (1979). *Piaget's Theory of Intellectual Development,* 2nd ed. Englewood Cliffs, NJ: Prentice-Hall.

Glover, T.D. (2004). Social capital and the lived experience of community gardeners. *Leisure Sciences, 26,* 143–162.

Goodwin, M.H. (2001). Organizing participation in cross-sex jump rope: Situating gender differences within longitudinal studies of activities. *Research on Language and Social Interaction, 34,* 75–106.

Goodwin, M.H. (2002). Exclusion in girls' peer groups: Ethnographic analysis of language practices on the playground. *Human Development, 45*(6), 392–415.

Goomansingh, C. (2010, September 16). Doctors sound alarm on childhood obesity. Retrieved September 25, 2012, from http://www.childhoodobesitydeerpark.com/?paged=8

Gordon, A. (2011a, May 21). How daily exercise jogs the brain. *Toronto Star,* A11.

Gordon, A. (2011b, June 4). Fresh Cure for What Ails Us: Take a Hike. *Toronto Star,* A14.

Government of Ontario. (2007). Shaping our schools: Shaping our future environmental education in Ontario schools. Retrieved September 25, 2012, from www.edu.gov.on.ca/ curriculumcouncil/shapingSchools.pdf

Government of Ontario. (2009). Acting today, shaping tomorrow. Retrieved September 25, 2012, from www.edu. gov.on.ca/eng/teachers/enviroed/ShapeTomorrow.pdf

Greenman, J. (1988). *Caring Spaces, Learning Places: Children's Environments That Work.* Redmond, WA: Exchange Press.

Greenman, J. (2003). Making outdoor learning possible. *Child Care Information Exchange, 151*, 75–80.

Greenman, J. (2005). Places for childhood in the 21st century. Retrieved September 25, 2012, from http://www.naeyc.org/files/yc/file/200505/01Greenman.pdf

Greenman, J. (2007). *Caring Spaces, Learning Places Children's Environments That Work*. Redman, WA: Exchange Press.

Green Thumb, Growing Kids. (n.d.). Retrieved June 5, 2012, from http://www.kidsgrowing.ca/wiki/wiki.php?n=WinchesterPS.FrontPage

Guddemi, M.P. (2000). Recess: A time to learn, a time to grow. In R. L. Clements (ed.), *Elementary School Recess: Selected Readings, Games, and Activities for Teachers and Parents* (pp. 2–8). Boston: American Press.

Hammer, K. (2011, August 30). Study Suggests Traditonal Playgrounds Could Do More to Reduce Childhood Obesity. *The Globe and Mail*. Retrieved November 3, 2012, from http://www.theglobeandmail.com/life/parenting/study-suggests-traditional-playgrounds-could-do-more-to-reduce-childhood-obesity/article600300

Harriman, H. (2010). *The Outdoor Classroom: A Place to Learn*. Swindon, UK: Corner to Learn.

Hartig, T., Mang, M., & Evans, G.W. (1991). Restorative effects of natural environment experiences. *Environment and Behavior, 23*, 3–26.

Hayes, Jane. (April, 2011). Personal communication.

Health Canada. (2003). Industry guide to Canadian safety requirements for toys and related products. Consumer Product Safety Office. Retrieved October 24, 2012, from http://www.hc-sc.gc.ca/cps-spc/pubs/indust/toys-jouets/index-eng.php

Heidemann, S. & Hewitt, D. (1992). *Pathways to Play: Developing Play Skills in Young Children*. St. Paul, MN: Redleaf Press.

Henley, J. (2010). Why our children need to get outside and engage with nature. Retrieved September 25, 2012, from http://www.guardian.co.uk/lifeandstyle/2010/aug/16/childre-nature-outside-play-health

Herrington, S. (2008). Perspectives from the ground: Early childhood educators' perceptions of outdoor play spaces at child care centers. *Children, Youth and Environments*, 18(2). 64–87.

Herrington, S. (2009). *On Landscapes: Thinking in Action*. New York: Routledge.

Herrington, S. & Beach, J. (2007). Research, practices, and trends in child care centre design for outdoor play. Retrieved February 2, 2012, from http://vancouver.ca/commsvcs/socialplanning/initiatives/childcare/development3.htm

Herrington, S. & Lesmeister, C. (2006) The design of landscapes at child care centres: Seven C's. *Landscape Research, 31*(1), 63–82.

Herrington, S. & Nicholls, J. (2011). Outdoor play spaces in canada: The safety dance of standards as policy. Sage Journals Online: Critical Social Policy. Retrieved September 25, 2012, from http://csp.sagepub.com/content/27/1/128.abstract

Hestenes, L., Shim, J., & DeBord, K. (2007, March). The measurement and influence of outdoor child care quality on preschool children's experiences. Presentation given at the Biennial Conference for the Society for Research in Child Development, Boston.

Heschong, L., Wright, R.L., & Okura, S. (2002). Daylighting impact on retail sales performance. *Journal of the Illuminating Engineering Society, 31*(2), 21–25.

Heseltine, P. (1998). Introductory presentation by RoSPA's playground safety officer to the ILAM training seminar, "Inspecting Children's Playgrounds." Liverpool. In F. Brown (ed.). *Playwork: Theory and Practice* (p. 123). Philadelphia: Open University Press.

High Scope Early Childhood Curriculum. (2009). *Outside Time for Active Learners*. High Scope Press. Retrieved January 31, 2012, from www.highscope.org/file/PDFs/OutsideTimeDVD_guide.pdf

Hill, P. (1978). *Play Spaces for Preschoolers: Design Guidelines for the Development of Preschool Play Spaces in Residential Environments*. Ottawa: Central Mortgage and Housing Corporation, National Office.

Hines, D.A. & Malley-Morrison, K. (2005). *Family Violence in the United States: Defining, Understanding, and Combating Abuse*. Thousand Oaks, CA: Sage.

Hirsh-Pasek, K., Golinkoff, R.M., Berk, L.E., & Singer, D.G. (2009). *A Mandate for Playful Learning in Preschool: Presenting the Evidence*. New York: Oxford University Press.

Hohmann, M. & Weikart, D. (1995). *Educating Young Children*. Ypsilanti, MI: High Scope Press.

Holland Bloorview. (2004). Spiral Garden & Cosmic Bird Feeder Annual Report, 2004. Retrieved September 25, 2012, from http://www.hollandbloorview.ca/programsandservices/communityprograms/centreforthearts/documents/annualreport2004.pdf

Honig, A.S. (n.d.). Infants and toddlers: Let's go outside. Retrieved September 25, 2012, from http://www.scholastic.com/teachers/article/infants-toddlers-let39s-go-outside

Houghton, E. (2003). *A Breath of Fresh Air: Celebrating Nature and School Gardens*. Toronto: The Learnxs Foundation & Sumach Press, Toronto District School Board.

Hughes, B. & King, F. (2000). *Best Play: What Play Provisions Should Do for Children*. London, UK: National Playing Fields Association.

Hull, L. (2010). Green Museum, Retrieved June 7, 2012, from http://www.greenmuseum.org

Humber Nurseries. (n.d.). Green Thumb Guide—Container Gardening [Handout].

Humber Nurseries. Feng Shui Green Thumbs Guides. (n.d.). Retrieved October 24, 2012, from http://www.gardencentre.com/Information/GardeningTips/GreenThumbGuides/FengShui/tabid/175/Default.aspx

"I am the Hummingbird." (n.d.). Retrieved November 19, 2012, from http://wangari.greenbeltmovement.org/hummingbird

ING Direct. (2012). Making a Difference in Our Community. Retrieved September 25, 2012, from http://www.ingdirect.ca/en/aboutus/inthecommunity/index.html

Irwin, J.D., He, M., Sangster Bouck, M.L., Tucker, P., & Pollett, G.L. (2005). Preschoolers' physical activity behaviours: Parents' perspectives. *Canadian Journal of Public Health,* July–August(96), 4.

Janz, K.F., Burns, T.L., Torner, J.C., et al. (2010). Physical activity and bone measures in young children: The Iowa bone development study. *Pediatrics, 107*(6), 1387–1393.

Johnson, J.E., Christie, J.R., & Wardle, F. (2004). *Play, Development, and Early Education*. Boston: Pearson Education.

Kami, C. (1982). *Number in Preschool and Kindergarten: Educational Implications of Piaget's Theory*. Washington, DC: National Association for the Education of Young Children.

Kaplan, R. (1984). Wilderness perception and psychological benefits: An analysis of a continuing program. *Leisure Sciences, 6*, 271–290.

Kaplan, R. (2001). The nature of the view from home. Psychological benefits. *Environmental Behaviour, 33*(4), 507–542.

Kaplan, R. & Kaplan, S. (1989). *The Experience of Nature: A Psychological Perspective*. New York: Cambridge University Press.

Keeler, R. (2008). *Natural Playscapes: Creating Outdoor Play Environments for the Soul*. Redmond, WA: Child Care Information Exchange.

Kellert. S. (1983). Affective, evaluative and cognitive perceptions of animals. In I. Altman & J. Wohlwill (eds), *Behavior and the Natural Environment* (pp. 241–267). New York: Phenum Press.

Kernan, M. & Singer, E. (2011). *Peer Relationships in Early Childhood Education and Care*. New York: Routledge.

Kindersley, D. (2010). *Ready Set Grow! Quick and Easy Gardening Projects*. Toronto: Tourmaline Editions.

Kirkey, S. (2011, June 13). Parents targeted in fight against childhood obesity. Retrieved September 25, 2012, from http://www.canada.com/health/Parents+targeted+fight+against+childhood+obesity/4928002/story.html

Kirkey, S. (2012, January 23). Obese teen girls more likely to be bullies: Study. Retrieved September 25, 2012, from http://www2.canada.com/topics/bodyandhealth/story.html?id=6037749

Kritchevsky, S. & Prescott, E. 1977. *Planning Environments for Young Children,* 2nd ed. Washington, DC: NAEYC.

Kuhn, M. (1996). *Learning from the Roof Tops*. Toronto: Green Teacher.

Kuo, F.E. & Faber Taylor, A. (2004, August 27). Children with ADHD Benefit from Time Outdoors Enjoying Nature. Retrieved September 25, 2012, from http://news.illinois.edu/news/04/0827adhd.html

Kuo, F.E. & Faber Taylor, A. (2011). For kids with ADHD, regular 'green time' is linked to milder symptoms. *Applied Psychology: Health and Well-Being*, Vol. 3(3), 281–303.

Kuo, F.E. & Sullivan, W. (2001). Aggression and violence in the inner city: Impacts of environment via mental fatigue. *Environment and Behaviour, 33*(4), 543–571.

The Lancet. (May 5, 2012). Myopia. Retrieved November 23, 2012, from http://www.thelancet.com/journals/lancet/article/PIIS0140-6736(12)60272-4/abstract

Laporta R. & Rossie J.P. (2010). Play Scotland. Retrieved September 25, 2012, from http://www.playscotland.org/play-related-quotes

Laumann, K., Garling, T., & Stormark, K.M. (2001). Rating scale measures of restorative components of environments. *Journal of Environmental Psychology, 21*, 31–44.

Lear, L. (1998). *Lost Woods: The Discovered Writing of Rachel Carson*. Boston, MA: Beacon Press.

Learning and Teaching Scotland. (2010). Curriculum for Excellence Through Outdoor Learning. Retrieved June 3, 2012, from http://www.educationscotland.gov.uk/images/cfeoutdoorlearningfinal_tcm4-596061.pdf

Lee, J. (n.d.). Constructive and Preventive Philanthropy. Retrieved April 7, 2012, from http://www.archive.org/stream/constructiveand03riisgoog/constructiveand03riisgoog_djvu.txt

Leitch, K. (2007). *Reaching for the Top: A Report by the Advisor on Healthy Children and Youth*. Ottawa: Health Canada.

Lester, S. & Maudsley, M. (2006, August). Play naturally: A review of children's natural play. Retrieved June 15, 2012, from http://www.playday.org.uk/default.aspx?page=385

Lever, J. 1978. Sex differences in the complexity of children's play and games. *American Sociological Review, 43*(4), 471–483.

Lewis, C.A. (1992). Effects of plants and gardening in creating interpersonal and community well-being. In D. Relf (ed.), *The Role of Horticulture in Human Well Being and Social Development: A National Symposium* (pp. 55–65). Portland, OR: Timber.

Lieberman, G.A. & Hoody, L.L. (1998). *Closing the Achievement Gap: Using the Environment as an Integrated Context for Learning*. Ponway, CA: Science Wizards.

Lindsey, E.W. & Colwell, M.J. (2003). Preschoolers' emotional competence links to pretend and physical play. *Child Study Journal, 33*(1), 39–52.

Little Eyes on Nature. (2009, May 15). The strand of nature. Retrieved September 25, 2012, from http://eyesonnature.blogspot.ca/2009/05/strand-of-nature-1.html

Lohr, V.I., Pearson-Mims, C.H., & Goodwin, G.K. (1996). Interior plants may improve worker productivity and reduce stress in a windowless environment. *Journal of Environmental Horticulture, 14*, 97–100.

Louv, R. (1991). *Childhood's Future*. New York. Doubleday.

Louv, R. (1996). *The Web of Life, Weaving the Values that Sustain Us*. Newburyport, MA: RedWheel Publishing.

Louv, R. (2005). Favourite Nature Play Quotes. Green Hearts: Institute for Nature in Childhood. Retrieved February 14, 2012 from http://www.greenheartsinc.org/uploads/Copy_of_Favorite_Nature_Play_Quotes_for_website.pdf

Louv, R. (2008). *Last Child in the Woods. Saving Our Children from Nature-Deficit Disorder*. Chapel Hill, NC: Algonquin Books.

Louv, R. (2010). Why children (and the rest of us) need nature. Wilderness Ventures. Retrieved September 25, 2012, from http://www.wildernessventures.com/richard-louv-essay

Louv, R. (2011a). *The Nature Principle: Human Restoration and the End of Nature-Deficit Disorder*. Chapel Hill, NC: Algonquin Books.

Louv, R. (2011b, July 4). Nature, an inspiration for all learning. Little Eyes on Nature. Retrieved March 17, 2012 from http://eyesonnature.blogspot.ca

Louv, R. (2012, July 13), 10 Reasons Why We Need Vitamin N. Huffington Post. Retrieved October 24, 2012, from http://www.huffingtonpost.com/richard-louv/nature-health_b_1662755.html#slide=1219689

Lovejoy, S. (1999). *Roots, Shoots, Buckets, and Boots. Gardening Together with Children*. New York: Workman Publishing.

Lovejoy, S. (2003). *Trowel and Error. Over 700 Shortcuts, Tips and Remedies for the Gardener*. New York: Workman Publishing.

Malone, K. & Tranter, P. (2003). Children's environmental learning and the use, design, and management for school grounds. *Children, Youth and Environments, 13*(2). Retrieved May 17, 2012, from http://www.colorado.edu/journals/cye/13_2/Malone_Tranter/ChildrensEnvLearning.htm

Marano, H.E. (2004). Nation of Wimps. Retrieved February 7, 2012, from http://www.psychologytoday.com/articles/200411/nation-wimps

Marketwire.com Press. (2008, September 30). Canada's first forest preschool to launch in Ottawa Valley, September 30. Retrieved September 25, 2012, from http://www.marketwire.com/press-release/Canadas-First-Forest-Preschool-to-Launch-in-Ottawa-Valley-905166.htm

Marshall, B.A. (2005). Science and Preschoolers—A Natural Combination. Workshop presented at the High/Scope Educational Research Foundation International Conference, Ypsilanti, Michigan, June 9–10.

Martin, C.L. & Fabes, R.A. (2001). The stability and consequences of young children's same-sex peer interactions. *Developmental Psychology, 37*(3), 431–446.

Martin, F. & Farnum, J. (2002). Animal-assisted therapy for children with pervasive developmental disorders. Retrieved September 25, 2012, from http://wjn.sagepub.com/content/24/6/657.short

Massad, C. (1979). Time and space in space and time. In K. Yamamoto (ed.), *Children in Time and Space* (p. 293). New York: Teachers College Press

Mayesky, M. (2012). *Creative Activities for Young Children*, 10th ed. Independence, KY: Wadsworth Cengage Learning.

McCue, H. (2006). The learning circle: Classroom activities on First Nations in Canada—Ages 4–7. Ottawa, Indian and Northern Affairs Canada.

McDonnell, P.J. (2005, September). Are We No Longer a Nation Built Upon Risk? *Ophthalmology Times*. Retrieved September 25, 2012, from http://www.highbeam.com/publications/ophthalmology-times-p137627/september-2005

McGinn, Dave. (2011, December 4). Is your office chair killing you? *The Globe and Mail*. Retrieved September 26, 2012, from http://www.theglobeandmail.com/life/health/new-health/health-news/is-your-office-chair-killing-you/article2258518

McIlroy, A. (2009, November 6). See Jane run, see Jane play violin, see Jane's grades soar. *The Globe and Mail*, L1.

McIlroy, A. (2010, November 13). Young minds bloom in outdoor classrooms. *The Globe and Mail*, A4.

McMahon, T. (2011, November 16). Parents cry foul after elementary school bans balls over playground safety. *National Post*. Retrieved September 25, 2012, from http://news.nationalpost.com/(2011)/11/16/parents-cry-foul-after-elementary-school-bans-balls

Mental Health Foundation. (1999). *Bright Futures: Promoting Children and Young People's Mental Health*. Glasgow, Scotland: Mental Health Foundation.

Mercogliano, C. (2007). *In Defense of Childhood; Protecting Kids' Inner Wilderness*. Boston: Beacon Press.

Meyers, M. (1993). *Teaching to Diversity; Teaching and Learning in the Multi-Ethnic Classroom*. Don Mills, ON: Pearson Canada.

Miles, I., Sullivan, W.C., & Kuo, F.E. (1998). Prairie restoration volunteers: The benefits of participation. *Urban Ecosystem, 2*, 27–41.

Miller, K. (1989). Infants and toddlers outside. *Texas Child Care Quarterly*, Summer, 24–30.

Miller, K. (1999). *Simple Steps: Developmental Activities for Infants, Toddlers, and Two Year Olds*. Lewisville, NC: Gryphon House.

Minter, S. (1993). *The Healing Garden: A Natural Haven for Emotional and Physical Well-Being*. London, UK, Headline Publishing.

Mitchell, T.C. (2008). Special education. Exploring the great outdoors. *High Scope Extensions; Curriculum Newsletter of the High Scope Foundation*, Vol. 22(5).

Mohr, M. (1987). *Home Playgrounds: The Harrowsmith Guide to Building Backyard Play Structures*. Scarborough, ON: Camden House.

Montessori, M. (1932). *Education and Peace*. Geneva: International Bureau of Education.

Mooney, P. & Nicell, P.L. (1992). The Importance of Exterior Environment for Alzheimer Residents: Effective Care and Risk Management. *Healthcare Management Forum, 5*(2), 23–29.

Moore, L.L., Lombardi, D.A., White, M.J., Campbell, J.L., Olshan, A.F., & Ellison, R.C. (1991). Influence of parents' physical activity levels on activity levels of young children. *Pediatrics, 118*(2), 215–219.

Moore, R.C. (1993). *Plants for Play: A Plant Selection Guide for Children's Outdoor Environments* Berkeley, CA: Mig Communications.

Moore, R.C. (1996). Compact nature: The role of playing and learning gardens for children's lives. *Journal of Therapeutic Horticulture, 8*, 72–82.

Moore, R.C. (1997). The need for nature: A childhood right. *Social Justice, 24*(3), 203–220.

Moore, R.C. (2010). Loose parts = imagination + creativity. The Body Smart Blog. Retrieved September 26, 2012, from http://bodysmartblog.org/2010/08/11/loose-parts-imagination-creativity

Moore, R., Goltsman, S., & Iacofano, D. (1992). *Play for All Guidelines—Planning, Design and Management of Outdoor Play Settings for All Children*. St. John's, NL: Atlantic Books.

Moore, R.C. & Cosco, N. (2000). Developing an earth-bound culture through design of childhood habitats. Natural Learning Initiative. Paper Presented at A Global View of Community Gardening, University of Nottingham, UK, September 13–16.

Moore, R.C. & Marcus, C.C. (2008). Healthy Planet, Healthy Children: Designing Nature into the Daily Spaces for Childhood. In S.R. Kellert, J. Heerwagen, & M. Mador (eds), *Biophilic Design: The Theory, Science, and Practice of Bringing Buildings to Life* (pp. 115–203). Hoboken, NJ: Wiley.

Moore, R.C. & Wong, H. (1997). *Natural Learning—Creating Environments for Rediscovering Nature's Way of Teaching*. Berkeley, CA: MIG Communications.

Morris, K. 2000. *The Kids Can Press Jumbo Book of Gardening*. Toronto: Kids Can Press.

National Council for Curriculum and Assessment (NCCA). (2010). Geography: A sense of the world. Curriculum On Line. Retrieved June 1, 2012, from http://www.curriculumonline.ie/en

National Geographic. (2012). Versailles. Retrieved May 17, 2012, from http://travel.nationalgeographic.com/travel/world-heritage/versailles

National Play Fields Association, Children's Play Council and Playlink. (2000). Best Play: What Play Provision

Should Do for Children. London: National Playing Fields Association. Retrieved April 12, 2012, from http://www.playengland.org.uk/resources/best-play.aspx

Natural Learning Initiative. (n.d.). Retrieved May 21, 2012, from http://naturalearning.org

NC State University College of Design. (2012). Robin Moore. Retrieved September 26, 2012, from http://design.ncsu.edu/users/robin-moore

Nemy, E. (2005, October 17). Enid A. Haupt, philantropist, dies at 99. *The New York Times*. Retrieved September 26, 2012, from http://www.nytimes.com/2005/10/27/nyregion/27haupt.html?pagewanted=all

Nicholson, S. (1971). How not to cheat children: The theory of loose parts. *Landscape Architecture, 62,* 30–34.

Neill, P. (2008). Science and the outdoor classroom. High Scope extensions. *Curriculum Newsletter of the High Scope Foundation, 22*(5) 1–3.

Neumann Hinds, C. (2007). *Picture Science Using Digital Photography to Teach Young Children*. St. Paul, MN, Redleaf Press.

New, R. (1990). Excellent early education: A city in Italy has it. *Young Children, 45*(6), 4–10.

Nimmo, J. & Hallett, B. (2008, January). Childhood in the garden: A place to encounter natural and social diversity. *Young Children*, 3.

Nind, M. (2001). Enhancing the Communication Learning Environment of An Early Years Unit. Paper presented at the British Educational Research Association Annual Conference, University of Leeds, September 13–15 2001. Retrieved September 26, 2012, from http://www.leeds.ac.uk/educol/documents/00001920.htm

Nisbet, E.K., Zelenski, J.M., & Murphy, S.A. (2011). Happiness is in our nature: Exploring nature relatedness as a contributor to subjective well being. *Journal of Happiness Studies, 12,* 303–322.

Norman, N. (2003). *An Architecture of Play: A Survey of London's Adventure Playgrounds*. London: Four Corners Books.

North Coast Gardening. (2010, October 26). Designing a Landscape for Color Blind People: The Garden Designers' Roundtable on Therapy and Healing. Retrieved July 7, 2012, from http://www.northcoastgardening.com/2010/10/color-blind-garden-design

Obeid, J., Nguyen, T., Gabel, L., & Timmons, V.W. (2011). Physical activity in Ontario preschoolers: Prevalence and measurement issues. *Applied Physiology, Nutrition and Metabolism, 35,* 291–297.

Oesterreich, L. (1995). Ages & stages—Newborn to 1 year. In L. Oesterreich, B. Holt, & S. Karas (eds), *Iowa Family Child Care Handbook* (pp. 192–196). Ames, IA: Iowa State University Extension.

Ogden, C.L., Troiano, R.P., Briefel, R.R., Kuczmarski, R.J., Flegal, K.M., & Johnson, C.L. (1997). Prevalence of overweight among preschool children in the United States 1971 through 1994. *Pediatrics, 99,* E1.

Olds, A. (2001). *Child Care Design Guide*. Whitby, ON: McGraw-Hill.

One World for Children. (2010, Winter). Outdoor Play in Winter. Training Newsletter. Retrieved May 18, 2012, from www.owfc.com.au/training/newsletters/2010

Ontario Report Card Supplement. Active Healthy Kids Canada report card on physical activity for children and youth. (2011). Retrieved September 26, 2012, from http://dvqdas9jty7g6.cloudfront.net/resources/ONRC_ShortForm_singles_26SE11.pdf

Orlick, T. (1978). *The Cooperative Sports & Games Book: Challenge Without Competition*. New York: Pantheon Books.

Ottawa Citizen. (2010, April 10). From parking lot to paradise. Retrieved September 26, 2012, from http://www.househunting.ca/buying-homes/ottawacitizen/story.html?id=c49aea64-8bc2-4367-8a07-1a035f95e343

Our Children, Our Ways. Early Childhood Education in First Nations & Inuit Communities [video]. (2000). Red River College.

Pabayo, R., Gauvin, L., & Barnett, T.A. (2011). Longitudinal changes in active transportation to school in canadian youth aged 6 through 16 years. *Pediatrics, 128* (2), 404–413.

Parks, Recreation and Forestry. (2012). The Franklin Children's Garden. Retrieved September 26, 2012, from www.toronto.ca/parks/franklin

Pathways for Families. (2012). Montessori schools celebrate first 100 years. Retrieved September 26, 2012, from http://tsl.org/family/2010/04/this-is-the-1st-education

Patterson, B. 2000. *Build Me an Ark*. New York: Norton.

Pellegrini, A.D. (2005). *Recess: Its Role in Education and Development*. Mahwah, NJ: Erlbaum Associates.

Pellegrini, A.D. & Smith, P.K. (1993). School recess: Implications for education and development. *Review of Educational Research, 63*(1), 51–67.

Pereira, B., Fale, P., & da Guia Carmo, M. (2002). Playgrounds. Comparative study of six districts in the region of Cavado in the North of Portugal. Paper presented at the European Conference on Education Research, University of Lisbon, September 11–14.

Perlmutter, J.C. & Burrell, L. (1995). Learning through "play" as well as "work" in the primary grades. *Young Children, 50*(5), 14–21.

Piaget, J. (1936). *Origins of Intelligence in the Child*. London: Routledge & Kegan Paul.

Piaget, J. (1962). *Play, Dreams, and Imitation in Childhood* (G. Gattegno & F.M. Hodgson, Trans.). New York: W.W. Norton & Company.

Place, G. (2000). Impact of Early Life Outdoor Experiences on an Individual's Environmental Attitudes. Ph.D. Thesis. Indiana University.

Playday ICM Survey. Play Scotland. (2010). Retrieved September 26, 2012, from http://www.playscotland.org/play-related-quotes

Pollan, M. (1991). *Second Nature: A Gardener's Education*. New York: The Atlantic Monthly Press.

Poole, C., Miller, S., & Church, E.B. (2004). Working through that "It's mine" feeling. *Early Childhood Today, 18*(5), 28–32.

Potter, J. (1995). *Nature in A Nutshell for Kids*. Jossey-Bass.

Project Wild. (2003). *Conceptual Framework. Project Wild and Project Wild Aquatic K-12 Curriculum and Activity Guide*. Houston, TX: Council for Environmental Education.

Public Health Agency of Canada. (2009). Northwest Territories: Inuvik community greenhouse—building a strong sense of community through recreational gardening, food production, knowledge sharing, and volunteer support. Retrieved September 26, 2012, from http://www.phac-aspc.gc.ca/publicat/2009/be-eb/nwt-tno-eng.php

Pyle, R. (2002). Eden in a vacant lot: Special places, species and kids in community of life. In P.H. Kahn & S.R. Kellert (eds), *Children and Nature: Psychological, Sociocultural and Evolutionary Investigations*. Cambridge, MA: MIT Press.

Ratey, J. (2008). *The Revolutionary New Science of Exercise and the Brain*. New York: Little, Brown and Company.

Rawlings, R. (1998). *Healing Gardens*. London: Weidenfeld & Nicholson.

Ray, V. (1996). *All from Zen Gardening: A Down to Earth Philosophy*. New York: Berkley Books.

Redleaf, R. (2009). *Learn and Play the Green Way: Fun Activities with Reusable Materials*. St. Paul, MN: Redleaf Press.

Redleaf, R. (2010). *Hey Kids! Out the Door, Let's Explore!* Paul, MN: Redleaf Press.

Reed, T. (2000). Rough and tumble play during recess: Pathways to successful social development. In R.L. Clements (ed.), *Elementary School Recess: Selected Readings, Games, and Activities for Teachers and Parents* (pp. 45–48). Boston: American Press.

Restak, R. & Mahoney, D. (1998). *The Longevity Strategy: How to Live to 100 Using The Brain-Body Connection*. New York: The Dana Press.

Rice, J.S. & Remy, L.L. (1998). Impacts of horticultural therapy on psychosocial functioning among urban jail inmates. *Journal of Offender Rehabilitation, 26*, 169–191.

Richardson, B. (1998). *Gardening with Children*. Newtown, CT: Taunton Books.

Riley, J.G. & Jones, R.B. (2007). When girls and boys play: What research tells us. *Association for Childhood Education International, 84*(1), 38.

Rinaldi, C. (2000). Subjectivity and intersubjectivity in children's learning. Paper presented at the NAEYC Conference. Atlanta, November 7–10.

Rinaldi, C. (2006). *In Dialogue with Reggio Emilia: Listening, Researching and Learning*. New York: Routledge.

Rivkin, M. (1997). The schoolyard habitat movement. *Early Childhood Education Journal, 25*(1), 61–65.

Rivkin, M. (2000). *Outdoor Experiences for Young Children*. Charleston, WV: ERIC Clearinghouse on Rural Education and Small Schools.

Rosen, M.J. (2004). Stars in a Child's Universe. In M.R. Jalong (ed.) (p. 6). Olney, MD: Association for Childhood Education International.

RoSPA (Royal Society for the Prevention of Accidents). (2006–2007). Retrieved July 12, 2012, from http://www.rospa.com/about

Sager, B. (2010). Sager Family Travelling Foundation and Road Show. Retrieved September 26, 2012, from http://www.teamsager.org

Sams, M.J., Fortney, E.V., & Willenbring, S. (2006). Occupational Therapy Incorporating Animals for Children with Autism. American Occupational Therapy Association. Retrieved October 24, 2012, from http://ajot.aotapress.net/content/60/3/268.full.pdf

Schwab, E. (1879). *The School Garden. Being a Practical Contribution to the Subject of Education*. Trans. Mrs. Horace Mann. New York: M. L. Holbrook & Co.

Scott, J. (2000). When child's play is too simple; Experts criticize safety conscious recreation as boring. *The New York Times*. Retrieved February 21, 2012, from http:// www.nytimes.com/2000/07/15/arts/when-child-s-play-too-simple-experts-criticize-safety-conscious-recreation.html?pagewanted=all&src=pm

Search, G. (2002). *The Healing Garden: Gardening for The Mind, Body and Soul*. Etobicoke, ON: Winding Stair Press.

Shapiro, E. (1995). Restoring habitats, communities and souls. In J. Roszak, S. Homes, & P. Kanner (eds), *Ecopsychology: Restoring the Earth, Healing the Mind* (pp. 224–239). San Francisco: Sierra Club.

Shields, A., Dickstein, S., Seifer, R., Giusti, L, Magee, K.D., & Spritz, B. (2001). Emotional competence and early school adjustment: a study of preschoolers at risk. *Early Education and Development 12*(1), 73–90.

Sinclair, D. (2005). *The Spirituality of Gardening*. Kelowna, BC: Northstone Publishing.

Sobel, D. (1996). *Beyond Ecophobia: Reclaiming The Heart of Nature Education*. Great Barrington, MA: The Orion Society.

Sobel, D. (2004). *Children's Special Places—Exploring the Role of Forts, Dens, and Bush Houses in Middle Childhood*. Detroit, MI: Wayne State University Press.

Solomon, S.G. (2005). *American Playgrounds Revitalizing Community Space*. Lebanon, NH: University Press of New England.

Speakers' Spotlight. (n.d.). Severn Cullis-Suzuki. Retrieved September 26, 2012, from http://www.speakers.ca/cullis-suzuki_severn.html

Sroufe, L.A. (1995). *Emotional Development: The Organization of Emotional Life in The Early Years*. Cambridge, NY: Cambridge University Press.

Starbuck, S., Olthof, M., & Midden, K. (2002). *Hollyhocks and Honeybees Garden Projects for Young Children*. St. Paul, MN, Redleaf Press.

Statistics Canada. (2010). "Fitness of Canadian adults: Results from the 2007–2009 Canadian Health Measures Survey", and "Fitness of Canadian children and youth: Results from the 2007–2009 Canadian Health Measures Survey", part of Health Reports, Vol. 21, no. 1.

Stolley, M.R., Fitzgibbon, M.L., Dyer, A., Van Horn, L., Kaufer Christoffel, K., & Schiffer, L. (2003). Hip-hop to health jr., an obesity prevention program for minority preschool children: Baseline characteristics of participants. *Preventive Medicine, 36*, 320–329.

Stroink, M.L., Nelson, C.H., & McLaren, B. (2009). The learning garden: Place-based Learning for Holistic First Nations' Community Health. Thunder Bay, ON: Canadian Council on Learning.

Sutton, L. (2011). Adventure playgrounds: A child's world in the city. Retrieved September 26, 2012, from http://adventureplaygrounds.hampshire.edu/aboutme.html

Suzuki, D. & Knudtson, P. (1992). *Wisdom of the Elders—Honouring Sacred Native Visions of Nature*. Toronto: Stoddart Publishing.

Suzuki, D. & Moola, F. 2010. Outdoor Fun Is Good For Kids and The Planet. Retrieved June 15, 2012, from http://www.davidsuzuki.org/blogs/science-matters/2010/07/outdoor-fun-is-good-for-kids-and-the-planet

Suzuki, D. & Vanderlinden, K. (1999). *You Are the Earth—From Dinosaur Breath to Pizza from Dirt*. New York: Sterling Publishing.

Symons, C.W., Cinelli, B., James, T.C., et al. (1997). Bridging student health risks and academic achievement through comprehensive school health programs. *Journal of School Health, 67,* 220–227.

Tennessen, C. & Cimprich, B. (1995). Views to nature: Effects on attention. *Journal of Environmental Psychology, 15,* 77–85.

Theemes, T. (1999). *Let's Go Outside: Designing the Early Childhood Playground.* Ypsilanti, MI: High Scope Press.

Thorne, B. (1993). *Gender play: Girls and boys in school.* New Brunswick, NJ: Rutgers University Press.

Timmons, B.W., LeBlanc, A.G., Carson, V., & Tremblay, M.S. (2011). Physical activity and sedentary behaviour guidelines for preschool-aged children. *Interaction, 25*(2), 31–34.

Tobin, A.M. (2011, July 5). Kids from poorer families more likely to walk or bike to school. *Toronto Star,* E12.

Tribal Thunder. (n.d.). Retrieved November 19, 2012, from http://tribalthunder.com

Tucker, P. (2008). The physical activity levels of preschool-age children: A systematic review. *Early Childhood Research Quarterly, 23,* 547–558.

Tucker, P. (2010). Childcare and Outdoor Play—An Opportunity to Support Healthy Active Behaviours, Presentation. Places of Natural Discovery [conference], Humber College. May 13.

Tucker, P., Gilliland, J., & Irwin, J.D. (2007). Splashpads, swings, and shade: Parents' preferences for neighbourhood parks. *Canadian Journal of Public Health, 98*(3) 198–202.

Tucker, P. & Irwin, J.D. (2009). Physical activity behaviors during the preschool years. *Child Health and Education, 1*(3), 134–145.

Tucker, P., Irwin, J.D., Sangster Bouck, L.M., He, M., & Pollett, G. (2006). Preventing paediatric obesity: Recommendation from a community-based qualitative investigation. *Obesity Reviews, 7,* 251–260.

UNICEF. (2009). Designing for children with focus on play + learn: Design of play spaces in the context of modern dwellings. Retrieved September 26, 2012, from http://www.designingforchildren.net/papers/anirudh-natuu-designingforchildren.pdf

United Nations. (1989). United Nations Convention on the Rights of the Child. Retrieved September 26, 2012, from http://www2.ohchr.org/english/law/crc.htm

University of the Incarnate Word. (2012). Frost Play Research Collection. Retrieved September 25, 2012, from http://www.uiw.edu/frost/joefrost.html

Van Hoorn, J., Monighan Nourot, P., Scales, B., Rodriquez, K., & Alward, B. (2003). *Play at the Centre of Curriculum,* 3rd ed. Boston, MA, Pearson Education.

Vieira, G. (2012, May 28). The Eyes Don't Have It. *Maclean's.* Retrieved June 4, 2012, from http://www2.macleans.ca/author/gvieira/page/2

Vieth, R. (2010). Dark-skinned immigrants urged to take vitamin D. Retrieved July 4, 2012, from http://www.cbc.ca/news/health/story/2010/02/12/ottawa-immigrants-vitamin-d.html

Vygotsky, L.S. (1977). Play and Its Role in the Mental Development of the Child. In M. Cole (ed.), *Soviet Developmental Psychology* (pp. 76–99). White Plains, NY: M.E. Sharpe.

Wangari Wuta Maathai. (n.d.). Retrieved from http://wangari.greenbeltmovement.org

Ward, J. (2008). *I Love Dirt!* Boston, MA: Trumpeter Books.

Warde, B.F. (1960). John Dewey's theories of education. *International Socialist Review, 21*(1). Retrieved September 26, 2012, from http://www.marxists.org/archive/novack/works/1960/x03.htm

Wasserman, S. (1992). Serious play in the classroom. *Childhood Education, 68*(3), 133–139.

Waterfront Toronto. (2011). Sherbourne Common. Retrieved September 26, 2012, from http://www.waterfrontoronto.ca/sherbourne_common

Weinstein, J., Przybylski, A.K., & Ryan, R.M. (2009). Can nature make us more caring? Effects of immersion in nature on intrinsic aspirations and generosity. *Personality & Social Psychology Bulletin, 35,* 1315–1329.

Wells, N.M. (2000). At home with nature: Effects of greenness on children's cognitive functioning. *Environment and Behaviour, 32*(6), 775–795.

Wells, N.M. & Evans, G.W. (2003). Nearby nature: A buffer of life stress among rural school children. *Environment and Behavior, 35*(3), 311–330.

White, R. (2004). Young children's relationship with nature: Its importance to children's development and the earth's future. Retrieved September 26, 2012, from http://www.whitehutchinson.com/children/articles/childrennature.shtml

White, R. & Stoecklin, V. (2008). Nurturing children's biophilia: Developmentally appropriate environmental education for young children. http://www.whitehutchinson.com/children/articles/nurturing.shtml

Whitebread, D. (2000). *The Psychology of Teaching and Learning in the Primary School.* Abingdon, UK: Routledge.

Wilson, E.O. (1984). *Biophilia.* Cambridge, MA: Harvard University Press.

Wilson, L. (2001, Spring/Summer). Creating magical outdoor play spaces for young children: Resources in early childhood education. A publication of the Gerrard Resource Centre, 1–3.

Wilson, R. (2007). *Nature and Young Children—Encouraging Creative Play and Learning in Natural Environments.* London and New York: Routledge, Taylor and Francis Group.

Wilson, R. (2008). *Nature and Young Children: Encouraging Creative Play and Learning in Natural Environments.* London and New York: Routledge, Taylor and Francis Group.

Wilson, R. (2009, May/June). Wonder. Becoming whole—Developing an ecological identity. *NACC Newsletter.* Retrieved September 26, 2012, from http://ccie-media.s3.amazonaws.com/nacc/wonder_may11.pdf

World Forum Foundation. (n.d.). Connecting the World's Children with Nature Advocacy. Powerpoint Presentation. Nature Action Collaborative for Children. Retrieved August 31, 2012, from http://worldforumfoundation.org/wf/wp/initiatives/nature-action-collaborative-for-children/environmental-action-kit/advocacy-tools/multimedia

World Health Organization. (n.d.). Information Series on School Health. Document 2: The Physical School Environment—An Essential Component of a Health-Promoting School. Department of Protection of the Human Environment and the Department of Noncommunicable Disease Prevention and Health Promotion. Retrieved November 25, 2012, from http://www.who.int/school_youth_health/media/en/physical_sch_environment.pdf

World Health Organization. (2002). Sun Protection: An Essential Element of Health Promoting Schools. Retrieved from www.who.int/school_youth_health/media/en/456.pdf

Worpole, K. (2006, February 13). The playgrounds and the city, Aldo van Eyck. Retrieved September 26, 2012, from http://www.opendemocracy.net/arts/playgrounds_3260.jsp

Wortham, S.C. (2002). *Early Childhood Curriculum*. Upper Saddle River, NJ: Merrill/Prentice Hall.

Xinhua. (2012). English news. Retrieved November 23, 2012, from http://news.xinhuanet.com/english/health/2012-02/28/c_131434648.htm

Yantzi, N. (2009). Centre for Rural and Northern Health Research (CRaNHR) Health Care Research Seminar Series 2008–2009: Evaluating the Accessibility and Inclusiveness of Sudbury Playgrounds for Children with Physical Disabilities. Laurentian University, March 19.

NATURE ORGANIZATIONS

1. Evergreen http://www.evergreen.ca/en
2. Children and Nature Network http://www.childrenandnature.org
3. Learning through Landscapes www.ltl.org.uk
4. National Wildlife Federation www.nwf.org/schoolyard
5. The Natural Learning Initiative www.naturalearning.org
6. Back to Nature Network http://www.back-2nature.ca_
7. Children's Nature Institute http://www.childrensnatureinstitute.org/newsite
8. Child and Nature Alliance of Canada http://www.childnature.ca_
9. Nature Canada http://www.naturecanada.ca_
10. Canadian Wildlife Federation http://www.cwf-fcf.org/en/index.html
11. Sharing Nature Worldwide: Joseph Cornell http://www.sharingnature.com/about-us/joseph-cornell.php
12. Earthplay www.planetearthplayscapes.com
13. Nature Action Collaborative for Children http://worldforumfoundation.org/wf/wp/initiatives/nature-action-collaborative-for-children
14. Linking Food, Culture, Health and the Environment http://www.ecoliteracy.org/books/big-ideas-linking-food-culture-health-and-environment
15. Nature Conservancy Canada http://www.natureconservancy.ca/en
16. Eekoworld http://pbskids.org/eekoworld
17. Nature Child Reunion http://www.naturechildreunion.ca
18. Project Wild http://www.projectwild.org
19. Environmental Earth Angels www.earthangels.ca
20. Earth Rangers www.earthrangers.ca
21. David Suzuki Foundation http://www.davidsuzuki.org/what-you-can-do
22. The Green Squad http://www.nrdc.org/greensquad/intro/intro_1.asp
23. The Big Blue Bus (Fisheries and Oceans Canada) http://www.dfo-mpo.gc.ca/canwaters-eauxcan/bbb-lgb/index_e.asp
24. Get to Know (Robert Bateman) http://www.gettoknow.ca
25. Ducks Unlimited http://www.ducks.ca
26. Earth Care http://www.earthcarecanada.com/earthcare_resources/websites.asp
27. Northwest Territories Department of the Environment and Natural Resources http://www.enr.gov.nt.ca/_live/pages/wpPages/education.aspx
28. Eco Kids Environmental Education Site http://www.ecokids.ca/pub/index.cfm
29. Environment Canada Action (Free Educational Resources for Educators) http://www.ec.gc.ca/education/default.asp?lang=En&n=D3D10112-1
30. Green Learning http://www.greenlearning.ca
31. Natural Life Magazine http://www.naturallifemagazine.com
32. Ontario Healthy Communities Initiative http://www.ohcc-ccso.ca/en/what-makes-a-healthy-community
33. Winnipeg, Manitoba's Discovery Children's Centre http://discoverycentre.homestead.com/dcc.html
34. Kids Planet http://www.kidsplanet.org

GARDENING RESOURCES

35. American Horticultural Society www.ahs.org
36. You Grow Girl http://www.yougrowgirl.com/tips
37. LEAF (Local Enhancement and Appreciation of Forests www.yourleaf.org
38. TreeCanada http://www.treecanada.ca
39. Trees for Peace Project http://www.bsworldpeace.org/en/index.php?bcr=12
40. Children of the Earth http://www.childrenoftheearth.org_
41. LifeCycles http://lifecyclesproject.ca/initiatives/growing_schools/school_garden.php#curriculum

42. The Edible Schoolyard
http://www.edibleschoolyard.org

43. The Learning Garden
http://www.thelearninggarden.org/aboutus.html

44. Square Foot Gardening (for Small Spaces/
People with Disabilities)
http://www.squarefootgardening.com

45. Urban Agriculture Notes (Urban Gardening)
http://www.cityfarmer.org

46. KidsGardening http://kidsgardening.org

47. Ontario Ministry of Natural Resources
http://www.mnr.gov.on.ca/en/Business/
Biodiversity

48. Compost Council of Canada
http://www.compost.org/English

49. Agriculture and Agri-Food Canada
www.agr.gc.ca

50. Environment Canada www.ec.gc.ca

51. Natural Resources Canada
www.nrcan-rncan.gc.ca

52. The Countryside Alliance Foundation
http://www.countryside-alliance.org/ca/
campaigns-education

53. Intergenerational Landed Learning on the
Farm for the Environment
http://m2.edcp.educ.ubc.ca/landedlearning

54. EcoLeague www.ecoleague.ca

55. Project Flow www.r4r.ca/en/project-flow

56. Recycle City
http://www.epa.gov/recyclecity/mainmap.htm

57. Sustainability and Education Academy
http://lsf-lst.ca/en/projects/education-sustain-
able/schools/seda

58. GardenImport (Canadian mail-order plant and
bulb company) http://www.gardenimport.com

PHYSICAL PLAY ORGANIZATIONS

59. International Play Association
www.ipaworld.org

60. ParticipACTION
http://www.participaction.com/en-us/Home.aspx

61. US Play Coalition http://usplaycoalition.
clemson.edu

62. Canadian Partnership for Children's Health
and Environment
http://www.healthyenvironmentforkids.ca

63. Active8—Module for 4- to 5-Year-Olds
http://www.activehealthykids.ca

64. Fun and Physical Activity, Toronto Public Health
http://www.toronto.ca/health/newfun.pdf

65. Growing Healthy Canadians: A Guide to
Positive Child Development
www.growinghealthykids.com

66. OPHEA http://www.ophea.net/order

67. Mothers in Motion
www.caaws.ca/mothersinmotion

68. Moving and Learning
www.movingandlearning.com

69. Active Kids Club
http://www.activekidsclub.com

70. Let's Go Outside Revolution http://www.lets-
gooutsiderevolution.com/wordpress

TEACHER RESOURCES

71. Environmental Education
Ontario http://www.eeon.org

72. Humber Arboretum
http://www.humberarboretum.on.ca

73. Natural Curiosity—A Resource for
Teachers
http://www.naturalcuriosity.ca

74. Aboriginal Resources for Teachers
http://www.aboriginalcanada.gc.ca/acp/site.
nsf/eng/ao31045.html

75. Council of Outdoor Educators of Ontario
http://www.coeo.org

76. School Garden Wizard (Downloadable
Teaching Resources)
http://www.schoolgardenwizard.org

77. Step Outside http://www.r4r.ca/en/step-outside

78. Green Teacher http://www.greenteacher.com

79. Institute for Outdoor Learning
http://www.outdoor-learning.org

80. Girls Outdoors: A Resource for Women in
Outdoor Education and Recreation
http://www.girlsoutdoors.org

81. Classroom Resources for Teachers
http://www.r4r.ca

82. Canadian Forestry Association Teaching Kits
http://www.canadianforestry.com/html/
education/cfa_kits_e.html

83. Parks Canada Teacher Resource Centre http://
www.pc.gc.ca/apprendre-learn/prof/index_e.asp

84. Michelle Obama Initiative, Active Schools
http://www.letsmove.gov